TORT LAW LIBRARY

DAMAGES IN TORT

AUSTRALIA
LBC Information Services
Sydney

CANADA and USA
Carswell
Toronto

NEW ZEALAND
Brooker's
Auckland

SINGAPORE and MALAYSIA
Sweet & Maxwell (Asia)
Singapore and Kuala Lumpur

44 0511998 4

/

TORT LAW LIBRARY

DAMAGES IN TORT

by

David K. Allen, MA (Oxon); LL.M (McGill)
of the Middle Temple, Barrister-at-Law
Vice President Immigration Appeal Tribunal
Honorary Visiting Fellow, Department of Law,
University of Leicester
General Editor, Personal Injuries and
Quantum Reports

John T. Hartshorne, LL.B (Exeter); LL.M (Leicester)
of the Inner Temple, Barrister-at-Law
Lecturer in Law, University of Leicester

Robyn M. Martin BA; LL.B; M.U.R.P. (Adel.)
Professor of Law, University of Hertfordshire

London
Sweet & Maxwell
2000

First Edition 2000

Published in 2000 by
Sweet & Maxwell Limited of
100 Avenue Road
London NW3 3PF
http://www.sweetandmaxwell.co.uk
Typeset by Wyvern 21, Bristol
Printed and bound in Great Britain by
MPG Books Ltd, Bodmin, Cornwall

No natural forests were destroyed to
make this product: only farmed timber
was used and replanted

ISBN 0 421 58310 X

A catalogue record for this book is available
from the British Library

PREFACE

In this book we have sought to provide a clear and full analysis of the principles governing the assessment of damages where a tort has been committed.

It seemed to the authors that clarity would be best served by approaching the subject thematically; that is by examining the rules of quantum as they concern different types of interest, rather than tort by tort, given the risk of overlap such an approach would entail.

Wherever possible we have adopted a critical approach to the law, interpretation of law and practice of damage allocation and assessment, and have sought to place the rules we examine in their broader social, political and economic context.

It is intended that this study of damages be of interest to a wide range of readers. Practitioners who work with cases in which issues of damages arise will, we hope, find in this book a single accessible source of law on damages for all types of tort. The book may also prove useful to students, particularly students taking specialist postgraduate options on issues related to compensation and restitution, as well as to researchers in these areas. We also hope that anyone interested in why the law on damages is as it is, and the merits and flaws in the law, will find in these pages a comprehensive and coherent picture of the operation of tort compensation.

Anyone writing on damages cannot fail to acknowledge the major contributions of McGregor, Burrows and Ogus to this area of the law. In addition we have been able to take account of the views of the Law Commission, which has now concluded its review of the law of damages, and whose reports contain a wealth of research and reform proposals.

David Allen would like to thank Robyn Martin and John Hartshorne for joining him in this project at short notice, and for their uncomplaining meeting of deadlines. He is also grateful to colleagues, both at the University and in Chambers for help and advice over the years. He would also like to thank Jo Goacher and Kath Lloyd for their patient, good-humoured and extremely professional typing of his share of the manuscript. He would especially like to thank his wife and children for their support. John Hartshorne would like to thank Rachael Ambus for her patience and support.

Robyn Martin would like to thank her co-writers for the opportunity to share ideas on an area of law that she continues to find fascinating. She would also like, as always, to thank her patient husband and six beautiful girls for making everything worth doing.

We have endeavoured to state the law, as we understand it to be, as at January 1, 2000 though it has been possible to incorporate one or two developments at proof stage.

CONTENTS

ABBREVIATIONS

A. & E. *and* Ad. & E. = Adolphus & Ellis
A.C. = Appeal Cases (Law Reports)
A.L.R. = Australian Law Reports
All. E.R. = All England Law Reports
Asp.Mar.Law Cas. = Aspinall's Maritime Law Cases

B. = Baron (Exchequer)
B. & Ad. = Barnewall & Adolphus
B. & S. = Best & Smith
B.G.H.Z. = Entscheidungen des Bundesgerichtshofesin Zivilsachen
B.M.L.R. = Butterworths Medico-Legal Reports
Bing. N.C. = Bingham, New Cases
Black. Wm. = Blackstone, W.
Burr. = Burrow

C. & J. = Crompton & Jervis
C. & K. = Carrington & Kirwan
C. & P. = Carrington & Payne
C.A. = Court of Appeal
C.B. = Common Bench
C.B., N.S. = Common Bench, New Series
C.C.R. = Crown Cases Reserved
C.J.Q. = Civil Justice Quarterly
C.L.J. *and* Camb.L.J. = Cambridge Law Journal
C.L.R. = Commonwealth Law Reports
C.L.Y. = Current Law Year Book
C.P.R. = Crown Prosecution Rules
Camp. = Campbell
Ch.D. = *see* L.R.Ch.D.
Cmnd. = Command Papers
Conv. = The Conveyancer and Property Lawyer
Crim.L.R. = Criminal Law Review

De G.J. & S. = De Gex, Jones & Smith, Chancery
D.L.R. = Dominion Law Reports

E. = East's Term Reports
E. & B. = Ellis & Blackburn
ECJ = European Court of Justice
E.C.R. = European Court Reports

E.G. = Estates Gazette
E.G.L.R. = Estates Gazette Law Reports
E.H.H.R. = European Human Rights Reports
E.L.Rev. = European Law Review

F. = Federal Court
F. & F. = Foster & Finlayson
F.L.R. = Family Law Reports
F.S.R. = Fleet Street Reports
Fam. = Family Division (Law Reports)

H. & N. = Hurlstone & Norman
H.L.Cas. = House of Lords Cases (Clark)
H.L.R. = Housing Law Reports
Har.L.R. = Harvard Law Review

ICJ = International Court of Justice
I.C.L.Q. = International and Comparative Law Quarterly
I.C.R. = Industrial Case Reports
I.R. = Irish Reports (Eire)
I.R.L.R. = Industrial Relations Law Reports

J. *and* JJ. = Justice, Justices
J.P.I.L. = Journal of Personal Injury Litigation

K.B. = King's Bench (Law Reports)
K.I.R. = Knight's Industrial Law Reports

L.J. = Law Journal Newspaper *or* Lord Justice
L.J.C.P. = Law Journal Reports, Common Pleas
L.J.Ch. = Law Journal Reports, Chancery
L.J.Q.B. = Law Journal Reports, Queen's Bench
L.Q.R. = Law Quarterly Review
L.R. = Law Reports First Series
L.R.C.P. = Common Pleas Cases
L.R.Ch.App. = Chancery Appeal Cases
L.R.Ch.D. = Chancery Div.
L.R.P.C. = Privy Council Appeals
L.R.Q.B. = Queen's Bench
L.T. = Law Times
Ld. Ray. = Raymond, Lord
Lev. = Levinz
Lush. = Lushington

M. & W. = Meeson & Welsby
M.L.R. = Modern Law Review
M.R. = Master of the Rolls
Med. L.R. = Medical Law Reports
Moo. N.S. = Moore, E.F., New Series

N.I. = Northern Ireland Reports
N.I.L.Q. = Northern Ireland Legal Quarterly
N.L.J. = New Law Journal
N.Z.U.L.R. = New Zealand Universities Law Review

O.J. = Official Journal (European Community)
O.J.L.S. = Oxford Journal of Legal Studies
OUP = Oxford University Press

P. = Probate, Divorce and Admiralty (Law Reports)
P.D. = *see* L.R.P.C.
P.I.Q.R. = Personal Injury and Quantum Reports
Pea. (2) = Peake's Additional Cases

R.P.C. = Reports of Patent Cases
R.S.C. = Rules of Supreme Court
R.T.R. = Road Traffic Reports

S.J. = Solictor's Journal
S.L.T. = Scots Law Times
Sc. N.R. = Scott's New Reports
Stark. = Starkie
Str. = Strange J. (ed. by Nolan)
Swab. = Swabey

Q.B. = *see* L.R.Q.B.

Taunt. = Taunton
T.L.R. = Tasmanian Law Reports

U.T.L.J. = University of Toronto Law Journal

V.R. = Victorian Reports

W.L.R. = Weekly Law Reports
Wils. = Wilson's King Bench Reports
Wm. Bl. = Sir William Blackstone
Wm. Rob. = W. Robinson's Reports

TABLE OF CASES

All references are to paragraph numbers

TABLE OF STATUTES

TABLE OF STATUTORY INSTRUMENTS

E.C. LEGISLATION

INTERNATIONAL LEGISLATION

INTERNATIONAL CONVENTIONS

CHAPTER 1

INTRODUCTION

This book focuses on tortious damages. Damages are all about money—money as compensation for a loss suffered. Not just any loss gives rise to damages, and not just any money given in response to a loss qualifies as damages. The person who suffers brain damage after a stroke is not as the law stands a contender for a damages award. The charity funds raised to benefit the victims of the Hillsborough football disaster, although intended to alleviate the victims' loss, do not constitute damages.

1–001

The determination of eligibility for damages, the procedure for claiming damages and the calculation of the value of those damages are very complex issues. These issues become even more complex when different types of loss are examined—the law's approach to damages for financial loss, property loss, personal injury harm and harm to intangibles such as reputation or privacy is very different. This book aims to bring together analyses of all types of tortious damage awards and to identify in a single study the range of factors which dictate when damages will be awarded and how those damages are to be calculated. It is not intended that details of causes of action giving rise to damages awards will be covered—that is the remit of studies in tort. However, as we shall see, some consideration of liability will be necessary when the basis of that liability has implications for the type and range of damages awarded.

1–002

(1) The nature of damages

Damages are firstly money paid in satisfaction of an obligation to pay—not just a moral obligation but a legal obligation. Damages may result from the finding of a court, but might equally result from negotiation and agreement to pay, or from a mediated resolution of a dispute about payment, or from a concession by one person (or the insurer) of an obligation to pay. The important point is that the payment was made in recognition of a legal obligation. Any discussion of damages cannot therefore be divorced from some discussion of the bases of liability which give rise to that obligation. Thus in this examination of damages it will be necessary to venture at times into determination of when liability arises.

1–003

Secondly, damages are that amount of money which the law calculates as appropriate to the loss suffered. Any payment over and above that ceases to be classified as damages and falls into the category of charity or generosity. Not all losses resulting from an obligation-creating act are recognised as worthy of compensation. A young aspiring surgeon who severely injures

1–004

her hands when an errant driver crashes into her motorbike may suffer not only the cost of medical expenses, loss of earnings and loss of career opportunities, but also incalculable pain and suffering, the disappointment of not following in the career-steps of a beloved parent, or perhaps the devotion of a suitor to whom her status as a surgeon was part of the attraction. She will be disadvantaged for the rest of her life by her injuries; she may not be able to hold and caress her baby, she may not be able to take up tennis or water-colour painting; she may even be disadvantaged in escaping from a burning building because her disabilities prevent her from pushing open the fire doors. All of these consequences of the original event may be of enormous significance to the victim herself, but the law will pick and choose which of the injuries to recognise and which to ignore, which to rate as significant and which to disparage as trivial. So any discussion of damages necessitates a discussion of the rules and guidelines of calculation, including identification of which losses are to be taken into account in the calculation, who has the power to determine the calculation, and at what point in time the damages are to be calculated.

1–005   Thirdly, it must always be borne in mind that damages are not awarded in a vacuum. The award of damages is designed to serve particular functions. There is no value-neutral, scientifically correct determination of the appropriate damages for particular loss—the award is made in accordance with the norms and values of the society in which it is enforced and is therefore subject to socio-legal analysis. Even within western Europe there is considerable diversity as to what loss warrants a payment of damages and when, and it is unlikely, and perhaps even undesirable, that any commonality of damage awards will be reached.[1] So any discussion of damages will involve identification of why damages are awarded and some examination of what external influences will dictate payment and quantum of those damages.

1–006   Finally, no examination of damages would be complete without recognition that the procedure by which damages are claimed and obtained plays a crucial part in the determination of damages. Just because the law recognises that, in theory, the victim of loss is entitled to damages on the facts of the misadventure which led to the loss, does not guarantee that the victim will be compensated. There is many a procedural hurdle to overcome between recognition of a legal right to claim and the payment of an award of damages. Indeed few claimants overcome all the hurdles and emerge from the legal process with their full entitlement of damages, and even fewer emerge unscathed by the emotional stresses, frustrations and disappointments attendant on the legal process. It would not give an accurate picture of the law on damages to omit discussion of these procedural hurdles which face claimants for damages from initial claim form to final resolution. It is not intended within the scope of this book to provide detailed coverage of damages procedure, but issues of procedure cannot be ignored when they impinge on liability for, or quantum of, damages.

---

[1] See J. Holding and P. Kaye, *Damages for Personal Injuries: A European Perspective* (Chancery 1993).

(2) Some other terminology

There are no formal legal definitions of terms such as "accident", "victim", "liability" or "compensation", so it would be useful to specify how such terms are to be used in this book. **1–007**

(a) Accident

The issue of damages usually arises after an accident where somebody **1–008**
has suffered some harm, whether it be a harm to property (to car, house, clothes, possessions), a harm to the person (to the physical person, the mind or to feelings, emotions or reputation) or financial harm. "Accident" is defined in the Oxford Paperback Dictionary as "an unexpected or undesirable event, especially one causing injury or damage". An accident might be an event which occurs with or without human intervention. Any human intervention which is relevant may be deliberate, it may be reckless, it may be unintentional, it may even be the action of an automaton. Some accidents will attract the attention of the law; other accidents will be regarded as outside the scope of law. In this book the term "accident" will be used to cover any event which results in harm regardless of cause or state of mind of the participants.[2] Indeed in the context of a study of damages, the term "accident" might also encompass an inaccurate statement which causes another an economic loss, or a published statement which causes harm to reputation.

(b) Victim/claimant/plaintiff

The person who suffers harm as a result of the accident is often termed **1–009**
a victim of the accident. The word "victim" has connotations of innocence, the person who has been hard done by. But of course the person whose actions precipitated the accident, the person that the law might classify as the defendant in a claim for damages, might also be a victim of the accident if she or he were to suffer loss too. It would be useful to use some more value-neutral word in place of victim, but possible alternatives such as "loss bearer" are clumsy. In this book the term "victim" will be used without prejudice to liability for the loss, and more often the term "claimant' will be used to indicate the person who is seeking damages for loss suffered as a result of the accident. The choice of "claimant" over the more traditional "plaintiff" will also be used in line with the recommendations of Lord Woolf[3] and the simplified language used in the Civil Procedure Rules 1998.

---

[2] See also Cane, *Atiyah's Accidents, Compensation and the Law* (6th ed., Butterworths, 1999), where the authors choose to use the term "accident" in this wide sense.
[3] Woolf, *Access to Civil Justice* (1996).

(c) Liability

1–010   Damages arise as a result of liability for an accident. The criteria of liability and their relevance to damages will be discussed in Chapter 2, but for the purposes of definition, the term "liability" will be taken to mean an obligation imposed by law. Moral obligation and social accountability, while relevant to an analysis of damage awards, do not satisfy this definition of liability.

(d) Compensation

1–011   Compensation is difficult to define. We could use compensation in the narrow sense of the damages that the court chooses to award the claimant in a legal claim. Then "compensation" and "damages" would be interchangeable. Or we could use "compensation" in the wide sense of any redress which might make the victim feel satisfied that justice had been done for the consequences of the accident. This latter interpretation might, for example, include criminal punishment for the behaviour which caused the accident, or revenge. In this book, compensation will be taken to mean something in between. Compensation is a financial redress, an amount of money which will make the victim feel that she or he has been justly treated. This amount of money may, indeed probably will and should, differ from the damages the court chooses to award, recognising that in some circumstances the damages which the law awards represent inadequate compensation for the loss suffered, and recognising that at times damages will represent reduced compensation to take into account such matters as the claimant's contribution to the accident or collateral benefits resulting from the accident.

(3) Different types of loss

1–012   There are many different ways in which someone might suffer loss as a result of an accident. There might be physical injury to the person, either traumatic injury or a slow-developing condition or disease. There might be injury to the mind, taking the form of a medically-diagnosable psychiatric injury, or a less specific disturbance of the mind or depression, or grief or injury to emotions such as loss of confidence or humiliation. There might be damage to personality, such as loss of reputation or loss of privacy. There might be injury to property, such as damage to a house or to equipment or to a car, or to a watch or clothing. And finally there might be financial loss, which could take the form of financial loss consequent on personal injury or property damage, such as loss of earnings or loss of income from damage to equipment; or could be a pure economic loss unrelated to other damage, such as loss resulting from reliance on inaccurate advice, loss resulting from closure of a road or the cutting of an electricity supply, or loss of the expectation of some future financial benefit, an inheritance for instance.

Any one of these forms of loss will be distressing to the sufferer, and the 1–013
victim may well feel justified in demanding compensation from the person
who caused the loss. The law in the context of tort however does not treat
these types of loss equally. Regardless of the value of the loss to the victim,
the law has, as case law has developed since 1932,[4] created a hierarchy of
losses, and the claimant's chances of obtaining damages with respect to the
loss suffered depend on where the loss fits into this hierarchy.

At the top of the hierarchy is traumatic personal injury. If a negligent 1–014
car driver runs over a pedestrian the law very readily compensates for any
broken bones or invasions of the body which result. The chances of
recovering damages for this type of loss are good. Solicitors will be keen to
take on cases of this sort even where the claimant cannot afford to pay
solicitor's fees in advance.[5] Legal aid was once readily available for traumatic personal injury cases, and now conditional fee agreements[6] will be
easy to negotiate.

Second in the hierarchy is property damage. Again the law is sympathetic 1–015
to a claim for property damage resulting from an accident and the claimant
has every chance of recovery. The advantage of property damage is its ease
of calculation. The damage is usually done once and for all, and future,
speculative losses are rare. Nor is there likely to be risk of a floodgate of
actions.

Third in the hierarchy is consequential economic loss. Once liability for 1–016
a personal injury or a property damage can be established, liability for a
truly consequential economic loss follows without further difficulty.[7] This
consequential loss is limited in scope by requiring that it is related to a
physical damage, and is usually comparatively easy to calculate.

Fourth, and surprisingly given the law's reluctance to recognise non- 1–017
physical injury, is the unique damage of interference with beneficial use of
land which is protected by the law of nuisance. Provided that the interference has been substantial, a measurement which is not absolute but rather
depends on detriment to the claimant's existing standard of amenity, establishing liability for nuisance is not problematic. The explanation for this is
that nuisance can be described as a land-protecting tort, not a person-
protecting tort. The interest which is recognised by the law in nuisance is
an interest in land, which in the history of the development of English law
has been held in high regard. Non-physical damage which results from
interference with personal interests is not given the same protection.

Next there is iatrogenic (non-traumatic) personal injury. Establishing a 1–018
causative relationship between the accident and slow-developing injury can

---

[4] The first judicial recognition of a general duty of care in tort was in *Donoghue v. Stevenson*
[1932] A.C. 562.
[5] *Thai Trading Co v. Taylor* [1998] N.L.J. 405 makes clear that a solicitor can take on a
case on a speculative basis, without entering into a conditional fee agreement. The solicitor
cannot however then charge an uplifted fee. In cases with good prospects of success, this
practice has always been not uncommon.
[6] Courts and Legal Services Act 1990, s. 58; Conditional Fee Agreements Regulations 1995
(S.I. 1995 No. 1675); Conditional Fee Agreements Order 1995 (S.I. 1995 No. 1674).
[7] *Spartan Steel v. Martin* [1972] 1 Q.B. 27.

often prove fatal to the claim[8] and there are many pitfalls on the road to compensation for such a claim.[9]

1–019   Sixth in the hierarchy is diagnosable psychiatric injury. Although modern medicine might regard psychiatric injury as equivalent to personal injury, the law remains suspicious of psychiatric harm and imposes additional limitations on recovery of damages for such injury.[10] These limitations mean that very few victims who suffer psychiatric injury as a result of an accident attributable to a defendant, even if they can prove their damage, prove negligence (or intention) and establish causation, will be awarded damages unless they fall within what might be described as arbitrary categories of victim. These categories are based on formal relationships and on geography and may bear no relationship to the reality of the suffering in an individual case.[11]

1–020   Seventh there is pure economic loss. Liability in negligence for pure economic loss fluctuates with changing political and economic policy, but generally allows some recovery of pure economic loss resulting from negligent statements,[12] and more restricted liability for pure economic loss resulting from a negligent act.[13] The distinction between negligent statements and negligent acts is difficult to define,[14] and the denial of liability for economic loss appears to be an issue of political policy rather than of logic.[15]

1–021   Then, injury to reputation, which the law does recognise, but creates additional hurdles such as a wide range of defences. Funding of such claims has always been problematic,[16] jury trials are still common for defamation, and the claimant takes a huge risk on the question of costs.[17]

1–022   Last in the hierarchy are the more non-specific types of damage, which tend to be difficult to prove and difficult to quantify: emotional suffering, damage to privacy and personal integrity, loss of expectation of future benefits and the like. The law rarely provides a remedy for these types of loss unless they are consequent on a damage further up in the damage hierarchy, regardless of how personally devastating the loss might be to the victim.

1–023   From the point of view of the victim, aspects of this damage hierarchy are both illogical and unjust. Why should property damage be rated higher than psychiatric injury? Why is pure economic loss less worthy of protec-

---

[8] For example *Wilsher v. Essex Area Health Authority* [1998] 2 W.L.R. 557 and *Loveday v. Renton* [1990] 1 Med. L.R. 117.

[9] See Stapleton, *Disease and the Compensation Debate* (Clarenden, 1986).

[10] *Alcock v. Chief Constable of South Yorkshire Police* [1992] 4 All E.R. 907; *White v. Chief Constable of South Yorkshire Police* [1999] 1 All E.R. 1.

[11] See criticisms of the law in Law Commission Consultation Paper, *Liability for Psychiatric Illness* (No. 137, 1995) and Law Commission, *Liability for Psychiatric Illness* (No. 249, 1998).

[12] For example *White v. Jones* [1995] 1 All E.R. 691.

[13] See *Murphy v. Brentwood* [1990] 1 A.C. 378.

[14] For example *Ross v. Caunters* [1980] Ch. 297—an act or a statement?

[15] Particularly in the case of defective premises. English law is out of line with that of all other commonwealth jurisdictions. See R. Martin, "Delivering Common Law—Invercargill goes to the House of Lords" (1997) 60 M.L.R. 94.

[16] The defendants in *Macdonald v. Steel The Times* June 16, 1997 were unable to obtain legal aid for their defence.

[17] For example the unsuccessful action by the former politician, Jonathan Aitken against *The Guardian* newspaper, unreported.

tion than consequent economic loss? Why does the law provide no remedy for grief or interference with privacy? Some explanations of the law's approach are historical; lack of medical expertise on diseases of the mind has meant that courts have traditionally been less impressed by evidence of mental injury as compared with physical injury. Some explanations are cultural; for example as a society we have not valued privacy in the same way as some other European cultures which provide legal protection against interference. Some explanations are political; for example the decision in *Murphy*[18] which denied liability for pure economic loss resulting from a negligent act on the premise that it is the responsibility of individuals to make provision for the insurance of their own property, and not of the local authority to enforce building regulations. And often the restriction on recovery of damages is a practical one: where there is any risk of liability giving rise to a multitude of actions the law will take a cautious approach to the award of damages, and some types of injury are more vulnerable than others to the floodgates argument. Whatever the justification for categorising types of damage in this way, the existence of the damage hierarchy means that classification of the type of loss is an important element in the victim's strategy in a claim for damages.

(4) One bite at the cherry

A particular feature of damages awards in this jurisdiction which distinguishes our law from that of most other European jurisdictions[19] is that damages, whatever their nature, are awarded as a lump sum. Once an award has been made by a court or agreed by the parties in settlement of a claim, then regardless of the way the loss progresses, there can be no further consideration of damages. If the claimant were to make a miraculous recovery after the damages award, then the claimant has received a windfall which cannot be recouped by the defendant. If the claimant were to develop complications of the injury which result in significantly greater disability and expense, the claimant cannot come back for a further award. Thus the question of when to bring the damages claim to a climax becomes an important part in the claimant's strategy of claim—too early and the full implications of the loss or injury may not yet be apparent; too late and the claimant has suffered the emotional and financial hardship of waiting for resolution of the claim longer than was necessary. Indeed the long and stressful period of waiting for resolution of the claim can in itself give rise to a claim for damages if the claimant develops symptoms of stress which amount to recognised compensation neurosis.[20]

1–024

This is more than a procedural issue. The question of when to resolve a damages claim can impact on the parties' motivation to pursue the claim

1–025

---

[18] n. 13.

[19] See for example R. Redmond-Cooper, "Aspects of the French Law of Damages", in *Damages for Personal Injuries: A European Perspective* (Holding and Kaye, Chancery, 1993).

[20] See C. Vincent and I. Robertson, "Recovering from a Medical Accident: the Consequences for Patients and their Families", in *Medical Accidents* (C. Vincent, M. Ennis and R. Audley ed., Oxford, 1993).

or defence of the claim, can influence settlement or protraction of the claim, and can dictate how much in damages will be awarded.

1–026   The "one bite at the cherry" approach of English law means that inevitably damages awards will be inaccurate. Except in minor personal injury cases, where the claimant will be well recovered by the time of resolution of the claim, and in most property damage claims where the damage is done once and for all, the exercise of damage calculation will involve estimation of what loss will be suffered in the future. The more serious the injury or loss, the more difficult that future calculation will be. In some cases of personal injury or damage to reputation the calculation is made all the more difficult by the fact that the loss is an exacerbation of an existing damage rather than an entirely new damage. In cases of medical negligence for example, the negligent act may have been performed in the course of treating an already ill person. In a case of defamation, the defamatory comments may exaggerate an already blemished reputation. The damages in such cases will need to reflect not the entirety of the loss but that part of the loss which can be attributed to the legally recognised cause, requiring a consideration not just of what will happen in respect of the loss, but what would have happened had the accident not occurred.

1–027   The difficulties of prediction were summed up by Lord Scarman in *Lim Poh Choo v. Camden and Islington Area Health Authority*:[21]

> "The award is final; it is not susceptible to review as the future unfolds, substituting fact for estimate. Knowledge of the future being denied to mankind, so much of the award as is to be attributed to future loss and suffering—in many cases the major part of the award—will almost surely be wrong. There is really only one certainty: the future will prove the award to be either too high or too low."

1–028   More recently the House of Lords in *Wells v. Wells*[22] agreed:

> "It is the nature of a lump sum payment that it may, in respect of future pecuniary loss, prove to be either too little or too much."

The lump sum rule can work unfairly on both claimant and defendant. The rule applies not only to court awards but also to negotiated settlements of claims. In a case which received much media coverage in 1997, a Health Authority settled a claim against it by a child who suffered severe injuries at birth. A few days after the settlement was agreed, the child died. The settlement had included a considerable sum for future medical care. The defendants were unable to undo the settlement and the money went to the child's parents as beneficiaries.

1–029   There are many critics of the lump sum rule[23] on the basis of the inac-

---

[21] [1980] A.C. 174.

[22] [1999] 1 A.C. 345.

[23] See for example Pearson, Report of the Royal Commission on Civil Liability and Compensation for Personal Injury, Cmnd. 7054 (1987, Vol. 1, Ch. 14); Rowley, "Public Choice and the Economic Analysis of Law", in *Law and Economics* (Mercuro, ed., Kluwer, 1989); B. Markesinis and S. Deakin, *Tort Law* (4th ed., Clarenden Press, 1999).

curacy of awards and the injustice of refusal to correct inappropriate awards. The award of a very large single sum of money to someone who then has the responsibility of managing and wisely investing that sum to provide for the future, creates stresses of its own. Research suggests that lump sums are not always invested wisely with the result that the money runs out well before the need for support, and some recipients treat the award in the way they might a lottery win.[24] In *Wells v. Wells*[25] the House of Lords recognised that claimants of damages awards did not have the investments skills and facilities of prudent stock market investors and that it should be assumed that the recipient of a damages award would not get the same rate of advantage on money invested as a player on the stock market.

Once the claimant has received the award, the law takes no further interest in how the money is spent. The claimant who successfully convinces the court that costs of private medical treatment should be awarded[26] is not obliged once the award is made to show that the money was actually used on medical treatment. The claimant who chooses to spend the entire award on a holiday or gambling is not then disentitled to social security and support, with the result that there is in effect double recovery of loss. **1–030**

The strongest criticism of the lump sum rule in recent years comes from Lord Steyn in *Wells v. Wells*[27] where he said: **1–031**

> "The court ought to be given the power of its own motion to make an award for periodic payments rather than a lump sum in appropriate cases. Such power is perfectly consistent with the principle of full compensation for pecuniary loss. Except perhaps for the distaste of personal injury lawyers for a change to a familiar system, I can think of no substantial argument to the contrary. But judges cannot make the change. Only Parliament can."[28]

However there can be advantages to the lump sum. The up-front payment of the full award gives to the claimant freedom to do as she wishes with the money—indulge in a holiday or repay the generosity of friends for example. A lump sum may enable the claimant to change a way of life— to move to another country where the weather is warmer, to move back to be near relatives, to start a new venture or business. **1–032**

The most significant advantage of the lump sum rule is its finality. The House of Lords in *Mulholland v. Mitchell*[29] made clear that final resolution of litigation was essential to the smooth running of our legal system and that it was undesirable to leave damage awards hanging, or to reopen awards unless there were exceptional justifying circumstances. It is in **1–033**

---

[24] See D. Harris ed., *Compensation and Support for Illness and Injury* (Clarenden, 1984) Ch. 3; H. Genn, *Hard Bargaining* (OUP 1987); Cane, *supra*, n. 2 p. 115; Law Commission, *Personal Injury Compensation: How Much is Enough?* (No. 225, 1994).
[25] See n. 22.
[26] Law Reform (Personal Injuries) Act 1948, s. 2(4).
[27] See n. 22.
[28] at p. 502.
[29] [1971] A.C. 666.

lawyers' interests that some sort of lump sum payment remains to ensure they are paid for their services.[30] The insurance industry argues strongly for the continuation of the lump sum approach. Any system of periodic payment of damages would increase the administration costs of each claim and would involve the extra costs of claim reassessment with changing circumstances, so resulting in increased premiums. Indeed claimants themselves seem to prefer the lump sum approach, giving them autonomy over their money[31] and any system of court-awarded periodic payment might force claimants to settle for less than the claim is worth so as to preserve their right to dictate the form of the award.[32] The Pearson Commission recommendations included giving the claimant the option of taking the lump sum or asking for periodic payments.[33]

Having stated the lump sum rule of damage awards, there are several exceptions to note.

(a) Continuing wrongs

1–034   Most damages awards result from a single one-off incident—a car crash, a medical accident, an assault, the publishing of a statement, the giving of a piece of information. The lump sum rule applies to these one-off incidents. Some harms however are repeated, and may in the future continue to be repeated. A leakage of chemicals from a factory onto the claimant's land, a blocking of a right of way, a defamation which continues to appear in a newspaper or a continuing trespass over someone's land; all these are continuing wrongs for which a "once and for all" award of damages would be inappropriate. In these circumstances the claimant may return to claim damages for the further wrong.

(b) Provisional damages

1–035   The possibility of provisional damages was introduced in 1982[34] and came into force on July 1, 1985 to apply retrospectively. The amendments to the law were incorporated into the Supreme Court Act.[35] Provisional damages may only be awarded in very limited circumstances. Where there is

> "proved or admitted to be a chance that at some definite or indefinite time in the future the injured person will, as a result of the act or omission which gave rise to the cause of action, develop some serious disease or suffer some serious deterioration in his physical or mental condition"[36],

---

[30] Suggested by Markesinis and Deakin, *Tort Law* (Clarenden, 1999), p. 744.
[31] Law Commission, *Personal Injury Compensation: How Much is Enough?* (No. 225, 1994).
[32] Assuming that the settlement process remains subject to the common law rules on freedom of contract.
[33] See n. 23.
[34] s. 6, The Administration of Justice Act 1982.
[35] s. 32A, Supreme Court Act 1981.
[36] s. 32A (1).

then the court may make an award of damages which does not take into account the risk, but allows for the possibility that the claimant returns for a further award should the risk come off.

The provisional damages procedure is not often used, and appears to be restricted to those cases where the original injury gives rise to a risk of epilepsy from a head injury, or arthritis from a bone injury. Provisional damages must be pleaded by the claimant[37] rather than initiated by the court. There will only be one right to return, and the court may set a time limit within which the provisional claim must be made. 1–036

The criteria for a provisional damages award were set out in *Willson v. Ministry of Defence*.[38] There must be a measurable chance that a specific medical risk, which must be identified in some detail, will materialise at a future date. That risk must involve a serious deterioration of the claimant's condition. And thirdly the court must be satisfied that a "once and for all" award would be inappropriate in the circumstances. The plaintiff can only come back to the court once in respect of each type of deterioration specified in the order for provisional damages, so if for example a claimant were to develop arthritis over time in different parts of the body, once a provisional damages award had been made there would be no further right of recovery.

Another issue of concern in the context of provisional damages is whether the dependants of a person who had been awarded provisional damages were precluded from claiming under the Fatal Accidents Act 1976 by reason of the provisional damages award. This matter was considered by the Court of Appeal in *Middleton v. Elliot Turbomachinery Ltd*[39] but the judgment did not result in clarification. However the Damages Act 1996[40] now provides that an award of provisional damages to a person who subsequently dies as a result of the act or omission in respect of which damages were awarded does not bar a Fatal Accidents claim, although any damages awarded to the claimant which covered the period which in the event falls after their death will be taken into account in assessing the loss of dependancy of the dependants. Provisional damages are discretionary and *Willson* makes clear that courts will use the procedure cautiously. The result is that provisional damages provide only a severely restricted exception to the lump sum rule and do not fulfil the objective of providing reassessment in unjust cases.[41] Further discussion of provisional damages can be found in Chapter 9 at paras 9–096 *et seq*. 1–037

(c) Agreement between the parties

The law does, in theory, allow that awards can be made in the form of periodic payments if both parties agree,[42] although some doubt was cast 1–038

---

[37] See C.P.R. r. 16.4(1)(d) and the accompanying Practice Direction.
[38] [1991] 1 All E.R. 638.
[39] *The Times*, October 29, 1990.
[40] s. 3.
[41] See comments in Markesinis and Deakin, *Tort Law* (Clarenden, 1999) p. 474, and concerns expressed in Law Commission Consultation Paper (No. 125).
[42] *Fournier v. Canadian National Railway* [1927] A.C. 167.

on the power of the court to agree such an award.[43] However section 2 of
the Damages Act 1996 makes clear that with the agreement of the parties,
the court may make an order for damages which is wholly or partly in the
form of periodic payments. It was pointed out by Lord Steyn in *Wells v.
Wells*[44] that such agreement is rarely forthcoming, and that the "present
power to order periodic payments is a dead letter".[45]

(d) Interim payments

1–039   In cases where some liability is admitted or where the chances of establishing liability and substantial damages are good, the claimant may apply
to the court for an interim payment pending the final award. Interim damages may be awarded in respect of any claim for damages but are most
frequently awarded in personal injury cases. The court will require the
claimant to establish high probability of final success.[46] The defendant must
be in a position to pay (in other words be insured, be a public authority or
have other means),[47] but the claimant is not required to show whether or
why the money is needed.[48] There are no rules on how much can be
awarded as interim damages; the usual approach is to award half or two
thirds of an amount which the court envisages as the final value of the
claim, or any special damages which are easily quantifiable. There can be
more than one application for interim payments for the same claim.

1–040   The interim damages procedures are not frequently used by claimants[49]
and the decision of the Court of Appeal in *Campbell v. Mylchreest*[50] will
further inhibit applications. There it was made clear the that the court
would not be prepared to award interim payments where the application
was heard close in time to trial, where the payment of an interim award
would be too small to justify the court's time and the exercise of the court's
power, where the claimant was delaying in pursuing the claim and an
interim award would assist in the delay, and finally where the way the
money was to be used might prejudice the final award of damages.

1–041   There are some good reasons for not applying for an interim award.
Social security recoupment procedures (see Chapters 9 and 11) apply to
interim awards as to final awards, and so much of the interim payment
may go to the Compensation Recovery Unit. An interim payment may also
affect the claimant's entitlement to benefits by giving the claimant a capital
sum which will be taken into account in eligibility criteria.

The most obvious use for interim payments is in the case of split trials,[51]

---

[43] *Metcalfe v. London Passenger Transport Board* [1938] 2 All E.R. 352, 355.
[44] See n. 22.
[45] at p. 502.
[46] *Gibbons v. Wall, The Times*, February 24, 1998.
[47] See C.P.R. 1998, Part 25.
[48] *Stringman v. McCardle* [1994] 1 W.L.R. 1653.
[49] See J. Pritchard and N. Solomon, *Personal Injury Litigation* (9th ed., FT Law and Tax,
1997).
[50] [1999] P.I.Q.R. Q17.
[51] *Coenen v. Payne* [1974] 1 W.L.R. 984.

where the issue of liability is decided but the issue of quantum is delayed while further information about the damage is gathered.

(e) Structured settlements

The most important exception to the lump sum rule is a comparatively recent one: the introduction of the structured settlement[52] in the late 1980s[53] following developments in North America. This is not so much a legal development but a practice development which resulted from changes in the law on taxation of annuities. Structured settlements have been sufficiently successful to induce further accommodating changes in tax law[54] and to be formally recognised and facilitated within the Damages Act 1996.[55]

1–042

The details of structured settlements will be discussed in Chapter 9, paras 9–089 *et seq.*, but it is worth noting in this context that structured settlements allow the claimant not to take the awarded sum in lump form but rather to ask the defendant's insurer (or the defendant in the case of self-insured institutions such as health authorities) to purchase with the award money an annuity which will provide the plaintiff with an inflation proof income for as long as is needed. This can of course only be done with the co-operation of the defendant and the court cannot direct that a structured settlement be set up. What was originally a complex procedure has been simplified by the development of four "model agreements" between the Inland Revenue and The British Association of Insurers.

1–043

The significant issue about structured settlements is not the way in which they impinge on the lump sum rule—so few of the total number of claimants can take advantage of them that they have little effect on the overall picture. Rather the settlements are interesting in the way that they demonstrate that where the law is inadequate, practice finds a way of getting around the law, what Markesinis and Deakin call "bargains in the shadow of the law".[56] Law reform in the area of damages, particularly personal injury damages, has been excruciatingly slow despite numerous Law Commission consultation papers and a plethora of critical commentary.

1–044

Few would dispute that damage awards are inadequate,[57] that there is unnecessary complication and delay in the procedure leading to the award,[58] and that the methods of calculation of awards are archaic and fail to take account of more sophisticated actuarial techniques. Individual courts have been hesitant to make structural changes to long standing tradition in this area and have awaited legislative intervention.[59] When that

---

[52] See R. Lewis, *Structured Settlements: The Law and Practice* (Sweet & Maxwell, 1993).
[53] Structured settlements were first recognised by the courts in *Kelly v. Dawes, The Times,* September 27 1990.
[54] Finance Act 1995 and Finance Act 1996.
[55] ss. 2 & 4.
[56] Markesinis and Deakin, *Tort Law* (Clarenden, 1999) p. 747.
[57] Except perhaps Atiyah, see P. Atiyah, *The Damages Lottery* (Hart, 1997).
[58] See Woolf, *Access to Civil Justice* (1996).
[59] In *Wells v. Wells* (see n. 22) Lord Steyn criticises the inability of the courts to award periodic payments but points out at p. 502 that "judges cannot make the change. Only Parliament can solve the problem." In March 2000 the Lord Chancellor's Department

legislative intervention has failed to materialise, other types of reform have
developed to adapt practice to economic realities. Structured settlements
are one such example; the decision on investment rates in *Wells v. Wells*[60]
is another (see Chapter 9).

1–045   It may be the case that structured settlements will always be too complex
and too expensive to become mainstream in damages awards. They will
continue however to serve as a reminder that the lump sum rule is inappropriate and inadequate for all but minor loss, and have instigated a flurry of
Law Commission activity which may, eventually, lead to reform.

(5) Types of damages

1–046   To pluck a lump sum of damages from the air in each case would be an
impossible task. To make calculation more manageable the lump sum is
divided into types and categories of damages, and each category has
developed its own rules and guidelines on calculation in accordance with
recognition of the principle of *restitutio in integrum*.

(a) Nominal damages

1–047   Some wrongs are actionable *per se*; that is the claimant need only establish that the wrong was committed, and not that damage was caused by
the wrong, to have a right of action; for example assault, battery, libel, and
possibly breach of confidence.[161] Other wrongs however, such as negligence
and nuisance, require that the claimant has suffered some damage before
the law will recognise the wrong.

Where a wrong is actionable *per se* but no actual damage has resulted,
nominal damages may be awarded to give token recognition to the existence of the wrong. Nominal damages are traditionally a "peg . . . on which
to hang costs",[62] although now that the award of costs is within the discretion of the court[63] it is not necessarily the case that because the claimant
was awarded nominal damages, there will also be an award of costs.

1–048   If the claimant in the case of a wrong actionable *per se* suffers actual
damage then there is no need to consider a nominal damages award, and
the court will award compensatory damages. There can be no nominal
damages award where the wrong was not actionable *per se*. Nominal damages may be only very token, especially when the court thinks the legal
action was a waste of time. If the court accepts that the claimant was
libelled for example, but takes the view that the libel was trivial, then a
derisory, token amount of damages will be awarded to reflect annoyance

---

issued a Consultation Paper canvassing, *inter alia*, views on the options for reform of the
lump sum system.
[60] See n. 22.
[61] *Attorney General v. Guardian Newspapers Ltd (No 2)* [1989] 1 All E.R. 1089.
[62] *Beaumont v. Greathead* [1946] 2 Q.B. 494, 499.
[63] Supreme Court Act 1981, s. 51.

that such a trivial matter should be brought into the public arena.[64] This may also have costs implications for the claimant.

(b) Compensatory damages

Compensatory damages are damages which are intended to compensate for the actual harm which the claimant has suffered as a result of the accident. If an action is framed in tort, the purpose of compensation is to make good to the claimant as nearly as possible "that sum of money which will put the person who has been injured . . . in the same position as he would have been if he had not sustained the wrong".[65]   1–049

Details of calculation of compensatory damages will be considered in more detail throughout this book in relation to particular types of loss. Meanwhile, it would be useful to define the two components of compensatory damages.   1–050

(i) Special damages

As a rule of thumb, special damages are those damages which cover the period between the date of the accident and the date of trial or final agreement of award. Because they are past damages they must be specified in detail and can be easily calculated. Some special damages will cover money that the victim has outlaid and wants recouped, and others will cover money that the victim expected to receive in that time but which the accident prevented. Special damages will therefore include such things as any property damage, travel expenses, necessary equipment, the cost of extra home help. They will also include net loss of income consequent on the accident. The advantage to the claimant of a complete special damages claim is that special damages attract greater interest than other heads of damage (see below).   1–051

(ii) General damages

Again as a rule of thumb, general damages tend to cover losses which are predicted to occur after the trial date. The exception to this is the award for pain and suffering which cannot easily be divided into pre-trial and post-trial suffering and so all pain and suffering is included in the general damages category. Another way of looking at general damages is that they cover those losses whose value cannot be specified by the claimant and to which the court must attach a value.   1–052

Some commentators divide general and special damages differently. Pritchard and Solomon[66] for example define special damages to include future loss of earnings and appear to limit general damages to the award for pain,

---

[64] For example see *Pamplin v. Express Newspapers (No. 2)* [1988] 1 All E.R. 282.
[65] *Livingstone v. Rawyards Coal Co* (1880) 5 App. Cas. 25, 39.
[66] J. Pritchard and N. Solomon, *Personal Injury Litigation* (FT Law and Tax, 1997) p. 73.

suffering and loss of amenity. The distinctions we use in the course of this book are however the more commonly accepted definitions.[67]

1–053   Details of general damage awards will be discussed in Chapter 9. The types of loss which might be compensated by general damages are, as well as pain, suffering and loss of amenities, loss of future earnings (including "lost years" earnings—that is those earnings which will have been lost because of a shortened life expectancy) and the cost of future medical care and attention.

(c) Aggravated damages

1–054   In some circumstances the court may award, either instead of or in addition to the compensatory damages discussed above, aggravated damages. These are awarded to reflect the gross nature of the wrong done or the effect the wrong has had on the feelings or reputation of the claimant. In an public assault and battery for example, where the claimant was frightened, humiliated and embarrassed but suffered no real bodily harm, the court might award aggravated damages to reflect injury to feelings and to show disapproval of the defendant's behaviour. In one sense these damages are also compensatory in that they compensate for harm that does not readily fall into the categories of bodily harm, property damage or economic loss. In another sense, while these damages are clearly not intended to be punitive, they go further than straight compensation into the area of public recognition of disapproval of behaviour.[68]

1–055   While there seems no good reason why aggravated damages should not be awarded in respect of all wrongs, the law as it stands limits aggravated damages awards to the intentional torts, defamation and some statutory wrongs such as discrimination, but not negligence or nuisance[69]. The future of aggravated damages as a separate head of damages may be in doubt if Law Commission recommendations[70] are implemented.

(d) Exemplary damages

1–056   Exemplary, or punitive, damages, sit on the cusp of the distinction between tort law and criminal law. They are clearly not compensatory, and are awarded to prevent the defendant from benefiting in any way from the wrong committed. They do not focus on the effect of the wrong on the claimant, but rather on the behaviour of the defendant. The scope of exemplary damages has been greatly limited and now can only be awarded where there has been oppressive, arbitrary or unconstitutional behaviour on the part of servants of the government, where the defendant might benefit financially from the commission of the tort, or where justified by

---

[67] See for example Jones, *Textbook on Torts* (5th ed., Blackstones, 1996) p. 514; Markesinis and Deakin, *Tort Law* (Clarenden, 1999) p. 724.
[68] *Joliffe v. Willmett & Co* [1971] 1 All E.R. 478; *Broome v. Cassell & Co* [1972] A.C. 1027; *Appleton v. Garrett* [1996] P.I.Q.R. 1.
[69] *Kralj v. McGrath* [1986] 1 All E.R. 54; *AB v. South West Water* [1993] 1 All E.R. 609.
[70] Law Commission, *Aggravated, Exemplary and Restitutionary Damages* (No. 247, 1997).

statute.[71] Such damages are most commonly awarded in cases of trespass or defamation and will be dealt with more fully in Chapter 5. Suffice to say at this point that there may be changes afoot in this area if the Law Commission recommendations take effect.[72]

---

[71] *Rookes v. Barnard* [1964] A.C. 1129.
[72] See n. 70.

CHAPTER 2

DAMAGES IN PERSPECTIVE

It would be unwise and misleading to examine issues of liability and **2–001** quantum of damages as though these issues were divorced and separable from the context in which they are awarded. Damages for loss are a small component of a legal system which poses its own constraints and values on the way in which laws are framed and in which they operate. That legal system is in itself part of a wider framework of political policy, economic policy and cultural values which have more than a passing influence on how laws work and who benefits from them. It would also be misleading to consider issues of compensation for loss in a purely national context. The globalisation of health risks, issues of free movement of goods and migration, the growing import and export market and the rapid development of world-wide technology (the internet for example) mean that any discussion of damages must take account of the European and international influences on the development of national law.

1. CONSTRAINTS OF THE LEGAL SYSTEM

Modern law has a long history. The way that English law (and con- **2–002** sequently the wider common law) has developed is by the drip method— over time each individual case has built on the body of previous law on a particular issue to create a stalagmite of law which stands independent of the bodies of law on other issues. There has been no major overhaul of law along the lines of that in other Western European countries[1] nor any overarching conceptual restructuring of the huge variety of individual laws which together make up the legal system.

Hence modern English laws are still hidebound by medieval causes of **2–003** action. The rules of precedent in the common law, far from providing the flexibility to adapt to modern circumstances, frequently serve to entrench positions which are at odds with the modern world. Why does the claimant for damages in private nuisance need to have a legal interest in land[2] whether suing for property damage or interference with comfort and convenience, whereas the claimant in *Rylands v. Fletcher*[3] need satisfy no such

---

[1] For example the French Civil Code of 1804, the German Burgerliches Gesetzbuch (BGB) of 1896, the Swiss Civil Code of 1907, the Italian Civil Code of 1942, the Portuguese Civil Code of 1967 and the Dutch Nieuw Burgerlijk Wetboek (NBW) of 1992.
[2] *Malone v. Laskey* [1907] 2 K.B. 141; *Hunter v. Canary Wharf* [1997] 2 W.L.R. 684.
[3] (1866) L.R. 1 Ex 265.

requirement? Why must a trespass be direct, so that the claimant for an indirect, intentionally caused injury (for example where the wrongdoer deliberately scatters tacks on the road with the intention that the cyclist, who is due to ride along the road later that day, will puncture a tyre, fall and suffer injury) must resort to arguments based on *Wilkinson v. Downton*?[4]

2–004   Why does it matter where the person who was hit on the head by a flying loose chimney pot was standing when the injury occurred? If the claimant was on the same property there would be a remedy in Occupier's Liability; if on a public highway any remedy would be in public nuisance; if he was the owner of neighbouring property and standing on his own land the remedy would lie in private nuisance; but if the claimant was on neighbouring land without a legal interest in that land the only remedy would be to attempt an argument in negligence or *Rylands v. Fletcher*. Chances of success, and therefore recovery of damages, will depend on which remedy the claimant is able to use. Should it really matter where the chimney fell?

2–005   The rigid distinction between tort and contract in English law also creates inconsistency in damages awards. Damages are awarded in contract on the basis of the position the claimant would have been in had the contract been performed, while damages are awarded in tort on the basis of the position the claimant would have been in before the tort was committed. Contract damages thus include recognition of, for example, loss of expectation, while tort damages purport to be compensatory for loss already suffered only. The rules of limitation also differ between contract and tort.[5] Thus in terms of the damages recovered it can make a significant difference in law whether the action to claim damages is framed in tort or contract. That significance might not be immediately obvious to, or comprehensible by, the claimant. If a ferris wheel at a fairground is carelessly operated such that someone is injured, should it matter when it comes to calculation of the damages whether the injured person has bought a ticket to enter the fair? If the owner of a house contracts building work to a main contractor and the main contractor subtracts to a subcontractor who performs the work carelessly, should the chances of recovery of damages for that careless work, or for damage which results from it, depend on whether the house owner has taken out a separate contract with the subcontractor?[6] The laws of other European jurisdictions are not trammelled by the tort/contract distinction in this way as they recognise a wider law of obligations encompassing both contract and tort.[7]

2–006   Rigidity of traditional classifications of law is further enforced by the hierarchy of English courts. Judges at first instance may well acknowledge that the law is anachronistic and unjust on a particular point but the judge is bound by decisions of higher courts. The judge who bravely decides contrary to precedent is likely to be appealed, and as defendants in damages

---

[4] [1897] 2 Q.B. 57.
[5] See Chapter 3.
[6] *Murphy v. Brentwood* [1990] 2 All E.R. 908.
[7] See M. Vranken, *Fundamentals of European Civil Law* (Blackstones, 1997).

cases are more likely than not to be insurance companies or other monied institutions, those defendants can afford to take the case to appeal. Indeed it is generally in their interest to do so if the out-of-line first instance judgment were to set a precedent of liability. Attempts by lower courts to make new law or adapt old laws to modern society are often thwarted by more conservative higher courts.[8]

The conservatism of English superior courts is unsurprising given the unique criteria for appointment to the Court of Appeal or House of Lords. These judges come from a very select group of barristers who have achieved the status of Queen's Counsel. The process of qualification for tenancy in barristers' chambers and qualification for appointment as Queen's Counsel has not yet fully addressed the issue of sex, race, class and state education representation. Even at circuit and high court level such representation is disproportional.[9] Other commonwealth jurisdictions, most of which operate a fused legal profession, appoint their judiciary from a far wider pool and are very conscious of wide representation. European judiciaries, while still not fully representative, are not characterised by school tie and class traditions in the same way.   2–007

The constitution of the judiciary is particularly relevant in the context of damages because civil claims for damages are decided by a judge (or on appeal several judges) without a jury. The homogeneity of the judiciary in this jurisdiction has influenced issues of both liability for and quantum of damages. The paucity of experience of unemployment, poverty, the diversity of family relationships and the hardships imposed by disability is evident in some judgments in which assumptions are made[10] and in which claimants are left uncared for not because they have failed to establish negligently caused injury, but because of reverence for the technical niceties of law.[11]   2–008

---

[8] For example the judgment in *Khorisandijan v. Bush* [1993] 3 W.L.R. 476, which attempted to widen the range of plaintiffs in a private nuisance action suing for interference with comfort and convenience (in that case harassing telephone calls), was rejected by the House of Lords in *Hunter v. Canary Wharf* [1997] 2 W.L.R. 684, which restored the traditional, but anachronistic, requirement that only persons with legal interest in the land are entitled to protection.

[9] For example of the 85 judges appointed since 1997, only seven were women and only one of those women was appointed above circuit court level. Women represent only 6% of the judiciary despite the fact that there are now more women than men practising in the legal profession as a whole. No woman has ever sat on the House of Lords and only one woman has ever been appointed to the Court of Appeal. Ethnic minority groups are represented by only 1% of the judiciary; 79% of judges appointed since 1997 came from a public school background; 73% had an Oxbridge tertiary education. These figures are taken from the journal of the Labour Research Department, an independent trade union, and were reported in the *Guardian*, June 1, 1999. Since this report was published, one more woman has been appointed to the Court of Appeal.

[10] For example assumptions about the way in which female relatives or new wives will take over housecare and childcare responsibilities when a wife and mother is killed or disabled in an accident. See K. O'Donovan, Legal Recognition of the Value of Housework 8 F.L.R. 215; R. Greycar, "Women's Work: Who Cares?" (1992) 14 Sydney L.R. 86; R. Greycar and J. Morgan, *The Hidden Gender of Law* (Federation Press, Sydney, 1990).

[11] For example *Hunt v. Severs* [1994] 2 A.C. 350, where a very severely disabled claimant was denied the costs of care because her young husband, who had given up his job to provide the care, was the negligent party. This judgment ignored the reality that the defendant was the husband's insurer, he having paid premiums to protect against just such a circumstance. It was not recognised that the young husband may choose not to provide this intensive care for ever, and the claimant cannot then come back to court to ask for damages for the cost of care.

(1) Political constraints and the preferencing of certain types of injury

2–009   Not all accidents and not all injuries are treated the same in law. Even within the confines of a discussion of damages for personal injury, the liability for and quantum of damages will depend on where and how the accident happened and the type of personal injury suffered. Some of these differentials result not from any considered determination of the needs or merits of particular types of claimants but rather from the political context which surrounded the introduction of particular laws on damages.

2–010   One example is the issue of damages awarded to a worker injured while working in the course of employment. Such injuries have at various times been uncompensated,[12] been compensated according to a schedule of limited damages under statute,[13] been entitled to full compensation in accordance with the common law rules of negligence,[14] and been preferentially treated in social security compensation.[15] Explanation for these changing attitudes to workers injured at work lies in part at least in political attitudes to the rights of workers, to the political desire to protect the country's economy through the protection of industry, and also to the political power of trades unions.

2–011   Children who suffer brain damage after vaccination are another example. Common law is a very poor remedy in such cases, partly because of the difficulties of showing that the vaccination was negligently administered and partly the problem of establishing that the vaccination was the cause of the injury.[16] In the early 1970s public fears about the effects of the vaccine for whooping cough resulted in a significant decrease in the number of children taking up vaccination, with a consequent rise in the incidence of whooping cough. The Pearson Commission[17] recommended that strict liability for vaccine damage be imposed on the local authority which conducted the relevant vaccination programme, thus preferencing such children over children injured in other ways, through medical negligence at birth for example. The Pearson recommendations on vaccine damage were not followed, but to restore public faith in vaccination the government passed the Vaccine Damage Payments Act 1979 as an interim measure while further thought was given to the issue. That Act is still in place, and

---

[12] Before 1897 the doctrine of common employment and the common law rules of contributory negligence served to prevent any liability on the employer in most cases.

[13] Workmen's Compensation Act 1897.

[14] Since the doctrine of common employment was abolished in the Law Reform (Personal Injuries) Act 1948, and contributory negligence became proportionally assessed as a result of the Law Reform (Contributory Negligence) Act 1945, common law employer's liability has become feasible as a basis for damages claims for industrial injury. In fact the employee suing an employer is advantaged compared with other common law negligence claims in that the issue of duty is relatively straightforward—*Wilson & Clyde Coal v. English* [1938] A.C. 57.

[15] Under the industrial injuries scheme, which incorporates some of the provisions of the Workmen's Compensation Act into the scheme of benefits as a consequence of the National Insurance (Industrial Injuries) Act 1946 and the Social Security Contributions and Benefits Act 1992. See R. Lewis (1980) 43 M.L.R. 514.

[16] For example *Loveday v. Renton* [1990] 1 Med. L.R. 117.

[17] Report of the Royal Commission on Civil Liability and Compensation for Personal Injury Cmnd. 7054 (1978).

provides very little protection to the vaccine-damaged child. To qualify the child must establish 80 per cent disability and that the disability resulted from the vaccine. Even then the child is entitled only to £30,000 compensation, which is very significantly lower than common law compensation for an equivalent degree of injury.[18]

Public lack of confidence in vaccination programmes can have disastrous effects on public health programmes and is politically embarrassing for the government in power. The controversy over the MMR vaccine in 1999 has again resulted in public mistrust, and once again pressure groups[19] are calling for improved compensation for children who, it is claimed, have been injured by the effects of vaccination.[20]   **2–012**

Compensation for injury caused by a defective product has also been affected by political intervention. The common law is a poor remedy provider for injuries caused by some defective products, particularly defective medicinal drugs. Problems of causation are usually insurmountable, and whereas common law can deal adequately with the situation where an individual product from a type of generally safe products causes injury, it copes poorly with the situation where the whole product design is inadequate and there are no safe comparators. When a large number of children worldwide (about 500 in Britain) suffered serious deformities as a result of the drug Thalidomide,[21] attention was turned to ways of compensating these children and the inadequacies of existing laws in this context. Product liability, particularly in relation to drugs, was also considered by the Pearson Commission[22] and by the Law Commission,[23] both of which recommended the introduction of strict liability for defective products. The Strasbourg Convention on Products Liability in 1977 also recommended strict liability for products.   **2–013**

It was in the event an EEC Directive[24] which forced the government's hand, requiring compliance by member states within three years. The Consumer Protection Act was passed in 1987 and came into force on March 1, 1988. However the government of the time was concerned not to alienate the drugs manufacturing industry, much of which was based in Britain. The Consumer Protection Act does not mirror the terms of the Directive, and in particular contains a defence, the development risks defence,[25] which enables the manufacturer of a product to escape liability if the state of scientific and technical knowledge at the time the product was supplied, was not such that such a manufacturer might be expected to have discovered the defect. Both this defence, and the definition of "defect"[26] in the   **2–014**

---

[18] In *Best v. Wellcome Foundation* [1994] 5 Med. L.R. 81 a claimant who was unusually able to satisfy the elements of an action in negligence was awarded £2.5 million in damages by an Irish court.

[19] Such as Association of Parents of Vaccine Damaged Children, and JABS.

[20] Such claims are particularly strong where the child was vaccinated not for his or her own benefit but for the good of the public as a whole, as in the case of boys being vaccinated against rubella.

[21] Taken by their mothers when pregnant to prevent morning sickness.

[22] See n. 17.

[23] Law Commission No 82, Cmnd. 6831 (1977).

[24] The European Community Directive on Liability for Defective Products 1985, 85/374.

[25] s. 4(1)(e).

[26] s. 3(1).

Consumer Protection Act, result in legislation that provides far from strict liability, and indeed appear to have introduced negligence by the back door. The victims of the Thalidomide drug would have little more chance of success under the Consumer Protection Act, which was intended to provide a remedy for just such a case, than they had in common law.

2–015 A further example of the political constraints of compensation lies in the chequered history of no-fault compensation in England, and in other commonwealth jurisdictions. No-fault compensation schemes enable the victim of an accident to recover compensation for loss caused by that accident regardless of proof of liability, although inevitably questions of causation must be addressed in some cases. Such schemes will generally compensate only for personal injury, leaving private insurance arrangements to protect against property damage and economic loss. Quantum of damages is usually capped to a level below that of common law damages, and most such schemes do not compensate for non-pecuniary loss (such as pain and suffering).

2–016 No-fault compensation attempts to remove the issue of accident compensation from the courts, setting up compensation boards to assess qualification and quantum, thus making the process far cheaper and faster to administer. However, removing the fault requirement enables significantly larger numbers of accident victims to recover compensation. The setting up of a compensation scheme requires government commitment to provision of the necessary funds and necessitates taxation to provide those funds.

Attention was first focused on the potential of no-fault compensation schemes to simplify accident compensation when New Zealand passed its Accident Compensation Act in 1972. This scheme purported to cover all personal injury arising from an accident,[27] and covered all types of accidents. It provided compensation which was less than would be available at common law but greater than would be available under the social security system. In exchange for this statutory protection from the consequences of accident, the New Zealand people were persuaded to relinquish their rights to pursue a claim in tort for compensation.

2–017 Many other jurisdictions have introduced no-fault schemes, though none as ambitious as the New Zealand scheme in its initial form. More commonly, no-fault schemes purport to address particular causes of injury such as medical accidents[28] and road accidents.[29] Most such schemes run parallel to tort remedies and allow the claimant to pursue legal action if they so choose.

---

[27] But not injury or disease which was perceived as arising from natural causes.
[28] See The Swedish No Fault Patient Insurance Scheme which came into effect in 1975. Similar schemes have been introduced in Finland (1987), Norway (1988) and Denmark (1992). For further on this see L. Fallberg and E. Borgenhammer, "The Swedish No Fault Patient Insurance Scheme" (1997) 4 European Journal of Health Law 279, R. Lahti, "The Finnish Patient Injury Compensation Scheme" in McLean ed., *Law Reform and Medical Injury Litigation* (1995) and P. Danzon, "The Swedish Compensation Scheme: Myths and Realities" (1994) 14 International Review of Law and Economics 435.
[29] Such as the full no-fault scheme introduced into Quebec in 1978 and now in place in several Canadian provinces, the modified no-fault schemes introduced into many North American jurisdictions in the mid 1970s, and the various no-fault schemes in place in Australia since the early 1970s.

It is no coincidence that the introduction of no-fault compensation 2–018
schemes in different jurisdictions tends to occur during a period of left-wing
political ethos. The financial commitment required by such schemes, and
the resultant cost to the public, require recognition of public rather than
private responsibility for the consequences of accident. It is true that in
New Zealand the original proposals for a compensation scheme came from
the National Party, but those proposals were very limited, covering only
motorvehicle accidents and providing protection only for earners. The government had set up a commission to consider issues of Workers' Compensation[30] and Mr Justice Woodhouse, who headed the Commission, had
taken it as part of his brief to look more widely at a comprehensive scheme
of accident compensation. The full Woodhouse proposals were not supported by the National Party, but shortly after the Act implementing this
original scheme was passed there was a change of government in New
Zealand. The incoming Labour government postponed the scheme to
enable supplementary legislation significantly expanding the scheme to
cover all accidents and to compensate all victims of accidents.

Since that time, as political commitment to the scheme has waned, there 2–019
has been corresponding erosion of the Woodhouse ideals incorporated in
the 1972 Act, to the point where it is arguable whether the scheme provides
any wider compensation than the common law would have done.[31] Meanwhile other jurisdictions have looked to the New Zealand experience and
there has been prolific critique of that system which has informed other
governments considering similar proposals. The most ambitious variation
on the New Zealand scheme was the Woodhouse Report in Australia[32]
which proposed a scheme expanded to include any sickness or disability
regardless of cause,[33] a scheme which it was estimated would cost five times
as much as an "accidents only" scheme.[34] These proposals were close to
implementation in Australia when there was an abrupt change of government, the Labour Party being dramatically dismissed by the Governor-
General. The incoming Liberal (conservative) Party failed to follow through
with the scheme and it lies in the history books.

Most other no-fault schemes, although inspired by the New Zealand Act,
have been far more modest in approach and aim to address particular
causes of injury which can be funded from within the industry,[35] so requiring less political courage to implement.

In December 1972 Edward Heath, Prime Minister of the time, set up a 2–020
Commission to consider compensation for personal injury in England and

---

[30] Royal Commission of Inquiry, *Compensation for Personal Injury in New Zealand*, Woodhouse Report (Government Printer, Wellington, Dec. 1997).
[31] See I. Campbell, *Compensation for Personal Injury in New Zealand: Its Rise and Fall*
(Auckland, 1996) and R. Mahoney, "Trouble in Paradise: New Zealand's Accident Compensation Scheme", in *Law Reform and Medical Injury Litigation* (McLean ed., 1995).
[32] National Committee of Inquiry, *Compensation and Rehabilitation in Australia* (Australia,
June 1997).
[33] The Woodhouse review of the New Zealand Scheme conducted in 1982 also proposed
extending the scheme to cover sickness unrelated to injury; Law Commission, *The Accident
Compensation Scheme—Interim Report on Aspects of Funding* (No. 3, 1987); Law Commission, *Personal Injury Prevention and Recovery* (No. 4, 1988).
[34] Cane, *Atiyah's Accidents, Compensation and the Law* (6th ed., Butterworths, 1999) p. 404.
[35] See n. 28 and 29 above.

Wales. The impetus for this commission was partly developments else-where, and partly the political fall-out from the Thalidomide tragedy which had been exposed in the press earlier that year.[36] The Commission, headed by Lord Pearson, although aware of the New Zealand scheme which was well established by the time the Pearson Committee reported in 1978, chose to limit its brief[37] to consideration of the tort system and did not contem-plate a comprehensive no-fault compensation as an option. Instead the Commission recommended instances of strict liability (product liability, medical research, vaccine damage for example) combined with a modified no-fault system for motor accidents and the fall back of a strong social security system. The Commission was much criticised[38] for its failure to grapple with the more profound issues of accident compensation, doing no more than tinkering with a system which had many flaws at a time when courts were calling for reconsideration of the compensation process.[39]

2–021   A further examination of accident compensation in the context of road accidents resulted in the Lord Chancellor's Department proposing a no-fault scheme to cover minor motor vehicle accidents (personal injury claims over £250 and under £2,500). Pedestrians and cyclists were not to be covered by the scheme, and only accidents occurring on a public highway would attract no-fault compensation.[40] The objective of this proposal was not to facilitate compensation to accident victims but rather to clear the legal system of troublesome and disproportionately expensive minor claims.

2–022   Any proposals for change were overtaken by the Woolf Report[41] and the subsequent Lord Chancellor's Report[42] which made recommendations for easier, cheaper and faster access to compensation. These reports did not endorse no-fault liability for road accidents, but did recommend that fur-ther consideration be given to a no-fault scheme for medical accidents.[43]

Assessment of the advantages and disadvantages of no-fault compensa-tion schemes depends on political perspective. No-fault compensation ensures that certain identified sufferers of injury receive some compensation quickly, without cost and without the stresses of confrontation. Injured persons who fall outside the scheme are however disadvantaged because they suffered the wrong sort of injury from the wrong cause, creating a hierarchy of disease preference which will need to be politically determined. No-fault compensation takes the responsibility of insuring against injury out of the private arena and makes compensation an issue of public responsibility. That public responsibility will need to be supported by a taxation and insurance system which imposes economic burdens on par-ticular groups such as road users or manufacturers or a particular profes-sional practice.

---

[36] See J. Conaghan and W. Mansell, *The Wrongs of Tort* (2nd ed., 1999) Ch. 5.
[37] Conaghan & Mansell *ibid.*
[38] Conaghan & Mansell *ibid.*
[39] See *Snelling v. Whitehead The Times*, July 31, 1975, per Lord Wilberforce.
[40] For details of the scheme see B. Markesinis and S. Deakin, *Tort Law* (4th ed., Oxford, 1999) Ch. 3.
[41] Lord Woolf, *Access to Civil Justice* (1996).
[42] Lord Chancellor's Department, *Review of Civil Justice and Legal Aid* (1997).
[43] Point 5.58, *Review of Civil Justice and Legal Aid*.

The considerations which influence what system will prevail will include   2–023
issues way beyond what is in the best interests of the accident victim. In
the end political and economic priorities of the government in power, pressure from interest groups, lobbying by the insurance industry, the power
of the legal profession and the social preferences and values of the majority
of the voting population will dictate whether, and what, changes will be
made to the compensation system in any jurisdiction.

(2) European and international constraints on damages

It is no longer the case that each legal jurisdiction can make and enforce   2–024
laws ignorant of, and without regard to, the domestic laws of other jurisdictions and the overarching framework of European or international law.
The movement of workers across jurisdictions has required English courts
to confront laws of the jurisdictions where accidents occur[44] or where the
worker originated,[45] and to consider issues of conflict of jurisdiction.[46] The
increase in tourism and international air travel has brought to domestic
courts issues of determination of international conventions[47] in claims for
damages. International business transactions and banking services have
also raised issues of enforcement of judgments for damages made in other
jurisdictions.[48] Medical science is becoming increasingly globalised, with
shared knowledge of techniques and risks of treatment, and movement of
patients according to facilities and expertise. Domestic courts will need to
grapple with the consequences of these treatments wherever they occur,
requiring knowledge and understanding of foreign legal systems and of any
applicable European law.[49] It has been said that

> "... with ever increasing ties being established between the United
> Kingdom and the rest of Europe, the plain fact is that personal injuries
> are always likely to be viewed as being at the forefront of develop-
> ments in international and transnational litigation."[50]

Nor can English courts any longer finally determine liability on matters   2–025
which are subject to the European Convention on Human Rights,[51] and the
coming into force of the Human Rights Act 1998 in England and Wales
will require courts to decide issues of liability for damages in the context
of the European convention in all domestic courts.

Even when deciding on issues of domestic law, courts are increasingly   2–026
looking to the laws of other jurisdictions to determine the direction of

---

[44] For example *Johnson v. Coventry Churchill International Ltd* [1992] 3 All E.R. 14.
[45] For example *Littrell v. United States of America* [1992] 3 All E.R. 218.
[46] For example *Lubbe v. Cape plc* (July 30, 1998, unreported).
[47] See for example *Sidhu v. British Airways* [1997] 2 W.L.R. 26.
[48] For example *Domicrest Ltd v. Swiss Bank Corporation* [1999] 2 W.L.R. 364.
[49] As in *U. v. W. (Attorney General Intervening)* [1997] 3 W.L.R. 739.
[50] P. Kaye, in *Damages for Personal Injuries: A European Perspective*, (F. Holding and P.
Kaye eds., Chancery, 1993), p. 1.
[51] See *A v. United Kingdom*, [1998] 2 F.L.R. 959 E.C.H.R.; *Stubbings v. United Kingdom*
[1997] 1 F.L.R. 105.

English law. In *White v. Jones*,[52] a case in which a disappointed beneficiary sought damages from the solicitor who failed to prepare a will before the death of the testator, Lord Goff looked to German law for guidance on how to fashion a remedy in tort for loss of expectation[53] and expanded English law of tort along these lines. German law also provides guidance on the possibility of introducing remedies for the breach of other, personal, interests which are presently not protected under English law. In *Kaye v. Robertson*,[54] an English privacy case, Bingham L.J. said in the Court of Appeal, "This case nonetheless highlights, yet again, the failure of both the common law of England and statute to protect in an effective way the personal privacy of citizens". He went on to point out that both French and German law provide remedies in this sort of case and recommended that Parliament step in to provide a similar remedy.

2–027   It is now common for English courts to refer to authority from Australia, New Zealand and Canada, and even from the United States. In *Kaye v. Robertson* Leggatt L.J. also lamented the inadequacy of English law on privacy and suggested looking to United States law for a remedy because there ". . . there is a wealth of experience of the enforcement of this right both at common law and also under statute". The development of structured settlements in this jurisdiction was prompted by similar developments in North America. In the *Rylands v. Fletcher* case of *Cambridge Water v. Eastern Counties Leather plc*[55] Lord Goff considered the direction taken by American courts on the development of *Rylands* to protect the environment and fashioned his judgment on those lines.

2–028   There is much to be learned from the practice of other jurisdictions. One matter on which academics and courts are looking to Europe is the question of periodic payment of damages. There is general recognition that the lump sum rule of damages has its drawbacks.[56] Other European states, France for example, have moved to index-linked payment of damages despite objections from the insurance industry and concerns that open-ended liability would have a destabilising effect on the franc.[57] Within the framework of these index-linked payments, damages awards can be re-opened in some circumstances to take into account the changing health of the accident victim. English courts are now considering alternatives to the lump sum along these lines[58] and the European experience will provide a model for change. Some attempt has already been made to achieve European commonality in aspects of damage awards. A standard scale of damages for non-pecuniary loss (pain, suffering and loss of amenities) was recom-

---

[52] [1995] 1 All E.R. 691. See also *Papamichalopoulos v. Greece* E.H.R.R., October 31, 1995 (on compensation for unlawful dispossession of land) and *Pressos Compania Navieroa SA v. Belgium* E.H.R.R., November 20, 1995 21 E.H.R.R. 301 (on damages for loss caused by harbour pilots).
[53] At 711.
[54] [1991] F.S.R. 62.
[55] [1994] 2 A.C. 264.
[56] See Introduction.
[57] See R. Redmond-Cooper, "Aspects of the French Law of Damages", in *Damages for Personal Injuries: A European Perspective* (F. Holding and P. Kaye eds., Chancery, 1993).
[58] See comments by Lord Steyn in *Wells v. Wells* [1998] 3 All E.R. 481, 502.

mended by the 1988 European Legal Symposium[59] on the basis that such awards are palliative and symbolic and not dependant on earnings levels or cost of living.

Courts in this jurisdiction are becoming more conscious of the recogni- **2–029** tion of European law in relation to domestic issues. Now that European law is considered a core component of a law degree by the Law Society, younger members of the legal profession are cognisant of the importance and relevance of European law, and are increasingly framing arguments on the basis of European law where domestic law is insufficient. In *R. v. Human Fertilisation and Embryology Authority, ex p. Blood*[60] it was argued, and conceded by the Court of Appeal, that although the treatment sought by the claimant was contrary to English law, Articles 59 and 60 of the E.C. Treaty gave the claimant an enforceable right to this medical treatment in another E.C. member state. European Directives such as those on compulsory insurance for motor vehicle accidents,[61] product liability[62] and environmental liability[63] have all impacted on damage awards in English law.

In the context of damages, the most important development in European **2–030** law has been the case of *Brasserie du Pecheur SA v. Germany; R. v. Secretary of State for Transport, ex p. Factortame Ltd*[64] in which the ECJ confirmed an earlier ruling[65] to the effect that a state could be held liable for damages for any loss arising from a failure of the state to implement a European Directive or any other Community law. Provided that the European law was intended to confer rights on individuals, provided that there was a serious breach of the law, and provided that a causative link could be established between the breach and the loss, an individual could claim damages in compensation of the loss. Claimants need not go to the European court to enforce their claim; United Kingdom courts are obliged to apply *Factortame*, although how such an action will be framed must still be sorted out.[66] It will be interesting to observe the degree to which *Factortame* influences courts' attitudes to other damages liability where the state might be held accountable.[67] The introduction of the European Convention on Human Rights to domestic law in England and Wales in the Human Rights Act 1998 will serve to focus attention on wider European recognition of individual rights and enforcement mechanisms for those rights, and may well result in a substantial rethinking of damages law in this jurisdiction.

Nor can wider international law be ignored when considering the frame- **2–031**

---

[59] See Allen, "Compensation for personal injury in Europe" (1989) P.M.I.L.L. (Vol. 5 No. 2).
[60] [1997] 2 W.L.R. 807.
[61] Directive 72/166 of April 24, 1972; Second Directive 84/5 of December 30, 1983; Third Directive 90/232 of May 14, 1990.
[62] Directive 85/374 of July 25, 1985.
[63] Convention on Civil Liability for Damage resulting from Activities Dangerous to the Environment, of June 21, 1993.
[64] [1996] All E.R. (E.C.) 301 (ECJ).
[65] *Francovitch & Bonfaci v. Italy* [1991] E.C.R. I-5357.
[66] See P. Craig, "Once More Unto the Breach: The Community, the State and Damages Liability" (1997) 113 L.Q.R. 67.
[67] For discussion of other decisions of the ECJ which will have relevance for damages law in this jurisdiction see W. Van Gerven, *Cases, Materials and Text on National, Supranational and International Tort Law* (Hart, 1998).

work of damages. The International Court of Justice[68] has been called upon
to decide on issues of liability arising from incidents such as the hostage
crisis in the United States Embassy in Tehran[69] and damage caused by vessels in international waters.[70] Threats to human health, to animal health
and to property from infectious disease, food additives and chemicals are
no longer issues only of national concern. The globalisation of food production and sophisticated techniques of preserving, ripening and exporting
of food products means that products of one country can be consumed all
over the world, and defects in those products will result in world-wide
damage. The manufacture of drugs for world-wide distribution raises issues
well beyond the confines of product liability. An issue of recent concern
has been the use of antimicrobials on food animal production[71] which has
been known to create antimicrobial resistance in consumers, prompting a
conference of the World Health Organisation[72] to discuss the implications
of the threats to health.

2–032   Indeed the role of the World Health Organisation and its use of international law, particularly in relation to infectious disease, AIDS, vaccination,
tobacco, artificial milk formula for babies, blood products, organs for
transplant and xenotransplantation as well as biological and pharmaceut-
ical products, is being reconsidered with the appointment of Dr Gro
Harlem Brundtland as Director-General and it is expected that the WHO
will in the future play a much more regulatory role in issues of health.[73]
The harm which is the fall-out from these transnational health risks will
need to be compensated, and an intra-jurisdictional approach to when and
how compensation is awarded will often be inappropriate. An awareness
of the legal treatment of harm from transnational threats to health across
jurisdictions will increasingly be called for in the determination of damages
awards in this jurisdiction.

2. ECONOMIC CONSTRAINTS ON DAMAGES

2–033   The role of law in damages awards is, in part, to provide economic security for the accident victim once the victim's immediate medical needs have
been seen to. What constitutes economic security depends very much on
the existing economic environment. In a jurisdiction with a highly
developed welfare system[74] there is already in place considerable economic

---

[68] For further discussion on the role of the ICJ see W. Van Gerven, n. 67 above.
[69] *United States Diplomatic and Consular Staff in Tehran, United States of America v. Islamic Republic of Iran* (I.C.J. May 24, 1980).
[70] *Corfu Channel case, United Kingdom v. Albania* (I.C.J. April 9, 1949).
[71] See D. Fidler, "Legal Challenges Posed by the Use of Antimicrobials in Food Animal Production" Microbes and Infection 29 (1999); D. Fidler, *International Law and Infectious Diseases* (OUP, 1999).
[72] WHO, Use of Quinlones in Food Animals and Potential Impact on Human Health, WHO Meeting June 2–5, Geneva (1998).
[73] See D. Fidler, "The Future of the World Health Organisation: What Role for International Law?" 31 Vanderbilt Journal of Transnational Law 1079 (1998).
[74] Such as Denmark, Sweden and Finland—hence the paucity of litigation for personal injury in those jurisdictions even prior to the introduction of no-fault medical injury schemes; see para. 2–017, n. 28 for commentary on this.

security and the role of courts or compensation schemes is limited to top-ping-up what is already in place. In jurisdictions where welfare provision is minimal or inadequate, the mechanisms for obtaining damages become crucial for the protection of the claimant. In a jurisdiction where medical care is largely provided by the state, calculation of damages will proceed on a different basis from one where medical care must be privately funded.

Where common accident causers (car drivers for instance) are required 2–034 by law to take out insurance, criteria of liability and calculation of damages can proceed on different assumptions than in the case of an uninsured defendant. In an environment where potential claimants are likely to be covered by first party insurance, the incentive to sue, and need to provide effective mechanisms for damages claims, are significantly reduced. The framework of insurance is more than just a background to the operation of law. The insurance culture of a jurisdiction will be influential in the creation and interpretation of law.[75]

But there is a much broader role for economics in the context of com-pensation law. Economic theory has been used in a positivist attempt to 2–035 explain and justify the law on liability and damages, and normatively to direct ways in which the law might develop.

Economic analysis of compensation is predicated on the understanding 2–036 that any compensation system must at the very least be economically effici-ent; efficient in the sense that the cost of accidents which do occur can be balanced in financial terms against the cost of avoiding accidents, and effi-cient in the sense that the cost of administration of compensation for those accidents can be balanced against the compensation costs themselves.[76] If laws are inefficient, then people affected by the law will be prepared to spend money litigating to have the law changed, and this process of change will, it is argued, continue until neither party to litigation is sufficiently disadvantaged by the law to warrant the investment.[77] So the law always tends towards economic efficiency. Indeed not only does the law work this way, but so it should. Economic efficiency requires the adoption of laws that will maximise the aggregate wealth of the society.[78]

The majority of accidents causing loss could be avoided but to do so 2–037 would be prohibitively expensive and members of society might not agree on the price we are prepared to pay for such a level of safety. If all cars were designed so that they could travel at a maximum of 20 mph, and were manufactured of the materials used to build spacecraft, then road accident injuries would plummet.[79] If doctors only performed treatments they were confident could be done safely and took no risks, then the medical accident rate would also plummet. Many more people would die from the natural process of disease of course, but if compensation is about loss resulting

---

[75] See the judgment of Lord Denning in *Nettleship v. Weston* [1971] 2 Q.B. 691; see also P. Cane, *Tort Law and Economic Interests* (Clarendon, 1996) Ch. 9.

[76] See for example G. Calabresi, *The Costs of Accidents* (Yale University Press, 1970).

[77] R. Posner, *Economic Analysis of Law* (Little Brown, 1986).

[78] Posner, *ibid.*

[79] For more on the debate on safety versus mobility see J. Mashaw and D. Harfest, *The Struggle for Auto Safety* (Harvard University Press, 1990).

from accident, then the more conservative the treatment the less need for compensation.

2–038   Economic analysis is one method of determining the balance between the price we are prepared to pay for safety and the risks we are prepared to take, and does so by attaching an economic value to the factors which go into the safety equation in order to identify the precise optimal point at which we feel we have paid enough for safety and from then on are prepared to take risks. We may want to build into our equation other factors, such as an incentive for deterrence from certain sorts of accidents by making the offender pay a prohibitive price for the privilege of causing the accident. Alternatively we may leave deterrence to the criminal law, but possibly allow into our equation contribution to the costs of criminal deterrence of the activity.

2–039   Once an accident has occurred, there are many ways of dealing with the costs arising from that accident. We could make the accident causer pay, we could let the loss lie where it falls or we could create ways of spreading or distributing the loss, through insurance premia or taxation for example. We could allow adversarial dispute over accidents, in the process discouraging trivial claims by the costs of dispute and framing the law such that only a proportion of disputes are successful. Or we could remove lawyers and litigation from the equation, making the administration costs cheaper but increasing the number of payouts. On this point economic analysis looks to determine, taking into account the administration costs (the transaction costs),[80] how most effectively to impose the economic burden which will inevitably arise.

2–040   Economic analysis has taken place at macro level (looking at the most efficient legal system and the most efficient laws) and at the micro level (looking at the most efficient outcome to a particular accident situation). In *United States v. Carroll Towing Co.*[81] Judge Learned Hand proposed a simple economic guide to the determination of individual accident liability. If the cost of the consequences of the accident multiplied by the probability of the accident occurring exceeds the cost of preventing the accident in a particular case, then the accident causer should be held liable for the accident and made to pay the costs of the consequences. If however the cost of avoiding the accident is greater than the factor of accident cost and probability of accident, then no reasonable person could be expected to pay the price of accident prevention, and there should be no liability for the accident. Judge Hand, and some critics, purport that this formula roughly approximates to the way in which judges in reality decide liability cases.

2–041   Of course the issue is much more complicated than this. There is always a range of options of behaviour, not just two (accident causing and non-accident causing) and when making a choice the potential accident causer must weigh the economic ramifications of this range of options. Hence what is relevant to the economic equation is not the cost of avoiding the accident as such, but the marginal cost,[82] that additional cost of one behavi-

---

[80] G. Calabresi, see *supra.* n. 76.
[81] 159F. 2d 169 (C.A. 2 1947).
[82] See R. Posner, *Tort Law—Cases and Economic Analysis* (Little, Brown and Co, 1982).

our over the other. And even if the formula were to establish that the costs of accident avoidance exceeded the accident costs, the participants in the accident (especially the victim) might still express a preference for the accident not to occur. Not all amounts of money might have the same value to spenders and receivers, and expectation of money (the money payable if the risk comes off) will probably not be valued in the same way as certain money (the cost of avoiding the accident in the first place).[83]

To some extent this correlation between the cost of avoiding accidents and the cost of paying for the consequences of accidents when they occur is distorted by insurance. The insurance industry, as well as undertaking the cost/benefit analysis which economists endorse, also has a commercial interest in keeping down the costs of accidents. This commercial interest may lead not so much to concern about accident avoidance but rather to concern about damage avoidance. Insurance resources are spent on evading the payment of compensation[84] and the tort litigation process facilitates this behaviour by matching the one-off claimant against the experience of the "repeat player" insurance defendants,[85] a match which disadvantages the claimant.   2–042

More recent attempts to analyse the law on compensation in an economic framework have downplayed economic efficiency as the overriding objective of a compensation system, and attempted to include the importance of less easily quantifiable goals such as justice and equity,[86] although they still assume that wealth is in itself a value which we as individuals, and the law, should pursue. These more complex and sophisticated analyses incorporate recognition of value judgments as to who is entitled to compensation, and whose rights should be protected by the law, such that the entitlement holder should be compensated for any violation of rights. These approaches place discussion of economic efficiency in a context of a normative theory of rights, distributive justice and corrective justice in order to determine liability for accidents.   2–043

A patient, for example, is entitled to expect a certain level of safety with respect to a medical procedure. The hospital is entitled to operate at a certain, societally agreed, level of safety which will not be a level of perfect safety, and which will allow for the possibility that some accidents will inevitably occur. If a patient wants a higher level of safety than the agreed entitlement, the patient must be prepared to pay for that greater entitlement, either as a taxpayer or by taking out private first-party insurance. If the hospital wants to operate at a lower level of safety than agreed, then the hospital must be prepared to pay for that lower level by paying damages when accidents occur.   2–044

Of course not everyone agrees that economic efficiency is a primary moral value. Much economic theory proceeds on the assumption that the overwhelming objective of a society is aggregate wealth maximisation, and   2–045

---

[83] Posner, *ibid.*
[84] See A. Dismore and F. Whitehead, "Personal Injury Law", in D. Bean ed., *Law Reform for All* (Blackstones, 1999).
[85] See H. Genn, *Hard Bargaining* (OUP, 1987).
[86] See for example A. Ogus and C. Veljanovski, *Readings in the Economics of Law and Regulation* (1984); C. Veljanovski, *The Economics of Law: An Introductory Text* (1990).

mainstream economic theory is not overly concerned with the inequities of wealth distribution. Sociologists and ethicists might well challenge that assumption and wish to substitute other societal objectives. Economic analysis tells us that the rational person always acts in such a way as to produce the greatest personal economic utility or satisfaction.[87] Critics of the economic analysis of accident compensation argue that we cannot assume that when people have a choice of behaviours they will act in this way.

2–046   The assumption of what is rational behaviour has traditionally been determined by a small but vocal cross section of society; educated, middle class, white men from a Western cultural background. Writers on law and economics tend to be drawn from this cross section. The behaviour of women, for example, may require different analysis.[88] Activities which have been traditionally ascribed to women, such as housework and nurturing, have been accorded no economic value and cannot easily be accounted for in assumptions of utility.[89] Economics as a discipline claims value neutrality and objectivity, that its methodology is rigorous and scientific, and that it is therefore a superior study of law to socio-legal or ethical analysis. But the assumptions made in the economic analysis of law reveal that it is underpinned by its own biases.

2–047   Values such as intimacy, attachment and responsibility, which cannot be measured in monetary equivalence, are ignored in the economic approach. Goodhart[90] gives the example of a noise dispute between a home owner and the owner of a neighbouring helicopter pad. From the point of view of economic analysis (and indeed the law), determination of damages entitlement is assessed without consideration of who moved in first. But to the home owner there is a difference between the situation where long quiet possession has been interfered with by the establishment of a new helicopter pad next door, and the situation where the home owner chose to move in next door to an existing helicopter pad. Primitive and deeply held feelings of ownership of peace and quiet and territoriality cannot be ignored and might well lead to the home owner being prepared to spend an inefficient sum of money to defend the right to quiet possession.

2–048   Nor can it be said that when we do maximise our wealth, either individually or as a society, we are better off. Wealth maximisation does not necessarily carry with it, as is claimed[91] other values such as respect for rights, human virtues and human instincts. The pursuit of wealth maximisation will give rise to some rights and values, but whether these are the "right" rights and values requires independent assessment based on other, morally determined, criteria.[92]

2–049   We cannot assume, as economists appear to do, that as individuals we

---

[87] See for example Veljanovski, *ibid.*

[88] See C. Gilligan, *In a Different Voice: Psychological Theory and Women's Development* (Cambridge, Mass., 1982).

[89] See M. Davies, *Asking the Law Question* (Sweet and Maxwell, 1994) p. 134.

[90] Goodhart, "Economics and the Law: Too Much One Way Traffic?" (1977) 60 M.L.R. 1.

[91] For example by R. Posner; see "Utilitarianism, Economics and Legal Theory" 8 J. Legal Stud. 103.

[92] See R. Dworkin, "Is Wealth a Value?" in *Lloyd's Introduction to Jurisprudence*, (1980) p. 454 and Posner's reply, "Dworkin's Critique of Wealth Maximisation" in the same volume at p. 459.

are able to make autonomous decisions, prioritising our own welfare at the expense of others. We are not all friendless orphans without dependants[93] and it would not be irrational, or even unusual, for us to make decisions which were contrary to our own economic interests but for the benefit of others. Indeed many of us, in our role as employees or spouses or patients for example, may not be in a position of sufficient power to make our own decisions on issues concerning our safety or economic advantage.

As a society we may also deliberately choose to adopt policies which are   2–050 economically inefficient but which achieve some other desirable goal such as the redistribution of wealth[94] or the protection of a vulnerable section of society. Taking in a large number of Eastern European refugees until they can return home safely is not economically efficient but we may nevertheless support the policy on other less quantifiable grounds. Equally we may support compensating children who develop serious injury following vaccination, bearing in mind that much vaccination is not for the benefit of an individual child but to create herd immunity and to work towards eradication of disease, even where no sufficient scientific causal relationship can be established between vaccination and injury.

Economic theory presumes that there is a discernible logic in compensa-   2–051 tion law, and is an intrepid attempt to track that logic. More cynical commentators would deny that any coherent value system, economic or otherwise, can explain the vagaries of our system of damages payment. Rather the compensation system in England and Wales is characterised by an illogic which benefits some and disadvantages others without reference to need or merit, and would more accurately be described as a lottery.[95]

Regardless of how convinced we might be by economic theory as an explanation or guide to compensation, we cannot choose to consider the issue of damages in an economic vacuum. Rightly or wrongly economics on both a macro and micro level does input into questions of both liability and quantum, and any discussion or critique of damages must acknowledge the importance of economic context even if the normative role of economics cannot be agreed.

3. CULTURAL CONSTRAINTS ON DAMAGES

Just as we cannot ignore the political and economic environments in   2–052 which damages awards are made, so we must take into account the cultural norms and values of the society in which damages awards are being considered if we are to attempt to explain the rationale of those damages.

A culture which regards self-sufficiency and independence as an identifier   2–053 of national character will, for example, be reluctant to accept a compensation system which is heavily reliant on social welfare. When the New Zealand people were considering adoption of their Accident Compensation

---

[93] Jinnett-Sack, "Autonomy in the Company of Others", in *Choices and Decisions in Health Care* (Grubb ed., 1993).
[94] See Davies *supra* n. 89.
[95] P. Atiyah, *The Damages Lottery* (Hart, 1997).

Scheme in exchange for relinquishing their right to sue in common law, it was an important issue in the political campaign to make clear that payment of damages under the scheme would be a right earned by taxation and not a charitable payment.[96] There was at the time a cultural shame about receipt of benefits, and many people entitled to benefits chose to live in poverty rather than claim them. In contrast, the Swedish and Finnish compensation schemes were introduced within "the Nordic ideology of the Welfare State"[97] where public health care and support were part of the culture and it was rare for patients to take legal action for damages, and so the new schemes were readily accepted.

2–054   Cultural attitudes to what constitutes loss or damage will also be relevant. Recognition of some sorts of loss, such as serious traumatic personal injury or visible property damage will be common to all cultures. Other sorts of loss are more problematic. Take for example the case of a negligently performed vasectomy which results in the birth of a healthy child. Have the parents suffered a loss? Should the negligent doctor be held legally accountable for that loss? How should the loss be measured in damages?

2–055   Even within the United Kingdom there has been disagreement about characterisation of the birth of a healthy child as a loss or damage, with courts originally refusing to recognise a loss,[98] then taking the view that the financial responsibilities of a child and the pain and suffering of pregnancy and birth were compensable,[99] and then returning to the view that to categorise a healthy child as a damage was inappropriate.[1]

2–056   Other categorisation of damage is also susceptible to cultural variation. The acceptance of psychological harm, shock, grief and depression as compensable damage[2] varies from culture to culture and is dependant on societal attitudes to mental and emotional illness. Recognition of cosmetic injury, loss of marriage prospects, loss of fertility and loss of sexual function as damage will differ according to the cultural importance of those faculties. Even recognition of some physical illness is culturally determined. Studies on illness, sickness and disease suggest that physical illness is more likely to be recognised when that illness prevents necessary activity, or when it differs from symptoms suffered by others in the community.[3] So in an environment where everyone already suffers from a particular type of injury or disease, bronchial disease from industrial pollution for example, only those persons who suffer significantly more seriously than others will be recognised as ill and therefore deserving of compensation. Liability will be resisted for the "ordinary" case of bronchial disease and even where

---

[96] See G. Palmer, *Compensation for Incapacity—A Study of Law and Social Change in New Zealand and Australia* (1979).

[97] R. Lahti, "The Finnish Patient Injury Compensation System", in *Law Reform and Medical Injury Litigation* Medico-legal Series (McLean ed., 1995).

[98] *Udale v. Bloomsbury AHA* [1983] 1 W.L.R. 1098.

[99] *Gold v. Haringey HA* [1988] Q.B. 481; *Allen v. Bloomsbury HA* [1993] 1 All E.R. 651.

[1] *Crouchman v. Burke The Times* October 10, 1997. *McFarlane v. Tayside Health Board* [1999] 3 W.L.R. 1301, House of Lords.

[2] For example the cultural reluctance in England to accept M.E. and "Gulf War Syndrome" as genuine illness.

[3] See Patrick & Scrambler, *Sociology as Applied to Medicine* (1986); Fitton & Acheson, *Doctor/Patient Relationship: A Study in General Practice* (1979).

liability is established, damages will be lower than for the same harm suffered elsewhere because of the expectation that the sufferer will return to work at an earlier level of recovery, and because there will be less recognition of pain and suffering.

New diseases or injuries will be more difficult to establish than those 2–057
traditionally accepted. Sufferers of Creutzfeldt-Jakob disease from growth hormone, or New-Variant Creutzfeldt-Jakob from BSE, and repetitive strain injury (RSI)[4] have had to overcome the reluctance of society, science and law to recognise both the existence and cause of damage. Women suffering burn injuries from new radiation or laser cancer treatments have also had difficulty in their claims for compensation.[5] The potential for injury of developing fertility treatments, xenotransplantation, modified food products and drugs will spawn novel damage claims which will be treated differently in different jurisdictions depending on their degree of cultural acceptance, until some common science and common jurisprudence emerges and the injuries become accepted into the literature on scientific medicine.

Cultural attitudes to the seeking of medical treatment for illness, and 2–058
tolerance of grief and pain behaviour vary, as do attitudes to taking time off work when ill. Care systems differ from society to society. Where there is commonly an extended family under one roof, or where the women of the family work within the home, then there is less recognition of the need for professional carers or substitute houseworkers. Where it is accepted that women's role is to marry and have children, injury inhibiting marriage and fertility will be taken more seriously. Where it is considered unacceptable for men to undertake housework or childcare, loss of a wife and mother will be more generously compensated.

Attitudes to the causes of accidents will also influence the approach to 2–059
compensation. Religious or cultural belief in fatalism, that accidents are predetermined by some higher power, will remove from the equation assignment of individual blame or responsibility for consequences of the accident. In such at environment a no-fault compensation system is likely to be more readily accepted. This cultural ethos would also be receptive to first-party insurance mechanisms, whereby each individual accepts the possibility of random accident and is prepared to pay for insurance to protect against the consequences of accidents.

Where however the culture emphasises personal responsibility and auto- 2–060
nomy, attribution of blame to the individual whose behaviour was the immediate cause of the accident will be an important component of the compensation system, and arguments based on the recognition of vindication and deterrence will be more convincing. Patrick Atiyah argues[6] that a "blame culture" has developed in this jurisdiction to the point that individuals have ceased to take responsibility for their own losses and expect always to pass loss onto someone to whom they can apportion blame. He argues that tort law is not only the product of the blame culture, but also

---

[4] RSI has now been recognised as a compensable injury by the House of Lords in *Pickford v. Imperial Chemicals* [1998] 1 W.L.R. 1189.
[5] See R. Rhodes-Kemp, "Breast radiation injury claims" (1996) 6 Medical Litigation 11; *Spry v. Calman* (unreported April 6, 1998) (radiotherapy for cervical cancer).
[6] P. Atiyah, *The Damages Lottery* (Hart, 1997).

that tort law encourages a blame culture by suggesting that it is other people's responsibility to take accident prevention measures, and by providing a strong financial incentive, through third-party insurance, to sue others for loss. Given this blame culture, the notion of first-party insurance for personal injury has been slow to catch on. Ironically, we are prepared to pay for first-party insurance for our cars (through comprehensive insurance cover) and our house and contents (through household insurance).

2–061   Recognition of cultural factors is important particularly when consideration is given to the adoption of a foreign system of accident compensation. Would the Swedish system of medical accident compensation work in Britain? Commentary suggests that the system works well enough in the Scandinavian countries but we cannot therefore assume that an imported system will work equally well in this jurisdiction. Sensitivity to national character and to cultural beliefs will be essential in proposals for change to any existing system.

4. A COMPENSATION SYSTEM TO WHAT END?

2–062   A further constraint on methods and quantum of compensation is the purpose of that compensation. The obvious first answer to the question "Why compensate?" is, to relieve the accident victim from the burden of medical costs, the costs of care, and to support the victim and any dependants financially during the period of disability. Most no-fault accident compensation systems are satisfied with this answer, and calculate the amount of compensation in each case accordingly. So an accident compensation system aims to protect individuals against the consequences of accidents and provides financial security regardless of why the accident happened, so long as a causal nexus can be established between the accident and the loss. Few accident compensation systems go beyond this to provide security against the financial costs of illness and disability;[7] that has traditionally been seen as the role of social security. This approach to compensation focuses more on the accident victim than the accident causer.

2–063   It has been argued[8] that the payment of compensation for injury should aim to achieve other ends. The philosophy of compensation may be bound up with societal beliefs about accountability and responsibility for behaviour, which dictate that the person who caused an accident should in some personal way be called to account for the consequences of it. This would justify treating injuries which result from human intervention differently from injury resulting from natural causes. Of course society could choose to recognise that accountability in different ways, calling for a public apology for instance, but the payment of damages has come to symbolise recognition of responsibility. The compensation is indeed symbolic given that in the majority of cases damages are paid not by the responsible party but by

---

[7] The proposed Australian no-fault disability scheme purported to provide this wider protection; see n. 32, para. 2–019.

[8] See for example Cane, *Atiyah's Accidents, Compensation and the Law* (6th ed., Butterworths, 1999), Ch. 18.

the insurer. This approach to compensation is more interested in the accident causer than in the accident victim and is likely to provide incomplete security against the consequences of accidents.

We might alternatively argue that society as a whole is responsible for 2–064 loss which is the inevitable by-product of activities we as a society choose to condone and benefit from (motorvehicles for example) and that therefore compensation for such injuries should come from the public purse through a public no-fault compensation system. Then risk arising from these activities is distributed amongst the beneficiaries. Equally society might be held responsible for illness arising from pollution, cigarette smoke, food additives, contraceptive use or any other activity which society condones for its convenience, and so these wider "non-accident" injuries should also merit compensation from the public purse. Cane[9] notes that damage done to private property during the Second World War was considered to be a burden to be publicly shared in this way.

Public responsibility for loss arising from misadventure is even more sup- 2–065 portable in a modern society where individuals have little say in risk exposure. Technological intervention in our daily lives is so complex and so overwhelming that we can no longer make rational choices about the risks we choose to take. We have been exposed to BSE and GM food, to medicinal drugs, vaccinations, infected blood products and to radiation, by paternalistic governments, professions and industries who decide what is good for us without offering us the information needed to make a choice. It is not always possible to identify an individual who can take legal responsibility for harm resulting from these interventions, and as the tort system is predicated on a named defendant who can be proved negligent, victims have found it very difficult to achieve compensation for their harm.[10] Recognition of collective responsibility would have been more appropriate.

These sorts of "organised irresponsibility"[11] risks create problems of 2–066 proving causation as well as attribution. Scientific knowledge is often insufficient to trace the side effects of new technologies and chemical products. Anthony Giddens suggest that in such cases we should adopt the "precautionary principle"[12] of prohibiting potentially risk-creating activities when there is scientific uncertainty about their effects. This would be a way of "reintroducing responsibility" for the manufacture and marketing of goods and processes, and inspiring wider responsibility to future generations. Meanwhile we should look to the development of the Welfare State, no longer as a means of reducing inequality, but rather as a form of "collective risk management" to cope with new forms of risk. Where there is no such collective approach to risk, we will see the emergence of a more litigious society, attempting to pin culpability wherever we can, "separating indemnity from causality".

Another view might be that individuals who carry out societally- 2–067

[9] *Atiyah's Accidents, Compensation and the Law*, p. 335.
[10] For example *Hope v. British Nuclear Fuels* (1994) 5 Med. L.R. 1; HIV Haemophiliac Litigation; Creutzfeldt-Jakob Disease Litigation.
[11] See A. Giddens, "Risk and Responsibility" (1999) 62 M.L.R. 1.
[12] Giddens, *ibid.* at p. 8.

approved activities in an unapproved and careless manner, and so cause injury, should be punished by being recognised as a wrongdoer and made to pay damages to the victim of the wrong. While punishment as an aim is purported to be confined to criminal law, there is often an expectation on the part of the victim of an accident that the court will publicly acknowledge that a wrong has been done and award damages as a symbol of that recognition. This attitude is particularly prevalent when the loss caused is one which cannot ordinarily be quantified in monetary terms, such as the death of a child, or where the behaviour of the wrongdoer is outside socially acceptable bounds of carelessness, such as drunk driving. Tort law preserves the right in some circumstances to satisfy the desire for recognition and retribution by the award of aggravated and exemplary damages,[13] but even within the bounds of compensatory damages there is arguably an element of vindication of wrong.

2–068   It is suggested that by making the accident causer pay, the accident causer and others will be deterred from further accident-causing behaviour. The deterrence objective of compensation is perhaps the strongest argument put forward by advocates of the tort system, recognising that a no-fault scheme, without related accountability measures, can have no deterrent effect at all. In the context of road accidents, where in reality the defendant is the insurer, and where the criminal law provides separate and parallel inducements to drive safely, it is questionable whether the prospect of civil legal action alters the behaviour of drivers. However Markesinis and Deakin[14] refer to research in Australia and New Zealand which suggests that there has been an increase in road traffic fatalities since the introduction of no-fault compensation schemes in those jurisdictions, although the direct correlation between the accidents and the absence of fault liability might be difficult to demonstrate. Where the insurance compensation scheme included financial penalties for accident causing, the increase in accidents was less noticeable. The argument for the deterrent effect of tort is more convincing in the context of professional negligence with the threat of loss of reputation and career prospects, and possibly in relation to defective products where the cost of rising insurance premia will influence product prices and competitiveness.[15]

2–069   Compensation through a tort, fault liability, route can achieve other less direct aims. The publicity of tort cases in the press and in specialist journals educates potential tortfeasors and potential claimants about rights to compensation and about the limits of legally acceptable behaviour. In the case of medical negligence, doctors can learn of treatments which have gone wrong and adjust their practices accordingly. Patients can discover that their mistreatment, failure to carry out a successful sterilisation leading to further pregnancy for example, is a basis for a damages claim.

Tort also provides a means of monitoring and regulating professional or industrial practice. The early case of *Donoghue v. Stevenson*[16] is an

---

[13] See Ch. 5.
[14] *Tort Law* (4th ed., Oxford, 1999) p. 301; they refer to D. Dewees, D. Duff and M. Trebilcock, *Exploring the Domain of Accident Law* (1996) Ch. 2.
[15] See discussion of economic constraints on damages above.
[16] [1932] A.C. 562.

example of the way in which the courts are able through tort litigation to stand over industrial practice and make clear what behaviour will prove acceptable to the court and what will give rise to a damages award. The Privy Council in *Edward Wong Finance v. Johnson, Stokes and Master*[17] used this market ombudsman role to force Hong Kong legal practice into line, providing an independent (or in this case, as it was the legal profession, semi-independent) overseer to an internally regulated profession.

Discussion of the purposes of compensation is not an issue of only theoretical interest. The purposes of compensation will dictate the basis on which damages are to be paid for loss, and the quantum of those damages. A system which prioritises the needs of the victims of accidents will provide wider, and possibly higher, damages than a system which is more concerned with the behaviour of the accident causer. A system which accepts societal responsibility for societal activities will compensate individuals who suffer loss from those activities more readily than a system committed to individual responsibility for actions. A system which is concerned with the wider aims of compensation (vindication, deterrence or education for example), will be prepared to sacrifice the financial security of individual loss sufferers to satisfaction of these wider objectives. 2–070

Attitudes to the objectives of compensation are not constant even within a particular jurisdiction: they alter with changing political ethos, with changing societal morality and with changing economic policy. The 1960s and 1970s in England and Wales and elsewhere saw an era of community responsibility and economic security which encouraged societal responsibility for loss arising from ordinary activities,[18] and spawned interest in no-fault schemes, strict liability, and *ex gratia* payment mechanisms for loss.[19] The late 1980s, after a period of world-wide economic recession and a predominance of right-wing politics, saw a concentration on individual responsibility for loss,[20] backtrack on payment schemes[21] and limitations on qualification for state assistance. More recently there has been a modified swing back to a recognition of community responsibility, coinciding with a strengthened economy in the West and the return to power of left-of-centre government in many English speaking and European jurisdictions. No-fault compensation is now back on the political agenda and there are moves in many jurisdictions to make the claiming of damages simpler, cheaper, and more cost effective.[22] 2–071

---

[17] [1984] A.C. 1296.

[18] For example the judgment of the House of Lords in *Anns v. Merton London Borough Council* [1978] A.C. 728, which imposed liability on a local council for failing to identify the negligent work of a builder, as a means of distributing the loss of individual property owners.

[19] For example the Criminal Injuries Compensation Scheme in England and Wales, introduced in 1964.

[20] The House of Lords in *Murphy v. Brentwood District Council* [1990] 2 All E.R. 908, on facts almost identical to *Anns* (see n. 18 above), overturned *Anns* and held that each property owner was individually responsible for insuring against loss.

[21] See the abortive attempts to fetter the scheme by the Home Secretary which were declared *ultra vires* by the House of Lords in *R. v. Secretary of State for the Home Department, ex p. Fire Brigades Union* [1995] 2 W.L.R. 1, and the amendments to the scheme in The Criminal Justice Act 1988 and the Criminal Injuries Compensation Act 1995.

[22] See for example the Australian Law Reform Commission, Review of the federal civil justice system discussion paper at www.alrc.gov/au/news/mb/19992008MB.html.

(1) Damages to what end?

2–072   What is the basis for the calculation of damages? Damages require an economic calculation of the value of the loss, so now we might be able to make use of the economic theory discussed earlier. The economists tell us that the system of damages awards should be at the least economically efficient in relation to the costs of preventing the accident from occurring such that both parties are sufficiently satisfied by the operation of the law as not to contest the law. One way of determining this might be to imagine what both parties, the accident causer and the victim, would have agreed in terms of damages if the two of them could have negotiated costlessly before the accident.[23]

2–073   Economic equilibrium between accident prevention costs and probability on the one hand, and costs of accident consequences on the other, may be sufficient to satisfy this efficiency requirement in some straightforward cases of replaceable property damage or economic loss. But in the case of personal injury or death, or in the case of damage to property which has a personal value over the top of its commercial worth, even if there were shown to be an economic advantage to being injured over paying the costs of prevention of injury, the victim of the accident might quite rationally choose the more expensive option of accident prevention. Indeed as well as the actual injury, there may additionally be an infringement of the "fundamental right of an individual not to suffer avoidable personal injury as a result of the actions of others"[24] which will also merit compensation. So a much higher payout on the side of accident costs would be necessary to achieve an outcome which will satisfy both parties. How should we go about the economic calculation of the value of the loss in such cases?

2–074   We could consider two alternative ways to calculate damages. We could measure our damages by asking the question, assuming the position was negotiable, how much would the victim have been prepared to pay to avoid the risk of suffering the harm?[25] This will give us a picture of what the risk of loss was worth to the victim, but the victim's answer to the question will be limited by the victim's resources. The wealthy will be able to pay more and so the starting point for their damages will be higher. This approach also puts the ball in the victim's court, suggesting that the victim has the onus of determining the value of avoidance of the risk of accident.

2–075   Or we could alternatively ask, how much we would have to pay the victim to volunteer to undertake the risk of accident and consequent harm? The victim can now name the price without reference to resources (although it may always be the case that the poor will be more tempted by an offer of payment). This approach may invite a more accurate valuation of the risk of loss suffered from the perspective of the victim. The onus with this approach lies with the accident causer, to offer the victim enough

---

[23] See R. Polinsky, "Economic Analysis as a Potentially Defective Product" (1974) 87 Harvard L.R. 1670.
[24] A. Dismore and F. Whitehead, "Personal Injury Law", *Law Reform for All* (D. Bean ed., Blackstones, 1996).
[25] See C. Veljanovski, *The Economics of Law: An Introductory Text* (IEA, 1990) at p. 44.

for the privilege of creating the risk of accident. Awards would be larger if this were taken as the starting point.

The law tends to take the former approach, and damages awards are referenced to the victim's own circumstances. In the sorts of cases where the victim would ask for more than the commercial value of the resultant loss to balance against accident risk prevention costs, the law recognises the value of that victim preference and builds this recognition into the award. So the purpose of a damages award in tort is purported to be to put the claimant back in the position he or she would have been in had the tort not been committed[26] to the extent that money can do so, to include not only recompense for all financial loss, but also a top up to compensate for some unquantifiable losses. This is the principle of full compensation.   2–076

The reality is however that the principle of full compensation is only a very general guide to damages awards. There are many instances where the law knowingly compensates beyond the level of loss suffered (for example the accumulation approach taken to some collateral benefits such as insurance payouts and charity funds), and others where the law knowingly undercompensates (for example where a relative gives up a well-paid job to act as carer for the injured person). A more accurate statement of the law's approach to damages awards was expressed by Lord Reid in *Parry v. Cleaver*[27]—the criteria for determining awards should be those of justice, reasonableness and public policy. Justice, reasonableness and public policy enable the courts to manipulate damages awards to achieve political, moral and economic ends, and to counterpoise any imbalance between accident prevention and consequences.   2–077

Damages are therefore both wider and narrower than compensation. They are wider in that they may aim to do more than to compensate the victim of the accident. They may for example attempt to exercise some social regulation by expressing disapproval of certain types of behaviour, or may implement some political or economic policy by forcing the parties into particular insurance positions. But damages are narrower than compensation in that an award of damages may not be sufficient to compensate the victim for the actual harm suffered. Indeed some types of loss (death for example) can never be truly compensated for by an award of damages if compensation is about putting the victim back into a pre-accident position. All that damages can do is replace what has been lost by providing some alternative goods which are equally desirable to what has been lost.   2–078

The calculation of damages is the determination of the value of those alternative goods. In his analysis of damages, Robert Goodin[28] distinguishes two types of compensation; means-replacing compensation and ends-replacing compensation. Means-replacing compensation is an award of damages which enables the accident victim to pursue the same ends as would have been pursued before the accident, for example, by providing an artificial limb, or providing a housekeeper, or by replacing a car. Ends-   2–079

---

[26] *Livingstone v. Rawyards Coal Co* (1880) 5 A.C. 25, 39.
[27] [1970] A.C. 1.
[28] R. Goodin, "Theories of Compensation", in *Liability and Responsibility* (R. Frey and C. Morris eds., Cambridge University Press, 1991).

replacing compensation works in circumstances where damages are unable to provide alternative means to the same end, and attempts to enable the victim to pursue other, different, ends which will leave the victim as well off overall. Examples would be by compensating for grief by paying for the victim to take an expensive holiday, compensating someone rendered paralysed by an accident for inability to play sports by paying for a computer and computer games, compensating a child who has lost her mother by paying for her to fly to America to stay with an aunt in her school holidays or replacing a precious piece of art work with another painting by an equally famous artist.

2–080   The law on tort damages is primarily concerned with means-replacing compensation, and other sources of compensation, social security for example, are concerned almost solely with means- replacing compensation. Traditional economic analysis of compensation is indifferent to the distinction and will always opt for the cheaper means of compensating the victim; it may sometimes be the case that providing alternative ends can be done at less cost than enabling the victim to achieve the same ends by other means. Some more sophisticated economic theories recognise that victim preference should be built into the measurement of utility, measuring utility not by the goods themselves but rather by the properties or characteristics of those goods.[29]

2–081   Goodin argues that where only ends-replacing compensation is possible, and victims are forced to change their life goals, then compensation is less appropriate to counter-balance the taking of the accident risk than where means-replacing compensation is possible. In such cases, we would be justified in spending more on accident prevention to avoid having to consider the calculation of ends-replacing compensation. We would also be justified in awarding higher damages for ends-replacing compensation, because of the importance of approximating the alternative ends as closely as possible to the original ends. So we should be prepared to award significant damages for rehabilitation costs, occupational therapy and retraining. Those who cause accidents resulting in the need for ends-replacing compensation should be prepared to pay more for the privilege of causing the accident than persons who cause accidents for which means-replacing compensation would be adequate.

2–082   While Goodin puts the moral argument for higher damages for personal injury and death which can be attributed to a negligent cause, others counter-argue that we should not advantage those who suffer injury from an identifiable cause over other sufferers of injury and disability. Atiyah[30] criticises the way in which tort law selects a tiny group of injured and disabled persons and generously compensates them, ignoring the remainder of sufferers, regardless of need or merit, but related rather to where the accident happened and whether there is an insured person on whom to pin the blame. Atiyah takes the view that those who can establish a claim in tort are given

---

[29] Goodin refers to K. Lancaster, (1966) 74 J. of Political Economy 132.
[30] P. Atiyah, *The Damages Lottery* (Hart, 1997).

"Rolls Royce treatment. Every penny of loss is carefully calculated by expert (and highly paid) doctors, consultants and rehabilitation experts. Expected future losses are calculated too. Something for pain and suffering and loss of amenities is thrown in. And . . . there is often a substantial duplication in entitlements so those who recover damages (especially in fatal cases) are sometimes better off financially after the accident than before."[31]

Atiyah's arguments have even more force when we consider damages for torts which are actionable *per se*, and where aggravated and exemplary damages are awarded.

The principle of full compensation which underlies tort damages has   2–083 been criticised by others[32] as overcompensating in some cases, particularly in the case of minor injuries where there has been no loss of earnings. Awards for pain and suffering in these cases are a windfall for the claimant, and insurance companies are often prepared to pay out without too much quibble to clear the cases from their books. Even in larger cases the claimant can benefit financially because some of the damages award will overlap with social security benefits and possibly also pension benefits and insurance. Cane[33] gives as an example of generous full compensation the case of *Davies v. Whiteways Cyder*[34] in which the court awarded, over and above a dependency award under the Fatal Accidents Act 1965, estate duty payable on substantial gifts of money given to a child before the accident, pointing out that any insurance payout from a policy taken out against the possibility of estate duty liability would not have been deducted from the award.

Some critics have argued that, particularly in the cases of severest injury,   2–084 we should look to providing functional compensation rather than full compensation. In *Lim Poh Choo v. Camden Health Authority*[35] a young Malaysian doctor suffered catastrophic brain injury as a result of medical negligence during minor surgery. In the Court of Appeal, Lord Denning argued that as the claimant did not have sufficient awareness of her injuries to suffer from them, it would be inappropriate to make an award for pain, suffering and loss of amenities, and the award of damages should reflect no more than the costs of her medical and care needs. The award for non-pecuniary loss was intended as a palliative to accident victims, to enable them to purchase some alternative pleasures to compensate for the pain suffered, but in this case there were no such alternative pleasures, and the award would eventually go to her beneficiaries. Functional compensation only was appropriate.

In the House of Lords on appeal[36] Lord Denning's view was rejected   2–085 and full compensation was awarded. The award for loss of amenities was considered to include an objective assessment of the amenity that had been lost which merited compensation even if the victim could not appreciate

---

[31] *ibid.* at p. 148.
[32] For example Markesinis and Deakin, *Tort Law* (4th ed., Oxford, 1999) p. 732.
[33] P. Cane, *Atiyah's Accidents, Compensation and the Law* (Butterworths, 1999).
[34] [1975] Q.B. 262.
[35] [1979] Q.B. 196.
[36] [1980] A.C. 174.

the award. It was not unjust that the money would eventually go to the beneficiaries; had she not been injured the young woman would have acquired capital which she would have wished to go to the beneficiaries. The degree of actual suffering could be reflected in the level of the award for pain and suffering.

2-086   The Law Commission also recommended full compensation[37] on the basis that the award was a conventional rather than a compensatory payment. To attempt to assess pain and suffering in any precise way, as functional compensation would require, would have the effect of transforming the non-pecuniary component into a type of quantifiable pecuniary loss. However where the victim was so badly injured as to be permanently unconscious, only a token conventional award would be appropriate. The Commission's recommendations have now been incorporated into The Judicial Studies Board Guidelines.[38]

2-087   Full compensation in cases of personal injury is a feature of tort damages in most jurisdictions.[39] The New Zealand Accident Compensation Scheme as it was first implemented also included awards for pain and suffering, but these awards have now been eroded, and it is a common feature of most accident compensation schemes that they aim to award functional rather than full compensation. Other sources of disability protection such as social security and private insurance also aim at functional awards. It is the principle of full compensation which differentiates personal injury victims of actionable accidents from other victims of disability and disease, and preferences this small group on the basis not of need or merit but of cause.

2-088   Where the damage is to property, even in tort there is no "top-up" award to reflect the personal consequences of the loss. If a much loved car is written off in an accident, the basis of compensation will be the commercial replacement value of that type of car, not the emotional value of the particular car to the claimant. Harm to items of emotional significance such as inherited trinkets can never be fully compensated in tort, and there is no conventional award in an attempt at full compensation. Any uncertain loss such as loss of expectation or enjoyment will not be taken into account. Damages awards for property loss are purely functional, as if what has been suffered is a pure economic loss. Insurance protection for property damage also takes a functional approach. When it comes to damages for harm to reputation however a tort award will take into account, to some extent at least, the subjective value of the harm to the claimant, particularly where the compensatory damages are accompanied by an aggravated damages award.

2-089   So even the question of quantum of damages is more than a mathematical calculation. There are calls for increase in damages awards, recognising

---

[37] The Law Commission, *Damages for Personal Injury: Non-pecuniary Loss* (1999, No. 257).

[38] The Judicial Studies Board, *Guidelines for the Assessment of General Damages in Personal Injury Cases* (Blackstones, 1998), which incorporated the earlier, provisional recommendations of the Commission.

[39] Even where the award is in the form of periodic payments; see for example the French Civil Code Art 1382 and the guidelines of the *Cour de Cassation* Civ. 2e civ. October 1954; see also R. Redmond-Cooper, "Aspects of the French Law of Damages", in *Damages for Personal Injuries: A European Perspective* (F. Holding and P. Kaye eds., Chancery, 1993).

the hardships of disability, the paucity of social security protection and the infringement of the right to personal safety from avoidable accident. On the other hand there are those who would argue for decrease in individual awards, recognising that recipients of tort awards represent a very small proportion of the ill and disabled, and reflecting concern about the cost of administering the tort system which is not built into the calculation of the awards. There is no common position on what damages awards are to achieve, and until a society can come to some consensus on these issues, there will continue to be a tension between the "too much" and "too little" camps.

(2) Some criticisms of the tort system of damages

There has been much written on flaws in the tort system of damages, and what follows is a brief overview of that critique.

The payment of damages violates the principle of proportionality 2–090 between the wrongfulness of the accident causer's conduct and the penalty imposed.[40] An accident may result from the most trivial, momentary negligence and be responsible for catastrophic damage. Yet a drunk driver driving at speed the wrong way down a one-way street may cause only minor property damage. Given that the tort system in most instances relates liability for damages to fault, there is no logical connection between the degree of fault and the level of damages. The doctrine of contributory negligence works equally disproportionately. This legal relationship between fault and liability has become, with modern industry and technology, even less tenable given that the "fault" often lies with corporate bodies or government departments rather than identifiable individuals. In such cases either the victim will have the added burden of trying to locate the entity to be held legally responsible and establish the causal connection between the fault and the damage, or legal liability will be imposed on persons who were not individually at fault.

If the fault/damage relationship is predicated on moral approbation of 2–091 behaviour, then the system of insurance considerably weakens the basis of that relationship. Richard Abel points out that most negligence litigation is settled without admission of fault, so severing the fault/liability link, contrasting "sharply with many non-Western societies, in which the response to injury focuses on the causal actor's admission of guilt, apology and pleas for forgiveness".[41] Arguments for relating liability to fault in our legal system no longer hold water, and Abel argues that the two should be divorced so as to provide a more efficient system of compensation, reaching a wider range of victim, while considering alternative ways to address the admission of, and personal responsibility for, fault.

Could it be argued that tort is not in fact about the simplistic determina- 2–092 tion of fault, but rather that it is a sophisticated system of risk allocation? The law allocates ordinary risks to the individual or body which steps

---

[40] R. Abel, "A Critique of Torts" (1994) Tort Law Review 99.
[41] *ibid.* at p. 100.

outside the societally accepted bounds of risk taking and causes damage (driving a car over the speed limit for example) by the fault principle, and allocates extraordinary risks with an imposition of strict (or in exceptional cases, absolute) liability. Strict liability invites legal responsibility not because there was any fault in the performance of an activity, but because the activity itself was one which created a societally unacceptable risk. Tort liability is thus a means of forcing risk creators to internalise the cost of risk.

2–093   The difficulty with seeing tort as a risk allocator is that the requirement of cause, problematic enough in fault liability, becomes insupportable. The employer is held strictly liable for the tort of the employee, but to argue that the employer caused the harm is to contrive the meaning of "cause". Another way of looking at fault and strict liability is as a loss distributor. Given that most defendants, especially in common accident situations such as roads, hospitals and industry, will be insured, allocation of legal liability is one way of spreading loss. If however the agenda of legal liability is loss distribution, why limit distribution to the small number of accidents which attract tort? Why place so many hurdles (duty, breach, causation, remoteness) in the path of the claimant? Loss distribution could be so much more effectively and cheaply administered by alternative compensation systems based on no-fault liability or social security or first-party insurance.

2–094   One of the major problems with the way the tort system of damages works is that it focuses on the behaviour of the tortfeasor and not on the needs of the victim. Support for the injured and ill is provided on the fortuitous identification of an insured defendant. The person who becomes paralysed after breaking his neck slipping on the wet supermarket floor is likely to be awarded damages to replace lost earnings and care expenses for life. The person who breaks his neck slipping on a country path is likely to be dependant on meagre social welfare payments and the charity of friends and relatives. If it were the case that serious thought had been given to the preferencing of some disabled on grounds of merit or justice or societal consensus[42] then such differentials might be supportable. As it is, they result from the historical development of the law combined with the exercise of political and economic power. The moral justification for allocating liability with fault loses its charm in the light of the moral injustice of distinguishing equally needy victims on the basis of where the accident occurred and who happens to be around to blame.

2–095   Even the no-fault systems in place in other jurisdictions discriminate against those who cannot establish that their disability arose from an accident. The child paralysed from birth will have the same needs as the accident victim but will fall outside both tort and an accident compensation scheme. Only the aborted Australian proposal[43] for a disability scheme would have fully addressed compensation on the basis of need.

2–096   Given that the tort system of damages favours those who suffer certain kinds of accidents, it is worth noting the profile of the typical victim of

---

[42] Along the lines of the Oregon experiment on resource allocation; see C. Newdick, *Who Should We Treat?* (Oxford, 1996) Ch. 1.
[43] See *supra* n. 32 at para. 2–019.

those types of accidents. The most readily compensable accidents are road accidents and industrial accidents. The most likely victims of such accidents are employed white men. Women, children, the unemployed, the elderly, the poor and racial minorities are far more likely to be victims of accidents in the home, victims of crime, or victims of poor health care or vaccine damage, all of which provide very limited opportunities for compensation.[44] Yet the best protected group is likely also to be protected by first-party property insurance and first-party disability insurance, the latter often as part of an employment package. These insurance payouts will not affect tort damages awards, leaving this group exceptionally well provided for. Is it then a co-incidence that employed white men constitute almost the entire judiciary, and a great majority of parliamentary and trade union power? The law will inevitably reflect the interests of the law makers.[45]

Even in those cases where liability can be established, the payout of dam- **2–097** ages reveals discrepancies which cause concern. Tort damages, based as they are on earnings, favour once again employed men. Housewives (whose work and contribution to the home and to the economy are barely recognised in damages awards), the unemployed, the poorly paid, children and the elderly will be awarded a significantly lower sum.[46] Assumptions are made about the ordering of society in the calculation of future loss. The unemployed will be assumed to stay unemployed. The housewife will be assumed to be stay out of the workforce. The grandparents who step in to provide emergency care will be assumed to be there whenever help is needed. The child of working-class parents will be assumed to leave school early. Any inequity in distribution of society's resources is replicated and magnified by the tort system of damage awards.

Ironically, the principle of equality is firmly upheld when it comes to **2–098** contributions to the damages pot. The wealthy will pay more or less the same third-party insurance premium in relation to a motorvehicle as the poor, safe in the knowledge that in the event of an accident the payout will not be related to contribution.

Other criticisms of tort damages focus on the procedure regulating a **2–099** damages claim. The Woolf Report[47] highlighted many of the obstacles to justice in damages awards including the disproportion between the costs of claim and the damages received, the unacceptable delay between accident and award, the unmeritorious defence of claims, problems of expert witnesses and lack of willingness to settle by solicitors. The Woolf proposals amounted in the main to fine-tuning of the system so as to reduce the

---

[44] R. Abel, "A Critique of Torts" (1994) Tort Law Review 99, p. 103, refers to an English study which found that 29% of road accident victims and 19% of industrial accident victims were likely to recover damages, but only 2% of other accident victims. Yet those other accident victims represented 86% of the accidentally disabled.

[45] See R. Martin, "A Feminist View of the Reasonable Man: An Alternative Approach to Liability in Negligence for Personal Injury" (1994) 23 Anglo-American Law Review 334.

[46] Abel *ibid*. p. 193; "Amongst English accident victims disabled for two weeks or more, men recovered tort damages almost twice as often as women, victims between the ages of 25 and 54 three times as often as those younger or older, the employed more often than the unemployed, and housewives less than a third as often as their proportion of the injured population would predict. The mean sick pay award to women was less than half that of men."

[47] Access to Justice (1996).

procedural barriers to damages, but in the context of medical negligence it was recognised that even fine-tuning would not solve the particular difficulties arising from legal action against a self-funded hospital trust. The Lord Chancellor's Report which followed recommended that immediate attention be given to the possibility of introducing a no-fault scheme in this context.[48]

2–100   Few would defend the damages system as it stands. Some would argue for retention of tort in an approved form.[49] Proposals for strict liability, first-party insurance[50] and reversed burden of proof[51] appear spasmodically. Some commentary supports consideration of no-fault schemes along the lines of those in Scandinavia with particular schemes designed to address particular types of accident[52] running parallel to the tort system, on the basis that although these schemes would not solve all the problems of inequitable support for disability, many of the problems of tort would be resolved and such schemes are at least politically and economically feasible. Others would still hold out for a full disability scheme[53] whereby all injured and ill were entitled to the same level of support whatever the cause. Of course the introduction of such a scheme would not preclude the operation of other means of provision, first-party liability and other welfare benefits for example.

2–101   Whatever the flaws in the system, the tort provision of damages is the lifeline of those who are injured in circumstances of negligence, strict liability or intention. It is the details of how that system works that this book is intended to address.

---

[48] Lord Chancellor's Department, *Review of Civil Justice and Legal Aid* (1997), Point 5.58.
[49] See A. Burrows, *Understanding the Law of Obligations* (Oxford, 1998).
[50] P. Atiyah, *The Damages Lottery* (Hart, 1997).
[51] E.C. draft Directive on liability for defective services (1988).
[52] Markesinis and Deakin, *Tort Law* (Oxford, 1999) appear to support such schemes for road and medical accidents.
[53] Cane, *Atiyah's Accidents, Compensation and the Law* (Butterworths, 1999) p. 418, supports such a proposal but recognises the difficulties of implementation; Abel (see para. 2–086) would also support such a proposal.

CHAPTER 3

FACTORS OF GENERAL RELEVANCE TO THE ASSESSMENT OF DAMAGES

The most significant constraint on an award of damages is the determina-   3–001
tion of a legal responsibility for damage caused. Legal responsibility is
dependant on the claimant establishing that the defendant has offended
against the rules of a specified tort or torts, and will be determined on
criteria of fault liability, strict liability or statutory no-fault liability according to the cause or causes of action pleaded. Until legal responsibility has
been agreed, or until a finding of legal responsibility has been made by the
court, the question of damages does not arise. Of course in the process of
negotiation for settlement of a claim, money may be paid by the defendant
to the claimant without admission or finding of liability, but such money
does not constitute damages. Rather it is an *ex gratia* payment made for
the purposes of ending the negotiations over the claimant's claim, such that
that claim is extinguished.

However there are other factors which can have the effect of negating,   3–002
limiting or increasing a claim for damages. The raising of a defence to the
defendant's behaviour, or the failure of the claimant to initiate the claim in
the appropriate time, can render an otherwise valid claim that the defendant be responsible for damage caused either null and void, or ensure that
the amount of damages awarded is significantly less than the assessed value
of the claimant's damage. Conversely, in the calculation of damages recognition will be given that money paid in damages will in part be compensation for money previously spent, and consequently interest will be added
to the calculation of damages to reflect the true value of the loss of that
money to the claimant. Any delay in proceedings will result in increased
interest payments which will increase the value of the total award.

An award by the court at the end of a hearing on compensation will   3–003
involve more than a sum of money to compensate for the claimant's loss.
The award will also include a recognition of the transaction costs[1] involved
in processing the claim, in particular the costs of legal advice and representation and the disbursements, such as the costs of medical assessment
and expert witnesses, necessary to facilitate the claim. Compensation for
transaction costs will not necessarily be awarded at face value. The issue
of assessment of costs must be considered in determination of the total
award.

---

[1] See Ch. 2 paras. 2–038 *et seq.*

This chapter will examine the effect of these constraints on the award of damages.

(1) The disclaimer defence

3–004   The law allows that in some circumstances potential defendants may disclaim or exclude their responsibility for damages in advance of the damage-causing act. This disclaimer may be expressed in form of an exclusion clause in a contract specifically governing the relationship between the defendant and the claimant, such as a condition written on the back of a train ticket or a term of a contract in relation to the purchase of goods. Alternatively the disclaimer may take the form of a notice of disclaimer addressed to the world at large or to a section of the public which includes the claimant, such as a sign at the entrance to a farmer's land or a notice in a car park.

3–005   The legal effect of a valid disclaimer or exclusion clause is that it serves to rebut completely any claim by the claimant that the defendant is legally responsible for the damage caused, even where the claimant is able to establish that the defendant has breached the legal duties imposed by the relevant tort.

3–006   Disclaimers may result from a genuine agreement between the parties as to where loss should lie in the event of misadventure, such as a negotiated clause of a commercial contract. However it is more likely to be the case that the disclaimer is imposed by a corporate or commercial defendant on an individual claimant who had no say in the terms of the contract. The passenger who wants or needs to travel on a train operated by a transport company has no power to negotiate the terms of carriage. The entrant to a fairground or theme park must either comply with the terms of the entrance ticket or stay away. Even where the claimant has not read the disclaimer and is unaware that liability is excluded, the disclaimer can exclude liability.[2]

3–007   The potential for injustice created by disclaimers has led both the courts and Parliament to impose restrictions on the consequences of disclaimers of liability for damages awards, particularly in cases of personal injury damage. At common law the courts require any attempt to exclude or disclaim liability to satisfy the criteria of notice, choice and construction. The notice criterion requires the defendant to have given adequate notice of the exclusion or disclaimer to the claimant. Any sign posted on land must be sufficiently large and clearly seen, and positioned such that the entrant to land is aware of the disclaimer at the point of entry onto the land.[3] Any term on a ticket must be written in large enough print on the ticket to be readable. There is no requirement that the claimant actually read the disclaimer or exclusion, as long as the defendant has made reasonable efforts to bring the exclusion or disclaimer to the claimant's notice and a reason-

---

[2]   *White v. Blackmore* [1972] 2 Q.B. 651.
[3]   *Ashdown v. Samuel Williams & Sons Ltd* [1957] 1 Q.B. 409.

able person in the claimant's position would have read and understood the notice.[4]

The claimant must have a choice whether or not to accept the terms of the exclusion or disclaimer. A claimant who is required by virtue of employment to enter property covered by a disclaimer has no real choice—she either enters the property or risks losing the job. The disclaimer would not absolve the defendant of liability in such case.[5] Similarly a rescuer who entered land to rescue someone from a burning building, or a doctor who stepped onto a bus to treat a passenger suffering a heart attack has entered into the relationship with the defendant as a result of economic or moral duty, and cannot therefore be said to have accepted, even in the widest sense, the terms of entry.[6] Of course it is arguable that in modern society none of us has completely free choice as to the risks we take. We must all get to work and we are encouraged to do so by public transport. We must all park our cars in car parks. We must all purchase the goods we need for modern daily life from the sources available to us. As these services are likely to be provided by large corporations and industries our bargaining power as to the terms and conditions of our use of these services is minimal. Common law interpretation of exclusions and disclaimers however, requires the claimant's choice to be limited by a specific moral or employment duty before that duty will be sufficient to rebut the exclusion or disclaimer. **3–008**

The third common law limitation is that of construction: the wording of the exclusion or disclaimer must clearly exclude the defendant's liability for the damage suffered. The wording must be in the language or languages which the defendant could reasonably expect would be comprehensible for potential entrants. The wording must make clear to the ordinary person the consequences of the exclusion of liability. Wording which might be alternatively construed, or which might without contortion be limited to particular types of liability and not others, will be narrowly construed against the defendant. For example a generally worded disclaimer may be interpreted to refer to liability under the Occupiers' Liability Act 1957[7] which clearly may be excluded, rather than to ordinary negligence. **3–009**

There are also statuary refinements on the operation of exclusion clauses and disclaimers. Some statutes specifically make clear that liability can be excluded; for example the Occupiers' Liability Act 1958,[8] the Maritime Conventions Act 1911,[9] the Congenital Disabilities (Civil Liability) Act 1976,[10] the Torts (Interference with Goods) Act 1977,[11] and the Merchant **3–010**

---

[4] *Bennett v. Tugwell* [1971] 2 All E.R. 248.
[5] *Burnett v. British Waterways Board* [1973] 2 All E.R. 631.
[6] Similarly under the Occupiers' Liability Act 1957 s. 2(6), a person who enters property under a right conferred by law (a policeman, fireman, social worker for example) is deemed to be a lawful entrant regardless of the permission of the occupier.
[7] s. 2(1).
[8] s. 2(1)—"the occupier is free to extend, restrict, modify or exclude his duty to the visitor by agreement or otherwise".
[9] s. 1(1)(c)—"nothing in this section shall affect ... the right of any person to limit his liability in the manner provided by law".
[10] s. 1(6)—"liability to the child may be treated as having been excluded or limited by contract made with the parent to the same extent as liability to the parent may be excluded or limited".
[11] s. 5(5)—"subject to any agreement varying the respective rights of the parties to the agreement".

Shipping Act 1979.[12] Some statutes include exclusions of liability within the statute itself; for example the British Telecommunications Act 1981,[13] the Civil Aviation Act 1982,[14] and the Pilotage Act 1987.[15] More commonly, other statutes declare that any agreements to limit or exclude liability shall be null and void; for example the Misrepresentation Act 1967,[16] the Employer's Liability (Defective Equipment) Act 1969,[17] the Carriage of Goods by Sea Act 1971,[18] the Defective Premises Act 1972,[19] the Health and Safety at Work Act 1974,[20] the Sex Discrimination Act 1975,[21] the Consumer Protection Act 1987[22] and the Road Traffic Act 1988.[23] Still other statutes are confusingly silent on whether or not liability can be restricted; for example the Occupiers' Liability Act 1984.

3–011   Undoubtedly the most important restrictions on the use of exclusion clauses and disclaimers for tortious liability are contained in the Unfair Contract Terms Act 1977 (UCTA). This Act recognises the imbalance of power which often exists, particularly in the commercial context, between defendants and the individuals who use their services, such that claimants are unlikely to have had any negotiating power in respect of exclusion of liability. The Act covers exclusions and disclaimers in both contract and tort. The provisions of the Act apply only to business liability, which is defined as liability arising from things done or to be done in the course of a business, or from the occupation of premises used for business purposes, although the determination of what is a business activity or occupation is often not a clear cut as this definition suggests.[24]

---

[12] Sched. 4, Arts. 1 and 2—"shipowners and salvors may limit their liability in accordance with the rules of this convention; ... claims in respect of loss of life, personal injury, damage to property or other loss resulting from infringement of rights may be subject to limitation of liability".

[13] s. 23—"no proceedings in tort shall lie against the Corporation in respect of any loss or damage suffered by any person by reason of failure, interruption or suspension of a telecommunication service".

[14] s. 76—"no action in trespass or nuisance will lie in respect of the flight of an aircraft over property at a reasonable height above the ground"; s. 77—"no action in nuisance will lie in respect of the noise of an aircraft or an aerodrome".

[15] s. 22(8)—"a competent harbour authority shall not be liable for any loss or damage caused by any act or omission by a pilot authorised under it by virtue only of that authorisation".

[16] s. 3—"if a contract contains a term which would exclude or restrict any liability resulting from the misrepresentation that term shall have no effect (subject to the Unfair Contract Terms Act 1977)".

[17] s. 1(2)—"in so far as any agreement purports to exclude or limit any liability of an employer arising under this Act, the agreement shall be void".

[18] Sched., Art. III, s. 8—"any agreement relieving the carrier or ship from liability for loss or damage to goods arising from negligence, fault or failure of duty shall be null and void and of no effect".

[19] s. 6(3)—"any term of an agreement which purports to exclude or restrict any liability arising by virtue of the provisions of this Act shall be void".

[20] s. 47(5)—"any term of an agreement which purports to exclude or restrict any liability shall be void, except in so far as health and safety regulations provide otherwise".

[21] s. 77(3)—"any term in a contract which purports to exclude or limit any provision of this Act shall be unenforceable by any person in whose favour the term would operate".

[22] s. 7—"the liability of a person to a person who has suffered damage caused by a defect in a product, or to a dependant or relative of such person, shall not be limited or excluded by any contract term, by any notice or other provision".

[23] s. 149(2)—"if any other person is carried in the vehicle, any antecedent agreement or understanding between them shall be of no effect in so far as it purports to negative or restrict the liability of the user".

[24] For more on this, see Markesinis and Deakin, *Tort Law* (4th ed., Clarenden, 1999) p. 322.

In respect of death or personal injury, the effect of the UCTA is to pro- **3–012** hibit any exclusion, disclaimer or limitation on liability in negligence. Any exclusion clause or disclaimer notice purporting to exclude such liability is consequently null and void. This is so even where the right to exclude liability is recognised by statute, such as the right of occupiers to limit or exclude liability provided in the Occupiers' Liability Act 1957.

The Unfair Contract Terms Act specifically includes the Occupiers' **3–013** Liability Act 1957 in its remit. What is less clear is the effect of the UCTA on disclaimers of liability to non-visitors (persons who do not satisfy the definition of lawful visitor for the purposes of the Occupiers' Liability Act 1957) under the Occupiers' Liability Act 1984. The 1984 Act explicitly provides that no duty is owed to any person in respect of risks willingly accepted by that person,[25] so recognising the defence of *volenti* (see below), but does not explicitly recognise, as the 1957 Act does, the right of occupiers to exclude liability to non-visitors. It seems unlikely and illogical that Parliament could have intended that occupiers be able to exclude liability to lawful visitors under the 1957 Act but be unable to exclude liability to non-visitors under the 1984 Act, as this would result in trespassers having greater protection than lawful visitors to premises. So it is generally assumed that a right of exclusion must be implied into the Act.

If this is the case however, the question arises as to the relevance of **3–014** UCTA to the 1984 Act. As UCTA was passed before the 1984 Occupiers' Liability Act, it makes no reference to the 1984 Act. Nor does the 1984 Act make reference to UCTA. If UCTA does not apply, then business occu- piers remain free to exclude liability to non-visitors for death or personal injury. Yet the intention of the 1984 Act has its origins in the "common duty of humanity" which was proposed by Lord Denning in *Herrington v. British Railways Board*[26] as the minimum duty owed by an occupier of premises to entrants to the premises. Lord Denning's view, echoed in the parliamentary debate leading to the 1984 Act, was that in contemporary society it was no longer appropriate for owners of premises to refuse to take responsibility for dangers presented by those premises, and that public policy favoured recognition of a minimum standard of care owed to all entrants. It is generally assumed that the failure to attach the provisions of UCTA to rights of exclusion under the 1984 Occupiers' Liability Act results from "defective drafting".[27]

The Unfair Contract Terms Act also limits the scope of exclusion clauses **3–015** and disclaimers in respect of negligently caused property damage or pure economic loss; such exclusions and disclaimers must satisfy the requirement of reasonableness to take effect. In the context of exclusions and dis- claimers in relation to property or economic damage caused by negligence, two questions arise: firstly, when does the disclaimer or exclusion come into play, and secondly, what constitutes a reasonable exclusion or disclaimer?

---

[25] s. 1(6).
[26] [1972] A.C. 877.
[27] See for example B. Markesinis and S. Deakin, *Tort Law* (4th ed., Clarenden Press, 1999), p. 323.

3–016   Liability for pure economic loss was first recognised in English law in *Hedley Byrne v. Heller & Partners*[28] in which the House of Lords acknowledged the existence of a potential duty of care between banker and enquirer, that duty being negated on the facts because the information was given "without responsibility". The test proposed in that case for determination of a duty of care in relation to statements giving rise to economic loss was based on determination of a special relationship between the parties. Indicators of a special relationship included reliance by the enquirer on the information given by the speaker, knowledge of that reliance on the part of the speaker, the fact that it was reasonable in the circumstances to rely on the words, and the absence of any disclaimer attached to the information. In other words, the presence or absence of the disclaimer is a vital factor in determination of the existence of any duty of care between speaker and enquirer.

3–017   The significance of this is that if the existence of the disclaimer or exclusion results in the absence of any duty of care between the parties at all, then in such cases the question will never arise as to the effect of any defence of exclusion of liability, and UCTA will not operate to prevent the exclusion or disclaimer. Thus UCTA will not work to protect claimants against unreasonable exclusion or disclaimer of liability. The Court of Appeal in *Harris v. Wyre Forest DC*[29] took this approach, finding that the very existence of the disclaimer could be sufficient to deny a duty of care in the first place. However on appeal, the House of Lords[30] referred to section 13(1) of UCTA which applies the provisions of the Act to "terms and notices which exclude or restrict the relevant obligations or duty", and concluded that exclusions and disclaimers must be considered as issues of defence rather than duty for UCTA to have any role in protection against unfair avoidance of liability.

3–018   On the question of reasonableness, UCTA gives no direction and we must look to common law interpretations of reasonableness in this context. The result is that issues of reasonableness come into play twice in the determination of liability for damage, once in the determination of the duty of care between the parties and again in evaluation of the reasonableness of the exclusion or disclaimer. There is no shortage of case law on the duty point,[31] but on the defence issue we must look to the decision of the House of Lords in *Smith v. Bush*.[32] Factors which will go to determine reasonableness will include an assessment of the imbalance of bargaining power between the parties (corporation or professional body versus an individual?), the accessibility of alternative sources of advice or information, the degree of knowledge or skill necessary in the giving of information or advice, and the economic consequences to the parties of recognition of the defence.

---

[28] [1964] A.C. 465.
[29] [1988] 1 Q.B. 835.
[30] *Harris v. Wyre Forest DC* and *Smith v. Bush* [1990] 1 A.C. 831.
[31] For example *Spring v. Guardian Assurance Ltd* [1995] 2 A.C. 296, *White v. Jones* [1995] 2 A.C. 207.
[32] See *supra* n. 30.

(2) The consent defence

Whereas disclaimers and exclusions are concerned with express consent   3–019
to limitations on the defendant's liability, the consent defence looks to the
actions of the parties to infer implied consent to such limitations. The consent defence provides a complete defence to any claim for damages.

As with express consent, some statutes specifically recognise that some   3–020
risks are willingly accepted. The Animals Act 1971 for example holds that
there will be no liability "for any damage suffered by a person who has
voluntarily accepted the risk thereof"[33] but makes clear that merely by
agreeing to work with animals the claimant is not to be held to have
accepted the risk of injury.[34] The Occupiers' Liability Act 1957 states that
the common duty of care does not impose any obligation with respect to
"risks willingly accepted as his by the visitor"[35] and the Occupiers' Liability
Act 1984 that no duty is owed to any person "in respect of risks willingly
accepted".[36] The Congenital Disabilities (Civil Liability) Act 1976 recognises the defence of consent in two contexts; where parents conceived a
child in the knowledge that there was a risk that the child would be born
with a disability,[37] or where parents conceived a child knowing that there
had been exposure of one of the parents to radiation which created a risk
of disability in the child.[38]

As well as these statutory recognitions of the *volenti* defence, common   3–021
law also continues to deny liability for willingly-accepted risks in relation
to a variety of torts, and of course even where statute does specifically
recognise the defence, the issue of what constitutes willing acceptance
remains open to judicial interpretation.[39] The Unfair Contract Terms Act
has no application to implied consent. However in the context of negli-
gently-caused road traffic accidents the Road Traffic Act 1988 states that
the fact that a passenger has willingly accepted the risk of negligence on
the part of the driver will not negate the driver's liability,[40] thus clarifying
the law which was unclear on the issue of passengers who knowingly accept
a lift with a drunk driver.[41]

Determination of what constitutes willing acceptance was considered by   3–022
Lord Denning in *Nettleship v. Weston*.[42] Mere knowledge of the risk was
not sufficient; the claimant must go further and by words or acts agree to
take responsibility for the consequences of any negligence on the part of

---

[33] s. 5(2).
[34] s. 6(5).
[35] s. 2(5).
[36] s. 1(6); see also *Ratcliff v. McConnell* [1999] 1 W.L.R. 1375.
[37] s. 1(4)—"the defendant is not answerable to the child if at the time (of conception) either
or both of the parents knew the risk of their child being born disabled . . .".
[38] s. 3(5)—"if the injury to the parent preceded the time of the child's conception and at that
time either or both of the parents knew the risk of the child being born disabled . . .".
[39] s. 1(6) of the Occupiers' Liability Act 1984 states that in relation to the statutory duty
imposed by the Act "the question whether a risk was so accepted was to be decided on the
same principles as in other cases in which one person owes a duty of care to another".
[40] s. 149(3).
[41] See for example *Dann v. Hamilton* [1939] 1 K.B. 509; *Insurance Commissioner v. Joyce*
(1948) 77 C.L.R. 39.
[42] [1971] 2 Q.B. 691.

the defendant. An example of such behaviour would be a pillion passenger actively encouraging a motorbike driver to drive dangerously as on the facts of *Pitts v. Hunt*.[43] In *Morris v. Murray*[44] a passenger who had been on a drinking spree agreed to fly in a light aircraft piloted by his even more drunk friend. When the pilot crashed the plane, an action in negligence by the claimant passenger failed because the claimant was sufficiently aware of events to have appreciated and accepted the risk of accident.[45] Had the claimant been too drunk to appreciate and accept the risk, the defence would not have been satisfied.

3–023   The consent defence applies to torts other than negligence. Anyone who consents to the non-natural user of a neighbour's land is denied a strict liability duty under the tort of *Rylands v. Fletcher*.[46] Similarly anyone who consents to an interference with the beneficial use of their land will be denied a remedy in nuisance.[47] Anyone who consents to the publication of a derogatory statement cannot complain in defamation.[48] However, the courts have been reluctant to recognise consent as a defence to an action for breach of statutory duty, particularly where the action is being brought by an employee against an employer, the exception being the case of *Imperial Chemicals v. Shatwell*[49] where there was a clear and knowing disregard by the employee of instructions to obey the statute.

3–024   Consent is a particularly important defence in the context of intentional harm to the person, such as battery and false imprisonment. The boxer who agrees to enter a fight consents to assaults on his person consistent with the rules of the game and cannot complain when he is landed a punch. However the boxer is entitled to expect that the rules of the sport will be upheld and that the organisers will take all reasonable steps to make the fights safe.[50] Patients are required to consent to any medical treatment to their person, and a competent patient is entitled to refuse unwanted treatment, even if in the doctor's view that treatment is in the patient's best interests.[51] The consent defence in the medical context has been muddied by court imposed limitations on what the patient needs in the way of information for the consent to be valid.[52] There is no recognition of the doctrine of "informed consent" in this jurisdiction equivalent to that in the United States, and courts in England and Wales have been reluctant to adopt the patient-focused compromise on issues of consent to medical treatment which has developed in other commonwealth jurisdictions.[53]

---

[43] [1991] 1 Q.B. 24, although as this was a road traffic accident the Road Traffic Act 1988 prevented the application of the consent defence.
[44] [1991] 2 Q.B. 6.
[45] The Road Traffic Act 1988 prohibition on the defence did not apply.
[46] For example *Rickards v. Lothian* [1913] A.C. 263.
[47] *Leakey v. National Trust* [1980] Q.B. 485.
[48] For example *Chapman v. Lord Ellesmere* [1932] 2 K.B. 431.
[49] [1965] A.C. 656.
[50] See *Watson v. British Boxing Board of Control* T.L.R. October 12, 1999.
[51] See *St George's Healthcare NHS Trust v. S* [1998] 3 All E.R. 673.
[52] See *Chatterton v. Gerson* [1981] 1 All E.R. 257, and *Sidaway v. Bethlem Royal Hospital Governors* [1985] 1 All E.R. 643.
[53] For example *Rogers v. Whitaker* (1992) 109 A.L.R. 625.

(3) The illegality defence

Where the claimant was injured in the course of an illegal or publicly   3–025
immoral activity then public policy might intervene to prevent a successful
claim for damages. In *Pitts v. Hunt*,[54] although the Road Traffic Act prevented the application of the consent defence, the fact that the pillion passenger was encouraging illegal behaviour was sufficient to preclude him
from damages award. In *Clunis v. Camden and Islington HA*[55] a man with
a history of mental illness was precluded from an award of damages when
he sued the health authority for not giving him the care he needed to prevent him from killing a stranger. However where the claim results from a
failure of the defendant to protect the claimant from self-infliction of harm,
the courts have recognised the effect of the Suicide Act 1961, and allowed
claims where there was a clear failure of a responsible person to prevent
the claimant from committing, or attempting to commit, suicide.[56]

(4) The necessity defence

The defence of necessity focuses on intentional acts designed to achieve   3–026
a justifiable end and again provides a complete defence to a damages claim.
For example a defence to trespass to land might be that the purpose of
trespass was to put out a fire.[57] The necessity defence is of its greatest
relevance in the context of medical treatment, where a patient is incapable
of expressing consent or refusal to that treatment and treatment is necessary to preserve the life or health of the patient.[58]

(5) The warning defence

Both the Occupiers' Liability Act 1957 and the Occupiers' Liability Act   3–027
1984 create specific defences of warning which have no direct correlation
in common law.[59] However, the requirements of the defence differ in the
two Acts. Under the 1957 Act, the warning to be effective must be sufficient
to enable the visitor to be reasonably safe in all the circumstances.[60] Under
the 1984 Act it is sufficient that the occupier take such steps as are reasonable in all the circumstances of the case to give warning of the danger or
to encourage the non-lawful visitor from incurring the risk.[61] Both defences
constitute a complete defence to a damages claim.

---

[54] See n. 43 para. 3–022.
[55] [1998] 2 W.L.R. 902.
[56] See *Kirkham v. Chief Constable* [1990] 2 Q.B. 283; *Commissioner of the Metropolitan
Police v. Reeves* [1993] 3 All E.R. 897.
[57] For example *Cope v. Sharpe (No 2)* [1912] 1 K.B. 496.
[58] See *Re F.* [1990] 2 A.C. 1.
[59] Although at common law, the existence of a warning might be evidence of consent to the
risk.
[60] s. 2(4)(a); see *Coupland v. Eagle Bros* [1969] 210 E.G. 581 and *White v. Blackmore* [1972]
2 Q.B. 651.
[61] s. 1(5).

(6) The contributory negligence defence

3–028   Contributory negligence at common law was, like the defences discussed
above, a complete defence to a claim in tort. However the effect of the Law
Reform (Contributory Negligence) Act 1945 was to make contributory
negligence a partial defence, enabling the court to apportion liability
between the parties "to such extent as the court thinks just and equitable
having regard to the claimant's share of responsibility for the damage".[62]

3–029   For a finding of contributory negligence it must be determined both that
the claimant was negligent, and that there is a causal relationship between
that negligence and the accident or the damage resulting from the accident.
At common law determination of claimant negligence followed the same
approach as determination of defendant's negligence: it assumed that the
claimant had a duty to take reasonable care to prevent self-harm and asked
whether the claimant had acted with all the care to be expected of a reasonable person in the circumstances. Determination of causal relationship followed the approach taken to tortious causation; on the balance of probabilities, would the claimant have suffered this injury but for her negligence?
It is arguable however that the 1945 Act gives the court greater flexibility
in making a finding of contributory negligence; the court may reduce the
award as it considers just and equitable according to the claimant's share
of responsibility for the damage. This suggests that the court may look at
the circumstances as a whole and award according to overall impression as
to responsibility rather than become too involved with the technicalities of
breach and causation.

3–030   Contributory negligence is concerned with more than the claimant's contribution to the accident; it looks also to the claimant's responsibility for
the damage resulting from the accident. Thus the claimant injured in a road
accident as a passenger in a car may have made no contribution to the
accident, but if the passenger suffers greater injury by failing to wear a seat
belt[63] or if a motorcyclist fails to wear a crash helmet[64] this will be taken
into account to reduce the damages award. The issue of seat belts and
motorcycle helmets is simplified by statutory requirements that they be
worn.[65] Where there is no such statutory requirement it is more difficult
to determine the consequences of negligence which contributes to the
damage but not to the accident. A follower of the Sikh religion wearing a
turban is exempted from the motorcycle helmet requirement.[66] Does this
mean that a helmetless Sikh who suffers from head injuries as a result of a
collision with another driver will not be found contributory negligent even
where it can be established that a helmet would have diminished his injuries? What of the helmetless bicycle rider? Attempts to argue contributory
negligence in the context of bicycle accidents have failed, in part because
there is no legal requirement to wear a helmet when riding a bicycle,

---

[62] s. 1(1).
[63] *Froom v. Butcher* [1976] Q.B. 286.
[64] *O'Connell v. Jackson* [1972] 1 Q.B. 270.
[65] ss. 15 and 16 of the Road Traffic Act 1988; s. 27 of the Transport Act 1981; the Motor
Vehicles (Wearing of Seatbelts) Regulations 1982 (S.I. 1982/1203).
[66] s. 16(2) Road Traffic Act 1988.

although it is accepted that helmets can prevent head injuries.[67] Arguments of contributory negligence based on failure to wear a seat belt in the rear seat of a car have been more successful,[68] based on the reasoning in *Froom v. Butcher*.[69]

Now that the Road Traffic Act 1988 prevents the defence of consent in 3–031 the context of road accident claims, the courts tend to deal with a passenger's willingness to travel in a vehicle with a drunk or unlicensed driver,[70] or in a vehicle known to be defective[71] as an issue of contributory negligence. It is not however open to the court to make a finding of 100 per cent contributory negligence to equate to the effect of the consent defence.[72]

Contributory negligence may also be a defence to some statutorily- 3–032 defined torts. The Occupiers' Liability Act 1957 implies rather than states that contributory negligence is a defence to a claim under the Act.[73] The Occupiers' Liability Act 1984 makes no mention of contributory negligence as a defence. However, in this context reference must be made to the decision in *Revill v. Newberry*.[74] This was not an action in occupiers' liability as such. The claimant was a burglar suing for injuries caused when the owner of an allotment he was trying to rob shot blindly through a small hole in a shed door. It was held that as the danger was not caused by a defect in the state of the premises, the action was more properly framed in ordinary negligence, but that the issue should be determined on the same lines as if it were an action brought under section 1 of the Occupiers' Liability Act 1984. Having held that there was a duty on these criteria, the court then proceeded to reduce the damages by two-thirds to reflect the claimant's contributory negligence, suggesting that had the action been framed under the Act, contributory negligence would have been an appropriate defence.

Contributory negligence is overtly stated to be a recognised defence in 3–033 any claim under the Nuclear Installations Act 1965,[75] the Employer's Liability (Defective Equipment) Act 1969,[76] the Congenital Disabilities (Civil Liability) Act 1976,[77] the Control of Pollution Act 1974[78] and the Fatal Accidents Act 1976.[79] Under the Animals Act 1971, the claimants's negligence will be a complete defence if the damage was "wholly due to the person suffering it",[80] and a partial defence if the claimant's negligence is

---

[67] *Williams v. Ashley* (1999) unreported; see Braithwaite (1999) 143 part 46 S.J. 1144.
[68] For example *Biesheuvel v. Birrell* [1999] P.I.Q.R. Q40.
[69] See n. 63 para. 3–030.
[70] See for example *Green v. Gaymer* June 25, 1999 (unreported) where a pillion passenger who rode with a drunk motorcycle driver was held to be 20% contributory negligent; see also *Owens v. Brimmell* [1977] Q.B. 859.
[71] *Gregory v. Kelly* [1978] R.T.R. 426.
[72] *Pitts v. Hunt* n. 43, para. 3–022.
[73] s. 2(3).
[74] [1996] 1 All E.R. 291.
[75] s. 13(6).
[76] s. 1(1)(b)—"without prejudice to the law relating to contributory negligence . . .".
[77] ss. 1(7) and 3(4).
[78] Section 88(4) makes clear that the Law Reform (Contributory Negligence) Act 1945 applies where there is a civil claim for the effects of pollution.
[79] s. 5.
[80] s. 5(1); see *Marlor v. Ball* (1900) 16 T.L.R. 239.

contributory.[81] The Torts (Interference with Goods) Act 1977 specifically excludes the defence of contributory negligence.[82]

3–034   It is unclear how the contributory negligence defence applies to claims under the Consumer Protection Act 1987. The European Directive which prompted the Act allowed for inclusion of the contributory negligence defence,[83] and section 6(4) of the Act appears to recognise the defence,[84] but given that the Act provides for strict liability for defective products it is difficult to see how the court can apportion comparative responsibility for the damage where no fault is required on the part of the defendant for *prima facie* liability to arise. It is true that the Animals Act, which also purports to impose strict liability, does specify the defence of contributory negligence, but the basis of liability under that Act is in reality far from strict and some measurement of comparative fault is at least theoretically possible.

3–035   Does contributory negligence apply to reduce the award of damages in cases of economic loss? There is some confusion as to whether the defence could be raised in cases of negligent misstatement. The test for duty of care in cases of misstatement includes consideration of whether the claimant was reasonable to rely on the words of the speaker,[85] and in the early negligent misstatement cases the claimant's behaviour was to be taken into consideration in determination of the *prima facie* duty in the same way as the existence of a disclaimer was considered an issue of duty rather than of defence. Although courts are now prepared to consider separately duty and defence issues,[86] there appears still to be reluctance to find contributory negligence where a duty has been found to exist on the facts as a whole.[87] Where the negligence on the part of the defendant was an act leading to pure economic loss rather than words, the law has been settled by the House of Lords in favour of recognition of the contributory negligence defence in *Platform Home Loans v. Oyston Shipways*.[88]

3–036   The defence of contributory negligence applies to actions for breach of statutory duty,[89] but will be applied cautiously in actions by employees against employers in recognition of the power imbalance in the relationship.[90] Contributory negligence may also serve as a defence to an action in nuisance or *Rylands v. Fletcher*,[91] but "coming to the nuisance" does not affect the claimant's claim. The application of contributory negligence to

---

[81] s. 10.
[82] s. 11(1).
[83] Directive 85/374 Art. 8(1).
[84] "Where any damage is caused partly by a defect in a product and partly by the fault of the person suffering the damage, the Law Reform (Contributory Negligence) Act 1945 . . . shall have affect as if the defect were the fault of every person liable by virtue of this Part for the damage caused by the defect".
[85] *Hedley Byrne v. Heller* [1964] A.C. 465.
[86] Since the Unfair Contract Terms Act 1977.
[87] *Smith v. Bush* [1989] 2 W.L.R. 790.
[88] [1999] 1 All E.R. 833.
[89] s. 4, Law Reform (Contributory Negligence) Act 1945.
[90] *Caswell v. Powell Duffryn Associated Collieries* [1940] A.C. 152; though see also *Robb v. Everard & Sons* unreported March 19, 1999.
[91] s. 4, Law Reform (Contributory Negligence) Act 1945—the Act applies to any "act or omission which gives rise to liability in tort".

claims in the intentional torts is controversial. Some authorities have denied the defence[92] although more recently courts appear to be more disposed to recognising contributory negligence in this context.[93]

The defence appears not to apply to actions in deceit. In *Alliance and Leicester Building Society v. Edgestop*[94] contributory negligence was found to be an inappropriate defence for deceit, and more recent attempts to argue to the contrary, despite some academic support,[95] have failed to bring about a change in approach. In *Nationwide Building Society v. Thimbleby*[96] the court held that had Parliament intended to introduce the defence of deceit in the Law Reform (Contributory Negligence) Act 1945 contrary to previous authority, it would have done so in clear terms, and that common law denying the defence remained good law. Contributory negligence does appear to apply to an action under the Misrepresentation Act 1967.[97]

(7) Calculation of interest on damages

Interest is normally awarded on damages to reflect loss on money paid out by the claimant in advance of recovery of damages. Courts have discretion to award interest on all tortious damages, and are required to award interest on damages for personal injury or death over the value of £200.[98] Section 35A of the Supreme Court Act provides that any sum of damages awarded shall include simple interest at a rate such as the court thinks fit unless the court thinks there are special reasons to the contrary. Interest is only awarded on past loss; there is no award on future loss such as loss of future earnings or damages for future medical care.   3–037

Interest on the award for pain, suffering and loss of amenity represents compensation for loss which is both past and future. There has been much controversy about the appropriate rate of interest on this award. In *Jefford v. Gee*[99] it was made clear that the rate of interest should be the same as that which is payable on money payable into court which is placed on a short-term investment account. This resulted in an interest rate of two per cent.   3–038

In *Wright v. British Railways Board*[1] the House of Lords confirmed authorities[2] following *Jefford v. Gee* which retained the two per cent rate, but did so on the basis not of the short term investment rate but on investment in Index Linked Government Securities (ILGS). The House added the qualification that this rate was a guideline only and not to be regarded   3–039

---

[92] For example *Lane v. Holloway* [1968] 1 Q.B. 379.
[93] See *Barnes v. Nayer*, *The Times* December 19, 1986; see also Childs (1983) 44 N.I.L.Q. 334.
[94] [1994] 2 All E.R. 38.
[95] For example, Howarth, *Textbook on Tort* (Butterworths, 1995) p. 661.
[96] [1999] E.G.C.S. 34.
[97] *Gran Gelato v. Richcliff Ltd* [1992] 2 W.L.R. 867.
[98] s. 35A, Supreme Court Act 1981; s. 69 County Court Act 1984.
[99] l[1970] 2 Q.B. 130.
[1] [1983] 2 A.C. 773.
[2] *Birkett v. Hayes* [1982] 2 All E.R. 70.

as a rule of practice. After *Wright* there was mounting criticism[3] of the inappropriateness of the two per cent rate, and the increasing recognition of Index Linked Government Securities as an advisable form of investment from the capital sum awarded in damages led to pressure to calculate interest rates in accordance with the investment rate in ILGS.

3–040   In *Wells v. Wells; Thomas v. Brighton Health Authority* and *Page v. Sheerness Steel*[4] the House of Lords proposed taking the investment rate in ILGS as the basis for calculation of the multiplier for future loss. The appeal in *Thomas* also required consideration of interest on the damages for the cost of providing a larger house. Although *Wright* was concerned with interest on non-pecuniary loss, Lord Lloyd in his discussion of *Thomas* found that "the point is the same"[5] as the issue of interest on special damages. Lord Lloyd pointed out that in *Wright* the House of Lords had used the ILGS as a guide to their imposition of an interest rate of two per cent, so for the purposes of calculating interest on the special damages in *Thomas*, present ILGS should be used to determine an interest rate of three per cent. As "the point is the same", this suggests that for non-pecuniary loss the interest rate is now established at three per cent. This was the view of Connell J in *Burns v. Davies*[6] and interest of three per cent was awarded on the general damages in that case. The interest on non-pecuniary loss is calculated from the date of service of the writ to date of judgment.[7]

3–041   The award of interest on damages for non-pecuniary loss is limited to personal injury claims. Awards for non-pecuniary loss resulting from a successful action in defamation, false imprisonment or deceit are not likely to have interest added[8] although the court retains discretion to award interest in appropriate cases.

Interest on special damages, that is pecuniary loss suffered by the time of trial, is now to be awarded at three per cent.[9] This interest covers the period from date of accident to date of trial.[10]

3–042   In the context of personal injuries, the question arises as to what special damages to base the interest award on. The issue is complicated by recoupment procedures[11] to reclaim social security benefits which had been paid to the claimant before trial. In *Wadey v. Surrey County Council*[12] it was made clear that the benefits were not to be deducted from the award for special damages before the interest was calculated.[13] This may result in a windfall for the claimant. Similarly, should the court award interest on special damages which include an award for lost wages, when those wages

---

[3] See for example Buchan, "Is it Time to Review Interest on General Damages at two per cent? Shouldn't it be three per cent?" (1998) J.P.I.L. 296.
[4] [1998] 3 All E.R. 481.
[5] At p. 499.
[6] [1999] Lloyd's Rep Med 215.
[7] *Jefford v. Gee* [1970] 1 All E.R. 1202.
[8] *Saunders v. Edwards* [1987] 2 All E.R. 651.
[9] *Wells v. Wells; Thomas v. Brighton Health Authority; Page v. Steel* [1998] 3 All E.R. 481.
[10] *Jefford v. Gee* [1970] 1 All E.R. 1202.
[11] Social Security (Recovery of Benefits) Act 1997.
[12] [1999] 2 All E.R. 334.
[13] s. 17 of the Social Security (Recovery of Benefits) Act 1997 reads "In assessing damages in respect of any accident, injury or disease, the amount of any listed benefits paid or likely to be paid is to be disregarded".

had been paid to the claimant by his employer and the claimant was under a contractual obligation to repay the wages? It was held in *Davies v. Inman*[14] that interest should be awarded on the full amount of special damages but that the interest on the wages was to be held in trust for the employer, who had lost the use of the wages money until repayment. The same approach is taken to awards to cover the cost of past care, which is also to be held in trust by the claimant to recompense the carer.[15]

Interest in the particular case of damage to ships is awarded in accordance with Admiralty practice.[16]   3–043

Interest may be awarded on costs from the date of the judgment or order[17] on the same basis as other special damages.   3–044

(8) Costs

Judges at all levels have a discretion to assess and award costs between the parties.[18] Costs have become a major component of damages awards, and were identified by Lord Woolf[19] as the most serious problem in our system of litigation. Most of Lord Woolf's proposals have been incorporated into the Civil Procedure Rules 1998 (CPR), replacing the rules as to costs formerly contained in the Supreme Court Rules (SCR) and County Courts Rules (CCR) from April 26, 1999. The new rules are aimed at controlling litigation costs, making them more proportionate to the value of the case and the means of the parties, and using costs as a sanction to enforce case management procedures. The overriding objective of the Civil Procedure Rules is to enable courts to deal with cases justly and requires parties to work towards this objective in the management of cases.[20]   3–045

Costs are awarded against the losing party to indemnify the successful party for the litigation expenses incurred. It is recognised that the successful party will have a legal obligation to pay his solicitor's charges, and these charges form the basis of the assessment of costs. It is only in an exceptional case that a court will exercise its discretion to refuse a costs award and such discretion must be exercised in accordance with reason and justice,[21] for example where the successful party has instituted or managed the litigation in a manner calculated to cause unnecessary costs.[22]   3–046

Costs may also not be awarded where the claimant fails to establish damage resulting from the tort. Any action in negligence will be fundamentally flawed by the absence of damage, such that the claimant will be unsuccessful in the negligence claim. Some negligence actions may be sufficiently

---

[14] [1999] P.I.Q.R. Q26.
[15] *Hunt v. Severs* [1994] 2 A.C. 350.
[16] In recent years the rate of interest in the Admiralty court has been equated with the rate awarded in the Commercial court.
[17] See Supreme Court Practice 1997, Vol. 1 para 62/35/9.
[18] Formerly R.S.C. Ord. 62 rule 7(4)(b); CCR Ord. 38 rules 3(3D) and 19(3); now CPR 1998 Part 47.
[19] Woolf, *Access to Justice* (1996).
[20] C.P.R. 1998, rule 1.1(a).
[21] See *Aiden Shipping Co Ltd v. Interbulk Ltd* [1986] A.C. 965; C.P.R. Rule 44.4.
[22] See *Smith v. Huntley* [1995] P.I.Q.R. p. 475; *Ritter v. Godfrey* [1920] K.B. 47; see also Part 47 C.P.R. 1998.

complicated in that there are a number of claims and counterclaims, or in that only some of many claims will be successful such that the court takes the view that a technically successful claimant has, taking the case as a whole, been unsuccessful.[23] This will be reflected in the costs award.

3–047   Some other torts such as assault, false imprisonment, defamation and breach of confidence are actionable *per se*, and allow for an award of nominal damages to reflect the technical breach of tortious obligation. In such cases the court may regard the absence of damage as an indication that the claimant has in reality lost the claim and thus refrain from an award of costs. Similarly a claimant who inflated the value of the claim to avoid the small claims jurisdiction may find that costs are not awarded. Legally-aided claimants will be awarded costs in the same way as claimants responsible for their own costs[24] subject to Part 47 Section VI of the CPR 1998.

3–048   Of equal importance to the question when can costs be awarded, is the question as to what costs will be awarded. The incidence and amount of costs expended must be reasonable. Determination of the appropriateness of costs was formerly termed "taxation of costs" but the Woolf changes now require the process to be called "assessment of costs".[25] This assessment requires costs to be proportional to the financial value of the claim,[26] recognising that in a small claim the costs may represent a higher proportion of the claim than in a large claim. Issues such as wasted costs and delay will go to assessment of costs. Another matter which will be relevant to assessment of costs will be the financial standing of each party.[27]

3–049   The overall principle guiding the assessment of costs however is the compensation principle: the total damages award aims to put the aggrieved party back in the position she would have been but for the commission of the tort, including allowance for transaction costs expended to enforce the party's legal rights. Despite this principle, it is not the case that the successful party will always be able to recover all the transaction costs expended. Only those costs which went to reasonable and efficient management of the case will be recoverable.

3–050   In the majority of cases the parties will agree costs. Where the losing party challenges the claim for costs the court may order a summary assessment of costs, or if it thinks appropriate, order a detailed assessment of costs by a costs officer. Costs may be awarded on a standard basis[28] (those costs are awarded which are proportionate to the matter and reasonably incurred, decided in favour of the paying party) or an indemnity basis (where doubts arise as to the reasonableness of costs, the benefit of doubt is given to the successful party, and proportionality is less relevant). Indemnity costs are less common, and are awarded to reflect court disapproval of the losing party's management of the case.

---

[23] For example *Pearless de Rougemont v. Pilbrow, The Times*, March 25, 1999.
[24] s. 31(1) Legal Aid Act 1988.
[25] See for example Rule 47, C.P.R. 1998.
[26] Rule 44.5 C.P.R. 1998.
[27] Part 1 C.P.R. 1998. Art. 6(1) of the European Convention on Human Rights, incorporated into the Human Rights Act 1998, may be relevant here: in the determination of his civil rights everyone is entitled to a fair and public hearing. See also *Ait-Mouhoub v. France* E.C.H.R. [1998] H.R.C.D. 976.
[28] Rule 44.4 (2) C.P.R. 1998.

The procedure for detailed assessment of costs is provided in Parts 47   3–051
and 48 of the Civil Procedure Rules 1998.[29] These procedures do not differ
substantially from those formerly contained in the SCR and CCR, hence
commentary on these old rules is still relevant.[30] The difference in the new
rules is that they focus on automatic costs sanctions for poor case management, provide costs limits and provide rigorous enforcement measures for
breach of procedural rules.

(9) Limitation periods

It is not enough for a claimant to have a valid case for the payment of   3–052
damages; the claimant must institute that claim within specified time limits
or the opportunity to claim compensation will be lost. The purpose of the
limitation periods is to prevent potential claims from hanging over the
defendant indefinitely, inhibiting financial decision-making. In addition, old
claims are harder to prove; evidence is lost and witnesses can give less
accurate accounts, prolonging litigation and making judgments on the facts
more difficult.

The issue of limitation works in essence as a procedural defence. The
party wishing to rely on limitation must specifically plead the limitation
issue.[31] As limitation is an issue of procedure it prevents the claimant from
pursuing a remedy in the courts but does not negate the claimant's legal
right under the tort. So if the defendant had paid money to the claimant as
part compensation for the tort in ignorance of the time bar, then the
defendant cannot recover that money.

The relevant time limits are laid down by statute and contained in the   3–053
Limitation Act 1980. Section 2 of the Limitation Act is a starting point for
consideration of limitation periods, and states that an action founded on
tort shall not be brought after the expiration of six years from the date on
which the cause of action accrued. The matter is however more complicated
than this, and in respect of individual torts, there have been statutory,
common law and even procedural[32] variations on the six-year rule. Where
an action is brought in libel, slander or malicious falsehood, any action
must be commenced within one year of the publication of that libel, slander
or falsehood.[33] There is however discretion for an exemption on the one-
year period where the court considers it equitable to proceed with the
case.[34]

Where an action is brought for product liability under the Consumer   3–054
Protection Act 1987 the action must be brought within three years of the
date of the damage, or of the date of the claimant's knowledge of the

---

[29] Assessment of costs was governed by Ord. 62 R.S.C. before April 26, 1999.
[30] See for example Pritchard & Solomon, *Personal Injury Litigation* (9th ed., FT Law and
   Tax, 1997) and Brennan, Curran and Kelly, *Personal Injury Handbook* (Sweet & Maxwell,
   1997); see also Osborne, *Civil Litigation* (Blackstones, 1999).
[31] C.P.R. 1998 Part 16 Practice Direction para 16.1.
[32] For example R.S.C. Ord. 53, r. 4, retained in force by CPR Sched. 1, governing applications
   for judicial review.
[33] See s. 4A of the Limitation Act 1980 as amended by the Defamation Act 1996.
[34] See s. 32A of the Limitation Act 1980 as amended by the Defamation Act 1996.

damage, subject to the court's discretion in the case of personal injury or death to extend the three-year limitation.[35] However, in respect of actions brought under the Consumer Protection Act there is a long-stop of ten years from the date at which the defendant put the product into circulation;[36] after this point no action can be commenced.

3–055   Any action brought under the Civil Liability (Contribution) Act 1978 to recover contribution to any legal liability for damages must be brought within two years from the date the right to contribution accrued;[37] any action by a dependant under the Fatal Accidents Act 1976 for recovery of loss of dependency must be brought within three years of the death, or within three years of the knowledge of the death by the claimant of the deceased;[38] any action to recover land must be commenced within 12 years from which the date of action accrued;[39] an action brought under the Defective Premises Act 1972 must be instituted within six years from the date of completion of the house.[40]

3–056   One of the major concerns with the interpretation of the provisions of the Limitation Act is determination of what constitutes the accrual of the cause of action. Torts such as assault, battery, false imprisonment and possibly breach of confidence which are actionable *per se* are not so problematic—the cause of action accrues at the point at which the tort is committed and time begins to run from that point. Where however the definition of the tort includes recognition of damage, as with negligence or an action in nuisance or *Rylands v. Fletcher*, the damage may occur some considerable time after the act which caused it. Does time begin to run at the date of commission of the tortious act or at the date the damage results from the tortious act? And if the latter, how can we determine, in cases of non-traumatic, slow developing or hidden damage, at what point the damage has occurred?

3–057   The application of the Limitation Act provisions to latent damage depends on the nature of the damage caused. Where the damage is a personal injury[41] resulting from negligence, nuisance or breach of a duty,[42] the limitation period is governed by section 11 of the Limitation Act: time begins to run either from the date of the commission of the tort, or from the date of knowledge of the person injured, which ever is the later. The time limit for commencement of the action is three years. Section 14 of the Limitation Act then attempts to define what is meant by "date of knowledge" for the purposes of section 11. The time begins to run from that date on which the claimant first had knowledge that the injury was significant, that the injury was attributable to the appropriate tortious act of

---

[35] s. 33 Limitation Act 1980.
[36] See s. 11A of the Limitation Act 1980 as amended by the Consumer Protection Act 1987.
[37] s. 10 of the Limitation Act 1980.
[38] ss. 11 and 12 of the Limitation Act 1980.
[39] s. 15—see also the qualifications to his rule in that section.
[40] s. 1(5) Defective Premises Act 1972.
[41] Defined in s. 38(1) of the Limitation Act to include any disease and any impairment of a person's physical or mental condition.
[42] The term "breach of a duty" does not include intentional torts, which are subject to the six-year limitation applying to all torts actionable *per se*; see *Stubbings v. Webb* [1993] 1 All E.R. 322.

the defendant, and the identity of the defendant.[43] If the claimant were to have died in this three year period without instituting a claim then the deceased's representatives have a further three years from the claimant's death.

What constitutes knowledge that the injury is significant is defined, with some circularity, in section 14(2): the injury is significant if the claimant would reasonably have considered it sufficiently serious to justify instituting proceedings against a defendant who did not dispute liability. The test is in part objective; it is based not on the knowledge the claimant in fact had but on the knowledge she could be deemed to have had and which she could be reasonably expected to have acquired. The test is also part subjective in that the characteristics of the claimant will be relevant to determination of reasonableness[44] although some doubt has been cast on the appropriateness of a subjective test.[45]   3–058

Knowledge that the damage was attributable to the act of the defendant is also determined by a subjective approach. If the claimant was aware in her own mind that the injury resulted from the defendant's act then time begins to run.[46] It is not necessary for the claimant to be aware that the defendant's action amounted to actionable negligence.[47] It is sufficient for the claimant to be aware that her injury was the result of the defendant's act on common sense principles.[48]   3–059

Interpretation of the knowledge requirements has resulted in claimants becoming time-barred before they were aware they had a right of action in relation to the injury. If the clamaint's solicitors have the requisite knowledge, that knowledge is attributed to the claimant and time begins to run from that point, even where the solicitors fail to inform the claimant.[49] Where the claimant's solicitors negligently advise the claimant not to pursue the claim, this does not suspend time until the claimant finds that the claim was viable after all.[50] The victim who makes no attempt to inquire about the causes of injury may also find herself time-barred. This is not uncommon in the case of medical misadventure, where the patient suffers complications after medical treatment but is not alerted to the fact that these complications might result from inappropriate treatment.[51] Time runs even where the patient is told by the defendant doctor that the complications are to be expected.[52]   3–060

Time limitations for actions in relation to personal injury are subject to section 33 of the Limitation Act which give the court power to extend time where it thinks equitable to do so. This will only be the case where the   3–061

---

[43] This interpretation resulted from criticism of the law on limitation expressed in *Cartledge v. Jobling* [1963] A.C. 758.
[44] See for example *McCafferty v. Metropolitan Police District Receiver* [1977] 1 W.L.R. 1073, and *Nash v. Eli Lilly* [1993] 4 All E.R. 383 where the claimant's level of intelligence was taken into account.
[45] See *Forbes v. Wandsworth Area HA* [1996] 3 W.L.R. 1108.
[46] *Spargo v. North Essex District HA* [1997] P.I.Q.R. P235.
[47] *Brookes v. Coates* [1984] 1 All E.R. 702.
[48] *Hallam-Eames v. Merrett Syndicates Ltd* [1995] 7 Med. L.R. 122.
[49] *Hayward v. Sherrard* unreported July 28, 1998, C.A.
[50] *Whitfield v. North Durham HA* [1995] 6 Med. L.R. 32.
[51] *Broadley v. Guy Clapham* [1994] 4 All E.R. 439.
[52] *Dobbie v. Medway HA* [1994] 1 W.L.R. 1234.

court considers the claimant to have acted promptly as soon as she had the requisite information to found a claim,[53] and where the delay had not substantially prejudiced the defendant's case.[54]

3–062   Where the damage resulting from the tort is a property damage or pure economic loss then the issue of time is governed by Section 14B of the Limitation Act which incorporates the provisions of the Latent Damage Act 1986. Recoverability of latent property damage, particularly in the context of defective buildings, where the defect is in law categorised as the economic cost of repair rather than as damage to the property, has been very problematic and the passing of the Latent Damage Act did little to clarify the position. While the House of Lords decision in *Murphy v. Brentwood DC*[55] remains good law,[56] such loss, along with much other pure economic loss tortiously caused, is unlikely to be recoverable for substantive reasons, so the issue of limitation for such damage is of little importance.

3–063   Section 14B of the Limitation Act results in there being three limitation periods in such cases. The claimant has six years from the accrual of the cause of action to institute proceedings, the cause of action accruing at the point at which damage is suffered. So in circumstances where there is clear property or economic damage resulting from the negligent act, the limitation period is six years. Where the damage is such that it is unobservable, the claimant has three years from the "starting date" of the damage, that date being a point where the claimant was aware that the seriousness of the damage was sufficient to warrant proceedings, was aware that the damage resulted from the defendant's negligence, and was aware of the identity of the defendant. Section 14B then imposes a long-stop limit of 15 years on such actions, that 15 years running from the date of the negligent act. There is no power given to extend this time.

3–064   Where the claimant is a minor, the time periods laid down do not begin to run until their eighteenth birthday. However the knowledge requirements will be fairly strictly interpreted for claims brought after the claimant turns 18.[57] It would be a rare case where such a claimant could argue that she was unaware of the cause of her injury.

3–065   Where the claimant is under a disability, in other words a person suffering from a mental condition within the terms of the Mental Health Act 1983, the time only begins to run at the point where the claimant ceases to be under that disability. In the case of claimants seriously brain-damaged as a result of the defendant's negligence that time will never be reached.[58]

---

[53] *Hodgson v. Imperial Tobacco Ltd* unreported, February 9, 1999; *Davis v. Camden and Islington HA* unreported, March 5, 1999, C.A.
[54] *Dale v. Michelin Tyre PLC* unreported, March 3, 1999.
[55] [1990] 3 W.L.R. 414.
[56] However see the decision of the Privy Council in *Invercargill CC v. Hamlin* [1996] 2 W.L.R. 367, which is a possible chink in the armour of *Murphy*; see Martin, Diverging Common Law—Invercargill Goes to the Privy Council (1997) 60 M.L.R. 94.
[57] See for example *Kelly v. Bastible* [1997] 8 Med. L.R. 15.
[58] See for example *Headford v. Bristol HA* [1995] 6 Med. L.R. 1 where the writ was issued 28 years after the accident.

There has been much criticism of the law on limitations.[59] This area of   3–066
law was described by the Law Commission[60] as needlessly complex, out-
dated and sometimes unfair. Why should it matter, for the purposes of
limitation, whether the action by the claimant is framed in negligence or
trespass? Why should the "discoverability of damage" rule apply to some
torts and not to others? The Report gives a list of examples of how the
present limitation periods might create injustice.[61] Law Commission proposals are based on an attempt to introduce coherence into the law in this
area and are based on a core regime which applies to all causes of action.

The main components of this core regime are firstly a *prima facie* limita-   3–067
tion period of three years for all civil actions, the time running from the
date when the claimant knows, or ought reasonably to know, that she has
a cause of action. Then there is proposed a ten-year long-stop running from
the date of the tort giving rise to the action, although for personal injury
actions that long-stop would be 30 years. The existence of a disability
would extend the limitation period, but in the case of adult claimants the
long-stop would still apply. Deliberate concealment of information by the
defendant would serve to extend the long-stop.

The intention is that these limitations would be applied in all cases and   3–068
there will be no discretion to extend them. Evidential difficulties which
arise in long-delayed cases inhibit the process of administering justice, particularly in abuse cases which revolve around repressed memory. It is to be
hoped that legislation results from this consultation process which will
greatly simplify the limitations issue.

---

[59] See for example Jones, *Limitation Periods in Personal Injury Actions* (Blackstones, 1995);
  and Mullany, "Reform of the Law of Latent Damage" (1991) 54 M.L.R. 349.
[60] Law Commission Consultation Paper, Making the Law on Civil Limitation Periods Simpler
  and Fairer (January 1998).
[61] Introduction, p. 1.

CHAPTER 4

LIMITATIONS TO THE PRINCIPLE OF COMPENSATION

In this chapter there follows discussion of the limitations to the principle   4–001
of compensation. Fairness, justice and public policy dictate that there
should be occasions when the claimant should not be put in the position
he would have been had the tort not been committed. For example, the
concept of remoteness of damage acts as a control mechanism which may
limit the extent of the defendant's liability where the full degree of the
claimant's actual loss could not have been foreseen. The existence of such
a concept rests upon the recognition that it may not always be fair to hold
the defendant liable for the full extent of the claimant's loss, even though
this will inevitably result in a net loss to the claimant. Furthermore, a just
system of compensation should not tolerate a claimant who sits back and
watches losses mount which could easily be avoided by the taking of reasonable action. The doctrine of mitigation of damage therefore provides the
defendant with an opportunity to argue that his liability should be reduced
to the extent that some, or all of it, has been caused by the claimant's
unreasonable inaction.

Throughout this chapter it will be observed that this area of the law   4–002
generates many decisions which are difficult to reconcile with both a guiding principle, and other decisions. To an extent this is an inevitable hazard
when the court is attempting to achieve a result which is fair and just and
in accordance with public policy. Moreover, it must never be forgotten that
the assessment of damages is essentially a factual exercise heavily reliant
upon the precise facts and circumstances of each individual case.

1. CAUSATION AND REMOTENESS OF DAMAGE

(1) Causation as a matter of fact

Except for those torts which are actionable *per se* without proof of   4–003
damage,[1] the claimant must prove not only that they have suffered damage,
but also on a balance of probabilities that the damage was caused by the
tort. In the majority of cases factual causation will not be in issue. A claim
for damages arising out of the negligent driving of a motorvehicle may
involve investigation of whether the driver fell below the standard of care,

---

[1] Such as trespass to land, goods and the person, libel and some slanders.

but the fact that the damage was caused by that negligent driving will usually be obvious. At the other extreme are cases where the damage may have been caused by a number of different factors, the tortious behaviour of the defendant being merely one of them. In this type of situation causation will be a fiercely contested battleground at trial.

4–004   The starting point is the so-called "but for" test. This test asks whether the damage would have occurred "but for" the actions of the defendant. It is a useful tool for weeding out obvious cases. So for example in *McWilliams v. Sir William Arrol & Co Ltd*[2] a workman who was employed to erect a steel tower fell to his death. In an unsuccessful claim by his widow it was alleged that the defendants were in breach of a statutory and common law duty by failing to provide the deceased with a safety belt. The court inferred from the evidence that the deceased would not have worn a safety belt even if one were available. It could not therefore be said that "but for" the failure to provide the safety belt, the deceased would not have fallen to his death.

4–005   The "but for" test becomes more difficult to apply where several factors may have caused the damage. A literal application of the "but for" test in this type of situation would require proof at trial that the defendant's actions were the *sole* cause of the damage. Evidentially this would be a stringent requirement as the facts of *Bonnington Castings v. Wardlow*[3] illustrate. The claimant was exposed to particles of dust through his employment which led to the onset of pneumoconiosis. The dust escaped from two sources in the claimant's workplace, one of them being created by the defendants' breach of statutory duty. The claimant was unable to prove that had his employers complied with their statutory duty, he would not have developed pneumoconiosis. Practically speaking it could not therefore be argued that "but for" the breach of statutory duty, the claimant would not have developed pneumoconiosis. The claimant could prove, however, that the extra dust created by the breach of statutory duty had at the very least made a "material contribution" to the onset of the disease. This was held by the House of Lords to be sufficient to establish causation in the case. On the issue of material contribution, Lord Reid said:

> "It appears to me that the source of his disease was the dust from both sources, and the real question is whether the dust from the swing grinders materially contributed to the disease. What is a material contribution must be a question of degree. A contribution which comes within the exception *de minimis non curat lex* is not material, but I think that any contribution which does not fall within that exception must be material. I do not see how there can be something too large to come within the *de minimis* principle but yet too small to be material."[4]

---

[2] [1962] 1 W.L.R. 295. See also to similar effect *Barnett v. Chelsea and Kensington Hospital Management Committee* [1969] 1 Q.B. 428.
[3] [1956] A.C. 613.
[4] *ibid.* at 621.

The House of Lords took matters a step further in *McGhee v. National* **4-006**
Coal Board[5] where it was held that causation was established where the
claimant could prove that the tort *materially increased the risk* of an injury
occurring. In this case a workman contracted dermatitis through skin exposure to brick dust whilst emptying brick kilns. It was argued that the
employers should have provided shower facilities to allow workers to wash
off the brick dust after finishing work. The issue for consideration was
whether the additional skin exposure to brick dust during the period
between finishing work and later washing off the brickdust at home, was
causative of the dermatitis. Expert evidence was to the effect that little was
known about the precise cause of dermatitis, and it was impossible to prove
that failure to provide shower facilities had caused the dermatitis. It was
agreed by the experts, however, that the additional exposure to the brick
dust had at the very least materially increased the chance or risk that dermatitis might set in. The House of Lords held that this was sufficient to
establish causation. The passages suggest that their Lordships could see no
distinction in practical terms between materially contributing to the
damage and materially increasing the risk that the damage may occur. Two
of their Lordships, Lord Reid and Lord Salmon, said so explicitly:

> "In the circumstances of the case, the possibility of a distinction
> existing between (a) having materially increased the risk of contracting
> the disease, and (b) having materially contributed to causing the dis-
> ease may no doubt be a fruitful source of interesting academic discus-
> sions between students of philosophy. Such a distinction is, however,
> far too unreal to be recognised by the common law."[6]

Despite these express assertions, it is clear in the light of the subsequent **4-007**
House of Lords' decision in *Wilsher v. Essex Area Health Authority*[7] that
McGhee did not lay down a principle that causation could be established
in all cases by merely demonstrating a material increase in risk.[8] Lord
Bridge in *Wilsher* described the reasoning of *McGhee* as follows:

> "Adopting a robust and pragmatic approach to the undisputed prim-
> ary facts of the case, the majority concluded that it was a legitimate
> inference of fact that the defender's negligence had materially contrib-
> uted to the pursuer's injury."[9]

This must be correct. In *McGhee* once it had been shown that exposure **4-008**
to brick dust was the probable cause of the dermatitis and that failure to
provide washing facilities materially increased the risk of dermatitis devel-

---

[5] [1973] 1 W.L.R. 1.
[6] Per Lord Salmon *ibid.* at 12H.
[7] [1988] 1 A.C. 1074.
[8] In *Page v. Smith (No. 2)* [1996] 1 W.L.R. 855, Sir Thomas Bingham M.R. at 858B
described *McGhee* as a "difficult decision" and said that there was force in the criticism
that the trial judge in *Page v. Smith* had been wrong when he referred to a material increase
in the risk rather than a material contribution to the damage.
[9] [1988] 1 A.C. 1074 at 1090D.

oping, it was legitimate to infer from the evidence that the breach of duty materially contributed to the development of dermatitis, and was thus legally causative of it.

4–009   The facts of *Wilsher* exposed the fallacy of any rule that causation could be established in all cases by merely demonstrating a material increase in risk. The claimant was born nearly three months prematurely. Due to an error by a junior doctor he was administered with excessive levels of oxygen. The claimant later developed a condition known as retrolental fibroplasia ("RLF") which resulted in near blindness. The condition could have been caused by the administration of excess oxygen, or could have been caused by four other medical conditions which afflicted the claimant. The House of Lords held that unless it could be proved on a balance of probabilities by the claimant that the administration of excess oxygen at least materially contributed to RLF, the defendants would not be liable.

4–010   *Wilsher* affirms that the burden of proof remains firmly upon the claimant to prove the causal link between breach and damage, but the decisions in *Bonnington Castings* and *McGhee* highlight the significance of drawing appropriate inferences from the available evidence in an area where concrete proof of causation may be an impossible task.[10] The importance of evidence of causation has been illustrated recently in the developing frontier of claims against local authorities. In *Phelps v. Hillingdon London Borough Council*[11] the claimant brought an action against the defendants for the alleged failure of an educational psychologist to diagnose, and take steps to alleviate, dyslexia. Allowing an appeal, the Court of Appeal held that the claimant had failed to establish that there was any deficit in her literacy which was actually attributable to the failure to diagnose. Further, in *Barrett v. Enfield London Borough Council*[12] the House of Lords commented upon the difficulties of proof facing a claimant who was attempting to sue for psychological injuries arising from alleged breaches of duty after being taken into care at the age of 10 months. However, as causation was a matter of fact, it was not felt to be appropriate to strike out the claim on this ground.

(a) Loss of a chance

4–011   A difficult issue within causation is whether it is possible to claim damages which represent loss of a chance. The authority governing this area is *Hotson v. East Berkshire Area Health Authority*.[13] The claimant fell from a tree sustaining an injury to his hip. The hospital which treated him failed to detect that the claimant had suffered a fracture to his hip joint and

---

[10] See for example *Kay v. Ayrshire and Arran Health Board* [1987] 2 All E.R. 417, where it was argued that an overdose of penicillin administered to a meningitis victim had led to the onset of deafness. Medically it was known that meningitis could cause deafness, but according to the accepted expert evidence an overdose of penicillin had never caused deafness. Failure to establish any link between the penicillin overdose and the deafness meant that the deafness had to be attributed solely to the meningitis.

[11] [1999] 1 W.L.R. 500.

[12] [1999] 3 W.L.R. 79.

[13] [1987] 1 A.C. 750.

discharged him. Five days later the claimant was taken back to the hospital and the injury to the hip joint was detected. The claimant went on to develop avascular necrosis, a condition of the hip joint which restricted mobility, caused general disability and which would lead to the development of osteo-arthritis. The trial judge made a finding that there was a 75 per cent chance that the claimant would have developed avascular necrosis even had the hip fracture been diagnosed on the first occasion. The trial judge nevertheless awarded the claimant damages for the loss of the 25 per cent chance that avascular necrosis would not have developed had the fracture been diagnosed, a decision confirmed by the Court of Appeal. The House of Lords allowed the Health Authority's appeal on the grounds that the judges below had confused the issues of causation of damage and quantification of damage. The real issue was causation of damage. Once the trial judge had made a finding that there was a 75 per chance that the claimant would have developed avascular necrosis as a result of the fall, in law[14] that made the onset of avascular necrosis a certain consequence of the fall; as soon as the claimant had fallen he had lost all chances of avoiding the onset of avascular necrosis. The breach of duty did not therefore lead to any loss of a chance which could be quantified.

That was enough to dispose of the appeal, but both Lord Bridge and Lord Mackay expressly left open the question of whether damages could ever be claimed for loss of a chance in a personal injury or medical negligence action. The Court of Appeal,[15] in contrast, had embraced such a principle with open arms. There Dillon L.J. had remarked: **4–012**

"I can see no reason why the loss of a chance which is capable of being valued should not be capable of being damage in a tort case."[16]

Similarly Sir John Donaldson M.R., in response to counsel for the defendants' submission that loss of a chance would not sound in damages, remarked:

"It has been said times without number that the categories of negligence are never closed and, subject to the rules relating to remoteness of damage which are not material in the instant case, I can see no reason why the categories of loss should be closed either."[17]

In quantifying the loss of the chance, the trial judge had awarded the claimant one quarter of the damages he would have been awarded had his claim been successful. The Court of Appeal described this approach, which had not been challenged on appeal, as one which did not necessarily follow, but which was nevertheless "convenient."[18]

---

[14] Lord Diplock's statement in *Mallett v. McMonagle* [1970] A.C. 166 at 176, was cited in support of this proposition: "In determining what did happen in the past a court decides on the balance of probabilities. Anything that is more probable than not it treats as certain."
[15] [1987] 1 A.C. 750.
[16] *ibid*. at 764D.
[17] *ibid*. at 761F.
[18] *ibid*. at 761H per Sir John Donaldson M.R.

4–013   In the House of Lords Lord Mackay said that much of the judgment of the Court of Appeal would remain for consideration in the future.[19] It is therefore conceivable that one day a claim for loss of a chance could be endorsed by the House of Lords. A hypothetical example could be a claim by someone who suffered from a degenerative spinal condition which would eventually lead to paralysis of the lower body. If they were to undergo a speculative operation which would lead to a 25 per cent chance that the condition could be reversed, but the operation was negligently performed destroying the chance, a claim could be mounted for loss of that chance.

(b) Losses requiring proof of hypothetical past events

4–014   Claims for loss of a chance in the sense discussed above should not be confused with claims for damages which are dependent upon demonstrating that a third party would have acted to confer a benefit or obviate a disbenefit. Such claims necessitate an analysis of the chances that a third party would have acted in a particular way, and the correct approach to this issue is that set out in the judgment of Stuart-Smith L.J. in *Allied Maples Group Ltd v. Simmons & Simmons*.[20] The defendants were acting as the claimants' advisers in relation to the takeover of the third party. The defendants failed to advise the claimants that the takeover agreement provided insufficient protection against liabilities which the third party later incurred. In an action against the defendants to recover for losses incurred in meeting those liabilities, the defendants argued that the claimants would only succeed if on a balance of probability it was shown that the claimants would have successfully negotiated greater protection from the third party had they been properly advised. Stuart-Smith L.J. held that there was a three-stage approach to the issue. First, proving on a balance of probability that but for the defendants' breach the claimants would have sought to negotiate for greater protection from the third party. Secondly, proving that there was a substantial chance rather than a speculative one that the third party would have agreed to greater protection. Finally, evaluating the chance that the third party would have agreed to greater protection. The Court of Appeal held that the first two issues had been established by the claimants. The third issue did not need to be decided as the trial had been one on liability only.

4–015   *Allied Maples* confirms that where proof of the claimant's loss is dependent upon the hypothetical action of a third party, the claimant will succeed provided he shows there was a substantial chance rather than a speculative chance that the third party would have acted in the manner desired. Once a substantial chance is proved, evaluation of that substantial chance is an issue for quantification of damage. On the question of what is a substantial chance, Stuart-Smith L.J. said that it may be less than 50 per cent but did not think that it would be helpful to lay down in percentage terms when

---

[19] [1987] 1 A.C. 750.
[20] [1995] 1 W.L.R. 1602.

a chance would just qualify as substantial on the one hand, and reach near-certainty on the other.[21]

Despite the emphasis in cases such as *Hotson* and *Wilsher* upon the need for the claimant to prove causation on a balance of probability, *Allied Maples* demonstrates that some aspects of causation can in fact be proved to a lower standard. *Allied Maples* was applied by the Court of Appeal in *Stovold v. Barlows*.[22] Here the claimant lost the sale of his house after the defendant solicitors mistakenly sent the title deeds and draft contract of sale to a tailors' shop rather than to the purchaser's solicitors. The trial judge approached the case on the basis that the claimant had to satisfy the court on a balance of probability that the sale would have gone ahead had the documents arrived on time. If he could demonstrate this he would recover his full loss; if he could not discharge this burden he would get nothing. The Court of Appeal held that this was the wrong approach to the question of causation where the loss depended upon the actions of a third party; the correct approach was to evaluate the loss of the chance that the sale would have gone ahead. It was held that there was a substantial chance that the purchaser would have gone ahead with the sale, quantified as 50 per cent.   4–016

Significantly, the principle in *Allied Maples* has now been extended beyond cases dealing purely with the hypothetical actions of third parties. In *Doyle v. Wallace*[23] the claimant argued that she would have qualified and obtained employment as a teacher four years before trial had it not been for the serious injury which she suffered. The Court of Appeal upheld the correctness of evaluating this past loss by reference to the loss of a chance, assessed by the trial judge as 50/50.   4–017

The approach enunciated in *Allied Maples* and *Doyle v. Wallace* appears to share support in the House of Lords. In *Spring v. Guardian Assurance plc*[24] an employer provided a negligent reference in respect of an ex-employee which it was alleged led to a rejection of employment. The view was expressed *obiter* by Lord Lowry that the claimant would only have to show that he had lost a reasonable chance of employment which would have to be evaluated; he would not have to prove that, but for the negligence, he would have been employed.[25]   4–018

The discussion thus far has concentrated upon causation of past loss. The position as regards causation of future loss equally involves the assessment of chances, and an approach based upon the balance of probabilities is inappropriate. In *Davies v. Taylor*[26] Lord Reid said: 4–019

"You can prove that a past event happened, but you cannot prove that a future event will happen and I do not think that the law is so foolish as to suppose that you can. All that you can do is to evaluate the chance."[27]

---

[21] [1995] 1 W.L.R. 1602 at 1612A and 1614D.
[22] *The Times*, October 30, 1995.
[23] [1998] P.I.Q.R. Q146.
[24] [1995] 2 A.C. 296.
[25] *ibid.* at 327.
[26] [1974] Q.B. 207.
[27] *ibid.* at 213B.

The assessment of future losses normally arises in the context of personal injury and Fatal Accident Act claims. Discussion of assessment of these future losses is therefore deferred until Chapters 9 and 10 respectively.

(c) Consecutive damage

4–020   This section deals with the situation where the claimant has been the victim of consecutive damage, for example where the defendant causes damage to the claimant, but before trial the claimant suffers further damage, either at the hands of a third party or through the occurrence of some natural event such as illness. Here the court has to decide whether the defendant should remain liable for the specific damage which they have caused, or whether the infliction of subsequent damage should lessen or even negate the defendant's liability entirely. The correct approach in this type of situation is not entirely clear. In *Baker v. Willoughby*[28] the claimant suffered an injury to his left leg due to the defendant's negligent driving. Shortly before the case was due to be tried the claimant was shot in the same leg during an armed robbery, the leg then having to be amputated. The House of Lords held that the damages payable by the defendant for the original leg injury should not be reduced to take account of the amputation. Lord Reid, who gave the leading judgment, said that the claimant was not being compensated for the leg injury, but for the loss he would suffer as a result of that injury, namely the inability to lead a full life, the inability to enjoy those amenities which depend upon freedom of movement, and the inability to earn as much as he could have earned if there had been no accident. The amputation did not diminish any of these. If the second injury either reduced the original disability or shortened the period over which that disability would be suffered, however, then the damages should be reduced.

4–021   A different approach was adopted in the later House of Lords' decision of *Jobling v. Associated Dairies Ltd.*[29] The claimant suffered a back injury in the course of his employment and claimed for future loss of earnings. Before trial the claimant was found to be suffering from myelopathy, a natural back disorder unconnected with the injury, which would in any event have proved totally disabling about three years after the accident. The House of Lords held that the decision in *Baker v. Willoughby* should be restricted to situations where the infliction of subsequent damage was due to a tortious act. In other cases, the court should normally take into account the vicissitudes of life when assessing damages, and the onset of natural conditions such as myelopathy was one of them. If the object of an award of damages was to put the claimant into the position they would have been in had the tort not been committed, the court must take account of factors that would have occurred in any event, such as an illness which has manifested itself by trial.

4–022   *Baker v. Willoughby* was arguably a decision motivated by policy and a

---

[28] [1970] 2 W.L.R. 50.
[29] [1982] A.C. 794.

desire to see that the claimant was not left without compensation through the misfortune of being the victim of an unidentified, and presumably impecunious, assailant. But as was pointed out by Lord Edmund-Davies in *Jobling*, in *Baker* there was no consideration of the possibility of the claimant being compensated through the Criminal Injuries Compensation Scheme. The existence of alternative avenues of compensation such as this makes it more palatable to view being the victim of a tort as much a vicissitude of life, as being the victim of a disabilitating illness. The continued authority of *Baker* must therefore be open to question.

Both of the above cases dealt with damages for personal injuries. The   4–023
position as regards damage to property broadly reflects the stance adopted in *Jobling v. Associated Dairies Ltd* of aiming to compensate the claimant for the loss actually suffered. To illustrate, in *Carslogie Steamship Company Ltd v. Royal Norwegian Government*[30] the claimants' ship was damaged in a collision with another vessel, but before permanent repairs could be effected the ship suffered heavy weather damage rendering her unseaworthy. Repairs to the collision and weather damage were carried out concurrently, occupying 30 days in dry dock. The collision damage repairs took 10 days to complete, but even without this damage it would still have taken 30 days to repair the weather damage. The claimants claimed loss of chartered hire for the 10 days necessary to effect the collision damage repairs. The House of Lords held that the claimants had suffered no loss because the ship would still have been off hire for those 10 days due to the weather damage repairs.

All of the cases discussed so far have related to situations where the   4–024
defendant inflicted the initial damage. An illustration of the court's approach where the defendant inflicts subsequent damage is to be found in *Performance Cars Ltd v. Abraham*,[31] where the defendant's car negligently collided with the claimant's car causing damage to a front wing. To repair the damage the whole lower part of the vehicle would require respraying. The defendant argued that he was not liable to pay for the respray as prior to the collision the car had been involved in another accident which would require the same part of the car to be resprayed. The Court of Appeal held that the defendant was not liable to pay damages in respect of the second collision. The need for a respray existed at the time of the second collision, therefore the second collision had imposed no additional burden on the claimant. Had the second collision caused damage requiring repairs more extensive than was previously necessary, the situation would have been different and the defendant would have been liable for the additional damage.

(2) Remoteness of damage

Even though it may be possible for the claimant to establish to the requis-   4–025
ite standard that there is a factual link between the tort and the damage,

---

[30] [1952] A.C. 292. See *infra* Ch. 6 in relation to damages for loss of profit-earning goods.
[31] [1962] 1 Q.B. 33.

damages will not be awarded for consequences which are regarded in law as too remote. The exception relates to intended consequences which are never regarded as too remote.[32] Remoteness is the judicial control mechanism which regulates the extent of the defendant's liability. It is a mechanism which is susceptible to manipulation to achieve what is perceived as being justice in the case.[33]

4-026   The touchstone of the test of remoteness is the decision of the Privy Council in *Overseas Tankship (UK) Ltd v. Morts and Dock Engineering Co. Ltd (The Wagon Mound)*,[34] which confirmed that damage will not be too remote if it is of such a kind as the reasonable man should have foreseen. The Privy Council expressed its disapproval of the earlier decision of the Court of Appeal in *Re Polemis Furniss Withy and Co.*,[35] which held that a defendant bore liability for all the direct consequences of his negligence, whether those consequences were reasonably foreseeable or not. Whilst not specifically overruling *Polemis*, the Privy Council nevertheless said that it "should no longer be regarded as good law".[36]

4-027   In *The Wagon Mound* the appellants were the charterers of the *Wagon Mound* and whilst taking on fuel at Caltex Oil Company's wharf the appellants' servants carelessly caused an oil spillage which was carried towards the respondents' wharf. Another vessel, the *Corrimel*, was moored alongside the respondents' wharf undergoing refitting, for which purpose welding work was being carried out at the time. The respondents' works manager became aware of the oil spillage in the vicinity and ordered welding to cease until he had made inquiries of the manager of Caltex Oil Company whether it was safe to continue. The results of the inquiry, coupled with his own belief as to the inflammability of furnace oil in the open, led him to think that it was safe to continue welding. Next day molten metal from the welding operations fell onto a piece of rag or cotton which lay upon floating debris under the wharf, setting it alight and in turn igniting the oil spillage, causing severe damage to the respondents' wharf. It was held that the appellants were not liable in negligence for the fire damage, as it had been found by the trial judge that the appellants could not reasonably have foreseen that the oil would catch fire.

(a) Remoteness of damage in torts other than negligence

4-028   *The Wagon Mound* test of foreseeability has been confirmed as the correct approach in torts other than negligence, such as nuisance[37] and

---

[32] See for example *Scott v. Shepherd* (1773) 2 Wm. Bl. 892.

[33] See *infra* the discussion in relation to *Tremain v. Pike* [1969] 1 W.L.R. 1556 and *Hepworth v. Kerr* [1995] 6 Med. L.R. 139. An alternative control mechanism in negligence claims is the concept of duty of care. In *Banque Bruxelles Lambert v. Eagle Star Insurance Co.* [1997] A.C. 191, Lord Hoffman emphasized the importance of determining what kind of loss the defendant was subject to a duty of care to prevent.

[34] [1961] A.C. 388.

[35] [1921] 3 K.B. 560.

[36] Per Viscount Simonds [1961] A.C. 388 at 422.

[37] Both public and private: *Overseas Tankship (UK) v. Miller SS Co. (The Wagon Mound (No. 2))* [1967] 1 A.C. 617 and see also *Cambridge Water v. Eastern Counties Leather* [1994] 2 A.C. 264.

Rylands v. Fletcher type liability.[38] However, in relation to claims in deceit it was held in *Doyle v. Olby (Ironmongers) Ltd*[39] that damages directly flowing from the deceit were recoverable and that "it does not lie in the mouth of the fraudulent person to say that they could not reasonably have been foreseen."[40] Furthermore, in *Smith New Court Securities Ltd v. Citibank NA*[41] Lord Steyn said that "The exclusion of heads of loss in the law of negligence, which reflects considerations of legal policy, does not necessarily avail the intentional wrongdoer."[42] This suggests that *The Wagon Mound* test is the correct approach for unintentional torts, but that in relation to intentional torts the defendant is liable for all the direct consequences flowing from the tort.[43]

In relation to those torts where remoteness of damage is governed by the principles established in *The Wagon Mound*, there are a number of further issues which require consideration concerning the circumstances in which damage will be regarded as reasonably foreseeable.   4–029

(b) Foreseeability of the likelihood that the kind of damage would be caused

Whilst *The Wagon Mound* confirmed that the test of remoteness for most torts was foreseeability of damage, what was not made clear was what degree of likelihood of the damage occurring had to be foreseen. The position was clarified by the Privy Council in *The Wagon Mound (No. 2)*,[44] where Lord Reid spoke in terms of whether a reasonable man would foresee a "real risk" of the damage occurring. There would be a real risk if it was one that would occur to the mind of a reasonable man in the position of the defendant, and which would not be brushed aside as far-fetched.[45] In *Koufos v. C. Czarnikow Ltd*[46] Lord Reid reiterated this view: 4–030

"The defendant will be liable for any type of damage which is reasonably foreseeable as liable to happen even in the most unusual case, unless the risk is so small that a reasonable man would in the whole circumstances feel justified in neglecting it."[47]

In *The Wagon Mound (No. 2)*[48] the respondents were the owners of two vessels damaged in the fire created by the spillage of oil from the *Wagon*   4–031

---

[38] *Cambridge Water v. Eastern Counties Leather* [1994] 2 A.C. 264.
[39] [1969] 2 Q.B. 158, approved by the House of Lords in *Smith New Court Securities Ltd v. Citibank NA* [1997] A.C. 254. See *infra* Ch. 7 in relation to damages for untrue statements.
[40] Per Lord Denning M.R. [1969] 2 Q.B. 158 at 167D.
[41] [1997] A.C. 254.
[42] *ibid.* at 279G.
[43] In relation to torts of strict liability, the question would be whether the damage was a reasonably foreseeable consequence of the breach, even if the breach itself could not have been foreseen. See *Galashiels Car Co. Ltd v. Millar* [1949] A.C. 275.
[44] [1967] 1 A.C. 617.
[45] *ibid.* at 643G.
[46] [1969] 1 A.C. 350.
[47] *ibid.* at 385G.
[48] [1967] 1 A.C. 617.

Mound, and proceedings were commenced against the appellants in negligence and nuisance. The Privy Council held that the evidence demonstrated that a reasonable man possessing the knowledge and experience to be expected of the appellants' chief engineer would have known that there was a real risk of the oil catching fire, and the fact that the risk would only materialise in very exceptional circumstances was irrelevant.

(c) Kind of damage

4–032   The requirement that the kind of damage which occurred should have been reasonably foreseeable places an important restriction upon liability. In *The Wagon Mound* there was a clear distinction drawn between damage by fire and damage by fouling, only the latter arguably being foreseeable. Sometimes the damage that should have been foreseen is defined in very narrow terms by the courts. In *Tremain v. Pike*[49] the claimant contracted Weil's disease, a rare disease caused through contact with rat's urine, in the course of his employment as a herdsman on the defendant's farm. It was held that it was unforeseeable that the claimant could contract Weil's disease. Payne J. refused to classify the kind of damage that should have been foreseen as risk of disease generally through exposure to rats in the course of employment. Disease contracted through contact with rat's urine was entirely different in kind from the effect of a rat bite, or food poisoning through the consumption of food or drink contaminated by rats. The decision how narrowly to define the kind of damage that should have been foreseen seems to have more to do with policy and justice than anything else. A suitable case to contrast with *Tremain v. Pike* is *Hepworth v. Kerr*[50] where the claimant suffered a spinal stroke after the defendant employed an unorthodox anaesthetic procedure upon him during surgery. It was known that the procedure could cause complications in the brain and major organs, but there was no specific reported risk of danger to the spine or central nervous system. McKinnon J. nevertheless held that what happened was "but a variant of the foreseeable" and "within the risk created by the negligence."[51]

4–033   In the sphere of psychiatric injuries caused by nervous shock, it is not necessary where the claimant is a primary victim that psychiatric injury should be foreseeable. It is sufficient that the defendant should foresee that his conduct will expose the claimant to a risk of personal injury, even if the claimant does not subsequently suffer any physical injury.[52] "Personal injury" for these purposes was described by Lord Lloyd in *Page v. Smith* as "any disease and any impairment of a person's physical or mental condi-

---

[49] [1969] 1 W.L.R. 1556.
[50] [1995] 6 Med. L.R. 139.
[51] *ibid.* at 171. See also *Bradford v. Robinson Rentals* [1967] 1 W.L.R. 337: claimant developed frostbite in the course of employment, a rare condition in England. Held: sufficient that it was foreseeable that the claimant would suffer injury through prolonged exposure to extreme cold.
[52] *Page v. Smith* [1996] 1 A.C. 155.

tion."[53] Where the claimant is a secondary victim of nervous shock, however, it remains a requirement that psychiatric injury in a person of normal
fortitude should be foreseeable.[54]

(d) Foreseeability of the extent of the loss

(i) Foreseeability of the extent of the kind of damage

As long as some damage of the kind suffered was foreseeable, there will   4–034
be liability for the full amount even if the damage is greater in extent than
should have been foreseen. This point is illustrated by *Hughes v. Lord
Advocate*,[55] discussed in more detail below, where some degree of burns
injury was foreseeable, but the full extent was not. An illustration in the
sphere of damage to property is *Vacwell Engineering Co. Ltd v. BDH
Chemicals Ltd*[56] where the claimants' laboratory was severely damaged by
a chemical explosion after a chemical supplied by the defendants reacted
with water. It was held that it was foreseeable that the chemical may come
into contact with water and cause a violent reaction or possible explosion,
which may result in some damage to property. That being the case, it was
irrelevant that the magnitude of the explosion and the extent of the damage
could not have been foreseen.

(ii) Foreseeability of the extent of the value of the damaged item

Consistent with the approach described above, provided that damage to   4–035
an item was foreseeable, the defendant will incur full liability if the item in
fact transpires to be more valuable than could have been foreseen. This
point is covered by the famous dictum of Scrutton L.J. in *The Arpad*:[57]

> "In the cases of claims in tort, damages are constantly given for con-
> sequences of which the defendant had no notice. You negligently run
> down a shabby-looking man in the street, and he turns out to be a
> millionaire engaged in a very profitable business which the accident
> disables him from carrying on; or you negligently and ignorantly injure
> the favourite for the Derby whereby he cannot run. You have to pay
> damages resulting from the circumstances of which you have no notice.
> You have to pay the actual loss to the man or his goods at the time of
> the tort, which is fixed by the circumstances at the time of the
> demand."[58]

---

[53] *ibid.* at 190C, approving the definition of "personal injury" found in s. 38(1) of the Limitation Act 1980.
[54] *Page v. Smith* [1996] 1 A.C. 155.
[55] [1963] A.C. 837.
[56] [1971] 1 Q.B. 88.
[57] [1934] P 189.
[58] *ibid.* at 203.

(iii) Foreseeability of the extent of consequential losses

4–036   It is foreseeable that if damage is caused to a profit-earning chattel, there will be consequential loss associated with the use for which the chattel was intended. What is unclear is whether as long as *some* consequential loss was foreseeable, the full extent of the actual loss can be recovered, including exceptional losses associated with lucrative projects or contracts.[59] In the light of the above discussion, there would seem no reason in principle why the full extent of the loss should not be recovered, as long as some loss of that kind was foreseeable. However, in this area policy may come to the fore, and it is submitted that it would be open to argue that an exceptional loss may be regarded as a loss of a *different kind*, which was unforeseeable. This approach is reflected in the dictum of Butler-Sloss L.J. in *Saleslease Ltd v. Davis*,[60] a decision concerning consequential loss in conversion:

> "In my view a consequential loss which is special to the circumstances of the particular claimant and which is not known to the tortfeasor may be regarded as too remote."[61]

(e) The manner in which the damage was inflicted

4–037   Provided that the factual causation is established, liability will still ensue if the kind of damage caused by the defendant's act was foreseeable, even if the precise chain of events which caused it was unforeseeable. This is vividly illustrated by *Hughes v. Lord Advocate*.[62] A boy was severely burned when he knocked a paraffin lamp into an unguarded manhole which exploded and caused the boy to fall into the manhole. It was argued by the respondents that it was unforeseeable that the boy could have been burned in this way. The House of Lords held that it was sufficient that it was foreseeable that the boy may suffer burns from playing with the unattended paraffin lamp, for example if he knocked it over and burnt himself. The fact that the burns were inflicted in a manner which could not have been foreseen and were greater in extent than could have been foreseen was irrelevant.

4–038   *Hughes v. Lord Advocate* was considered by the Court of Appeal in *Doughty v. Turner Manufacturing Co. Ltd*,[63] where the asbestos cover of a cauldron of hot liquid was inadvertently knocked into the cauldron resulting in an eruption of liquid, injuring the claimant. The Court of

---

[59] Dictum often cited for and against this proposition is that of Lord Wright in *Owners of Dredger Liesbosch v. Owners of Steamship Edison* [1933] App. Cas. 449 at 463, a case involving loss of a ship: "The true rule seems to be that the measure of damages in such cases is the value of the ship to her owner as a going concern at the time and place of the loss. In assessing that value regard must naturally be had to her pending engagements, either profitable or the reverse"; and Lord Herschell in *The Argentino* (1889) 14 A.C. 519 at 523, a case involving damage to a ship: "the loss of the fair and ordinary earnings of such a vessel on such an adventure appear to me to be the direct and natural consequence of the collision." Both dicta precede *The Wagon Mound* and are therefore open to question.

[60] [1999] 1 W.L.R. 1664.

[61] *ibid.* at 1677H.

[62] [1963] A.C. 837.

[63] [1964] 1 Q.B. 518.

Appeal held that the defendants could not have known that the chemical reaction of asbestos with the liquid would cause an eruption, so there was no negligence. It was argued for the claimant, however, that knocking the cover into the cauldron was negligent and gave rise to a foreseeable risk that the claimant would be injured by a splash as it fell. If injury by splash was foreseeable in such circumstances, then applying *Hughes v. Lord Advocate*, injury by eruption was also foreseeable. The Court of Appeal disagreed, holding that it would be quite unrealistic to describe the accident as a variant of the perils from splashing. The decision illustrates how in answering the question "what damage was foreseeable", the court must take account of the nature of the duty to take care. In *Hughes* the duty was to protect persons such as children from hazards associated with leaving paraffin lamps unattended. It was foreseeable that the lamp could ignite causing burns, and an explosion was merely a variant of this. In *Doughty* the duty was to protect employees against the hazards associated with inadvertently knocking the asbestos lid into the cauldron, namely displacement of water as the lid hit the water. Displacement of water caused by the mixing of asbestos with the liquid was not a variant of this. It was a completely different kind of damage altogether.

(f) The "eggshell skull" rule

Allied to the principle that the precise extent of the resulting damage does not have to be foreseen is the principle that extensive damage suffered as a result of the claimant's bodily sensitivity does not have to be foreseen. This is known as the "eggshell skull" rule and rests upon the principle that the defendant must take the claimant as he finds him. To illustrate, in *Robinson v. Post Office*[64] the claimant slipped and lacerated his shin whilst descending a ladder in the course of his employment. The wound was treated by a doctor who administered an anti-tetanus injection, an allergic reaction to which caused the onset of encephalitis. It was held that it was foreseeable that the defendants' breach may cause a slippage and resultant injury which may require an anti-tetanus injection. The fact that the onset of encephalitis could not have been foreseen was held to be irrelevant. The defendants had to take the claimant as they found him, namely a person with an allergy to anti-tetanus serum. This principle allows the claimant to recover for kinds of damage which are not strictly foreseeable. As long as the damage which triggers the additional consequences is foreseeable, however, this is of no consequence.[65]

4–039

The principle applies with equal rigour to claims for psychiatric harm. In *Page v. Smith*[66] Lord Lloyd said "There is no difference in principle . . . between an eggshell skull and an eggshell personality."[67] In this case the claimant was involved in a car accident, sustaining no physical injuries. He

4–040

---

[64] [1974] 1 W.L.R. 1176.
[65] A similar illustration is to be found in *Smith v. Leech Brain & Co. Ltd* [1962] 2 Q.B. 405: burn on pre-malignant lip in course of employment causing cancer and death.
[66] [1996] 1 A.C. 155.
[67] *ibid.* at 189F. See also *Brice v. Brown* [1984] 1 All E.R. 997.

had throughout life suffered spasmodic bouts of chronic fatigue syndrome of varying degrees of severity, but it was held that the accident had caused the development of permanent chronic fatigue syndrome which made it unlikely that he would undertake permanent employment again. Damages of £162,153 were awarded.

(g) Loss due to claimant's own lack of resources

4-041   According to the decision of the House of Lords in *Owners of Dredger Liesbosch v. Owners of Steamship Edison*,[68] a defendant is not liable for any damage caused by the claimant's own lack of resources, rather than the defendant's tort. Here the appellants' dredger the *Liesbosch* was employed on a harbour construction project, and sank as a result of the negligent navigation of the respondents' vessel the *Edison*. Owing to their own lack of resources the appellants were unable to purchase a replacement dredger and instead were forced to hire one at a high rate of hire. Lord Wright, with whom the other Law Lords agreed, held that the hire expenses could not be recovered from the respondents:

> "The respondents' tortious act involved the physical loss of the dredger; that loss must somehow be reduced to terms of money. But the appellants' actual loss in so far as it was due to their impecuniosity arose from that impecuniosity as a separate and concurrent cause, extraneous to and distinct in character from the tort; the impecuniosity was not traceable to the respondents' acts, and in my opinion was outside the legal purview of the consequences of these acts ... In the present case if the appellants' financial embarrassment is to be regarded as a consequence of the respondents' tort, I think it is too remote, but I prefer to regard it as an independent cause, though its operative effect was conditioned by the loss of the dredger."[69]

4-042   The House of Lords held that the true measure of compensation in the case was that of the replacement value of a dredger comparable to the *Liesbosch*, and incidental expenses. The decision appears to suggest that the hire charges could not be recovered either because they were not caused by the defendants' tort, or because they were too remote, but in *Dodd Properties v. Canterbury City Council*[70] Donaldson L.J. observed that in modern terms Lord Wright would have said that the damage was unforeseeable.[71] On that basis the decision is difficult to reconcile with the rules that a defendant must take his victim as he finds him, and that the full extent of damage need not be foreseen to be recoverable.[72] Lord Wright said, however, that the former of these rules went to the extent of actual

---

[68] [1933] A.C. 449. See *infra* Ch. 6 in relation to damages for destruction of goods.
[69] *ibid.* at 460.
[70] [1980] 1 W.L.R. 433. See *infra* Ch. 6 in relation to damages for injury to property.
[71] *ibid.* at 459.
[72] Criticisms made by Donaldson L.J. in *Dodd Properties v. Canterbury City Council* [1980] 1 W.L.R. 433 at 458.

physical damage and the latter to interference with profit-earning capacity, whereas impecuniosity was something extrinsic.[73] Whatever the merits of that distinction, the principle which the *Liesbosch* case enunciated has been whittled down over the years by a series of decisions to the extent that its continued authority must now be open to question.[74] In several cases the principle has been avoided on the basis that extra damage due to the claimant's impecuniosity was in fact foreseeable. For example, in *Perry v. Sidney Phillips & Son*[75] the claimant claimed damages for distress, worry and inconvenience caused through having to live in a house with a number of defects which a surveyor's report had failed to identify. The defendants argued that this damage could have been avoided had the claimant possessed the funds to have the defects remedied; the loss was therefore due to his impecuniosity. The Court of Appeal ruled in favour of the claimant. According to Kerr L.J.:

"If it is reasonably foreseeable that the plaintiff may be unable to mitigate or remedy the consequence of the other party's breach as soon as he would have done if he had been provided with the necessary means to do so from the other party, then it seems to me that the principle of *The Liesbosch* . . . no longer applies in its full rigour."[76]

This approach has been followed in other cases, subject to the proviso that the claimant's actions which have incurred the extra expense whilst awaiting compensation must have been reasonable. Examples include a taxi driver who claimed loss of income due to inability to purchase a replacement taxi whilst awaiting compensation,[77] and a motorist who hired a replacement vehicle until the third party's insurance company paid for repairs to her own vehicle.[78]   **4–043**

The *Liesbosch* principle was further refined in *Dodd Properties v. Canterbury City Council*,[79] where the claimants refrained from undertaking repairs to their building until damages had been received, on grounds of "commercial prudence", one reason being financial stringency. In the period between the damage becoming apparent and the case reaching trial the cost of the repairs rose considerably. The Court of Appeal held that the inflation of the damages was not attributable to what could be described as impecuniosity. Where damages were inflated as a result of a decision made on grounds of commercial good sense, financial stringency being merely one factor in the decision, the *Liesbosch* principle had no application. The *Liesbosch* principle will also have no application where it is the defendant's breach which has actually created the impecuniosity.[80]   **4–044**

---

[73] [1933] A.C. 449 at 461.
[74] Although the principle was seemingly accepted by the Court of Appeal without criticism in *Ramwade Ltd v. W. J. Emson & Co. Ltd* [1987] R.T.R. 72, a decision later distinguished by the subsequent Court of Appeal decision *Mattocks v. Mann* [1993] R.T.R. 13.
[75] [1982] 1 W.L.R. 1297.
[76] *ibid.* at 1307.
[77] *Mason v. British Railways Board*, C.A. unreported, October 6, 1992.
[78] *Mattocks v. Mann* [1993] R.T.R. 13. See also *Martindale v. Duncan* [1973] 1 W.L.R. 574.
[79] [1980] 1 W.L.R. 433.
[80] *Archer v. Brown* [1985] 1 Q.B. 401.

It seems, therefore, that provided the claimant can demonstrate that the incurring of extra losses was in the circumstances both foreseeable and reasonable, the *Liesbosch* principle is now capable of avoidance.

(3) Intervening events

4–045   Even though the damage that the claimant has suffered can as a matter of fact and history be traced back to an act on the part of the defendant, the defendant will not be held responsible for the damage if it is deemed to have been caused by an intervening event. The term normally given to such an intervening event is a *novus actus interveniens*, or break in the chain of causation. It is useful to categorise the types of event which may break the chain of causation, and discuss each in turn.

(a) Natural events

4–046   The occurrence of a natural event will frequently break the chain of causation. In *Carslogie Steamship Company Ltd v. Royal Norwegian Government*,[81] the claimants' ship was damaged in a collision with another vessel, but before permanent repairs could be effected the ship suffered heavy weather damage rendering her unseaworthy. Had it not been for the collision the claimants' ship would never have embarked upon the voyage which ultimately resulted in the heavy weather damage; in a "but for" sense, therefore, the unseaworthiness was caused by the collision. As a matter of law, however, the House of Lords held that the weather damage was not a consequence of the collision. The heavy weather had to be treated as a supervening natural event occurring in the course of a normal voyage.

4–047   Damage caused through the occurrence of a natural event may not always break the chain of causation, however. For example, if it was the very duty of the defendant to provide protection against the effects of a natural event, it could hardly be said that there was a break in the chain of causation if the damage was inflicted by a natural event following breach of that duty.

(b) Acts of a third party

4–048   Here the issue is whether the defendant should be held responsible for damage which has been caused by the act or omission of a third party. As an illustration, in *Knightley v. Johns*[82] the claimant police-motorcyclist was injured after he was ordered by an inspector to seal the entrance of a road tunnel, following an earlier accident, by riding his bike against the flow of traffic in the tunnel. The Court of Appeal held that the order to ride against the flow of traffic was negligent. The driver responsible for the original accident was therefore not liable for the claimant's resulting injuries; the

---

[81] [1952] A.C. 292. See *infra* Ch. 6 in relation to damages for loss of profit-earning goods.
[82] [1982] 1 W.L.R. 349.

negligence of the inspector had broken the chain of causation between the accident and the claimant's injury.

The approach adopted by the courts towards this issue is whether the 4–049 sequence of events which flowed from the defendant's act, encapsulating the actions of the third party, is to be regarded as the natural and probable consequence of the defendant's act, and therefore a reasonably foreseeable consequence of it.[83] Determining whether the actions of the third party were innocent, negligent or wilful may assist in deciding whether they break the chain of causation, but this will not necessarily be conclusive of the issue, as Stephenson L.J.'s comments in *Knightley v. Johns*[84] illustrate:

> "Negligent conduct is more likely to break the chain of causation than conduct which is not; positive acts will more readily constitute new causes than inaction. Mistakes and mischances are to be expected when human beings, however well trained, have to cope with a crisis; what exactly they will be cannot be predicted, but if those which occur are natural the wrongdoer cannot, I think, escape responsibility for them and their consequences simply by calling them improbable or unforseeable. He must expect the risk of some unexpected mischances ... But what mischances? The answer to this difficult question must be dictated by common sense rather than logic on the facts and circumstances of each case."[85]

(i) Mistakes in the face of a crisis

As an example of the treatment by the courts of a mischance in the face 4–050 of a crisis, in *The Oropesa*[86] a collision occurred between the *Oropesa* and the *Manchester Regiment*, following which the Master of the *Manchester Regiment* decided to board the *Oropesa* to discuss salvage arrangements. En route the lifeboat containing the Master and several of his crew capsized in heavy seas resulting in loss of life. In an action by a member of the crew's parents against the owners of the *Oropesa*, it was held that the Master had acted reasonably in the face of the emergency; his decision to cross to the *Oropesa* was not a *novus actus interveniens* but a natural consequence of the emergency in which he was placed by the negligence of the *Oropesa*. Lord Wright said that to break the chain of causation

> "it must be shown that there is something which I will call ultroneous, something unwarrantable, a new cause which disturbs the sequence of events, something which can be described as either unreasonable or extraneous or extrinsic."[87]

Involuntary actions have been treated in the same way. In *Scott v. Shep-*

---

[83] *Weld-Blundell v. Stephens* [1920] A.C. 956.
[84] [1982] 1 W.L.R. 349.
[85] *ibid.* at 366H.
[86] [1943] P. 32.
[87] *ibid.* at 39.

herd[88] a lighted squib was thrown into a market place where it was thrown from stallholder to stallholder as each tried to avoid injury, until it eventually exploded, blinding the claimant. The involuntary actions of the stallholders did not break the chain of causation.

(ii) Negligent and reckless conduct

4–051   Negligent conduct is more likely to break the chain of the causation, as *Knightley v. Johns* illustrates, but that it will not automatically do so can be seen from the decision in *Rouse v. Squires*.[89] The third party's lorry jack-knifed on a motorway, obstructing two of the three lanes, and another lorry parked short of the scene of the accident to illuminate the accident with its headlights and warn other road users. The defendant, who was driving his lorry towards the scene of the accident, failed to realise that the vehicles were stationary and drove his lorry into the rear of the parked lorry, projecting it forward and knocking down R. who was standing in the lorry's path. In a claim by R.'s widow the Court of Appeal held that the defendant's negligent driving had not broken the chain of causation between the third party's negligence and R.'s death. The third party's share of the damage was fixed at 25 per cent and the defendant's at 75 per cent. The reason why negligence in this instance did not break the chain of causation can be discerned in the following extract from the judgment of Buckley L.J.:

> "Anyone who by a negligent act creates a danger on a highway to other users of the highway can be liable to another user if damage results from the danger so caused. The question whether there is a danger is to be determined by the ordinary test of foreseeability. But for that purpose, when considering how other road users can reasonably be expected to use the road, you are not entitled to assume that they will all exercise the proper degree of care. For instance, one should not proceed upon the assumption that every driver will be able to stop within the limits of his own vision, because common experience shows that people do not always drive in that way. But when there is ample visibility and ample opportunity for the driver of an oncoming vehicle to see and appreciate the nature and extent of an obstruction and to take evasive action, then the obstruction does not constitute a danger, and in such a case there is a break in the chain of causation."[90]

4–052   Sometimes, therefore, a negligent act by a third party can be considered reasonably foreseeable. This is particularly so as regards the standard of driving that can reasonably be expected of third parties. Cairns L.J. in the same case suggested by contrast that deliberate or reckless acts by third parties would break the chain of causation.[91] This dictum was applied in

---

[88] (1733) 2 Wm. BL. 1 892.
[89] [1973] Q.B. 889.
[90] *ibid.* at 901A.
[91] [1973] Q.B. 889 at 898D.

the later Court of Appeal decision of *Wright v. Lodge*.[92] A Mini broke down in fog, obstructing the nearside lane of a dual carriageway, and was hit from the rear by a lorry being driven recklessly. The lorry crossed the central reservation and obstructed the opposite carriageway, where several vehicles drove into the obstruction. The Court of Appeal held that the driver of the Mini was not responsible for creating the obstruction on the opposite carriageway. By driving above the speed limit in fog, the lorry driver had acted recklessly and this recklessness had caused the obstruction and broke the chain of causation.

(iii) Wilful conduct

Wilful acts of damage by a third party are likely to break the chain of causation, although it is important to disentangle the discussion from those cases where the defendant was subject to a duty of care to guard against the wilful actions of the third party. So in *Stansbie v. Troman*[93] a decorator left a house unlocked whilst he went out to buy some supplies. During the decorator's absence a thief entered the house and stole items of property. It was held that the risk of thieves entering placed upon the decorator a duty to take reasonable care with regard to the security of the premises if he left them during performance of his work.[94] 4–053

If the matter is to be dealt with as one of remoteness of damage, then

> "In general . . . even though A. is in fault, he is not responsible for injury to C. which B., a stranger to him, deliberately chooses to do. Though A. may have given the occasion for B.'s mischievous activity, B. then becomes a new and independent cause."[95]

In *Weld-Blundell v. Stephens*[96] the claimant sent a letter of instruction to the defendant to investigate a company. The letter, which contained libellous statements concerning two officials of the company, was left by the defendant's partner in the company's office where it was read by the company's manager. He communicated its contents to the two defamed officials who sued the claimant for libel. The claimant subsequently sought to recover from the defendant the damages he had been ordered to pay, but it was held that the deliberate disclosure by the company's manager had broken the chain of causation.

The dictum of Lord Sumner cited above suggests that there are some exceptional cases where the deliberate actions of a third party will not break the chain of causation. In *Dorset Yacht Co. v. Home Office* Lord Reid had remarked *obiter* that 4–054

> "where human action forms one of the links between the original

---

[92] [1993] 4 All E.R. 299.
[93] [1948] 2 K.B. 48.
[94] See also *Smith v. Littlewoods Organisation Ltd* [1987] A.C. 241 and *Dorset Yacht Co. v. Home Office* [1970] A.C. 1004.
[95] *Weld-Blundell v. Stephens* [1920] A.C. 956 per Lord Sumner at 986.
[96] *ibid.*

wrongdoing of the defendant and the loss suffered by the plaintiff, that action must at least have been something very likely to happen if it is not to be regarded as *novus actus interveniens* breaking the chain of causation."[97]

The issue was extensively considered by the Court of Appeal in *Lamb v. Camden London Borough Council*[98] where the defendants broke a water main which allowed water to undermine the foundations of the claimant's house, leading to subsidence and the need to vacate the property. The house subsequently fell victim to inhabitation by squatters who caused extensive damage to the property. The Court of Appeal held that the damage caused by the squatters was too remote a consequence of the broken water main. Watkins L.J. and Lord Denning M.R. declined to follow Lord Reid's dictum. Watkins L.J. held that the issue should be determined through a robust and sensible application of *The Wagon Mound* test of foreseeability. On that approach, his Lordship had an "instinctive feeling that squatters' damage is too remote."[99] Lord Denning preferred to look at the issue from the standpoint of policy, particular consideration being given to the question of who should more appropriately bear any loss. Oliver L.J. had more sympathy with Lord Reid's dictum, but felt that

> "he may perhaps have understated the *degree* of likelihood required before the law can or should attribute the free act of a responsible third person to the tortfeasor ... It may be that some more stringent standard is required. There may, for instance, be circumstances in which the court would require a degree of likelihood amounting almost to inevitability before it fixes a defendant with responsibility for the act of a third party over whom he has and can have no control."[1]

4–055   *Lamb* confirms that the situations in which a defendant will be fixed with responsibility for the wilful actions of a third party will be exceptional. The precise jurisprudential basis upon which such liability would be established is far from clear, however. *Lamb* was considered by Scott J. in the first instance decision of *Ward v. Cannock Chase District Council*,[2] where exceptionally it was held that the defendants were liable for some of the damage inflicted by third parties. Scott J. discerned that the common *ratio* of *Lamb* was that although reasonable foreseeability of damage should be taken as the starting point, something more would then need to be demonstrated. His Lordship thought that it would make little difference to the end result if the route of either Oliver L.J., Watkins L.J. or Lord Reid in *Dorset Yacht* were then followed. In *Ward* the defendants had allowed premises adjoining that of the claimants to fall into disrepair and eventually collapse, causing damage to the claimant's property and leading to its vaca-

---

[97] [1970] A.C. 1004 at 1030.
[98] [1981] 1 Q.B. 625.
[99] *ibid.* at 647D.
[1] [1981] 1 Q.B. 625 at 644C.
[2] [1986] 1 Ch. 546.

tion. Refusal by the defendants to effect repairs exposed the property to attacks from vandals to such extent that it eventually had to be demolished. Scott J. held that the vandal damage was not too remote, either because it was the very thing that was likely to happen, or (adopting Watkins L.J.'s approach) because there appeared to be a clear connection between the failure of the council to effect repairs and the eventual vandal damage. It should be emphasised that in *Ward* it was well known that there was prevalent vandal activity in the vicinity. The result may otherwise have been different.

(c) Acts of the claimant

The actions of the claimant may break the chain of causation depending upon the reasonableness of those actions. In *McKew v. Holland & Hannen & Cubitts (Scotland) Ltd*[3] the pursuer's left leg was injured as a result of negligence on the part of the defenders which made the leg prone to give way beneath him. Before this injury had time to heal the pursuer attempted to descend a steep flight of stairs with no handrail, but his leg gave way and in the subsequent fall he severely fractured his ankle. It was held that his unreasonable conduct in attempting to descend unaided a steep flight of stairs, with no handrail, broke the chain of causation between the original breach and the ankle injury. Unreasonable conduct was not the natural and probable result of the breach of duty, even though technically such action may have been reasonably foreseeable.   **4–056**

In contrast, on vaguely similar facts, in *Wieland v. Cyril Lord Carpets Ltd*[4] the claimant suffered an injury which necessitated the wearing of a neck collar, inhibiting neck movement. In consequence the claimant was unable to use her bi-focal spectacles with her usual skill and she fell whilst descending some stairs, injuring her ankles. It was held that it was foreseeable that one injury may affect a person's ability to cope with the vicissitudes of life and thereby be a cause of another injury. In this instance the chain of causation had therefore not been broken. Eveleigh J. held that the fall on the stairs was a fall in one of the ordinary activities of life, for which she had been rendered less capable by the defendant's negligence. The distinction with *McKew* is thus a fine one, although Eveleigh J. was influenced by the fact that the fall occurred very soon after the claimant had been fitted with the collar; the position might have been different if she had persisted in wearing the bi-focals for a long time after the injury and then sustained another injury. The effect of the original accident might then have been more difficult to demonstrate.   **4–057**

That reasonable actions of the claimant should not break the chain of causation was illustrated in rather stark fashion in *Emeh v. Kensington and Chelsea and Westminster Area Health Authority*[5] where a sterilisation operation was wrongly performed, resulting in the conception and birth of a child with congenital abnormalities. The child required constant medical   **4–058**

---

[3] [1969] 3 All E.R. 1621.
[4] [1969] 3 All E.R. 1006.
[5] [1985] 1 Q.B. 1012.

and parental supervision. In an action to recover damages for the pregnancy, birth and upkeep of the child, it was held that the claimant's decision not to undergo an abortion at 20 weeks was reasonable. Slade L.J. ruled that:

> "Save in the most exceptional circumstances, I cannot think it right that the court should ever declare it unreasonable for a woman to decline to have an abortion in a case where there is no evidence that there were any medical or psychiatric grounds for terminating the particular pregnancy."[6]

4–059   On other occasions the court may hold that the chain of causation has not been broken, but that the claimant's damages should be reduced on grounds of contributory negligence.[7] In *Sayers v. Harlow Urban District Council*[8] the claimant found herself locked in a lavatory cubicle. Having attempted unsuccessfully to attract attention, she decided to escape by climbing out of the cubicle. Realising that she would be unable to climb over the door, she attempted to lower herself again and was injured when she balanced on a toilet roll which revolved causing her to slip and fall. The Court of Appeal held that attempting to escape in the circumstances was not unreasonable, but attempting to balance on the toilet roll contributed to the injury and damages would be reduced by 25 per cent accordingly.

(d) "Rescue cases"

4–060   The "rescue cases" deserve separate treatment in any discussion of intervening causes. In *Haynes v. Harwood*[9] the defendants' servant negligently left a horse-drawn van unattended in a busy street, which bolted exposing women and children to danger. The claimant, a police constable, attempted to stop the horses and was injured in the process. Maugham L.J. held that the claimant had not unreasonably exposed himself to danger:

> "In deciding whether such a rescuer is justified in putting himself into a position of such great peril, the law has to measure the interests which he sought to protect and the other interests involved. We have all heard of the reasonable man whom the law postulates in certain circumstances; the reasonable man here must be endowed with qualities of energy and courage, and he is not to be deprived of a remedy because he has in a marked degree a desire to save human life when in peril."[10]

4–061   In other words the courageous act of the rescuer is regarded as the natural and probable consequence of a helpless person being put in danger, and

---

[6] [1985] 1 Q.B. 1012 at 1024H.
[7] The defence of contributory negligence is discussed in detail in ch. 3 *supra*.
[8] [1958] 1 W.L.R. 623.
[9] [1935] 1 K.B. 146.
[10] *ibid.* at 162.

should be regarded as foreseeable. Some acts may be regarded as foolhardy rather than courageous, however, and therefore not reasonably foreseeable:

"For example, one may imagine a horse bolting on a desolate country highway, as does happen sometimes; he would ultimately get tired and stop and graze by the side of the road without injuring anybody; if a person rushed out in those circumstances and was injured he might well not be entitled to a legal remedy against the negligent owner."[11]

Or to put it in a different context:

"It may be that circumstances can arise of attempted rescue where the risk to the rescuer is so great, and the chances of rescue so small, that it could not be expected that a rescue would be attempted."[12]

As an illustration of the above, in *Cutler v. United Dairies*[13] the claimant 4–062 was injured after answering a call for help to try and restrain an excited horse which had run loose into a field without its van driver. The Court of Appeal held that the claimant must have appreciated the risks associated with his actions, and his attempt to restrain the horse in circumstances where it posed no real danger amounted to a *novus actus interveniens*. The situation would have been different if the horse had posed a threat to the public.

As regards what is reasonable, the law must be astute not to judge the 4–063 issue with the benefit of hindsight. It is

"fatally easy to be wise after the event. It is not enough that, when all the evidence has been sifted and all the facts ascertained in the calm and deliberate atmosphere of a court of law, the rescuer's conduct can be shown ex post facto to have been misguided or foolhardy."[14]

In *Baker v. T.E. Hopkins & Son Ltd*[15] the defendants used a petrol 4–064 engine to pump water from a well. The petrol engine produced carbon monoxide fumes which built up to a lethal concentration inside the well. Two of the defendants' employees who had descended into the well were overcome by the fumes. A doctor was lowered into the well by a rope but he too was overcome by the fumes. In an action by his executors it was held that the doctor's rescue attempt was not a *novus actus interveniens*. Applying *Haynes v. Harwood*, the Court of Appeal said that it was the natural and probable result that if someone was overcome by carbon monoxide poisoning a doctor would be called in, and that such a doctor, having regard to the traditions of the profession, would descend the well for the purpose of attempting a rescue, even at the risk of his own safety.

Whilst it is plainly foreseeable that professional rescuers will attend the 4–065

---

[11] Per Maugham L.J. *Haynes v. Harwood* [1935] 1 K.B. 146 at 163.
[12] Per Ormerod L.J. *Baker v. T.E. Hopkins & Son Ltd* [1959] 1 W.L.R. 966 at 978.
[13] [1933] 2 K.B. 297.
[14] Per Willmer L.J. *Baker v. T.E. Hopkins & Son Ltd* [1959] 1 W.L.R. 966 at 984.
[15] [1959] 1 W.L.R. 966.

scene of an emergency and may be injured thereby,[16] the principles enunciated above still apply to amateur rescuers. So in *Chadwick v. British Railways Board*[17] it was held that the claimant (suing as administratix of her
late husband) could recover in respect of psychoneurosis which the husband
developed after assisting at the scene of a train disaster which occurred 200
yards from his home. It was foreseeable that someone might try and rescue
passengers put in peril by the defendants' negligence, and suffer injury in
the process.

4–066   Two limitations upon recovery require mention before leaving this section. First, any psychiatric harm suffered whilst acting as a rescuer can now
only be recovered if it was foreseeable that the rescuer might suffer physical
injury, following the House of Lords' ruling in *White v. Chief Constable
of South Yorkshire Police*.[18] Secondly, any damage suffered by the rescuer
that was not of a kind that was reasonably foreseeable will be irrecoverable.
In *Crossley v. Rawlinson*[19] the claimant, an Automobile Association Patrol
Man, tried to render assistance in extinguishing a fire on a lorry. As he was
running towards the scene with a fire extinguisher, he caught his foot in a
concealed hole and fell sustaining injury. It was held that no reasonable
man could have foreseen this injury occurring as a consequence of the fire.

2. THE REQUIREMENT TO MITIGATE

4–067   The claimant may not be able to recover all losses flowing from the
tort because of the fundamental requirement that the claimant should take
reasonable steps to mitigate his losses. This is a requirement for claims
framed in tort just as much as it is for claims framed in contract.[20] Although
mitigation is associated with mandatory expressions such as a "requirement" or "duty" to mitigate, in reality it is the defendant that bears the
onus of establishing that the claimant has failed to take reasonable steps to
mitigate his loss.[21] If the defendant can establish this, that part of the loss

---

[16] Although no claim will lie for psychiatric harm unless the rescuer was exposed to danger
of physical injury: *White v. Chief Constable of South Yorkshire Police* [1998] 3 W.L.R.
1509.

[17] [1967] 1 W.L.R. 912.

[18] [1998] 3 W.L.R. 1509.

[19] [1982] 1 W.L.R. 369.

[20] See for example *The Liverpool (No. 2)* [1960] 1 All E.R. 465 at 474F, where Lord Merriman P. stated that the requirement to mitigate in contract as stated by Viscount Haldane
L.C. in *British Westinghouse Electric & Manufacturing Co. Ltd v. Underground Electric
Rys. Co. of London Ltd* [1912] A.C. 673 at 688, applied equally, *mutatis mutandis*, to tort.
In *Standard Chartered Bank v. Pakistan National Shipping Corporation (No. 3)* [1991] 1
Lloyd's Rep. 747, Toulson J. confirmed that the requirement to mitigate applies to intentional torts such as deceit or conspiracy.

[21] *Roper v. Johnson* (1873) L.R. 8 C.P. 167; *Richardson v. Redpath* [1944] A.C. 62. In
Selvanayagam v. University of the West Indies [1983] 1 W.L.R. 585, the Privy Council
emphatically stated that the onus was upon the claimant to demonstrate that he had acted
reasonably in regard to his duty to mitigate his damage. McGregor (para. 299) suggests
that the decision was against the entire weight of authority and was arrived at *per incuriam*.
Subsequent decisions have continued to place the burden upon the defendant, for example
Metelman GmbH & Co KG v. NBR (London) Ltd [1984] 1 Lloyd's Rep. 614 at 631, per
Sir John Donaldson M.R.

that could have been avoided through taking reasonable steps will be deducted from the damages calculated as being due to the claimant. Whether the claimant has or could have taken reasonable steps to mitigate his loss is a question of fact[22] and this, coupled with the requirement that the steps must only be such as *this* claimant ought *reasonably* to have taken,[23] means that there is some danger in relying too heavily upon previous decisions. It may also explain why some decisions at face value appear difficult to reconcile. Nevertheless it is possible to discern several themes which have developed through the cases, which act as a guide in this area.

(1) Examples

Mitigation of damage can become an issue in relation to hire of a vehicle where the claimant's own vehicle has been damaged or written off by the defendant. In *Watson Norie, Ltd v. Shaw and Nelson*[24] the claimant company provided a Jensen car for the use of their managing director and chairman. The car was damaged by the negligence of the defendants and the claimants hired alternative vehicles for their managing director to use whilst repairs were being carried out. The vehicles hired were of a similar prestige value to the Jensen usually driven, and the hire charges were accordingly excessive. The Court of Appeal upheld the County Court Judge's refusal to award the claimants the full value of the hire costs, as a reasonable substitute car could have been obtained at substantially lower rates.   4–068

The Court of Appeal was less sympathetic to the defendant's arguments in *Mattocks v. Mann*[25] where it was argued that the claimant had acted unreasonably in hiring a four-door vehicle whilst she awaited compensation to pay for repairs to her two-door vehicle. The Court of Appeal concentrated on the actual hire costs of £130 per week, and held that these were reasonable in the circumstances, even though the claimant as a mother of children had enjoyed the extra benefit of a vehicle with four doors.   4–069

It was emphasised by the Court of Appeal in *Moore v. D.E.R. Ltd*[26] that the question of whether the claimant has acted reasonably in relation to the hire of a replacement vehicle is always one of fact. It was held that the claimant in this case had not acted unreasonably by insisting on purchasing a new replacement vehicle (because he *never* bought used ones), even though this had prolonged the period of hire. Where the claimant effects repairs to the vehicle himself, rather than waiting for an insurance company to do so, it has been held that having the car repaired at a cost which exceeds its market value, instead of attempting to replace it with a comparable car, is a failure to mitigate.[27] The situation may be different, however,   4–070

---

[22] *Payzu Ltd v. Saunders* [1919] 2 K.B. 581 approved in the tort context in *Moore v. DER Ltd* [1971] 1 W.L.R. 1476.
[23] *Moore v. DER Ltd* [1971] 1 W.L.R. 1476.
[24] [1967] 1 Lloyd's Rep. 515. See *infra* Ch. 6 in relation to damage to goods.
[25] [1993] R.T.R. 13.
[26] [1971] 1 W.L.R. 1476.
[27] *Darbishire v. Warran* [1963] 1 W.L.R. 1067. See *infra* Ch. 6 in relation to damage to goods.

if the vehicle is of a unique character and a replacement cannot reasonably be found.[28]

4–071   In the sphere of compensation flowing from personal injuries it has been held that damages or compensation payments may be reduced if the claimant unreasonably refuses to undergo an operation which would improve his condition, and render him fit for employment. Again, it is all a question of what is a *reasonable course of action* in the light of medical advice on the matter.[29] In *Steele v. Robert George and Company Ltd*,[30] a workman's compensation case, Viscount Simon L.C. ruled that:

> "the question whether the workman is unreasonable in refusing to undergo an operation is a question of fact to be decided by the judge of fact on the evidence, and that where the workman has been advised against the operation by a skilled medical man in whom he has confidence, it would be necessary to bring home to the workman an extremely strong body of expert advice to the contrary before the onus which rests on the employer of proving that the refusal was unreasonable should be regarded as discharged."[31]

4–072   In *Selvanayagam v. University of the West Indies*,[32] for example, the claimant, a diabetic, was held to have acted reasonably in his refusal to undergo surgery to improve a neck injury due to concerns about the risks of infection exacerbated by his diabetic condition. But in *McAuley v. London Transport Executive*[33] the Court of Appeal held that the claimant had been unreasonable in refusing to undergo an operation, in circumstances where he had not been advised by any doctor not to have the operation, which carried a 90 per cent chance of rendering the claimant's hand serviceable for ordinary work. Similar considerations apply where the claimant unreasonably refuses to undergo treatment for conditions such as anxiety which are rendering him unfit for work.[34]

4–073   The rule that the defendant must take his victim as he finds him applies to any decision not to undergo medical treatment, and provided that the claimant can be shown to have suffered from a psychological fear of hospitals before the accident, for example, this will be relevant to the reasonableness of the claimant's refusal. Absent evidence of a pre-accident or accident-induced psychological fear, however, the test of what is reasonable remains objective.[35]

4–074   Further illustrations relate to the reasonableness of a refusal to institute legal proceedings which could have mitigated loss. In *Pilkington v. Wood*[36] Harman J. was of the opinion that:

---

[28] *O'Grady v. Westminster Scaffolding Ltd* [1962] 2 Lloyd's Rep. 238.
[29] *Richardson v. Redpath, Brown & Co. Ltd* [1944] A.C. 62.
[30] [1942] A.C. 497.
[31] *ibid.* at 501.
[32] [1983] 1 W.L.R. 585.
[33] [1957] 2 Lloyd's Rep. 500.
[34] *Marcroft v. Scruttons Ltd* [1954] 1 Lloyd's Rep. 395.
[35] *Morgan v. T. Wallis Ltd* [1974] 1 Lloyd's Rep. 165.
[36] [1953] 1 Ch. 770.

"the so-called duty to mitigate does not go so far as to oblige the injured party ... to embark on a complicated and difficult piece of litigation against a third party."[37]

Here the claimant purchased the freehold in a property but owing to the negligence of the defendant solicitor, it was not identified that the vendor was a trustee of the property and had committed a breach of trust in purchasing the property for himself. In an action against the defendant it was argued that the claimant should have mitigated his losses by suing the vendor in respect of the defective title. Harman J. held that it was no part of the claimant's duty to embark on such litigation in order to protect his solicitor from his own negligence.[37a]

Pilkington v. Wood was approved by the Court of Appeal in *London and South of England Building Society v. Stone*[38] where the defendant valuer failed to identify to the claimant mortgage lenders that a property suffered from serious subsidence. The claimants had the subsidence damage made good at their own expense, even though they could have had recourse to a covenant obliging the borrowers to do so. Stephenson L.J. held that the principle in *Pilkington v. Wood* extended to litigation which may be reasonably certain to result in judgment for the claimant, but where there is no certainty that the judgment would be satisfied. Moreover, as one of the reasons for the claimants' decision to effect repairs themselves was to protect their public relations, this made the decision not to pursue the borrowers all the more reasonable.[39]   **4–075**

Finally, unreasonable refusal of offers of assistance from the defendant or others following the tort, which may reduce the claimant's losses, may be deemed a failure to mitigate. In *Warren Hastings Anderson v. Adrian Hoen, The "Flying Fish"*,[40] the respondent's vessel was damaged following a collision with the appellant's vessel and ran ashore. Thereafter the Master refused all offers of assistance from the coastguard to help her reach harbour, and the vessel subsequently broke up. It was held that the Master had acted unreasonably in refusing these offers of assistance.   **4–076**

(2) Claimant's impecuniosity

It is accepted that damages should not be reduced for failure to mitigate if the failure is as a result of the claimant's impecuniosity. The dictum of Lord Collins in *The Clippens Oil Company, Ltd v. The Edinburgh and District Water Trustees* is apposite here: **4–077**

---

[37] *ibid.* at 777.
[37a] By contrast in *Walker v. Medlicott & Son* [1999] W.L.R. 727, the Court of Appeal held that a beneficiary under a negligently-drafted will ought to have mitigated his loss by issuing proceeding for rectification of the will: rectification proceedings would in the circumstances have been no more complicated and difficult than bringing a claim in negligence.
[38] [1983] 1 W.L.R. 1242.
[39] Approving the rule in McGregor para. 330 that a claimant need not prejudice his commercial reputation: *Banco de Portugal v. Waterlow & Sons* [1932] A.C. 452.
[40] (1865) 3 Moo. N.S. 77.

"[I]n my opinion the wrong-doer must take his victim *talem qualem*, and if the position of the latter is aggravated because he is without the means of mitigating it, so much the worse for the wrongdoer, who has got to be answerable for the consequences flowing from his tortious act."[41]

It is difficult to reconcile this statement with the principle discussed earlier, that losses will be regarded as too remote if they stem from the claimant's impecuniosity, as established in the *Liesbosch* case.[42] Lord Wright in the *Liesbosch* case referred to Lord Collins' dictum in *Clippens Oil Company* but declared that:

"I think it is clear that Lord Collins is here dealing not with the measure of damage, but with the victim's duty to minimise damage, which is quite a different matter, the dictum is not in point."[43]

This suggested that there could not be deduction from the claimant's damages for failure to mitigate on grounds of impecuniosity, but that nevertheless the claimant would not be awarded damages for those losses which were due to his own impecuniosity.

4–078   As discussed earlier, the principle in *Liesbosch* has been subjected to considerable criticism and has been distinguished in several decisions, calling into question its continued authority.[44] The relationship between the two principles is far from clear, however, and the rather unsatisfactory position appears to be that the court has a choice of whether to define the issue as one of remoteness or mitigation, with differing results. Certainly this appeared to be the basis upon which the *Liesbosch* was distinguished by John Stephenson J. in *Robbins of Putney v. Meek*,[45] and in *Dodd Properties Ltd v. Canterbury County Council*[46] the Court of Appeal decided the issue by distinguishing the *Liesbosch* case, or alternatively viewing the issue as one of mitigation.[47]

(3) Costs incurred through mitigation

4–079   Costs incurred through reasonable attempts to mitigate the claimant's losses will be recoverable from the defendant, even if the reasonable mitigation attempt itself was unsuccessful and in fact increased the claimant's overall losses.[48] Reasonable hire charges for a replacement vehicle whilst a damaged one is being repaired represent a classic example.[49] An illustration

---

[41] [1907] A.C. 291 at 303.
[42] *Owners of Dredger Liesbosch v. Owners of Steamship Edison* [1933] A.C. 449.
[43] *ibid.* at 461.
[44] See discussion of these cases *supra* paras. 4–042, 4–044.
[45] [1971] R.T.R. 345.
[46] [1980] 1 W.L.R. 433.
[47] Per Megaw L.J. at 453B and Donaldson L.J. at 495F *ibid.* See also *Bunclark v. Hertfordshire County Council* [1977] 2 E.G.L.R. 114.
[48] *Lloyds and Scottish Finance Ltd v. Modern Cars and Caravans (Kingston) Ltd* [1966] 1 Q.B. 764.
[49] As for example in *Mattocks v. Mann* [1993] R.T.R. 13.

of unsuccessful mitigation costs being recovered is *Esso Petroleum v. Mardon*,[50] where the defendant leased a petrol station from the claimants following an oral representation regarding potential petrol sales. The defendant invested large sums of money in the venture but the projected sales never materialised, and instead the defendant suffered losses. Nevertheless the defendant took out a subsequent tenancy, but the situation did not improve and eventually he was unable to meet payments under the lease. The claimant issued proceedings for possession, and the defendant counterclaimed for breach of warranty or negligent misrepresentation. The Court of Appeal held that entering the second agreement was a reasonable attempt to mitigate losses flowing from the first agreement. Indeed the claimants were anxious for him to stay on as their tenant. Accordingly the loss sustained under the second agreement was attributable to the original oral representation, and was recoverable.

(4) Determining when losses have been reduced or avoided through "mitigation"

Not every action taken by the claimant after the tort which reduces or even obviates the loss will be viewed as an act of "mitigation". In *Salih v. Enfield Health Authority*[51] Butler-Sloss L.J. on this matter cited the statement in *McGregor on Damages* (15th ed., 1988, para. 326) that a "matter completely collateral and merely *res inter alios acta* cannot be used in mitigation of damage."[52] For example, in *Hussey v. Eels*[53] the claimants purchased a bungalow in reliance upon the misrepresentation that the property had not been subject to subsidence. They paid £53,250 but the property was in fact worth £17,000 less than this. Two years later the claimants sold the land for £78,500, complete with attached planning permission for demolition of the bungalow and erection of two buildings. In an action against the defendants claiming the £17,000 diminution in value, the Court of Appeal had to decide whether the subsequent action of selling the land with the attached planning permission amounted to mitigation of the damage. Mustill L.J. held that:

4–080

> "Ultimately, as with so many disputes about damages, the issue is primarily one of fact. Did the negligence which caused the damage also cause the profit—if profit there was? I do not think so . . . It seems to me that when the plaintiffs unlocked the development value of their land they did so for their own benefit, and not as part of a continuous transaction of which the purchase of land and bungalow was the inception."[54]

---

[50] [1976] 1 Q.B. 801.
[51] [1991] 3 All E.R. 400.
[52] *ibid.* at 405D. This statement is to be found in the current edition of McGregor on Damages (16th ed., 1997), at para. 337.
[53] [1990] 2 Q.B. 227.
[54] *ibid.* at 241B. See also *Dominion Mosaics and Tile Co. v. Trafalgar Trucking Co.* [1990] 2 All E.R. 246.

4–081   On the other hand, in *Bellingham v. Dhillon*,[55] as a result of an operation for a back injury caused by the defendant, the claimant lost the opportunity to negotiate purchase of a special driving simulator for use in his driving school. He claimed for the loss of profits he would have earned through use of the machine during a 41-month period. The period was limited to 41 months because the claimant was subsequently able to purchase a simulator at a greatly reduced price compared to that which it had been originally. Forbes J. held that the profit made through being able to purchase the simulator at a greatly reduced price had to be taken into account, eradicating this head of damage entirely. The actions of the claimant were those of a reasonable and prudent man of business in pursuit of his duty to mitigate his damage.

4–082   Ultimately, as with all issues of mitigation, the issue is one which must be determined according to the facts of each individual case. The "continuous transaction" approach adopted by the Court of Appeal in *Hussey v. Eels*[56] found favour in the later Court of Appeal decision of *Gardner v. Marsh & Parsons*[57] where the claimants purchased a lease on a maisonette in reliance on a negligently-prepared full structural report which failed to identify a serious structural defect. The defect was made good by the landlords pursuant to the activation of a repair covenant. The claimants were awarded damages for the diminution in value assessed at the date of purchase. The defendants' arguments that the repairs by the landlord should be taken into account in the assessment of damages were rejected by the Court of Appeal. Applying *Hussey v. Eels*, the Court of Appeal defined the issue as whether the repairs could be viewed as part of a continuous transaction of which the purchase of the lease in reliance upon the defendants' report was the inception. It was held that the benefit came about by reason of the performance of a contractual obligation by a third party, and was too remote from the defendants' negligence.

3. DEDUCTION FOR COMPENSATING ADVANTAGES

4–083   In *Hunt v. Severs*[58] Lord Reid said:

> "The starting point for any inquiry into the measure of damages which an injured plaintiff is entitled to recover is the recognition that damages in the tort of negligence are purely compensatory. He should recover from the tortfeasor no more and no less than he has lost."[59]

4–084   If the aim of an award of damages in tort was literally to put the claimant in the position he would have been but for the commission of the tort, with

---

[55] [1973] Q.B. 304.
[56] [1990] 2 Q.B. 227.
[57] [1997] 1 W.L.R. 489. For criticism of this decision see D. Allen and M.P. Thompson, "Surveyor's negligence and collateral benefits" (1998) Conv. 303.
[58] [1994] 2 A.C. 350.
[59] *ibid.* at 357H.

no more and no less than he has lost being recovered, then account would have to be taken of any benefits or advantages which the claimant has derived as a result of the tort. That this is not always the case can be gleaned from some of the decisions discussed above in relation to mitigation of damage, such as *Gardner v. Marsh & Parsons.*[60] Moreover, it will be seen in Chapter 9 that there are some situations where benefits which are received by the claimant as a direct consequence of the tort are not deducted from an award of damages, for example payments received pursuant to a policy of insurance. Our task here is to discover what, if any, principles make it acceptable that in some cases the purely compensatory aim should be departed from, leaving the claimant in a better position as a result of the tort.

(1) The relevance of causation

An essential notion in this area is to attempt to compensate the claimant   4–085 in a manner which is fair, just and reasonable. Fairness dictates that any benefits or advantages derived pursuant to the tort should only be taken into account if their occurrence could be said to have been caused by the tort in a legal sense. Factual causation therefore plays a role in the delineation of those circumstances where any benefits or advantages derived should be ignored in the assessment of damages. So, for example, sick payments received following an injury at work are an obvious benefit which the claimant has been caused to receive as a result of the tort. On the other hand, if the injury and subsequent incapacity for work has caused the claimant to pursue a new activity such as attending bingo, a lucrative bingo win could hardly be said to be a benefit which the claimant has been caused to receive as a result of the tort.

Causation also arguably explains the results in the decisions discussed   4–086 earlier, such as *Hussey v. Eels*,[61] in the context of what is, and what is not, an act of mitigation. If the benefit is held to have been received in an attempt to mitigate, it is deducted. If it is held not to have been received in an attempt to mitigate, it is not deducted, and the claimant is in fact left better off as a consequence of the tort. In these latter circumstances, therefore, the court is acknowledging that the claimant was not caused to receive the benefit as a result of the tort, but as a result of some other factor, such as a desire to unlock the development potential of land.[62] But in an area where the court is seeking to achieve what it believes to be the fair, just and reasonable result, there will inevitably be some decisions which are questionable, such as *Gardner v. Marsh & Parsons.*[63] Indeed in this decision Peter Gibson L.J. dissented from the majority who held that the repairs carried out by the landlord were not part of a continuous transaction, the inception of which was the purchase of the lease five years earlier in reliance upon the defendants' negligently prepared report. Instead his

[60] [1997] 1 W.L.R. 489.
[61] [1990] 2 Q.B. 227.
[62] *Hussey v. Eels ibid.*
[63] [1997] 1 W.L.R. 489.

Lordship was persuaded that to allow the action to succeed would result in double recovery for the claimants, and this would be contrary to justice and common sense.[64]

4-087   The most difficult cases to reconcile with the compensatory aim are those exceptional situations where it is clear that the cause of receipt of a benefit or advantage was the commission of the tort, but where nevertheless damages are not offset to take account of their receipt by the claimant. In these cases there must be some other principle at work which justifies non-deduction from an award of damages.

(2) Public policy

4-088   In *Hussain v. New Taplow Paper Mills*[65] Lord Bridge, after stating the *prima facie* rule that the only recoverable loss in tort is the net loss, continued:

> "But to the *prima facie* rule there are two well established exceptions. First, where a plaintiff recovers under an insurance policy for which he has paid the premiums, the insurance moneys are not deductible from damages payable by the tortfeasor . . . Secondly, when the plaintiff receives money from the benevolence of third parties prompted by sympathy for his misfortune, as in the case of a beneficiary from a disaster fund, the amount received is again to be disregarded . . . In both these cases there is in one sense double recovery. If the award of damages adequately compensates the plaintiff, as it should, the additional amounts received from the insurer or from third-party benevolence may be regarded as a net gain to the plaintiff resulting from his injury. But in both cases the common sense of the exceptions stares one in the face. It may be summed up in the rhetorical question: 'Why should the tortfeasor derive any benefit, in the one case, from the premiums which the plaintiff has paid to insure himself against some contingency, however caused, in the other case, from the money provided by the third party with the sole intention of benefiting the injured plaintiff?' "[66]

4-089   This excerpt demonstrates that the compensatory aim may in appropriate circumstances have to be qualified to take account of competing public policy considerations, or to achieve what is considered to be the reasonable and just result in the circumstances. The exceptions referred to by Lord Bridge are worthy of closer inspection to gain some understanding of the forces that pull at the compensatory aim, occasionally forcing it to give way.

---

[64] For criticism of this decision see D. Allen and M.P. Thompson, "Surveyor's negligence and collateral benefits" (1998) Conv. 303.
[65] [1988] 1 A.C. 514.
[66] *ibid.* at 527G.

(a) Insurance payments

Ever since the decision of the Court of Exchequer in *Bradburn v. The*   4–090
Great Western Railway Company,[67] it has been accepted that if moneys
are received by a claimant, following a tort, under a policy of insurance,
this should lead to no deduction from an award of damages. The reason
offered by Lord Bridge in *Hussain* for this rule was that the claimant had
purchased these moneys for himself through the payment of premiums,
although an alternative reason advanced in *Bradburn*, which appears to
have fallen out of favour, is that it was not the tort but the contract of
insurance which was the cause of the payment.[68]

The principle established in *Bradburn* has been stated with approval on   4–091
many subsequent occasions by the House of Lords,[69] most recently in 1997
in *Longden v. British Coal Corporation*.[70] This exception was criticised,
however, in the Law Commission's Consultation Paper, Damages for Personal Injury: Collateral Benefits.[71] The Law Commission colourfully argued
that if damages were reduced to take account of insurance moneys

> "a plaintiff still receives the precise collateral benefit that he or she
> paid for: deduction of collateral benefits from damages which meet the
> same loss does not mean that plaintiffs are deprived of the fruit of
> their thrift, but that they do not receive that fruit twice."[72]

Moreover, deduction from damages would not mean that the claimant
would be deprived of all the benefits of his prudent investment: the insured
claimant could rely on early receipt of moneys and peace of mind compared
to the uninsured claimant, who may have to wait years for his compensation. In addition, the Law Commission noted that the rule in *Bradburn*
ignored the reality that those that take out personal accident insurance pay
for the security and peace of mind which possession of a policy offers, not
the prospect of double recovery. The peace of mind argument is emphasised
if one bears in mind that it is far more likely that the insured person will
be injured in circumstances where tort compensation will not be available.[73]
The peace of mind argument was discussed by McGregor,[74] who pointed
out that the existence of insurance may prove a blessing in those situations
where the tortfeasor is insolvent, or where the claimant prefers to rest with
their insurance proceeds and avoid the time, trouble and uncertainty which
is necessarily involved in bringing a lawsuit.[75] Finally, as noted by
McGregor, the rule in *Bradburn* is difficult to reconcile with the fact that

---

[67] (1874) L.R. 10 Exch. 1.
[68] Per Pigott, B., *ibid.* at 3.
[69] For example in *Parry v. Cleaver* [1970] A.C. 1, *Smoker v. London Fire Authority* [1991]
    2 A.C. 502, *Hussain v. New Taplow Paper Mills* [1988] 1 A.C. 514, and *Hunt v. Severs*
    [1994] 2 A.C. 350.
[70] [1997] 3 W.L.R. 1336.
[71] (1997) Consultation Paper No. 147.
[72] *ibid.* para 4.40.
[73] *ibid.* para 4.43.
[74] H. McGregor, "Compensation Versus Punishment in Damages Awards" (1965) 28 M.L.R.
    629.
[75] *ibid.* at 635–636.

"it is equally true of property insurance that the payment results from the plaintiff's thrift and foresight: yet in property insurance the insured is always held to an indemnity and no more."[76]

4–092   The principle established in *Bradburn* is therefore a good illustration of the public policy factors which may pull at the compensatory aim, occasionally forcing it to give way. Despite the Law Commission's criticisms of the rule, in its Final Report[77] the Law Commission recommended that there should be no change to the present law in this area due to a lack of consensus amongst the consultees as to the appropriate way forward.[78] The Law Commission's criticisms nevertheless raise questions concerning whether the policy factors which underpin this exception have any continuing justification.

(b) Benevolent gifts

4–093   The decision in *Redpath v. Belfast and County Down Railway*[79] established the exception that payments received as an act of benevolence are not taken into account in the assessment of damages. There would appear to be at least two separate reasons why this should be so. First, that the payment was made with the act of benefiting the claimant and not the tortfeasor: there would be public revulsion at the notion of a tortfeasor's liability being reduced on account of the charitable actions of others; secondly, that the cause of the payment was an act of a third party rather than the tort. As with the insurance exception, this exception has been approved on several subsequent occasions by the House of Lords.[80] Lord Bridge in *Hussain* explained this exception as one based upon an intention to benefit the claimant rather than to relieve the defendant. In *Parry v. Cleaver*[81] Lord Reid said that:

> "It would be revolting to the ordinary man's sense of justice, and therefore contrary to public policy, that the sufferer should have his damages reduced so that he would gain nothing from the benevolence of his friends or relations or of the public at large, and that the only gainer would be the wrongdoer."[82]

Another public policy reason advanced in *Redpath* itself in favour of no deduction was that if benevolent payments were taken into account in the assessment of damages,

---

[76] *ibid.* at 635. See also R. Lewis, "Deducting collateral benefits from damages: principle and policy" (1998) Legal Studies 15 at 26.
[77] Damages for Personal Injury: Medical, Nursing and other Expenses; Collateral Benefits (1999) Report No. 262.
[78] *ibid.*, part IX, para. 9.8, 9.9.
[79] [1947] N.I. 167.
[80] For example in *Parry v. Cleaver* [1970] A.C. 1, *Hussain v. New Taplow Paper Mills* [1988] 1 A.C. 514, and *Hunt v. Severs* [1994] 2 A.C. 350.
[81] [1970] A.C. 1.
[82] *ibid.* at 14D.

"the inevitable consequence in the case of future disasters of a similar character would be that the springs of private charity would be found to be largely, if not entirely, dried up."[83]

The public policy arguments in favour of this exception did not escape criticism by the Law Commission. Principally the Law Commission said that compensation should focus on putting the claimant in the position he would have been had the tort not been committed—it should not focus upon punishing the tortfeasor. In that sense the fact that the tortfeasor's burden is relieved by the benevolent payment is irrelevant.[84] The Law Commission also observed that it is unlikely that those making donations are aware of the rules governing the assessment of damages. If they were, it is arguable that they would be equally discouraged from donating if they knew that the claimant was to be compensated by an award of damages in tort. The donor might well think their money better spent in providing support to those with no prospect of recovering tort damages.[85] Moreover, it was doubted whether the "provider's intentions" argument was sound. In many cases the donor will have had no intention with regard to the tortfeasor; even in those cases where the donor did not intend to relieve the tortfeasor, this argument would be unsound unless the donor also intended that the claimant should enjoy the benefit of double recovery.[86]   **4–094**

Once again the Law Commission's criticisms raise questions concerning whether the policy factors which underpin this exception have any continuing justification. The policy in this area must take account of the modern conditions in which compensation is paid. The growth of insurance means that few defendants these days feel a judgment against them in their pockets. Any argument that there would be public revulsion at the spectre of benevolent moneys being used to lessen the tortfeasor's liability must recognise that in reality it is a society of tax and insurance premium payers that ultimately bears the costs of double recovery.   **4–095**

(c) Other types of benefit

In *Hussain v. New Taplow Paper Mills*[87] Lord Bridge said: **4–096**

"There are, however, a variety of borderline situations where a plaintiff may receive money which, but for the wrong done to him by the defendant, he would not have received and where there may be no obvious answer to the question whether the rule against double recovery or some principle derived by analogy from one of the two classic exceptions to that rule should prevail. Some of these problems have been resolved by legislation, sometimes in the form of a compromise solution providing that a proportion only of certain statutory benefits

---

[83] Per Andrews L.C.J. [1947] N.I. 167 at 170.
[84] (1997) Law Com. No. 147, paras 4.31–4.33.
[85] *ibid*. para 4.34.
[86] *ibid*. para 4.47.
[87] [1988] 1 A.C. 514.

is to be taken into account when assessing damages. But where there is no statute applicable the common law must solve the problem unaided and the possibility of a compromise solution is not available. Many eminent common law judges, I think it is fair to say, have been baffled by the problem of how to articulate a single guiding rule to distinguish receipts by a plaintiff which are to be taken into account in mitigation of damage from those which are not. Lord Reid aptly summed the matter up in *Parry v. Cleaver* when he said [1970] A.C. 1, 13H: 'The common law has treated this matter as one depending on justice, reasonableness and public policy.' "[88]

4-097   From this passage it should now be clear that there are no guiding principles (causation aside) which make it acceptable that in some cases the purely compensatory aim should be departed from, leaving the claimant in a better position as a result of the tort. Instead the matter is determined by what is just, reasonable and in the interests of public policy. Whilst this approach has the advantage of being flexible, it also carries the disadvantage of making it difficult to predict how the court may decide to treat a particular benefit in the assessment of damages. As will be seen in Chapter 9, whether or not a particular benefit is deductible has been resolved on a piecemeal, case-by-case basis which has inevitably created numerous areas of uncertainty, in addition to generating many appeals.

4-098   A good example of how the courts have treated a benefit other than insurance moneys or benevolent payments is to be found in pension payments. In *Parry v. Cleaver*[89] the House of Lords held by a majority that no account should be taken of payments received pursuant to a disability pension, be they contractual or purely voluntary. The reasoning of the majority was not harmonious, but the judgment of Lord Reid probably represents the *ratio* of the case as it is understood today.[90] His Lordship could see no difference between pension payments and insurance payments. In respect of both the claimant had paid the premiums for the moneys: in the case of pension payments these premiums had been paid for by the claimant's past work:

> "But the true situation is that wages are a reward for contemporaneous work, but that a pension is the fruit, through insurance, of all the money which was set aside in the past in respect of his past work. They are different in kind."[91]

Public policy therefore made it just that no account should be taken of pension payments in the same way that no account is taken of insurance

---

[88] [1988] 1 A.C. 514 at 528E.
[89] [1970] A.C. 1.
[90] *Parry v. Cleaver* was later unanimously approved by the House of Lords in *Smoker v. London Fire Authority* [1991] 2 A.C. 502. Lord Templeman, who delivered the leading judgment, approved of the approach adopted by Lord Reid in *Parry v. Cleaver*.
[91] [1970] A.C. 1 at 16H.

payments. *Parry v. Cleaver* was later unanimously approved by the House of Lords in *Smoker v. London Fire Authority*.[92]

In Lord Bridge's words in *Hussain*, the decision in *Parry v. Cleaver* is **4–099** therefore based upon "some principle derived by analogy from one of the two classic exceptions"[93] to the rule against double recovery. As was pointed out by the Law Commission, however, the decision in *Parry v. Cleaver* creates a tension between the treatment of different types of benefit, which in turn raises difficult questions of policy over whether it is justifiable to treat what may be intrinsically identical benefits on a separate footing. For example, in *Hussain* itself the claimant received payments pursuant to the defendants' permanent health insurance scheme, which made payments equal to half the claimant's pre-accident earnings for so long as the claimant remained an employee and was unable to work. Lord Bridge held that the payments were indistinguishable in character from sick pay, and were the very antithesis of a pension which is payable only after employment ceases. The Law Commission noted that:

> "The House of Lords deducted long-term sickness benefit from damages for loss of earnings because it was paid prior to the termination of employment, although apart from this detail it was indistinguishable from a disablement pension. The decision comes close to treating differently two collateral benefits, which are by their nature very similar, because one is called disablement pension and the other is called long-term sickness benefit."[94]

(3) Reform

It was noted earlier that in its Final Report[95] the Law Commission recom- **4–100** mended that there should be no change to the present law relating to the deductibility of collateral benefits for personal injuries, due to a lack of consensus amongst the consultees as to the appropriate way forward.[96] It is nevertheless informative to briefly look at the Law Commission's options for reform of this area of the law.[97] The most radical option favoured allowing all the major benefits which may be received by the claimant, as discussed in Chapter 9, to be taken into account in the assessment of damages. The exceptions to this rule would operate where the provider of the benefit had a right to recover the value of the benefit from the victim in the event of a successful tort claim, or where the provider could recover the value from the tortfeasor by being subrogated to the victim's undischarged

---

[92] [1991] 2 A.C. 502.
[93] [1988] 1 A.C. 514 at 528C.
[94] (1997) Law Com. No. 147, para 2.108.
[95] Damages for Personal Injury: Medical, Nursing and other Expenses; Collateral Benefits (1999) Report No. 262.
[96] *ibid.*, Part IX, para. 9.8, 9.9.
[97] The position as regards collateral benefits in Fatal Accident Act claims was dealt with separately by the Law Commission. See Claims for Wrongful Death (1999) Report No. 262, Part V.

tort claim.[98] A second option would operate as above but would continue to ignore benevolent payments in the assessment of damages.[99] A further option favoured allowing the benefit to be deducted except where the provider intended the benefit to be in addition to tort damages, although it was acknowledged that there may be problems of certainty associated with this option.[1]

4–101   Adoption of the first option for reform would inject some welcome clarity into this area of the law and operate in a way which would be fair to claimants, defendants and providers of benefits. It would meet squarely the aim of just compensation, not more or less, to the victims of torts. Despite lack of consensus by consultees, the recommendations of the Law Commission might be taken forward by a Government committed to a policy of cutting (or redistributing) the costs of the tort system,[2] and they should certainly act as a major influence upon the development of the common law in this area.

---

[98] (1997) Law Com. No. 147, paras 6.6–6.8.
[99] *ibid.* para. 6.9.
[1] *ibid.* para. 6.10.
[2] *ibid.* para. 9.10.

CHAPTER 5

NON-COMPENSATORY DAMAGES

Quite apart from the difficulties of determining what losses are to be com-   5–001
pensated, and to what extent, the law of tort, in admitting that in certain
circumstances damages may be awarded for purposes other than compensation, has as a consequence had to grapple with the problem of establishing
the limits to the basic compensatory function of tort damages. Determining
the precise ambit of this exception is, as we shall see, no easy task, and
inevitably the appropriateness of awarding non-compensatory damages has
been hotly debated, especially in recent years.[1] The main exception to the
compensatory function is to be found in cases where exemplary (also
known as punitive) damages are awarded. Given the historical (and indeed
continuing) confusion between exemplary and aggravated damages, we
have thought it best to include discussion of the latter in this chapter
although, as we shall see, they clearly have a compensatory object. It may
also be questioned whether nominal and contemptuous damages are truly
non-compensatory, but the question is sufficiently open to justify their
inclusion in this chapter. Restitutionary damages are concerned to remove
gains from a wrongdoer rather than to compensate his victim, hence their
inclusion in this chapter.

1. NOMINAL DAMAGES

Nominal damages may be awarded where, in the words of Lord   5–002
Halsbury L.C. in *The Mediana*:

"there is an infraction of a legal right which, though it gives you no
right to any real damages at all, yet gives you a right to the verdict or
judgment because your legal right has been infringed."[2]

Nominal damages may be awarded against a defendant who has committed a tort which is actionable *per se, i.e.* where damage need not be proved.
The relevant torts are trespass to the person, trespass to goods, trespass to

---

[1] See *e.g.* A. Burrows, *Remedies for Torts and Breach of Contract* (2nd ed., 1994) pp. 282–
5; A. Ogus, *The Law of Damages* (1973) pp. 32–34; Anderson (1992) 11 C.J.Q. 233; Law
Com. Consultation Paper No. 132 (1993): "Aggravated, Exemplary and Restitutionary
Damages" Part V; Law Com. No. 247 (1997) (the subsequent report), Todd (1998) 18
N.Z.U.L.R. 145.
[2] [1900] A.C. 113 at 116.

land, defamation (limited in the case of slander to the four categories of slander which are actionable *per se*),[3] malicious prosecution, interference with contract and interference with other intangible interests, such as trade marks and copyright. In such cases the claimant is, of course, entitled to compensation for such losses as he suffers, but, as has been said,[4] for nominal damages to be awarded, loss to the claimant must be neither proved nor presumed, and hence, as in *Constantine v. Imperial Hotels Ltd*,[5] an award of nominal damages will be made where the court is of the view (surely erroneously in *Constantine*) that no loss has been suffered by the claimant. An award may also be made where the claimant has shown that a loss occurred, but the necessary evidence as to its amount is not given.[6]

5–003   Two particular functions of nominal damages have been identified.[7] The first is that of declaring or establishing a right, as in *Hanfstaengl v. W.H. Smith*,[8] an action for infringement of copyright in a painting, where the court supported the claimant's right to take action in order to avoid future more serious infringements. Today, of course, injunctive or declaratory relief would be the more effective and appropriate remedy. The second function is the provision of "a mere peg on which to hang costs",[9] though given that today costs are in the discretion of the court, and, as was pointed out by Devlin J. in *Anglo-Cyprian Trade Agencies v. Paphos Wine Industries*[10] ". . . a plaintiff who recovers nominal damages ought [not] necessarily to be regarded in the ordinary sense of the word as a 'successful' plaintiff", and, if not so regarded, as for example, if he did not have a good reason for suing, he might find the award of costs going against him. Neither of the traditional functions of nominal damages may necessarily be appropriate or beneficial to the claimant today, therefore.

2. CONTEMPTUOUS DAMAGES

5–004   Where damages are at large since the loss, usually non-pecuniary, is difficult to assess, a derisory sum, usually referred to as "contemptuous damages" may be awarded. Defamation cases provide the main illustrations of this.[11] The award illustrates the court's attitude to the claimant's conduct;

---

[3] *i.e.* the imputing of (a) a criminal offence punishable corporally (*i.e.* by punishment with at least imprisonment in the first instance); (b) some disease tending to exclude the party defamed from society; (c) in the case of a woman, unchastity; (d) calculated to disparage the party defamed in any office, profession, calling, trade or business held or carried on by him at the time of publication. Clerk & Lindsell on Torts (17th ed., 1995) para 21–28.

[4] See Ogus *op. cit.* pp. 22–23.

[5] [1944] K.B. 693.

[6] *e.g. Dixon v. Deveridge* (1825) 2 C. & P. 109; *Twyman v. Knowles* (1853) 13 C.B. 222. See McGregor on Damages (16th ed., 1997) paras 423–424.

[7] See Ogus *op. cit.* pp. 24–25; McGregor *op. cit.* paras 426–429.

[8] [1905] 1 Ch. 519. See also *Pindar v. Wadsworth* (1802) 2 E. 154 (action by commoner for injury done to the common, although he himself had suffered trifling harm); *Bower v. Hill* (1835) 1 Bing N.C. 549 (obstruction to navigable (albeit for many years blocked up) drain).

[9] Per Maule J. in *Beaumont v. Greathead* (1846) 2 c.B. 494 at 499.

[10] [1951] 1 All E.R. 873 at 874.

[11] See *e.g. Newstead v. London Express Newspaper* [1940] 1 K.B. 377; *Pamplin v. Express Newspapers* (1985) 129 S.J. 188 and 190.

admitting the technical victory, but condemning the bringing of the action. The award is usually in the form of the lowest coin of the realm (currently 1p), and the sanction is likely to be in the area of costs, the claimant being deprived of his own[12] and risking being liable for the defendant's also.[13] It is suggested that the justification of this exceptional form of award lies in its ability to declare the claimant's rights, while admonishing him at the same time.[14]

3. EXEMPLARY DAMAGES

The clearest exception to the compensatory principle is to be found in the ability of the court to award exemplary[15] damages in certain circumstances, to be described below. In such cases, the object of the award of damages is to punish and deter the defendant. Until relatively recently damages for punitive purposes were awarded in a fairly wide range of torts, e.g. trespass to the person,[16] trespass to land,[17] breach of copyright,[18] and in relatively large sums.[19] The fact that for many years juries sat in civil cases generally meant that, at least in cases where damages were at large, the opportunity existed for a punitive element to form part of the award, though this possibility was subject to directions made by the judge to the jury concerning the appropriateness or otherwise of a punitive award. Unfortunately the law was significantly bedeviled by a confusion between exemplary and aggravated damages, thereby failing to clarify and distinguish the punitive from the compensatory element of the award. Thus, in *Butterworth v. Butterworth*[20] it was said that, where exemplary damages were awarded;

> "there are really three distinct heads of damage—namely, (a) pecuniary loss; (b) compensation for wounded feelings and injured pride; and (c) a sum of money of a penal nature in addition to the compensatory damage given for either pecuniary or physical and mental suffering."[21]

In *Rookes v. Barnard*[22] the House of Lords had the opportunity to consider the authorities on exemplary damages, and Lord Devlin sought to

5–005

5–006

---

[12] See *e.g. Martin v. Benson* [1927] 1 K.B. 771.
[13] See *e.g. Red Man's Syndicate v. Associated Newspaper Ltd* (1910) 26 T.L.R. 394 at 395 per Phillimore L.J.
[14] Burrows *op. cit.* at p. 270.
[15] Also known as punitive damages.
[16] *Loudon v. Ryder* [1953] 2 Q.B. 202. See below para. 5–008.
[17] *Merest v. Harvey* (1814) 5 Taunt. 422.
[18] *Williams v. Harvey* [1960] 1 W.L.R. 1072.
[19] *e.g. Huckle v. Money* (1763) 2 Wils. 205, where the claimant was held in custody for six hours by the defendant, a King's Messenger, on suspicion of having published the "North Briton". During his period of custody, the defendant "used him very civilly by treating him with beef-steaks and beer, so that he suffered very little or no damages" (*ibid.*), yet £300 was awarded by the jury, and the Lord Chief Justice did not regard this as excessive.
[20] [1920] P. 126.
[21] *ibid.* at 137 per McCardie J.
[22] [1964] A.C. 1129.

identify the types of cases where exemplary damages could appropriately be awarded, and to clarify the distinction between such cases and where aggravated damages could be awarded. Lord Devlin concluded that cases, such as *Loudon v. Ryder*,[23] in which the injury to the plaintiff had been aggravated by malice or the manner of doing the injury, should be regarded as cases of aggravated rather than exemplary damages, and that the cases in which exemplary damages could be awarded were to be restricted to three categories.

5–007   The first category consisted of cases where there had been oppressive, arbitrary or unconstitutional action by the servants of the government. Cases where that sort of oppression was perpetrated by some other powerful entity, such as a corporation, might give rise to aggravated damages, where the oppression was a source of humiliation, but not to exemplary damages. The second category consisted of cases where the defendant's conduct was calculated by him to make a profit for himself which might well exceed the compensation payable to the plaintiff. This might extend beyond money-making in the strict sense to cases where the defendant sought to gain, at the claimant's expense, some object which he was either unable to obtain at all or obtain at a price higher than that which he wished to pay. The final category comprised those cases in which exemplary damages are expressly authorised by statute.

5–008   We shall return to consider each of these categories in due course. First of all we must examine to what extent Lord Devlin was successful in elaborating a clear distinction between exemplary and aggravated damages. Having identified the three categories of cases in which he considered exemplary damages could be awarded, he went on to consider a number of authorities[24] in which the injury to the claimant was aggravated by malice or by the manner of doing the injury. No statement of principle was revealed by those cases, and he concluded that they were best regarded as cases of aggravated damages. In two more recent cases,[25] though the term exemplary damages was used in connection with the award of damages, the sums awarded could be more easily justified in the result as cases of aggravated damages. *Loudon v. Ryder*[26] where the claimant, a young girl into whose flat the defendant broke and tried to turn her out, was awarded £1,500 for trespass, £1,000 for assault and £3,000 by way of exemplary damages, was held to be wrong, and was overruled, on the basis that there should have been no award of exemplary damages; the compensatory damages awarded were at least as high as any jury could properly have awarded on the facts of the case.

5–009   However, Lord Devlin, in speaking of these cases of aggravated damages, clearly regarded the way in which the injury was caused, *i.e.* the insolence or arrogance which accompanied it, as being a necessary element to the

---

[23] *supra* n. 16.
[24] *i.e. Tullidge v. Wade* (1769) 3 Wils. 18; *Leith v. Pope* (1779) 22 Wm. Bl. 1327; *Merest v. Harvey* (1814) 5 Taunt. 442; *Sears v. Lyons* (1818) 2 Stark. 317; *Williams v. Currie* (1845) 1 C.B. 841 and *Emblen v. Myers* (1860) 6 H. & N. 54.
[25] *Owen and Smith (trading as Nuagin Car Services) v. Reo Motors (Britain) Ltd* (1934) 151 L.T. 274 and *Williams v. Settle* [1960] 1 W.L.R. 1072.
[26] [1953] 2 Q.B. 202.

award, albeit that he subsequently described exemplary and compensatory damages as being essentially different. The difficulty impeding a clear delineation between exemplary and aggravated damages lies in the fact that the nature of the defendant's conduct is regarded as a necessary element for both.

The continuing significance of the defendant's conduct as a factor in the award of aggravated damages risks introducing a punitive element into what should be purely a compensatory award. Thus, in *Messenger Newspapers Groups Ltd v. National Graphical Association (1982)*[27] Caulfield J. held that aggravated damages (as well as exemplary damages) could be awarded to a company (a publishing company, which claimed damages and an injunction against the defendant trade union for unlawful interference with its business and intimidation), stating that: 5–010

> "injured feelings of the plaintiff is only one aspect in considering aggravated damages. The more important element is where the injury to the plaintiff has been aggravated by malice or by the manner of doing the injury; that is, the insolence or arrogance by which it is accompanied."

Quite apart from the appropriateness of an award of aggravated damages to a company, which, with respect, seems questionable, the emphasis in this case seems very much to be concerned with the conduct of the defendant rather than its effect on the claimant.

In *Appleton v. Garrett*[28] Dyson J. adopted the following summary of when aggravated damages were available.   5–011

> "In *Rookes v. Barnard* Lord Devlin said that aggravated awards were appropriate where the manner in which the wrong was committed was such as to injure the plaintiff's proper feelings of pride and dignity or gave rise to humiliation, distress, insult or pain. Examples of the sort of conduct which would lead to these forms of intangible loss were conduct which was offensive or which was accompanied by malevolence, spite, malice, insolence or arrogance. In other words the type of conduct which had previously been regarded as capable of sustaining a punitive award. It would therefore seem that there are two elements relevant to the availability of an aggravated award, first, exceptional or contumelious conduct or motive on the part of the defendant in committing the wrong and second, intangible loss suffered as a result by the plaintiff, that is injury to personality."[29]

Despite the emphasis by Lord Devlin in *Rookes v. Barnard*, and other judges subsequently, that aggravated damages are purely compensatory, there remains some confusion as to whether such an award contains a punitive aspect, hence the inclusion of aggravated damages in this chap-   5–012

---

[27] [1984] I.R.L.R. 397.
[28] [1996] P.I.Q.R. P1 at P4. See also *Ministry of Defence v. Meredith* [1995] I.R.L.R. 539 at 542.
[29] Law Com. Consultation Paper No. 132 para 3.3 "Aggravated, Exemplary and Restitutionary Damages" (1993).

ter. The main reason for this apparent confusion lies in what the Law Commission describes as the "exceptional conduct" requirement,[30] *i.e.* the first of the two elements in the above quotation adopted by Dyson J. in *Appleton*. Such focusing on the defendant's conduct as a criterion of the making of an award of aggravated damages inevitably risks at least the appearance of a punitive aspect unless the court is careful; thus, in *Appleton* Dyson J. emphasised the compensatory function of aggravated damages.[31] However, in *Thompson v. Commissioner of Police of the Metropolis*[32] the Court of Appeal noted that there could be a penal element in the award of aggravated damages, but they were primarily compensatory; however the court went on to emphasis the compensatory nature of aggravated damages. It is suggested that the relevance of the "exceptional conduct" test is that it is the cause of the increased injury to the claimant's feelings. As it has been helpfully expressed by the Law Commission: "if the loss that the plaintiff has actually suffered is exacerbated or aggravated by the conduct of the defendant, he or she should be compensated for it."[33]

5–013   A further factor conducive to confusion is that aggravated damages may be awarded as well as damages for mental distress. On the face of it, if damages for mental distress are compensatory, the award of aggravated damages risks being seen as essentially punitive. That the two can co-exist however can be seen from *Thompson v. Commissioner of Police of the Metropolis*,[34] where is was said that aggravated damages

> "can be awarded where there are aggravating features about the case which would result in the plaintiff not receiving sufficient compensation for the injury suffered if the award was restricted to a basic award ... the total figures for basic and aggravated damages should not exceed what [the jury] consider is fair compensation for the injury which the plaintiff has suffered."[35]

Again, the "exceptional conduct" is the factor which augments the injury to feelings and hence increases the overall award, but again clear language must be used by the court.

5–014   Aggravated damages have been awarded for a number of torts, including trespass to the person,[36] trespass to land,[37] false imprisonment,[38] malicious

---

[30] See Law Com. No. 247 "Aggravaged, Exemplary and Restitutionary Damages" at 2.3 n. 11 (1997).
[31] [1996] P.I.Q.R. P1 at P7.
[32] [1998] Q.B. 498 at 512.
[33] Law Com. No. 247 (1997) at 2.19.
[34] [1998] Q.B. 498.
[35] *ibid.* at 516. See also *Appleton v. Garrett* above n. 28; *Prison Service v. Johnson* [1997] I.C.R. 275.
[36] *Appleton v. Garrett* [1996] P.I.Q.R. P1; *W. v. Meah* [1986] 1 All E.R. 935.
[37] *Drane v. Evangelou* [1978] 1 W.L.R. 455; *Merest v. Harvey* (1814) 5 Taunt. 442.
[38] *Thompson v. Commissioner of Police of the Metropolis* [1998] Q.B. 498.

prosecution,[39] defamation,[40] deceit,[41] discrimination,[42] intimidation,[43] unlawful interference with business[44] and nuisance.[45] However, in *Kralj v. McGrath*[46] it was held that aggravated damages could not be recovered in a claim for negligence.[47] This was a case of medical negligence where the expert evidence, accepted by the judge, described the doctor's conduct as "horrific" and "completely unacceptable". Woolf J. considered it to be entirely inappropriate to award aggravated damages in a case of negligence, since the object of the award of damages in such a case was to compensate the claimant for the loss she had suffered, rather than "treating these damages as being a matter which reflects the degree of negligence or breach of duty of the defendant."[48] The Court of Appeal in *A. B. v. South West Water Services*[49] endorsed this view, holding, in a case concerning an allegation of a negligently-committed public nuisance, that the anger and indignation experienced by the claimants were not a proper subject of compensation, being neither pain nor suffering. Clearly though, in the case of torts such as defamation and malicious prosecution, where anger and indignation are recognised as recoverable heads of loss, aggravated damages would be recoverable. As the Law Commission points out,[50] given that damages for mental distress are recoverable in cases of negligently-inflicted personal injury, in the form of the award of general damages for pain and suffering, it is not easy to understand why aggravated damages should not be recoverable in negligence where it is mental distress of a recoverable kind rather than anger or indignation that is experienced by the claimant. It may be that the court in *A. B.* was doing no more than emphasising the irrecoverability of aggravated damages in negligence for anger and indignation rather than endorsing Woolf J.'s broader approach in *Kralj*;[51] certainly the matter is ripe for reconsideration by the Court of Appeal, given the Law Commission's persuasive reasoning.

It is established that conduct subsequent to the tort may justify an award **5–015** of aggravated damages. In cases of defamation matters such as failure to apologise, repetition of the libel and pleading justification with no prospect of success will all risk an increase in the award.[52] Likewise, further victimising the claimant after discriminatory behaviour[53] may lead to aggravated

---

[39] *ibid.*
[40] *Broome v. Cassell & Co* [1972] A.C. 1027; *A.B. v. Southwest Water Services Ltd* [1993] Q.B. 507 at 533. And also malicious falsehood: see *Khodaparast v. Shad* [2000] 1 All E.R. 545.
[41] *Mafo v. Adams* [1970] 1 Q.B. 548 at 558; *Archer v. Brown* [1985] Q.B. 401 at 426.
[42] *Prison Service v. Johnson* [1997] I.C.R. 275 (race discrimination); *Duffy v. Eastern Health & Social Services Board* [1992] I.R.L.R. 251.
[43] *Messenger Newspaper Group Ltd v. National Graphical Association* [1984] I.R.L.R. 397.
[44] *ibid.*
[45] *Thompson v. Hill* (1870) L.R. 5 C.P. 564. See Law Com. No. 247 at 2.10 n. 61.
[46] [1986] 1 All E.R. 54.
[47] Nor for breach of contract, which was also pleaded.
[48] [1986] 1 All E.R. 54 at 61.
[49] [1993] Q.B. 507.
[50] Law Com. No. 247 (1997) para 2.36.
[51] Though Stuart-Smith L.J. quoted the broad approach of Woolf J. with approval, and his brethren agreed with his reasoning.
[52] See *Sutcliffe v. Pressdram Ltd* [1991] 1 Q.B. 153 at 184.
[53] See *Duffy v. Eastern Health & Social Services Board* [1992] I.R.L.R. 251.

damages being awarded, and in cases of discrimination,[54] malicious pro-secution[55] and false imprisonment[56] the defendant's conduct during the course of litigation and at trial may have the same effect.

5-016   In *Thompson v. Commissioner of Police of the Metropolis*[57] the Court of Appeal, in the course of setting out guidelines to juries assessing damages in civil actions against the police, included some guidance concerning aggravated damages, some aspects of which have been examined above. It was said that where it was appropriate to award aggravated damages the figure was unlikely to be less than £1,000. It was not thought to be possible to indicate a precise arithmetical relationship between basic damages and aggravated damages, as the circumstances would vary from case to case, but aggravated damages would not usually be as much as twice basic damages, unless perhaps the basic damages were modest.[58] In *Appleton v. Garrett*[59] Dyson J. adopted a mathematical approach, awarding 15 per cent of the award (for the trespass to the person) for pain, suffering and loss of amenity, for aggravated damages, bearing in mind that, broadly speaking, the greater the pain, suffering and loss of amenity the greater the injury to feelings; and that, though this approach was not necessarily accurate the evidence did not enable him to distinguish the degree of actual pain and suffering and loss of amenity experienced.

5-017   The Law Commission in its Consultation Paper[60] favoured the abolition of the "exceptional conduct" requirement, with aggravated damages being assimilated within a compensatory framework, but in its 1997 Report[61] no longer held this view, fearing that the availability of mental distress damages would be limited if "aggravated damages" were abolished. The losses compensated by an award of aggravated damages might not be compensated under another already-recognised head of damages. The Commission now favours legislation emphasising the compensatory, non-punitive nature of aggravated damages, employing wherever possible the label "damages for mental distress" rather than "aggravated damages" thus enabling a more coherent perception, and thus development, of the law on damages for mental distress. Such an approach is to be commended, given that as recently as 1998 the Court of Appeal stated "there can be a penal element in the award of aggravated damages".[62] It can thus not be assumed that the judiciary will always recall the need for aggravated damages to be regarded as exclusively, rather than primarily, compensatory.

5-018   Before proceeding to a detailed examination of the three categories identified by Lord Devlin in *Rookes v. Barnard* it is necessary to bear in mind that, even if the case in question falls within one of these categories, it does not necessarily follow that exemplary damages will be awarded. The award

---

[54] See *Duffy v. Eastern Health & Social Services Board* [1992] I.R.L.R. 251..
[55] *Thompson v. Commissioner of Police of the Metropolis* [1998] Q.B. 498.
[56] *ibid.*
[57] *ibid.*
[58] *ibid.* at 516. See also *W. v. Meah* [1986] 1 All E.R. 935 at 942.
[59] [1996] P.I.Q.R. P1 at P7.
[60] Consultation Paper No. 132 (1993).
[61] Law Com. No. 247 (1997).
[62] *Thompson v. Commissioner of Police of the Metropolis* [1998] Q.B. 498 at 512.

of exemplary damages is essentially discretionary. The various restrictions will be examined below, following an analysis of the three categories.

(1) Oppressive, arbitrary or unconstitutional action by the servants of the government

The origins of this category (indeed, it seems, the origins of exemplary   5–019
damages also) lie in the eighteenth century, in cases arising out of the publication of the "North Briton". Thus, in *Wilkes v. Wood*[63] where the house in which it was alleged the offending publication was printed was searched under an illegal general warrant, £1,000 was awarded by the jury, which was directed by Pratt C.J. that damages served not only to satisfy the injured person, but also to punish the guilty. Lord Devlin saw the value of this category in the reinforcement of the principle that the use of the power of servants of the government must always be subordinate to their duty of service. In *Broome v. Cassell*[64] Lord Diplock doubted the value of awarding exemplary damages in such cases, in view of the development of prerogative writs and declarations in recent years, but since his opinion was delivered there has been a growth in the use of exemplary damages in this category, largely in actions against the police in cases of assault, false imprisonment and malicious prosecution. In *Holden v. Chief Constable of Lancashire*[65] it was held, in a case where there had been no oppressive behaviour on the part of the police, that nevertheless wrongful arrest could give rise to an award of exemplary damages, though the absence of oppression in the arrest might well be a factor for the jury to bear in mind.[66] It would seem therefore that conduct which is no more than unconstitutional may give rise to an award under this head, though it may be that some improper use of constitutional or executive power must have occurred.[67] The essence of this category, as was explained by Sir Thomas Bingham M.R. in *A.B. v. South West Water Services Ltd*,[68] is "gross misuse of power, involving tortious conduct, by agents of government".

The question of who is an agent of government for the purposes of this   5–020
category, has tended to be answered quite broadly. Lord Reid in *Broome v. Cassell*[69] considered that it covered all those exercising functions of a governmental character, by common law or statute. It has been held to extend to solicitors executing an *Anton Piller*[70] order, since in so doing they

---

[63] (1763) Lofft. 1. See also *Huckle v. Money* (1763) 2 Wils. 205, *Benson v. Frederick* (1766) Burr. 185.
[64] [1972] A.C. 1027.
[65] [1987] Q.B. 380. See also *White v. Metropolitan Police Commissioner* [1982] C.L.Y. 898; *The Times* April 24, 1982; *Smith v. Commissioner for Metropolitan Police* [1982] C.L.Y. 899. More recently, see *Treadaway v. Chief Constable of the West Midlands* [1994] C.L.Y. 1468 (£40,000 awarded for conduct amounting to torture).
[66] The idea that negligent conduct could give rise to an award of exemplary damages was disapproved in *Barbara v. Home Office* (1984) 134 N.L.J. 888. Cf. *Coloca v. B.P. Australia Ltd* [1992] 2 V.R. 441.
[67] *Holden v. Chief Constable of Lancashire supra* n. 65 at 388.
[68] [1993] Q.B. 507 at 529.
[69] [1972] A.C. 1027 at 1088.
[70] *Columbia Pictures Inc. v. Robinson* [1987] Ch. 38 at 87.

act as officers of the court, and to a local authority when considering a job application.[71] However in *A.B. v. South West Water Services Ltd*[72] it was held that the defendant, a nationalised body set up under statute for the commercial purpose of supplying water (and subsequently privatised), did not comprise a servant of the government, as it was not exercising executive power derived from government, and it did not follow that it was exercising such power simply because it was an emanation of the state for the purpose of direct enforcement of E.C. Directives. Nor was the question of the defendant's susceptibility to judicial review a relevant factor.

5–021   In *Rookes v. Barnard* Lord Reid made it clear that the essence of this category is not the imbalance of power *per se* between the parties, but the fact and the nature of government power, and in particular the duty of service implicit in that power. Oppressive action by private corporations or individuals could not, therefore, give rise to an award of exemplary damages.

5–022   This view has been powerfully criticised,[73] on the basis that the status of the defendants was not central to the decisions in *Wilkes*, *Huckle* and *Benson*, and that oppressive conduct should be the key element rather than status, especially in an era of increasing privatisation of publicly owned enterprises. It should be borne in mind that Lord Devlin in *Rookes* was concerned to restrict the range of situations in which exemplary damages were to be awarded, and, on the whole, the courts since then have exhibited a preference for such a restrictive view, (such that it is very unlikely that in the future English law will focus on the conduct rather than the status of the defendant). Somewhat paradoxically, however, the principles of vicarious liability[74] make it likely that in many cases the public as a whole rather than the individual government servant will bear the cost of the misconduct.

(2) Cases in which the defendant's conduct has been calculated by him to make a profit for himself which may well exceed the compensation payable to the claimant

5–023   Lord Devlin saw this category as extending beyond moneymaking in the strict sense to cases where the defendant was seeking to gain some object at the expense of the claimant, and where, it was necessary to teach a wrongdoer that tort does not pay. *Broome v. Cassell*[75] provides a clear example of this category. The defendants published a book which blamed the claimant in part for a war-time disaster. The evidence was that the defendants had known from a very early stage that the claimant objected to various passages in the book and threatened a libel action, but the

---

[71] *Bradford City Metropolitan Council v. Arora* [1991] 2 Q.B. 507. The Court of Appeal rejected the suggestion that the council was acting in a private capacity, but suggested that the carrying out of some duty by a junior officer of a council might not necessarily be properly regarded as the exercise of a public function.

[72] [1993] Q.B. 507.

[73] See the judgment of Taylor J. in *Uren v. John Fairfax & Sons Pty. Ltd* (1966) 117 C.L.R. 118. See also the remarks of Viscount Dilhorne in *Broome v. Cassell* [1972] A.C. 1027 at 1108.

[74] See *infra* paras. 5–041 *et seq.*

[75] [1972] A.C. 1027.

defendants proceeded to publication with only a few minor amendments to the relevant passages. The claimant was awarded £15,000 compensatory damages and £25,000 exemplary damages.

The award of exemplary damages in cases falling within this category is not simply designed to reflect the extent to which the defendant was unjustly enriched,[76] but it must be shown that he went ahead, knowing his conduct was wrong, or recklessly indifferent as to whether it was wrong, because the likelihood of material benefit outweighed the risk of material detriment.[77] In *John v. Mirror Group Newspaper Ltd*,[78] a defamation case, it was said that the jury must be satisfied that the publisher had no genuine belief in the truth of what he published, and must have acted in the hope or expectation of material gain. He must have believed that he would be better off financially if he violated the claimant's right than if he did not; mere publication of a newspaper for profit not being enough. The fact that the conduct in question took place in a business context would not, *per se*, bring a case within this category however.[79] Other than cases of defamation, cases in this category have not infrequently concerned landlords wrongfully evicting tenants with a view to making a more profitable use of the property.[80] In *Ramdath v. Daley*[81] it was held that an award of exemplary damages could not be made against a person who was managing premises on behalf of a landlord, on the basis that he did not have a sufficient interest in the matter.

It would seem that exemplary damages can also be awarded under this head for wrongful interference with the claimant's business. Thus, in *Messenger Newspapers Group Ltd v. National Graphical Association*[82] an award of exemplary damages was made against the defendant trade union for unlawful interference with the claimants' business, intimidation and public and private nuisance. This decision has been convincingly criticised by Burrows[83] on the basis that it is difficult to see what material gain the defendants sought to obtain from their conduct. A more satisfactory example can be seen in *Bell v. Midland Railway Company*,[84] one of the cases cited by Lord Devlin in describing this category in *Rookes v. Barnard*. In *Bell* the defendant wrongfully prevented trains running to a wharf occupied by the claimant, with the result that his tenants ceased to use his wharf, and took their business to the defendant's wharf. Wilkes J. considered it to be an obvious case for an award of exemplary damages, since:

"The defendants have committed a grievous wrong with a high hand and in plain violation of an act of parliament; and persisted in it for

5–024

---

[76] Se [1972] A.C. 1027 at 1130, per Lord Diplock. The problem of assessment of exemplary damages is considered *infra* paras. 5–037 *et seq*. See also McGregor *op. cit.* at para 422.
[77] [1972 A.C. 1027 at 1079, per Lord Hailsham L.C.
[78] [1997] Q.B. 586.
[79] *ibid*.
[80] See *e.g. Drane v. Evangelou* [1978] 2 All E.R. 437; *Guppys (Bridgport) Ltd v. Brookling and James* (1983) 269 E.G. 846.
[81] [1993] 20 E.G. 123.
[82] [1984] I.R.L.R. 397. See also earlier discussion at para. 5–014.
[83] *op. cit.* p. 277.
[84] (1861) 10 C.B. (N. S.) 287. Nuisance was also a significant basis of the claim.

the purpose of destroying the plaintiff's business and securing gain to themselves."[85]

5-025   An award of exemplary damages under this head appears to have a restitutionary aspect. As has been persuasively pointed out by the Law Commission, however,[86] it would be erroneous to equate the two forms of damages, since in particular (a) this category of exemplary damages focuses on the improper motive of the defendant, whereas restitutionary damages are awarded on the basis that the defendant has actually made a profit.[87] Hence an award of exemplary damages may, though it is perhaps unlikely, be awarded where the profit contemplated is not actually achieved, whereas there must be a profit for restitutionary damages to be awarded; (b) the latter are geared to the profit, whereas exemplary damages may exceed the profit (though again this may be more theoretical than practical).

(3) Cases where exemplary damages are expressly authorised by statute

5-026   In *Rookes v. Barnard* Lord Devlin cited section 13(2) of the Reserve and Auxiliary Forces (Protection of Civil Interests) Act 1951, which makes provision for an award of exemplary damages in actions for damages for conversion in respect of goods falling within the statute. This may well however be an example of the older, broader usage of the term "exemplary damages" since, as Lord Kilbrandon pointed out in *Broome v. Cassell*, section 13(2) applies to Scotland, by virtue of section 13(6), and Scots law does not allow for awards of exemplary damages.

5-027   A stronger example may be section 97(2) of the Copyright, Designs and Patents Act 1988.[88] In *Williams v. Settle*[89] exemplary damages were awarded against a photographer for breach of copyright in photographs of a murder victim. The copyright belonging to the deceased's son-in-law, the photographs having been taken at his wedding. Lord Devlin in *Rookes v. Barnard* left open the question whether the predecessor to section 97(2) authorised an award of exemplary damages. Lord Kilbrandon in *Broome v. Cassell* did not consider the subsection authorised an award of exemplary damages.[90] The wording of the subsection, authorising the award of "such additional damages as the justice of the case may require" having regard to all the circumstances, and in particular the flagrancy of the infringement and any benefits accruing to the defendant as a consequence of the infringement, does not make the matter clear, and it is suggested that as a matter of principle clear

---

[85] (1861) 10 C.B. (N.S.) 287 at 307. In fact the damages awarded by the jury seem to have been compensatory only. See 301 *ibid*.
[86] Law Com. No. 247 (1997) paras 4.16–4.19.
[87] See *infra* paras. 5–057 *et seq*.
[88] Previously s. 17(3) of the Copyright Act 1956. See also s. 22(3) of the Act (design right) and s. 191 J. of the COPA 1988 Act (performer's property rights).
[89] [1960] 2 All E.R. 806.
[90] See also *Beloff v. Pressdram Ltd* [1973] 1 All E.R. 241 at 265–266 per Ungored-Thomas J.

words must be used in a statute to authorise the infliction of an exemplary award.[91]

(4) Further restrictions on the award of exemplary damages

(a) The cause of action test

Though the matter was not canvassed in *Rookes v. Barnard* a number   5–028
of members of the House of Lords in *Broome v. Cassell* considered that, since Lord Devlin in *Rookes* intended to restrict the availability of exemplary damages, he did not intend in the words of Lord Diplock, "to extend the power to award exemplary ... damages to particular torts for which they had not previously been awarded, such as negligence and deceit."[92] These dicta found the support of the Court of Appeal in *A.B. v. South West Water Services Ltd*,[93] where it was held, *inter alia*, that the defendant water authority, which was held (on the assumed facts) liable to the claimants in negligence and public nuisance, was not liable to an award of exemplary damages, since such damages had not been awarded for either of those torts prior to 1964. Cases such as *Bradford City Metropolitan Council v. Arora*,[94] where exemplary damages were awarded for race and sex discrimination, had proceeded on the assumption that exemplary damages could be awarded for a tort for which such an award had not been made prior to 1964, and were not binding.

It follows that, in addition to the limitations inherent in Lord Devlin's   5–029
three categories, it is necessary to look to the tort in question to see if exemplary damages had been awarded in connection with its commission before *Rookes v. Barnard* was decided. It is suggested that, though this may appear somewhat arbitrary, it is consistent with the general tenor of *Rookes v. Barnard* in emphasising the highly exceptional nature of exemplary damages. As a consequence, it is possible to list the torts in connection with which, subject to the three categories, exemplary damages can be awarded.

These are: defamation; trespass (to land, goods or the person),   5–030
private nuisance[95] and intimidation and unlawful interference with business.[96] Malicious prosecution has been said to be a tort for which

---

[91] Uncertainty over the meaning of the phrase "additional damages" can be seen from the contrasting decisions in *Cala Homes (South) Ltd v. McAlpine Homes (East) Ltd (No. 2)* [1996] F.S.R. 36 (held to be akin to exemplary damages) and *Redrow Homes Ltd v. Bett Brothers plc* [1997] S.L.T. 1125 (held to be aggravated damages).

[92] [1972] A.C. 1027 at 1131. See also *ibid.* at 1076 (per Hailsham L.C.) at 1114A (per Lord Wilberforce).

[93] [1993] Q.B. 507. See also *Catnic Components Ltd v. Hill & Smith Ltd* [1983] F.S.R. 512, where it was held that exemplary damages could not be awarded for infringement of a patent since that had not been done in any pre-*Rookes v. Barnard* case.

[94] [1991] 2 Q.B.507. See also *Alexander v. Home Office* [1988] 2 All E.R. 118.

[95] In *A.B. v. South West Water Services Ltd* the Court of Appeal seem to have thought that *Bell v. Midlands Railway Co.* (1861) 10 C.B. (N. S.) 287, *supra* n. 84 could be regarded as a case of nuisance.

[96] See *Bell v. Midland Railway Co. supra* n. 84. Whether inducing breach of contract and conspiracy also pass the cause of action test depends upon whether the fact that damages have been held to be at large in such cases (see *G.W.K. Ltd v. Dunlop Rubber Co. Ltd*

exemplary damages may be awarded[97] and this view is sufficiently entrenched that a contrary view is now unlikely to be taken, though such authorities as exist are, to say the least, equivocal.[98]

5-031   As a corollary, it is clear that exemplary damages are not available in cases of discrimination,[99] negligence, deceit,[1] and infringement of intellectual property rights (except where authorised by statute). *A.B. v. South West Water Services Ltd* therefore represents a significant further restriction on the availability of exemplary damages.[1A]

(b) Defendant punished by the criminal law for the same conduct

5-032   In *A.B.* the defendants had already been convicted and fined. The court saw a serious risk of injustice if an award of exemplary damages were also to be made in such a case. In *Archer v. Brown*[2] Peter Pain J. considered that an award in such circumstances would offend the basic principle that a man should not be punished twice for the same offence. However, it has been argued[3] that where the criminal penalty is regarded as inadequate, or if the case falls within Lord Devlin's first category, it should not be regarded as axiomatic that previous punishment by the criminal law precludes an award of exemplary damages.

(c) The conduct of the claimant

5-033   In *Holden v. Chief Constable of Lancashire*[4] Purchas L.J. emphasised the discretionary nature of exemplary damages, which included the inducement by the claimant of the commission of the tort. In *O'Connor v. Hewitson*[5] the provocative conduct of the claimant resulted in no award being made.

(d) Absence of aggravating circumstances

5-034   In *Holden* Purchas L.J. also suggested that the absence of aggravating circumstances such as cruelty in the mode of arrest, insolence, assault or

---

(1926) 42 T.L.R. 376 on the former, and *Quinn v. Leatham* [1901] A.C. 495 on the latter) is regarded as sufficient. It is suggested that it is not, though it emphasises starkly the random effect of the Court of Appeal's decision in *A.B.*

[97] See *White v. Metropolitan Police Commissioner, The Times*, April 24, 1982; *Bishop v. Metropolitan Police Commissioner, The Times*, December 5, 1989, and most recently, *Thompson v. Commissioner of Police of the Metropolis* [1998] Q.B. 498.

[98] *Leith v. Pope* (1779) 22 Wm. Bl. 1327; *Chamber v. Robinson* (1726) 2 Str. 691. See Law Com. Consultation Paper No. 132 (1993) p. 69 n. 265.

[99] See *e.g. Deane v. Ealing London Borough Council* [1993] I.C.R. 329.

[1] *Cf. Archer v. Brown* [1985] Q.B. 401, where it was considered that an award could be made (though on the facts of the case no award was made).

[1A] See *Kuddus v. Chief Constable of Leicestershire* [2000] P.I.Q.R. Q187, [2000] W.L. 468, in which, by a majority, the Court of Appeal held that exemplary damages may not be awarded for the tort of malfeasance in public office. Leave has been granted for an appeal to the House of Lords. The dissenting judgement of Auld L.J. is of particular interest. We are grateful to Nicholas George Esq., junior counsel for the appellant, for providing us with a transcript of the judgment.

[2] *supra* n. 1, para. 5-031.

[3] See Law Com. Consultation Paper No. 132 (1993) pp. 79-80.

[4] [1987] 1 Q.B. 380; *supra* n. 65.

[5] [1979] Crim. L.R. 46.

prolonged imprisonment was a matter that the jury could be invited to consider when contemplating an award of exemplary damages. This, like the conduct of the claimant, may lead either to a reduction in the amount awarded[6] or to no award being made.

(e) Adequacy of compensatory award

It was stated by Lord Devlin in *Rookes* that there should only be an   5–035
exemplary award if the compensatory award is inadequate as a punishment, a deterrent and a mark of the jury's disapproval. Whether the award has to reflect all of these features is unclear. Lord Kilbrandon in *Broome* emphasised the deterrence aspect, but generally judges have referred to punishment as the essential element.

(f) The claimant must be the victim of the punishable behaviour

This restriction on the availability of exemplary damages was stated by   5–036
Lord Devlin in *Rookes*. It has perhaps unsurprisingly, not proved to be a contentious issue in the case law. Presumably it is intended to ensure that opprobrious conduct by the defendant which is separate from the conduct *vis à vis* the claimant which gives rise to his claim cannot be the basis of an exemplary award, at least in his favour.

(5) Assessment of exemplary damages

As with any case where the assessment of damages is the province of the   5–037
jury, which is the case for most of the torts for which an exemplary award can be made,[7] much criticism has been levelled at exemplary awards. A degree of control has been provided by section 8 of the Courts and Legal Services Act 1990, which empowers the Court of Appeal to substitute for the award made by a jury such sum as appears to it to be proper. Recently, in *Thompson v. Commissioner of Police of the Metropolis*[8] the Master of the Rolls set out guidelines as to the directions to be given to a jury assessing damages in civil actions against the police. Exemplary damages were unlikely to be less than £5,000, otherwise the conduct probably did not justify an award. The conduct would have to be particularly deserving of condemnation for an award of £25,000 to be made, and an award of £50,000 should be regarded as the absolute maximum, involving directly officers of at least the rank of superintendent. An aspect of the guidance provided by the Court of Appeal in *Thompson* is the intention, in providing guideline figures, to establish a relationship between those figures and personal injury awards. Given the prevalence of jury trial in cases where exemplary damages may be awarded, quite apart from the inherent problems of

---

[6] Se *infra* p. 5–037 *et seq.* on quantum in cases of exemplary damages.
[7] s. 69(1) of the Supreme Court Act 1981 provides for a presumption in favour of jury trial in cases of libel, slander, malicious prosecution and false imprisonment.
[8] [1998] Q.B. 498. See [1964] A.C. 1227–8 for an early anticipation of this development.

quantifying a non-compensatory award, any minimising of the unpredict-ability of exemplary awards is a positive step, and this approach may, by analogy, be extended in the future to other cases where exemplary damages can be awarded. It is however somewhat difficult to see why a punitive award should be related to a personal injury award, given the essentially different functions of the two. In cases where the relevant tort also com-prises criminal conduct, a better analogy might be the appropriate level of fine for such an offence. Inevitably, though, a significant element of discre-tion must remain, to reflect the individual circumstances of the case.

5–038　　Certain principles, in addition to the guidelines in *Thompson*, have emerged. Lord Devlin in *Rookes* emphasised the need for restraint in awards, which is surely incontestable, given the exceptional nature of exem-plary damages. He also stressed the significance of the parties' means. It is far from clear, however, how this is to be determined. Unless it is to be done on a very impressionistic basis, it would require a detailed investigation, presumably by way of discovery, which, both in terms of time and expense might be entirely disproportionate to the issues involved.

5–039　　In *Broome v. Cassell* Lord Hailsham L.C. made it clear that an award of exemplary damages in the case of joint defendants should reflect the lowest figure for which each/any of them could be liable.[9] It must follow from this that if one defendant is not liable to an award, exemplary dam-ages can not be awarded at all. Where there are multiple claimants, it was held in *Riches v. News Group Newspapers Ltd*[10] that it is necessary to determine first the total sum the defendant ought to pay by way of exem-plary damages and divide that amongst the claimants. Though the defend-ant might deserve a heavier punishment for infringing a number of persons' rights than one person's only, the total amount of the exemplary award should not be unreasonable and excessive to show disapproval of his con-duct and deter repetition.

5–040　　As a consequence of the enactment of the Human Rights Act 1998, breach of Article 10(1) of the European Convention for the Protection of Human Rights and Fundamental Freedoms is justiciable, which presents especial problems where large jury awards of exemplary damages are made. The exercise of the right of freedom of expression, enshrined in Article 10(1) may be subject, in Article 10(2), to

> "such formalities, conditions restrictions or penalties as are prescribed by law and are necessary in a democratic society . . . for the protection of the reputation or rights of others."

In *Rantzen v. Mirror Group Newspapers Ltd*[11] the Court of Appeal con-sidered: "that the grant of an almost limitless discretion to a jury fails to provide a satisfactory measurement for deciding what is 'necessary in a democratic society' . . ." Justification for these concerns can be seen in *Tol-*

---

[9] At 1063 he also considered that this principle applied generally, and in particular to aggrav-ated damages.
[10] [1986] Q.B. 256.
[11] [1994] Q.B. 670 at 690.

stoy Miloslavsky v. United Kingdom[12] where the European Court of Human Rights held that an award of £1.5 million in compensatory damages, coupled with the lack of adequate judicial safeguards at trial and on appeal against disproportionately large awards at the time comprised a breach of the applicant's rights under Article 10. It may be argued that the power the Court of Appeal now has under section 8(2) of the Courts and Legal Services Act 1990 and R. S. C. Ord. 59 r. 11(4) (re-enacted in 1998 by CPR, Pt. 50) to substitute its own award for that of the jury where it considers the jury's award to be excessive, together with increasing autonomous appellate control over jury awards,[13] has rectified the problem, but the matter will surely fall to be considered domestically in due course once the Human Rights Act is in force.

(6) Vicarious Liability

Prima facie the usual rules on vicarious liability in tort apply to cases where an exemplary award is made: the employer (if there is one) is liable for torts committed by the employee in the course of his employment. Clearly the employee's conduct may take him outside the course of his employment, and thereby render him personally liable, as in *Makanjuola v. Commissioner of Police for the Metropolis*,[14] where a police officer sexually assaulted the claimant, having threatened her that if she did not submit to the assault he would make a report which would result in her deportation. In *Racz v. Home Office*[15] it was held that a prison officer whose unauthorised acts comprised the tort of misfeasance in a public office was acting outside the scope of his authority, and the Home Office was not vicariously liable. Misfeasance in a public office does not, however, appear to be a tort for which exemplary damages were awarded before *Rookes v. Barnard*, but where such conduct, as in *Makanjuola*, amount to such a tort, the defendant may render himself personally liable. The emphasis in *Weldon*[16] on acting in bad faith, and deliberately acting outside the scope of authority may, as has been suggested[17] have the effect of removing the protection of vicarious liability from a number of servants of the government whose actions fall within Lord Devlin's first category.   5–041

The lack of clarity concerning the function of exemplary damages is illustrated by the fact that, as a consequence of section 1(2)(a) of the Law Reform (Miscellaneous Provisions) Act 1934 no claim for exemplary damages can be included in any damages recoverable for the benefit of the estate of a deceased person. If punishment is the purpose of exemplary damages, it can clearly not serve that purpose when, as a consequence of the chance fact that the victim has died, no award can be made. Nor can   5–042

---

[12] (1995) 20 E.H.R.R. 442. The case was heard before *Rantzen* reached the Court of Appeal.
[13] See *Rantzen v. Mirror Group Newspapers Ltd* [1994] Q.B. 670 (defamation); *John v. Mirror Group Newspapers Ltd* [1997] Q.B. 586 (defamation); *Thompson v. Commissioner of Police of the Metropolis* [1998] Q.B. 498 (false imprisonment and assault).
[14] [1989] C.L.Y. 3527.
[15] [1992] T.L.R. 627. See also *Weldon v. Home Office* [1992] 1 A.C. 58 at 164.
[16] *supra* n. 15.
[17] Law Com. Consultation Paper No. 132, para 3-107.

the deterrence function be said to be served, nor can it be said that the court's disapproval of the defendant's conduct is in some way assuaged by the death of the claimant. It would seem that the effect, at least in this instance, is to place emphasis on the retributive function, insofar as that is a justification for a punitive award. It is difficult to avoid the conclusion that it is the absence of a person to compensate that lies behind this exclusion, inconsistent though that is with the idea of a punitive award.

5–043   The standard of proof where exemplary damages are sought is an issue that has tended to be ignored. However, in *Mafo v. Adams*[18] Sachs L.J. stated: "In cases where exemplary damages are being claimed, the court must be careful to see that the case for punishment is as well established as in other penal proceedings." In the absence of anything more weighty than a few dicta, it is likely that the standard of proof required is no more than the balance of probabilities, especially bearing in mind the absence of other protections of the criminal law, such as sentencing by a judge, effective rights of appeal and the protection of the rules of criminal evidence.[19] The potential difficulties for the jury in applying different standards of proof for the compensatory and exemplary aspects of the award should not be underestimated.[20]

(7) The Future of Exemplary Damages

5–044   In 1997 the Law Commission issued its report on "Aggravated Exemplary and Restitutionary Damages",[21] following its earlier Consultation Paper[22] and a supplementary consultation paper, which was issued in 1995. As regards exemplary damages, the law was considered by the Commission to be in need of reform, a view concurred in by most of its consultees. A fundamental issue canvassed was whether exemplary damages should be abolished and if not, what changes to the law required to be made. Before examining the Commission's views on reform, it is worth setting out the arguments identified by the Law Commission, for and against exemplary damages.

(a) Arguments in favour of exemplary damages

5–045   (a)   "There are certain categories of cases in which an award of exemplary damages can serve a useful purpose in vindicating the strength of the law and thus affording a practical justification for admitting into the civil law a principle which ought logically to belong to the criminal."[23]

---

[18] [1970] 1 Q.B. 548 at 556. There are also suggestions in *Riches v. News Group Newspapers Ltd* [1986] Q.B. 256 at 274, 278 and 285, that the standard of proof may be higher then the balance of probabilities.

[19] See Lord Reid's judgment in *Broome v. Cassell op. cit.* at 1087.

[20] See Law Com. Consultation Paper No. 137, para 3.112.

[21] Law Com. No. 247 (1997).

[22] (1993) Consultation Paper No. 132.

[23] Per Lord Devlin in *Rookes v. Barnard op. cit.* at 1226. See also Lord Hailsham L.C. in *Broome v. Cassell op. cit.* at 1077.

However, in *Broome* Lord Reid disagreed with this view, which he did not regard as forming an essential step in Lord Devlin's argument. He regarded exemplary damages as highly anomalous, but as being so firmly embedded in English law that only Parliament could remove them. The kind of case which perhaps best reflects Lord Devlin's point is one falling within his second category, where, in the words of Lord Diplock, it is necessary "to teach a wrong-doer that tort does not pay."[24]

(b) *Exemplary damages are freely available in other common law jurisdictions*[25].   5–046

In Australia the High Court in *Uren v. John Fairfax & Sons Pty. Ltd.*[26] did not accept the restrictions of *Rookes v. Barnard* and preferred a broader view, extending the availability of exemplary damages to cases where the conduct of the defendant displayed "conscious wrongdoing in contumelious disregard of another's rights."[27] Likewise, the Supreme Court of Canada in *Vorvis v. Insurance Corporation of British Columbia*[28] preferred a broader view to *Rookes v. Barnard*, but restricted awards to cases involving conduct deserving of condemnation and punishment and extreme in its nature. In the USA exemplary awards are quite widely available, no doubt in part as a consequence of the fact that there is no category of aggravated damages, though control mechanisms such as capping the potential award and increasing the standard of proof are increasingly being introduced.

(c) "... there is much to be said before one can safely assert that   5–047
the true or basic principle of the law of damages in tort is compensation ... still less that it ought to be, an issue of large social import, or that there is something inappropriate or illogical or anomalous (a question-begging word) in including a punitive element in civil damages, or conversely, that the criminal law, rather than the civil law, is in these cases the better instrument for conveying social disapproval, or for redressing a wrong to the social fabric ..."[29]

This quotation raises fundamental questions about the function of the award of damages in the law of tort and is central to the case for retaining exemplary damages.

(d) The inadequacy of the criminal law and other enforcement mech-   5–048
anisms

Under this heading it is argued that some forms of reprehensible conduct, such as ordinary defamation, nevertheless fall outside the

---

[24] In *Broome* at 1130.
[25] See Law Com. Consultation Paper No. 132, paras 4.1–4.17.
[26] (1966) 117 C.L.R. 118.
[27] Per Knox C.J. in *Whitfield v. De Lauret & Co. Ltd* (1920) 29 C.L.R. 71 at 77.
[28] (1989) 58 D.L.R. (4th) 193 at 208.
[29] Per Lord Wilberforce in *Broome v. Cassell op. cit.* at p. 1114.

ambit of the criminal law, and that criminal law sanctions where they exist are sometimes inadequate or insufficiently employed.

(b) Arguments against exemplary damages

5–049   (a) *Damages in the law of tort are designed to compensate, not to punish*

This argument raises fundamental issues about the function of damages in the law of torts, which historically has not concerned itself exclusively with compensation, as the cases on exemplary damages show, and there is two hundred years of weight behind the argument that retribution, deterrence and condemnation are legitimate functions of the law of tort—in the words of Winderyer J. in *Uren v. John Fairfax & Sons Pty. Ltd*:[30] "the roots of tort and crime in the law of England are greatly intermingled." However, it is suggested that this is at best a slender justification for maintaining an overtly punitive element in the law of tort in the late twentieth century. The procedural and evidential rules developed over many years to protect the person accused of a criminal offence are signally lacking in cases where exemplary damages are at issue,[31] and the determination of the punishment by the jury rather than the judge is a further anomaly. It has been argued however[32] that there are significant differences between the consequences for the defendant of a criminal prosecution and a civil action where exemplary damages may be awarded; the risk of imprisonment and the damaging potential effect on employment prospects being present in the former but lacking in the latter. Though there is some force in this argument, the rules of criminal procedure and evidence are not only applicable in cases where the defendant may be imprisoned, and surely it is the penal nature of the sanction rather than the particular punishment which is the essential element. This objection to exemplary damages remains a strong one, even if legislation corrected such anomalies as the punishment being determined by the jury, and the claimant, rather than the State, being the recipient of the exemplary award.

5–050   (b) If the criminal law and other enforcement mechanisms are inadequate, then arguably they should be reformed and rendered adequate rather than accepting their flaws and creating an exception to the general function of tort damages of compensating the claimant. As has been argued,[33] insofar as the police and landlords are major targets of exemplary damages claims, adequate sanctions already exist or could readily be created to punish their defaults;

---

[30] (1966) 117 C.L.R. 118 at 149.
[31] See the powerful argument of Lord Reid in *Broome v. Cassell* [1972] A.C. 1027 at 1087.
[32] Law Com. Consultation Paper No. 132.
[33] Burrows *op. cit.* p. 284.

and, as can be seen elsewhere,[34] restitutionary remedies exist which are well able to ensure recoupment from a defendant of profits obtained in cases falling under the second category expounded by Lord Devlin.

(c) Though exemplary damages are generally available throughout the common law world, they appear to be unknown to the civil law. Though it would be far-fetched to suggest that European law is likely to require U.K. law to harmonise with other E.U. countries in this regard, there is no doubt that European private law is likely to be increasingly influential on U.K. law, and the argument that abolishing exemplary damages would put U.K. law out of step with other common law jurisdictions is one that is likely to carry diminishing weight.   5–051

The Law Commission ultimately came to the view that the case for retention was stronger than the case for abolition. As regards the fundamental issues of whether exemplary damages confuse the civil and criminal functions of the law, the Commission considered that civil punishment is a different form of punishment from criminal punishment, being enforced by an individual victim of wrongdoing rather than by the state, and not carrying the stigma associated with criminal punishment. This distinction entailed that the objections listed above[35] fell away as necessary objections. The Commission regarded the argument as being finely balanced, but noted that overall over 70 per cent of its consultees favoured the retention of exemplary damages. The Commission also recommended that renaming exemplary damages as "punitive damages" would be clearer and more straightforward.   5–052

Having decided that exemplary damages (as we shall continue to call them) should be retained, the Commission, again reflecting the responses of consultees to the Supplementary Consultation Paper, which set out three alternative reform proposals, favoured expanding the availability of exemplary damages to all torts (and equitable wrongs, but not breaches of contract) committed with, or accompanied or followed by conduct evincing a deliberate and outrageous disregard of the claimant's right. The "cause of action" restriction set out in *A. B. v. South West Water Services Ltd* would therefore be removed, and torts such as negligence would be included, though the nature of the conduct that would give rise to an award of exemplary damages under the Commission's proposals would seem to arise but rarely in a case of negligence.   5–053

The potential breadth of these proposals is mitigated by a variety of restrictions set out by the Law Commission. These include: leaving it to the judge (not the jury—if any) to decide on the availability and quantum of exemplary damages; only permitting an award to be made if the other remedies awarded are inadequate to punish and deter the defendant; allowing exemplary damages to be awarded only exceptionally where the defendant   5–054

---

[34] *infra*. paras. 5–057 *et seq.*
[35] *supra* paras. 5–049 *et seq.*

has been convicted of a criminal offence in respect of the conduct concerning which exemplary damages are claimed; establishing a statutory structuring of the court's assessment of awards by means of overriding principles of "moderation" and "proportionality" and by a non-exhaustive list of factors, such as the defendant's state of mind, the nature and extent of (a) the harm to the claimant that the defendant caused or intended to cause; (b) the benefit which the defendant derived or intended to derive from his wrongdoing; the nature of the right or rights infringed by the defendant, *e.g.* bodily integrity is seen as more important than property rights.

5–055   Other proposals include allowing insurance against the risk of liability to pay exemplary damages as not being contrary to public policy, retaining vicarious liability to pay exemplary damages, amending the Law Reform (Miscellaneous Provisions) Act 1934 so as to allow claims for exemplary damages to survive for the benefit of the estate of a deceased victim, and so as to prevent exemplary damages from being available against a wrongdoer's estate. Sections 97(2) 191J and 229(3) of the Copyright, Designs and Patents Act[36] are recommended to be repealed.

5–056   These are bold proposals, which some may see, despite the various safeguards described above, as extending the ambit of exemplary damages too far. The proposals do however, have the particular merit of placing exemplary damages on a principled basis and removing anomalies, and form an important part of the Law Commission's overall strategy on non-compensatory damages.

4. RESTITUTIONARY DAMAGES[37]

5–057   The principles of restitution based on reversing unjust enrichment go well beyond the range of circumstances where a restitutionary remedy may be available for a tort, and indeed, since unjust enrichment is not restricted to cases where a tort or breach of contract has occurred, but extends to what has been called "autonomous unjust enrichment,"[38] there may be cases where this principle is the basis of a restitutionary claim rather than a claim founded on the tort.[39] In this chapter we are however concerned with the situations where the claimant who is the victim of a tort may be able to recover from the defendant not his own losses but the defendant's gains which arise from the tort. As such the claimant is not seeking compensation for his own loss, though it may be assumed that in choosing the restitutionary rather than the compensatory remedy his aim is to secure at least

---

[36] Discussed *supra* paras. 5–049 *et seq.*
[37] See generally Goff & Jones, "The Law of Restitution" (4th ed., 1993); Burrows, "The Law of Restitution" (1992). Law Com. Consultation Paper No. 132: "Aggravated, Exemplary and Restitutionary Damages" (1993) part VII; Burrows, "Remedies for Tort and Breach of Contract" (2nd ed., 1994) Ch. 6.
[38] See Birks, "An Introduction to the Law of Restitution" (1989) pp. 314–315.
[39] See Chitty on Contracts (27th ed., 1994) at 29–048 for discussion of whether liability only arises where a tort has been committed or whether such cases fall within a broader restitutionary principle.

redress for any losses he may have suffered, though, as we shall see, a claim may in some circumstances be made in restitution even though the claimant can not be shown to have suffered a loss.

The term "waiver of tort" is frequently used to describe the situation 5–058
where the claimant elects a restitutionary remedy rather than a tortious one. Burrows[40] argues that the term is ambiguous as it may be used either to describe the case where the claimant sues on the tort but seeks a restitutionary remedy rather than compensatory damages or the case where he ignores the tort and founds his claim on autonomous unjust enrichment. The Law Commission[41] emphasise however that the distinction would appear to be of no practical importance, the main issue being that of the available remedy, a matter to be discussed in due course.

A number of historical reasons motivated claimants in suing in restitution 5–059
rather than in tort. Thus matters such as differences in limitation periods,[42] and immunity from suit in tort[43] might lead a claimant to prefer, or to be required, if he wanted a remedy, to opt for a restitutionary claim. In addition, a restitutionary claim might be more profitable; for example, in a case of conversion it may be more profitable to claim in restitution for money had and received than in tort.[44]

An important question is that of the nature of the enrichment which can 5–060
be claimed from the defendant. The most straightforward case is that where the defendant's benefit comprises the claimant's property which he has tortiously obtained; thus in *Lamine v. Dorrell*[45] the defendant, pretending to be administrator of an estate, obtained debentures belonging to the claimant and sold them. The claimant was held to be entitled to waive the tort and recover the price for which the debentures were sold in an action for money had and received. This was followed in *Phillips v. Homfray*,[46] where the defendant made unauthorised (and hence trespassory) use of roads and passages under the claimant's land in order to transport coal. The Court of Appeal held that in a case of trespass to land an action for money had and received would only lie where "property, or the proceeds or value of property, belonging to another, have been appropriated . . . and added to his own estate or moneys".[47] Thus no award could be made in respect of

---

[40] *op. cit.* n. 1 p. 289. See also Birks *op. cit.* n. 2 at 315–6. Both authors refer also to a third possible meaning of the phrase: the principle of agency law whereby the victim of a tort can choose to forgo his right to sue for the tort by treating the tortfeasor, assuming he purported to act in the capacity of the claimant's agent, as in fact being authorised so to act, and then employing the standard remedies available against an agent to recover the profit made: see *Verschures Creameries Ltd v. Hull and Netherlands SS Co. Ltd* [1921] 2 K.B. 608.

[41] *supra* n. 1 at 7.11.

[42] s. 113 of the Law of Reform (Miscellaneous Provisions) Act 1934 provided for a six-month limitation period for "tort actions" against a wrongdoer's personal representatives. This could be circumvented by a restitutionary claim: see *Chesworth v. Farrar* [1967] 1 Q.B. 407. It seems unlikely that this has survived the Proceedings Against Estates Act 1970.

[43] *e.g.* the immunity of the Crown prior to the Crown Proceedings Act 1947 (Chitty *op. cit.* para 29-048 n. 83).

[44] See *Bavins & Sims v. London and South Western Bank Ltd* [1900] 1 Q.B. 270.

[45] (1705) 2 Ld. Ray. 1216. See also *United Australia Ltd v. Barclays Bank Ltd* [1941] A.C. 1.

[46] (1883) 24 Ch. D. 439.

[47] *ibid.* at 454.

the expenses saved by the defendant in the use he made of the claimant's land. Baggallay L.J. dissented, arguing:

> "I cannot appreciate the reasons upon which it is insisted that although executors are bound to account for any accretions to the property of their testator[48] derived directly from his wrongful act, they are not liable for the amount or value of any other benefit which may be derived by his estate from or by reason of such wrongful act".[49]

This view has found powerful support,[50] the majority being regarded as having adopted an unduly narrow approach to the notion of "benefit", though the decision has never been judicially contradicted,[51] and it can at least be said to be clearly established that an action for money had and received will lie and the tort may be waived where the defendant has converted the claimant's property[52] or trespassed on his land, *e.g.* to mine coal[53] reversing the benefit comprised by the claimant's property and its proceeds. A negative benefit will not suffice.

5–061   However, the narrow interpretation by the majority in *Phillips* has to an extent been superseded by the award in a number of cases of tortious damages which have a restitutionary rather than a compensatory object. An early illustration of this can be seen in the decision of the Court of Appeal in *Whitwham v. Westminster Brymbo Coal and Coke Co*,[54] where the defendant trespassed on the claimant's land by tipping refuse from its colliery on to part of the land. Chitty J. at first instance[55] held that, as to that part of the land which had been used for tipping, the defendant must pay on the footing of the value of the land to it for tipping purposes; as regards the rest of the land it had to pay the diminished value of the land to the claimant. The former part of the award, based on what has been conveniently described by Nicholls L.J. in *Stoke on Trent City Council v. W. J Wass Ltd*[56] as "the user principle", can be traced back to the wayleave cases,[57] where the defendant trespassed by carrying coals on an underground way through the claimant's mine. The value of the claimant's land was not diminished by the trespass, but he was awarded damages equivalent to what he would have received if he had been paid for a wayleave. Lindley L.J in *Whitham*[58] stated the principle thus: ". . . if one person has

---

[48] It seems clear that the principle in *Phillips* is not restricted to actions against an executor, but applies generally, see especially *ibid*. at 460–1.
[49] *ibid*. at 471.
[50] See *e.g.* Law Com. *op. cit.* n. 1 para 7.9; Burrows (Damages) p. 292; Goff and Jones *ibid*. n. 1 pp. 717–720.
[51] Indeed, it has been applied, as, *e.g.* in *Att.-G. v. De Keyser's Royal Hotel* [1920] A.C. 508 at 533; *Morris v. Tarrant* [1971] 2 Q.B. 143 at 162.
[52] See *e.g. Chesworth v. Farrar* [1967] 1 Q.B. 407. See also *Oughton v. Seppings* (1830) 1 B. & Ad. 241.
[53] See *e.g. Powell v. Rees* (1837) 7 Ad. & E. 1 426.
[54] [1896] 2 Ch. 538.
[55] [1896] 1 Ch. 894.
[56] [1988] 3 All E.R. 394 at 402. See *infra* para. 5–066 for discussion of this case.
[57] See *e.g. Martin v. Porter* (1839) 5 M. & W. 351; *Jegon v. Vivian* (1871) L.R. 6 Ch. app. 742.
[58] [1896] 2 Ch. 538 at 541–2.

without leave of another been using that other's land for his own purposes, he ought to pay for such uses."

Lord Denning applied this reasoning in *Penarth Dock Engineering Co Ltd v. Pounds*[59] where the defendant committed trespass to the claimant's dock by failing to remove its pontoon. There was no question of the claimant being deprived of making a gain by letting out the dock to anyone else during the period in question, nor could it be said to have suffered a loss by not being paid the fee it would have charged the defendant for legitimate use of the dock; as it had no wish to allow the defendant to use the dock, legitimately or otherwise. Lord Denning assessed damages on the basis of the benefit the defendant had obtained by having the use of the dock, the award being based on what the defendant would have had to pay to rent an equivalent alternative dock.   5–062

The same approach was utilized by the Court of Appeal subsequently in *Swordheath Properties Ltd v. Tabet*[60] where tenants stayed on as trespassers in residential premises. The damages were calculated by reference to the ordinary letting value of the premises, albeit that there was no evidence that the claimant could or would have let the premises to someone else. Of special interest is *Ministry of Defence v. Ashman*[61] where a tenant wrongfully ignored a notice to quit her accommodation. It was said by the Court of Appeal that where a person is entitled to possession of land they can claim damages against the person occupying without consent, either on the basis of the loss suffered by them as a consequence of the trespass or on the basis of the value of the benefit received by the occupier. Hoffman L.J. clearly described the latter option as being a restitutionary remedy. Some further support for this approach may be derived from *Bracewell v. Appleby*[62] where the claimants sought an injunction to prevent the defendant from trespassing on their private road for the purpose of reaching his newly-built house. An injunction was refused, but damages in lieu were awarded. These were assessed on the basis that the claimant would have been willing to accept a fair sum for loss of amenity and increased use of the private road. It is arguable that the assessment of damages supports a restitutionary analysis, since the judge took account of the notional profit made by the defendant (£5,000) in deciding that he would have been prepared to pay £2,000 to obtain his right of way, and that was therefore the measure of damages awarded.   5–063

It may be argued therefore that in cases of trespass to land restitutionary damages may be awarded, though, as Hoffman L.J. stressed in *Ashman*,[63] the claimant must choose between a compensatory and a restitutionary award. Though the Court of Appeal in *Swordheath* did not expressly describe the basis of the award in that case as restitutionary, it is suggested that there is force in the argument[64] that the award of a reasonable letting   5–064

---

[59] [1963] 1 Lloyd's Rep. 359. He was sitting as a single judge of the Queen's Bench Division.
[60] [1979] 1 W.L.R. 285.
[61] (1993) 25 H.L.R. 513. See also *Ministry of Defence v. Thompson* (1993) 25 H.L.R. 552. See Cooke (1994) 110 L.Q.R. 420.
[62] [1975] Ch. 408.
[63] (1993) 25 H.L.R. 513 at 519.
[64] Chitty on Contracts (27th ed., 1994) at para 29-050.

rate can only realistically be regarded as compensatory if it is clear that the owner would have been willing to charge a fee, though it must be accepted that an award so based is capable of being regarded either as the saving of an expense for the defendant in not having to hire alternative property of that character (restitutionary) or as representing the rent the claimant has been deprived of the opportunity of charging (compensatory). The Court of Appeal in *Stoke on Trent City Council*[65] seems to have preferred the latter view, in contrast to its later decision in *Ashman*, and the matter may need to be resolved by the House of Lords.

5–065   As regards wrongful interference with goods, Denning L.J. (as he then was) in *Strand Electric Engineering Co Ltd v. Brisford Entertainments Ltd*[66] again nailed his colours firmly to the restitutionary mast. The defendant wrongfully detained portable electric switchboards owned by the claimant, which it usually hired out in the course of its business. Denning L.J. agreed with his brethren that the claimant was entitled to recover the full market rate of hire for the switchboards during the period of their wrongful detention. He said:[67]

> "The claim for a hiring charge is therefore not based on the loss to the plaintiffs but on the fact that the defendant has used the goods for his own purposes. It is an action against him because he has had the benefit of the goods. It resembles therefore, an action for restitution, rather than an action of tort."

Somervell and Romer L.JJ. however preferred a compensatory analysis, bearing in mind that the equipment was profit-earning property, which the claimant usually hired out in the course of its business, and a sum representing the reasonable hire of the goods during the period of wrongful detention represented the loss suffered by the claimant.[68]

5–066   In nuisance however the situation is less encouraging for devotees of the restitutionary approach. In *Stoke-on-Trent City Council v. W & J Wass*[69] the defendant operated a market unlawfully, in that it was closer to the claimant's statutory market than the law permitted. Nourse L.J. was of the opinion that the levying of an unlawful rival market comprised a nuisance.[70] The judge awarded damages on the basis that the claimant, though it had not suffered any loss, was entitled to an award on the basis that it could have demanded a licence fee based on profits from the defendant's market. Again, such an approach may be explained on either a compensatory basis (since the claimant might have granted such a licence)[71] or a restitutionary basis (relieving the defendant of its profit).

---

[65] *supra* n. 56. See *infra* para. 5–066.
[66] [1952] 2 Q.B. 246.
[67] *ibid.*
[68] See also *Hillesden Securities v. Ryjak Ltd and another* [1983] 1 W.L.R. 959.
[69] [1988] 3 All E.R. 394. See also *Carr-Saunders v. Dick McNeil Associates Ltd* [1986] 2 All E.R. 888 where, in a case of nuisance, damages in lieu of an injunction were awarded, it would appear, on a compensatory basis, there being no evidence of profit to the defendant, though Millett J. (*ibid.* at 896) indicated his willingness to take account of profits. See however Jackman (1989) 48 C.L.J. 302 at 305–6.
[70] *ibid.* at 397.
[71] On the facts this seems unlikely however.

However, the Court of Appeal was not prepared to award more than   5–067
nominal damages, distinguishing decisions such as *Penarth* and *Strand
Electric* on the basis that an unlawful use of the claimant's right to hold
his own market did not deprive him of the opportunity to hold one himself,
whereas in the trespass cases the defendant's use of the claimant's land
deprived him of any such opportunity. This distinction has been criticised
as "unconvincing",[72] and the approach of the court essentially embraces an
exclusively compensatory approach; Nourse L.J. concluding:[73]

> "It is possible that the English law of tort, more especially of the so-
> called 'proprietary torts', will in due course make a more deliberate
> move towards recovery based not on loss suffered by the plaintiff but
> on the unjust enrichment of the defendant: see Goff and Jones, *The
> Law of Restitution* (3rd ed., 1986, pages 612–614). But I do not think
> that process can begin in this case and I doubt whether it can begin at
> all at this level of decision."

This approach contrasts markedly with that of the Court of Appeal sub-   5–068
sequently in *Ministry of Defence v. Ashman*,[74] and this contrast in judicial
attitudes raises interesting questions as to the basis (if any) of the restitutionary aspect of tort damages, which has been considered by the Law
Commission[75] recently and is discussed by way of conclusion below.[76]

A restitutionary approach can also be seen in other proprietary torts, *i.e.*   5–069
in the intellectual property context, both in statutory and common law
torts. Here the remedy is by way of an account of profits, reflecting the
equitable roots of these torts. Thus, an account of profits may be ordered
in cases of passing off[77] infringement of patents,[78] infringement of design
rights,[79] infringement of copyright,[80] infringement of trademarks[81] and
infringement of performers' property rights.[82] In such cases the defendant
will be required to draw up an account of the net profits he has acquired
as a consequence of his tortious conduct, and pay that amount to the claimant. It should be borne in mind that, given the equitable nature of this form
of relief, the conduct of the claimant may be a relevant factor, and such
equitable defences as acquiescence may bar what would otherwise be a
successful claim for an account. In addition the state of mind of the defendant may be of relevance in determining whether or not he is liable to an
account. Thus, in a case of infringement of trademark, the defendant must

---

[72] Burrows, *The Law of Restitution*, (1993) p. 392.
[73] [1988] 3 All E.R. 394 at 402.
[74] *supra* para. 5–063.
[75] Law Com. No. 247, "Aggravated, Exemplary and Restitutionary Damages" (1997).
[76] *infra* paras. 5–073 *et seq.*
[77] See *e.g. Lever v. Goodwin* (1887) 36 L.N. Ch. d. 1; *My Kinda Town Ltd v. Soll and Grunts
    Investments* [1982] F.S.R. 147 (reversed on liability: [1983] R.P.C. 407).
[78] Patents Act 1977, s. 61(1)(d); *Siddell v. Vickers* (1892) 9 R.P.C. 152.
[79] Copyright, Designs and Patents Act 1988, s. 229(2).
[80] Copyright, Designs and Patents Act 1988, s. 96(2).
[81] *Edelsten v. Edelsten* (1863) 1 De G.J. & s. 185, *Slazenger & Sons v. Spalding & Bros*
    [1910] 1 Ch. 257.
[82] Copyright, Designs and Patents Act 1988, s. 229(2).

have known of the claimant's trademark for an account to be ordered,[83] and in passing off cases it seems that the defendant's innocence may limit the award of an account to the period after which he became aware of the true facts.[84] Strict liability will however apply to cases of infringement of copyright,[85] primary infringement of design right[86] and infringement of performer's property rights[87] where an account is ordered,[88] whereas in cases of patent infringement, the defendant may avoid an account[89] being ordered by showing that he did not know and had no reasonable grounds for supposing that the patent existed.

5–070   A particular difficulty in cases where an account is ordered is that of determining for which profits the defendant must account. It cannot be assumed, in a case of passing off, for example, that all the profits made by the defendant can be attributed to the tort. Thus, in *My Kinda Town v. Soll and Grunts Investments*[90] it was alleged that the defendant had passed off its chain of restaurants as the claimant's by using a similar name to that of the claimant's chain. The profits to be accounted for could only be the extra profits caused by customers being confused into believing the defendant's restaurants were the claimant's and could not comprise all the defendant's profits from the restaurants. Further examples of the need to ensure that only the profits attributable to the tort are recovered can be seen in cases of infringement of a trademark,[91] and patent infringement.[92] The task of calculation is clearly potentially highly problematic, especially given the courts' traditional view that an actual account has to be drawn up indicating the precise gains and losses. However Slade J. in *My Kinda Town*[93] considered that a reasonable approximation would suffice, an approach which would significantly enhance the likelihood that in future cases an account will be claimed more often.[94]

5–071   As regards non-proprietary torts, there is a dearth of cases where restitutionary damages have been awarded, though it is sometimes possible to waive the tort and claim for money had and received, as discussed above.[95] Recently, in *Halifax Building Society v. Thomas*[96] the Court of Appeal did not allow the claimant to succeed in a restitutionary claim to the gains made by the defendant in the tort of deceit. Peter Gibson L.J. said:

"I do not overlook the fact that the policy of the law is to view with

---

[83] See *Edelsten* and *Slazenger supra* n. 45.
[84] See *Spalding & Bros. v. A.W. Gamage Ltd* (1915) 84 L.J. Ch. 499.
[85] Copyright, Designs and Patents Act 1988, s. 97(1).
[86] Copyright, Designs and Patents Act 1988, s. 233(1).
[87] Copyright, Designs and patents Act 1988, s. 191J(1).
[88] But not where damages are the remedy; see Burrows (Remedies) at p. 302 for criticism of this distinction.
[89] Or damages (but not an injunction).
[90] [1982] F.S.R. 147. Reversed on liability at [1983] R.P.C. 407.
[91] See *Colbeam Palmer v. Stock Affiliates Pty Ltd* (1968) 122 C.L.R. 25 at 37.
[92] See *United Horse Shoe & Nail Co. Ltd v. Stewart & Co.* (1888) 13 App. Cas. 401 at 412–3.
[93] [1982] F.S.R. 147 at 159.
[94] Burrows (Remedies) at 305.
[95] *supra* para. 5–060. See *e.g. Kettlewell v. Refuge Assurance Co.* [1908] 1 K.B. 545 (deceit); *Universe Tankships Inc of Monrovia v. I.T.W.F.* [1983] 1 A.C. 366 (intimidation).
[96] [1996] Ch. 217.

disfavour a wrongdoer benefiting from his wrong, the more so when the wrong amounts to fraud, but it cannot be suggested that there is a universally applicable principle that in every case there will be restitution of benefit from a wrong".[97]

In any event as Glidewell L.J. pointed out,[98] a confiscation order had been made under Part VI of the Criminal Justice Act 1988, thus ensuring that the defendant would not benefit from his wrongdoing, and, as the Law Commission points out[99] that may be the true reason why restitution was inappropriate in that case, just as (if they had been pleaded) exemplary damages would have been inappropriate.

A further restitutionary straw in the wind can however be seen in sections   5–072
27 and 28 of the Housing Act 1988 which already creates a restitutionary remedy in cases of unlawful eviction. Damages are assessed according to the difference in value between the landlord's interest with the residential occupier continuing to have the right to occupy, and the landlord's interest with the tenant no longer having that interest.[1]

From the above it can be seen that restitutionary damages are available   5–073
in a number of cases where a tort has been committed though it is by no means the case that restitutionary damages are automatically available for any tort. Restitutionary remedies have thus far been restricted to the "proprietary torts" (i.e. trespass to goods, conversion, trespass to land) and the intellectual property torts but not for "personal torts" such as negligence, defamation and trespass to the person. At its broadest it may be argued that a restitutionary award should be available for all torts, there being no logical basis for distinguishing some from others on this basis, the only requirement being that of causation: the defendant would not have made his gain but for his tortious conduct.[2] Alternatively the proprietary/personal distinction may be argued to be justified on the basis that, as has been suggested, the law should protect "facilitative institutions", i.e. "power-confering facilities for the creation of private arrangement between individuals, such as . . . private property",[3] whereas, as Burrows suggests,[4] the interests protected by "personal torts", such as bodily integrity and reputation, are natural assets existing irrespective of rights given by law, and hence not in need of the same kind of protection. A further relevant factor which has been taken into account in some cases is the defendant's consciousness of his wrongdoing: thus, as we have seen, in cases of infringement of trademark and passing off the defendant's awareness of his wrongdoing is a crucial factor for the ordering of an account, though this is not

---

[97] [1996] Ch. 217 at 227.
[98] ibid. at 230.
[99] Law Com. No. 247 "Aggravated, Exemplary and Restitutionary Damages" (1997) at 3.27.
[1] See Jones & Lee v. Miah & Miah (1992) 24 H.L.R. 578; Melville v. Bruton (1997) 29 H.L.R. 319 infra para. 6–029. See also Seager v. Copydex Ltd (No. 2) [1969] 1 W.L.R. 809, where Lord Denning again seemed to favour a restitutionary approach, in a case of breach of confidence.
[2] See Goff and Jones: "The Law of Restitution" (4th ed., 1993) pp. 720–3.
[3] See Jackman (1989) 48 C.L.J. 302 at 304.
[4] Burrows (Restitution) p. 394.

a criterion of all intellectual property torts.[5] In its report on Aggravated, Exemplary and Restitutionary Damages,[6] the Law Commission concludes that development of the law on restitution for wrongs is best left to the courts except that restitutionary damages should be available where a defendant has committed a tort, an equitable wrong (*e.g.* breach of confidence) or a statutory civil wrong, and his conduct shows a deliberate and outrageous disregard of the claimant's rights.[7] For the sake of greater clarity the Law Commission recommends that the labels "action for money had and received" and "account of profits" should be abandoned in favour of the single term "restitutionary damages"[8] or "restitutionary award" though, as the Commission accept,[9] such a step, effectively fusing common law and equitable remedies, is open to the argument that it would entail the lack of flexibility that is a part of equitable relief.

5–074   If, as seems wise, future development of restitutionary damages in tort is to be left to the courts, what principles should govern this development? As Burrows argues,[10] it is easier to justify compensation for losses than restitution of gains. The former clearly serves the basic function of repairing a harm that has been done, whereas the latter, though it prevents a defendant from retaining a gain tortiously acquired, nevertheless enriches the claimant, profiting him rather than simply compensating him for his loss.[11] It seems logical to adopt the Goff and Jones approach, as with respect to Jackman's thesis, it smacks of rationalisation rather than *a priori* logic, and there seems no clear reason for allowing restitution for some torts and not others, albeit that the types of interest they seek to protect are different. However it is unlikely that the courts will move swiftly to embrace the inclusive approach of Goff and Jones, and it is suggested that the law is unlikely in the immediate future to move beyond the proprietary torts in making restitutionary awards in tort.

---

[5] See Burrows (Damages) p. 302 for convincing criticism of this inconsistency.

[6] Law Com. No. 247 (1997).

[7] At 3.49. This follows from the Commission's recommendations on exemplary damages: see *supra* paras. 5–052 *et seq.*

[8] *Cf.* Millett L.J. in *Co-operative Insurance Society Ltd v. Argyll Stores (Holdings) Ltd* [1996] Ch. 286 at 306.

[9] Law Com. No. 247 (1997) at 3.84.

[10] Burrows (Restitution) at 395–6.

[11] Though presumably, assuming he is faced with a choice between restitution and compensation, a claimant, if he elects the former, will do so on the basis that it is the larger amount; thereby his losses are, in effect, compensated. It is clear from *United Australia Ltd v. Barclays Bank Ltd* [1941] A.C. 1 at 30 that no question of election between the alternative remedies arises until judgment.

CHAPTER 6

DAMAGE/INJURY TO PROPERTY RIGHTS

1. INTRODUCTION

In this chapter we consider the principles governing the assessment of 6–001
damages where the defendant has infringed the property rights of the claimant. Such infringement may consist of destruction, damage or interference,
and may fall within the ambit of such torts as trespass, nuisance, negligence, passing off and infringement of copyright. The topic is divided into
consideration firstly of damage to land (which includes, and indeed is largely exemplified by, damage to or destruction of buildings), then wrongful
interference with land; subsequently we shall consider damage to, destruction of and appropriation of and interference with goods.

2. DAMAGE TO LAND

The two contrasting basic approaches to the measure of damages in such 6–002
cases are the cost of repair/reinstatement and the difference in value. The
basic *restitutio in integrum* principle does not suggest an obvious answer
to the question of how one chooses between the two, and a number of
factors are relevant in determining the choice to be made by the court.

As a example of the issues that may arise, in *Harbutt's "Plasticine" Ltd* 6–003
v. Wayne Tank and Pump Co Ltd[1] the claimant's factory was destroyed as
a result of the defendant's breach of contract. The claimant claimed that it
was entitled to the cost of replacement of the factory; the defendant argued
that the measure of damages should be the difference in value before and
after the fire. The Court of Appeal held that the claimant was entitled to
the cost of replacement.

> ". . . if no substitute for the damaged article is available and no reason-
> able alternative can be provided, the claimant should be entitled to the
> cost of repair. It was clear in the present case that it was reasonable
> for the claimants to rebuild their factory, because there was no other
> way in which they could carry on their business and retain their labour
> force."[2]

---

[1] [19870] 1 Q.B. 447; a claim in contract, but "the principles apply equally to the measure
of damages for tort" per Taylor L.J. in *Dominion Mosaics and Tile Co. Ltd v. Trafalgar
Trucking Co. Ltd* [1990] 2 All E.R. 246 at 249–250.
[2] [1970] 1 Q.B. 447 at 473 per Widgery L.J.

As this passage suggests, unsurprisingly the duty to mitigate is a relevant factor. It is clear also that the purpose for which the claimant owned the property is of significance.

6-004   The difference between the two measures in *Harbutt's* was around £30,000. In *Dominion Mosaics and Tile Co Ltd v. Trafalgar Trucking Co Ltd*[3] the diminution in value of the claimant's premises after fire had effectively destroyed the original premises was £390,000. In asserting that the choice between cost of reinstatement and difference in value depended on the circumstances of the case, the court, as in *Harbutt's Plasticine*, awarded the claimant the cost of acquiring the new premises, as clearly they required premises to carry on business, and thereby they mitigated the damage which would have been caused by the loss of profits (estimated at £300,000 a year) during the period of rebuilding that would otherwise have had to take place.

6-005   It should not be assumed however that the fact that the premises were owned for business purposes necessarily entitles the claimant to claim the cost of reinstatement. In *C.R. Taylor (Wholesale) Ltd v. Hepworths Ltd*[4] the claimants owned a disused billiard hall, which they essentially regarded as a site for potential redevelopment. The hall was destroyed in a fire, and the claimants claimed the cost of reinstatement, which greatly exceeded the diminution in the site's value (which in turn was entirely offset by the amount it would have cost to have the site cleared by a developer). As the claimants did not intend to occupy the premises in their existing condition or let them for occupation, it was held that the diminution in the site's value was the appropriate measure (no award was made under this head however because of the saving of the cost of clearance).

6-006   Where diminution in value is the appropriate measure, the problem may be, in the words of Russell L.J. in *Farmer Giles Ltd v. Wessex Water Authority*,[5] "how one goes about measuring that diminution in value." A wall of an industrial building belonging to the claimant collapsed in circumstances which, it was admitted, gave rise to liability on the part of the defendant. The judge held that the fair market value of the property without commercial potential was £10,000. Estimates of the cost of rebuilding varied between £117,000 and £155,000. The judge rejected reinstatement as an option. He accepted that, when the building collapsed, it was in such a condition that, with the expenditure of money on it, it could be refurbished so as to render it a viable commercial property capable of generating rent on a fairly substantial scale. He assessed the capitalised value of the rent that he held would have been obtained as £40,000, and deducted the probable costs of refurbishment and the value of the cleared site from this. The Court of Appeal held that this was the correct approach. The choice was not the stark one between market value and cost of complete physical reinstatement, but, in assessing the former (the alternative having been described, not surprisingly, by the judge as "grotesque"), on

---

[3] [1990] 2 All E.R. 246.
[4] [1977] 2 All E.R. 784. See also *Hole & Son (Sayers Common) v. Harrisons of Thurnscoe* [1973] 1 Lloyds Rep. 345.
[5] (1990) 1 E.G.L.R. 177.

the facts it was proper to include damages to compensate the claimant for his loss of profit less the costs rightly deducted by the judge.

The issue fell to be considered in the context of a dwelling house in **6–007** *Hollebone v. Midhurst and Fernhurst Builders.*[6] Considerable damage was caused to the claimant's house as a result of the defendant's negligence. By the time the case was tried the claimant had carried out the structural repairs and decorative work, at a cost exceeding the difference in value of some £4,000. It was held, given the unique nature of the house (site, location, features) that the claimant had acted reasonably in reinstating it, and he was awarded the cost of repair. More recently, in *Ward v. Cannock Chase Council*[7] Scott J. emphasised the need, if reinstatement damages are to be awarded, for the claimant to show that he intends to rebuild or has reasonably rebuilt the damaged/destroyed structure, and that the case is an exceptional one where justice requires that he be awarded the cost of reinstatement. The presumption (as it in effect appears to be) in favour of the diminution in value measure was rebutted in *Ward* as the court accepted that the property and land in question comprised a land holding of special and particular value to the claimant. It consisted of two cottages at the end of a terrace, together with 1.5 acres of adjoining land on which the claimant kept livestock and dismantled vehicles. The cottages were seriously damaged over a period of time as a consequence of a breach of duty by the defendant. The unique value of the land to the claimant essentially comprised the 1.5 acres of land, which was of a size to enable him to keep his livestock, indulge his desire for an agricultural smallholding and provide space for his children's recreation, also enabling him to assist in his agricultural or other activities. He would not have been able to purchase anywhere remotely similar if merely awarded diminution in value. There was, however, a *caveat*. The award was conditional on the claimant obtaining planning permission to rebuild the cottages or, if permission were refused, to convert a nearby property which he also owned. In the absence of planning permission for either, he could only be awarded the diminution in value. The conditional nature of the judgment is explained by the fact that the basis of the award of damages was being tried as a preliminary issue.

By contrast in *Munnelly v. Calcon*,[8] a decision of the Supreme Court of Ireland, which it is thought that an English court would decide the same way, the diminution measure was held to be appropriate. The house of an auctioneer, where he carried on his business, was irreparably damaged. The court was satisfied that he genuinely intended to rebuild a new house on the site of the old, but there was a £30,000 difference between the cost of reinstatement and the diminution in value. The court concluded that the claimant's intention should not be the determining factor, and that, whereas the diminution in value measure would be both compensatory and reasonable, the reinstatement measure would unjustifiably profit the claim-

---

[6] [1968] 1 Lloyds Rep. 38.
[7] [1985] 3 All E.R. 537. See also *Munnelly v. Calcon Ltd* [1978] I.R. 387. See also *Scutt v. Lomax* [2000] W.L.R. 394.
[8] [1978] I.R. 387.

ant and unfairly penalise the defendant. In effect therefore the presumption in favour of diminution in value was not rebutted.

6–008   Two interesting associated issues fell to be considered in *Dodd Properties (Kent) Ltd v. Canterbury City Council*[9] The first is the point in time at which the cost of reinstatement should be taken. The case concerned serious structural damage caused by the defendants to a building respectively owned and occupied by the first and second claimants. Liability was not admitted until shortly before the hearing of the action in 1978. The first claimants, the owners of the land, had not carried out any repairs at the date of the hearing, arguing that to have done so in 1970 (the earliest date when it was physically possible to carry out repairs) would have caused them a degree of financial stringency, and that in any event it would not have made commercial sense for them to have carried out repairs before they were sure of recovering the expenditure from the defendants. The Court of Appeal held that the claimants were entitled to be compensated on the basis of the cost of repairs being assessed at the earliest date when, having regard to all the circumstances, they could reasonably be undertaken, rather than the date on which the damage occurred. This was stated as a general principle, applicable to cases of tortious damage to buildings put in need of repair. On the facts of the case, the date of the hearing of the action (*i.e.* 1978) was the date at which the damages were to be assessed given the degree of financial stringency the claimants would have been caused had they effected the repairs in 1970, the commercial sense of postponing of repairs until the outcome of the action, the fact that the claimants were not in breach of any duty to mitigate, and the wrongful denial of liability by the defendants.

6–009   Where the case involves the diminution in value measure the general principle, as stated by Scott J. in *Ward*[10] is that the date the tort is committed is the date on which the damages are to be measured. However, Scott J. went on to say that where, as in that case, the breaches of duty had had continuing consequences leading eventually to the demolition of the property, the date of the demolition was the date at which the diminution in value should be measured.

6–010   The second point of interest in *Dodd* concerns the quality of reinstatement/repair that is appropriate. The general principle that the claimant is entitled to the cost of such repairs as are reasonable may need further refinement when, as was the case in *Dodd*, the parties are not in agreement as to what repairs are reasonable. Cantley J. at first instance[11] concluded that the claimants were not

> "entitled to insist on complete and meticulous restoration when a reasonable building owner would be content with less extensive work which produces a result which does not diminish to any or any significant extent the appearance, life or utility of the building, and when

---

[9] [1980] 1 All E.R. 928.
[10] *Supra* n. 7 at p. 559.
[11] [1979] 2 All E.R. 118 at 124. There was no appeal against this finding. See also *Lodge Holes Colliery Co. v. Wednesbury Corporation* [1908] A.C. 323.

there is also a vast difference in the cost of such work and the cost of meticulous restoration."

An associated issue is that of betterment, *i.e.* the question whether a sum 6–011 should not be deducted from the claimant's award (whether on a repair or replacement basis) to take account of the fact that the repaired or new property is more valuable than the property before the accident. Earlier authorities[12] favoured a reduction in damages to take account of betterment, though with little analysis of the problem, but more recently the view that has prevailed is that no allowance for betterment should be made, as this may well prevent the claimant from being fairly compensated.[13] In *Harbutt's "Plasticine" Ltd v. Wayne Tank and Pump Co Ltd*[14] Widgery L.J. considered that to require the claimants to give credit for betterment "would be the equivalent of forcing [them] to invest their money in the modernising of their plant which might be highly inconvenient to them."

The issue arose for detailed consideration in *Dominion Mosaics Co Ltd* 6–012 *v. Trafalgar Trucking Co.*[15] In that case the original premises were freehold, with rates of £10,000 per annum. The new premises were acquired initially on the 36-year residue of a lease (subsequently the claimant purchased the freehold for £60,000) with a ground rent of £2,500 per annum and rates of over £70,000 per annum. The court did not regard this as amounting to betterment; although the new premises comprised a "better building" (larger by some 5,000 sqare feet but in need of attention), the change brought additional burdens. Further, the fact that the claimant was subsequently able to sell the new premises for £690,000, having paid £390,000 for the lease and £60,000 for the freehold, was also not to be taken into account, the Court of Appeal concluding that a defendant was not entitled to the benefit of any successful dealings which the claimant might have had up to trial, and also agreeing with the trial judge that the claimant's gains were attributable to the inflationary rise in the value of real property at the time.

Difficulties might however arise where a factory in a poor state of repair 6–013 is destroyed in circumstances for which the defendant is responsible. In such a situation, as was stated by Cantley J. in *Bacon v. Cooper (Metals) Ltd*,[16] a case concerning replacement of a chattel, "the application of any general principle is inappropriate at the point where it would produce an absurdity", and it seems likely that in such a case the clear benefit to the claimant would have to be reflected in a deduction from the *prima facie* award of damages, though of course, as in the *C.R. Taylor* case, the appropriate measure in such a case might well be diminution in value, depending on the claimant's intentions.

---

[12] See *e.g. Lukin v. Godsall* (1795) Pea. (2) 15; *Hide v. Thornborough* (1846) 2 C. & K. 250 ("you ought not to give him a new house for an old one" per Parke B.).

[13] See *Hollebone v. Midhurst and Fernhurst Builders* [1968] 1 Lloyds Rep. 38, the court preferring authorities where the problem arose in the context of damage to ships, *e.g. The Gazelle* (1844) 2 Wm. Rob. 279.

[14] [1970] 1 Q.B. 447 at 473.

[15] [1990] 2 All E.R. 246 at 251–252. *Supra* para. 6–004.

[16] [1982] 1 All E.R. 397 at 400. See also the comments of Taylor L.J. in *Dominion Mosaics Co. Ltd v. Trafalgar Trucking Co.* [1990] 2 All E.R. 246 at 255.

In cases of diminution in value and cost of repair there may be consequential losses for which the claimant seeks to be compensated.

(1) Expenses

6–014   It is clearly established that, subject to the rules on remoteness and mitigation, expenses incurred by the claimant as a consequence of the defendant's tortious conduct can be recovered. Thus in *Grosvenor Hotel Company v. Hamilton*[17] damage caused by a landlord to his tenant's house
required the tenant to move his business. He was held to be entitled to
recover (in effect) the reasonable cost of removal and of obtaining and
adapting new premises. Removal and travel costs were also awarded to the
claimant in *Ward v. Cannock Chase District Council*.[18]

(2) Loss of Profits

6–015   A further aspect of loss for which the tenant successfully claimed compensation in *Grosvenor* was loss of profits, and a number of cases demonstrate the recoverability of this type of loss. For example, in *Dodd Properties (Kent) Ltd v. Canterbury City Council*,[19] the second claimants (the
tenants of the first claimants) were held to be entitled to loss of profits and
expenses during the time when the repairs would be carried out. However,
in *Ward v. Cannock Chase District Council*[20] a claimed loss of ability to
make money on land adjoining the claimant's damaged premises was held
not to be a foreseeable consequence of the defendant's breach of duty to
him.

(3) Non-pecuniary losses

6–016   A further aspect of the claim in *Ward* was a claim for discomfort, anxiety
and stress, as is not uncommon in cases of damage caused to domestic
premises. The claimant was compensated for the discomfort that he and
his family sustained; firstly for a period of two months during which their
house had a large hole in its roof; secondly for the period since then during
which they had been living in grossly-overcrowded council accommodation. Cases concerning local authority liability for damage caused by tree
roots[21] also illustrate the availability, in a appropriate case, of compensation under this head, though awards are generally fairly low.

---

[17] [1894] 2 Q.B. 836.
[18] [1985] 3 All E.R. 537; *supra* para. 6–007.
[19] *supra* n. 9.
[20] *supra* n. 7. See also *Bayoumi v. Protium Services Ltd*. (1998) 30 H.L.R. 785. Where, in a
claim under the Defective Premises Act 1972, the claimant was able to recover for damage
to furniture, loss of use and enjoyment of the premises and travel expenses in overseeing
repairs.
[21] *e.g. Bunclark v. Hertfordshire DC* (1977) 243 E.G. 381 and 455.

(4) Limited interest of claimant

Where the claimant has a limited interest in the land, he can recover   6–017
damage only to the extent to which his interest has been damaged. If, for
example, the claimant is a lessee, his damages (if any) will reflect the extent
to which the value of the lease has been diminished, and may extend to
allowing recovery of any loss he suffers in his enjoyment of the land. By
contrast, a reversioner may recover damages to reflect the harm caused to
his permanent interest in the land. Thus, in *Bedingfield v. Onslow*[22] the
defendant flooded the claimant's land destroying some two hundred timber
trees. The claimant was held to be entitled to recover for the damage to the
reversion; his tenant for the loss of shade, shelter and fruit of the trees.
Again, in *Moss v. Christchurch R.D.C.*[23] the claimant, whose house, let on
a weekly tenancy, was destroyed by a fire, held to comprise a nuisance on
the part of the defendant, was held to be entitled to recover the difference
between the money value of her interest before and after the fire.

The risk of over-compensation must be borne in mind when both rever-   6–018
sioner and tenant sue. In *Rust v. Victoria Graving Dock Co*[24] Cotton L.J.
stated that in such a case

> "all that they ought to be required to pay is damages for the injury
> caused directly to the whole estate . . . Having got at that, you have to
> consider how that sum ought to be apportioned among the persons
> interested in the property damaged . . ."[25]

It was also emphasised by the court that the damage to the reversioner's
interest must be permanent, *i.e.* that it will continue beyond the term of
the tenancy and into the time when the reversion becomes an estate in
possession.[26] Part of the claim concerned houses on the claimant's land
which had been erected by builders under building leases and which had
been damaged by a flood caused by the defendant's negligence. The court
held that the fact that the claimant had sold the reversion of those houses
in order to raise money to continue his speculation meant that he could
not claim for any depreciation in the selling value of the reversion, since it
was accepted that there was no damage to the land or the houses which
would still exist after the determination of the builders' leases. Such a claim,
it was held, could only succeed if it was shown that there was a recognised
trade or business in dealing with reversions in this way, and it had not been
demonstrated that such was the case.

A further aspect of the claim in *Rust* concerned part of the land in ques-   6–019
tion which the claimant had agreed to let to builders. He had contracted
to make, and had made advances to them on the security of the houses the
builders were in the course of constructing. Here, recognising the need to
take account of the claimant's security interest, the court decided that it

---

[22] (1865) 3 Lev. 209.
[23] [1925] 2 K.B. 750. See also *Hosking v. Phillips* (1848) 3 Ex. 168.
[24] (1887) 36 Ch. D. 113.
[25] *ibid.* at 130, 135.
[26] See *Mayfair Property Company v. Johnston* [1894] 1 Ch. 508 at 516–520.

was necessary to ascertain what sum would have been needed to repair the damage caused to the houses by the flood, then decide to what extent the houses, before they were repaired, would have been a sufficient security for the claimant's advances. If there was a deficiency then the claimant should be given such of the money needed to repair the houses as, when added to their value in their damaged state, would be enough to make good the advances.

3. WRONGFUL INTERFERENCE WITH LAND

6–020   Wrongful interference by a person with another's land will usually give rise to liability in trespass and/or nuisance. Such interference will usually (though not necessarily) be temporary, and the claimant's main interest will be in obtaining an order for the cessation of the nuisance or, in the case of trespass, recovery of his land in the action of ejectment, which can be coupled with a claim for damages in the form of an action for *mesne* profits.

(1) Temporary Deprivation

6–021   Where the loss of use of the land is temporary only, the usual measure of damages is the market rental value of the property for the period of wrongful deprivation. In *Stoke on Trent City Council v. W. & J. Wass Ltd*[27] Nicholls L.J. referred to the underlying principle in such cases as the "user principle", which, as we shall see, embraces elements of restitution as well as compensation.

6–022   The easiest cases are those where it can be shown that the land would have been rented out during the period of deprivation. Thus, in *Hall & Co Ltd v. Pearlberg*[28] the defendant wrongfully occupied two farms belonging to the claimant. Damages of £650 for trespass were awarded, representing one year's rent which the claimant would have charged to an incoming tenant. A further aspect of recoverable losses under this head may arise where, as a result of nuisance by the defendant, the claimant suffers a loss of custom, as in *Andreae v. Selfridge & Co Ltd*[29] where building operations carried on by the defendant caused a loss of custom at the claimant's hotel, which was held to be recoverable. As was pointed out by Lloyd L.J. in *Ministry of Defence v. Ashman*[30] if the market has risen the landlord may recover more than the previous rent; if it has fallen he will presumably recover less.

6–023   Greater difficulty arises in cases where it cannot be shown that the claimant would have let out the land during the period of deprivation. In *Whitwham v. Westminster Brymbo Coal and Coke Co*[31] the defendant had tres-

---

[27] [1988] 3 All E.R. 394.
[28] [1956] 1 All E.R. 297. There were also consequential losses (see below).
[29] [1938] Ch. 1.
[30] (1993) 25 H.L.R. 513 at 522, citing *Clifton Securities v. Huntley* [1948] 2 All E.R. 286.
[31] [1896] 1 Ch. 894 (Chitty J.); [1896] 2 Ch. 538 (C.A.).

passed on the claimant's land by depositing spoil from its colliery on it. Chitty J. held that on the authority of earlier authorities allowing damages in cases of trespass by unauthorised mining where no injury was done to the land,[32] damages were to be assessed on the basis of what would be a reasonable sum to be paid for the use of the claimant's land by the defendant for tipping purposes. The Court of Appeal upheld the award, the majority basing their reasoning on the loss sustained by the claimant, rather than taking account of any benefit to the defendant. The damages awarded represented the reasonable value of the land for tipping purposes with respect to the part of the land that had actually been used by the defendant for tipping.

Subsequently in *Penarth Dock Engineering Co v. Pounds*[33] Lord Denning M.R. chose to follow his own view in the detinue case of *Strand Electric Engineering Co Ltd v. Brisford Entertainers Ltd*[34] rather than the majority in that case and the majority in *Whitwham*, both of which espoused a compensatory approach, and awarded damages on a restitutionary basis. *Penarth*, where the claim was in breach of contract or trespass, concerned the failure by the defendant to remove a pontoon, which it had bought from the claimant dock company, from the dock premises. Damages were awarded representing what it would have cost the defendant to berth the pontoon on similar premises. There was no damage suffered by the claimant.   **6–024**

This case, and *Whitwham*, were cited by the Court of Appeal subsequently in *Swordheath Properties Ltd v. Tabet*[35] as authority for the proposition that, in a case where (as in the instant case) the claimant has established that the defendant has remained on as a trespasser, he is entitled   **6–025**

> "without bringing evidence that he could or would have let the property to someone else in the absence of the trespassing defendant, to have as damages for the trespass the value of the property as it would fairly be calculated; and in the absence of anything special in the particular case it would be the ordinary letting value of the property that would determine the amount of damages."[36]

This view was endorsed by the Judicial Committee of the Privy Council in *Inverugie Investments v. Hackett*[37] where the claimant was kept out of an hotel containing 30 apartments of which it was lessee for 15 and a half years by the defendant, and was held to be entitled to recover the market rent of all 30 apartments over the entire 15 and a half years. Lord Lloyd, who delivered the judgment of the Board, stated that, though it was sometimes said that such cases were an exception to the rule that damages in tort are compensatory, that was not necessarily so as it depended on how widely the "loss" suf-

---

[32] *e.g. Martin v. Porter* 5 M. & W. 351: *Jegon v. Vivan* (1871) L.R. 6 Ch. App. 742. Damages in such cases are assessed on the basis of a reasonable rent for the use of the passages in the mines, known as "wayleave".
[33] [1963] 1 Lloyds Rep. 359.
[34] [1952] 2 Q.B. 246.
[35] [1979] 2 All E.R. 240.
[36] *ibid.* at 242 per Megaw L.J.
[37] [1995] 3 All E.R. 841. See Watts (1996) 112 L.Q.R. 39.

fered by the claimants was defined. Referring to the term "user principle" employed by Nicholls L.J.[38] to describe the underlying principle, Lord Lloyd pointed out that, though the claimant ought not have suffered any *actual* loss by being deprived of the use of his property he was, under the user principle, entitled to recover a reasonable rent for the wrongful use of his property by the trespasser. Equally the fact that the trespasser had not derived any actual benefit from the use of the property did not prevent him from being obliged to pay a reasonable rent for the use he had enjoyed. "The principle need not be characterised as exclusively compensatory, or exclusively restitutionary; it combines elements of both."[39]

6–026   However, it appears that the claimant in a trespass case may have a choice between compensation and restitution (in so far as in the light of Lord Lloyd's remarks in *Inverugie* the two can be separated). The claimant in *Inverugie* did not assert a restitutionary claim as an independant cause of action. However, in *Ministry of Defence v. Ashman*[40] the issue arose directly for consideration. The defendant was an RAFwife, deserted by her husband, who stayed on in RAF accommodation after being given notice to vacate. The rent paid for the property was at a concessionary rate of £95 per month. The open market value of the property was about £500 a month. The cost of equivalent local authority accommodation was £145 a month. The claimant claimed *mesne* profits representing the market rent. The Court of Appeal held that the landlord was entitled to recover on the basis of the proper value to the trespasser of the use of the property. Hoffman L.J. considered that a person entitled to possession of land could choose to claim either for the loss he had suffered as a consequence of the defendant's trespass, the normal measure of damages in the law of tort, or for the value of the benefit which the occupier had received. The two were mutually exclusive and the claimant must make his choice between them before judgment. This approach was confirmed three weeks later in *Ministry of Defence v. Thompson*[41] by a differently constituted Court of Appeal (albeit again containing Hoffman L.J.). The effect in *Ashman* was that, the claimant having elected the restitutionary remedy, the subjective benefit to the defendant was, in the circumstances of the case awarded, this being the value of suitable local authority housing to which she was entitled (and which she in fact received), rather than the open market rental value of the property.

6–027   As Lloyd L.J. pointed out in *Ashman*,[42] in the vast majority of cases the measure of damages in a claim for *mesne* profits will be at the same rate as the previous rent. *Prima facie* in the case of a tenant holding over, the compensation and the restitution approaches would lead to the same result, however, as has been pointed out,[43] though the saving to a business tenant may be the market rent, the value of the benefit to him may be far greater because of the goodwill associated with the premises; placing a precise value on the benefit to the defendant may be extremely difficult. In the light

[38] *Supra* n. 27.
[39] [1995] 3 All E.R. 841 at 845.
[40] [1993] 25 H.L.R. 513. See Cooke (1994) 110 L.Q.R. 420.
[41] (1993) 25 H.L.R. 552.
[42] (1993) 25 H.L.R. 513 at 522.
[43] Cooke (n. 49 *infra*) *ibid.* at 427 n. 44.

of *Inverugie* and *Ashman/Thompson* it would seem that a claimant has the option of claiming full market value by way of damages or, if the defendant has obtained a greater benefit, obtain that in a restitutionary claim.

(2) Permanent deprivation

Less commonly the claimant may be unable to recover his land, as for example, where an injunction is refused. In *Bracewell v. Appleby*[44] a small development of six houses was built forming a cul-de-sac around a private road. The road gave the only means of access to the houses, and the only right of way that existed was limited to the six houses. The defendant bought one of the houses, and subsequently also purchased a plot of land adjoining the grounds of his house. He began to build a house on the plot, and the claimants, who both owned houses in the cul-de-sac, sought a declaration that there was no right of way over the road to the plot and an injunction restraining him from using the road to reach the plot. The declaration was granted, but an interlocutory injunction was refused because of the claimants' delay in bringing proceedings until the house was built. Damages in lieu of an injunction were awarded, in an amount, in Graham J.'s words,[45] "which in so far as it can be estimated is equivalent to a proper and fair price which would be payable for the acquisition of the right of way in question." Graham J. related the award to the notional profit which the defendant had made, this being estimated at £5,000. He considered that the defendant would have been prepared to pay, relative to the notional profit, quite a large sum for the right of way and to achieve the building of the new house, and concluded that he would have been prepared to pay £2,000 and that the other house owners in the cul-de-sac ought to have been prepared to accept a fifth each of that sum. Again the result seems to be an amalgam of compensation (there is reference in the judgment to the sum being one which the claimants would accept as compensating them for loss of amenity and increased user) and restitution. The approach adopted in *Bracewell* was endorsed subsequently by Millett J. in *Carr-Saunders v. Dick McNeil Associates*,[46] a case concerning a right to light, though there was no evidence of the profit the defendant expected to make, and general damages of £8,000 were awarded. In *Snell & Prideaux v. Dutton Mirrors*,[47] however, damages in lieu of an injunction sought for infringement of a right of way were assessed on the basis of the difference in value of the claimant's premises with full rights of access as opposed to the current limited access. There was no discussion of a possible restitutionary claim.

6–028

(3) Housing Act 1988 sections 27 and 28

The restitutionary theme can however be seen in the statutory damages remedy created by sections and 27 and 28 of the Housing Act 1988. In

6–029

---

[44] [1975] Ch. 408.
[45] [1975] *ibid.* at 419.
[46] [1986] 2 All E.R. 888. See also *Deakins v. Hookings* [1994] 1 E.G.L.R. 190.
[47] [1995] 1 E.G.L.R. 253.

many ways the award of damages echoes the views of Lord Lloyd in *Inverugie* as being neither exclusively compensatory nor exclusively restitutionary, with the emphasis on the latter. The claim arises where a landlord unlawfully deprives the residential occupier of any premises of his occupation of the whole or part of the premises, or by unreasonable conduct causes the occupier to give up his occupation. Damages are assessed according to the difference in value between the landlord's interest with the residential occupier continuing to have the right to occupy and the landlord's interest with the tenant no longer having that right. The object of these sections was summed up by Leggatt L.J. in *Jones & Lee v. Miah & Miah*[48] as follows:

> "that sum [*i.e.* the award of damages under section 28] represents the financial advantages which the landlord has gained in respect of each respondent, and of which it is the purpose of sections 27 and 28 to deprive him."

It was emphasised by the Court of Appeal in *Melville v. Bruton*[49] that the comparison required by section 28 must necessarily involve valuing the unencumbered interest on a factual as opposed to a notional basis, otherwise the sum which the landlord is ordered to pay is not the value of the profit occasioned by his wrong but a fine, which may be far greater. In that case, on the facts there would have been no difference in value, so no award could be made under section 28. Provision is made in section 27(7) for a reduction in the award if the tenant's conduct makes it reasonable to do; thus, in *Regalgrand Ltd v. Dickerson & Wade*[50] a prima facie award of £12,000 was reduced to £1,500. Awards can be high: in *Tagro v. Cafane*[51] an award of £31,000 was made, the defendant calling no evidence to dispute the claimant's figure.

6–030   Quite apart from the Act, at common law it has long been the case that a person, such as a tenant, with a limited interest over land may be able to claim damages for wrongful interference with his interest in the land. Most[52] such cases concern claims by tenants against their landlords for wrongful eviction, damages being measured on the basis of loss of use. In addition compensation for inconvenience can be awarded. Awards of aggravated and exemplary damages are also not infrequently made in such cases.[53] It is provided by section 27(5) of the Housing Act 1988 that common law claims are not precluded by the statutory claim under section 27, but damages may not be awarded twice for the same loss. The relationship between the two claims fell to be considered by the Court of Appeal in *Nwokorie v. Mason*.[54] The judge had awarded £500 general damages, £1,000 exemplary damages and £4,000 under section 28. It was held that

---

[48] (1992) 24 H.L.R. 578 at 592.
[49] (1997) 29 H.L.R. 319.
[50] (1997) 29 H.L.R. 620. See also *Osei-Bonsu v. Wandsworth LBC* [1999] 1 W.L.R. 1011.
[51] [1991] 2 All E.R. 235.
[52] But not all; see *e.g. Moore v. Buchanan* (1966) 197 E.G. 565, a case concerning wrongful obstruction of a right of way.
[53] See *supra* Ch. 5. Leading cases include *Drane v. Evangelou* [1978] 2 All E.R. 437; *Guppys (Bridport) v. Brookling and James* (1983) 14 H.L.R. 1.
[54] (1994) 26 H.L.R. 60. See also *Francis v. Brown* (1998) 30 H.L.R. 143.

the £500, being in essence damages for wrongful eviction which deprived the claimant of the right to occupy the premises as his residence, fell to be set off against the award under the Act. The judge appeared not to have drawn any distinction between exemplary and aggravated damages, and the £1,000 award was to be treated as an award of aggravated rather than exemplary damages: it was not a case where the defendant had had a financial motive for the eviction, so it could not stand as an award of exemplary damages. As an award of aggravated damages it was still an award of damages in respect of the loss by the claimant of the right to occupy premises as his residence and ought therefore also to be set off against the statutory award. Whether the same would apply to an award of exemplary damages is not clear. Such an award is at best indirectly in respect of the loss of the right to occupy in such a case, being essentially geared to relieve the defendant of the profit he has sought to make out of his conduct. However, the essentially restitutionary nature of the award of exemplary damages in a case of this kind is likely to be seen as substantially overlapping with the similar purpose behind the award of damages under section 28, and it is thought that the better view is that any exemplary award would require to be set off against the statutory award.

A further issue of importance is the extent to which an award for loss of   6–031
use at common law is subsumed within the statutory claim. The former is compensatory; the latter essentially restitutionary, and hence there appears to be scope for an award under both heads in an appropriate case. Thus in *Sampson v. Wilson*[55] in addition to damages under section 27, the judge made an award for "substantial deprivation of beneficial enjoyment"[56] to the tenants for what they had to put up with before they left, which comprised the rent paid during the relevant period when the landlord was in breach of his repairing covenant and the property was uninhabitable. In addition an award of exemplary damages was made, again limited to the period before the tenants left.

4. DESTRUCTION OF GOODS

Liability in such cases may arise from a variety of torts, including negli-   6–032
gence, trespass, nuisance and strict liability (*e.g. Rylands v. Fletcher*). In considering the principles governing the award of damages for destruction of goods, it should be borne in mind that a literal destruction is not a prerequisite: if damage is so extensive as to make repair uneconomic, the principles applicable to destruction of goods rather than damage to goods will be applicable. A further preliminary point to note is that very many of the cases concerning destruction of (and damage to) goods involve ships. As the courts have regularly emphasised, however, the principles developed

---

[55] (1994) 26 H.L.R. 486. The basis of the award for common law damages was not disturbed by the Court of Appeal: [1997] 29 H.L.R. 18.
[56] [1994] 26 H.L.R. 486 at 505.

in these cases are not limited in their application to ships, but are of universal application.[57]

6–033   As regards the appropriate measure of damages, this will in general be the market value of the goods destroyed, as was emphasised by the House of Lords in the leading case; *Liesbosch Dredger v. S.S. Edison*.[58] It was emphasised in *Liesbosch* that compensation is not limited to the market value, but may extend to cover, in the words of Lord Wright,[59] "the value [of the ship] to her owner as a going concern at the time and place of the loss", thus permitting the recovery of consequential losses, contrary to the view expressed in earlier authorities.[60] The nature of the consequential losses recoverable in such cases is examined in detail below.

6–034   As regards the basic measure of damages, this is the market value at the time and place of destruction of the goods. Interest is awarded, in the case of ships in accordance with Admiralty practice, as was stated in *The Kong Magnus*;[61] in the case of other goods under section 35A of the Supreme Court Act 1981.[62]

6–035   Whether or not the cost of replacement will be awarded depends upon its reasonableness. Thus, in *Uctkos v. Mazzetta*[63] as a consequence of the claimant's negligence, the defendant's motor boat was destroyed. The defendant claimed that a replacement would cost over £5,000, as the destroyed vessel was irreplaceable and it would cost a great deal to obtain as speedy, seaworthy and commodious a vessel. Ormerod J. held that the defendant was not entitled to damages on the basis of cost of replacement, but was entitled to the reasonable cost of another vessel which reasonably met his needs and was reasonably in the same condition as the destroyed boat; and awarded a sum of £750, in the light of expert evidence that that was the reasonable replacement cost, plus £108 for fittings. It was no doubt relevant that the boat had only cost £600 when bought five years before the accident, had subsequently had £500 spent on it, and a further £780 was later spent on it to effect repairs after it sank in the dock on one occasion.

6–036   The concept of market value is not without its difficulties. Early authorities[64] restricted recovery to the market value of the ship just prior to the collision which caused its destruction, without allowing a claim to be made for consequential losses, such as the claim for twelve months loss of use and profits in *The Columbus*. This was justified by Dr. Lushington on the basis of the limitless difficulties the court would face in seeking to assess

---

[57] See *e.g. The Argentino* (1888) 13 P.D. 191 at 201, per Bowen L.J.; *The Kingsway* [1918] p. 344 at 356 per Pickford L.J.; *The Hebridean Coast* [1961] A.C. 545 at p. 562 per Devlin L.J.

[58] [1933] A.C. 449.

[59] *ibid.* at 464.

[60] *e.g. The Columbus* (1849) 3 Wm. Rob. (Adm.) 158; *The City of Rome* (1887) 8 Asp. Mar. Law Cas. 542n.

[61] [1981] p. 223; approved in *The Liebosch*. In recent years the rate of interest in the Admiralty Court has been equated with the rate awarded in the Commercial Court.

[62] Whether or not the goods are profit-earning: see *Metal Box Ltd v. Currys Ltd* [1988] 1 All E.R. 341.

[63] [1956] 1 Lloyd's Rep. 209. See also *Dominion Mosaics and Tile Co. v. Trafalgar Trucking* [1990] 2 All E.R. 246.

[64] See *e.g. The Columbus* (1849) 3 Wm. Rob. (Adm.) 158 and *The Clyde* (1856) Swab. 23.

the lost profits.[65] However a broader view developed of the particular application of the *restitutio in integrum* principle in this context. Thus, in *The Kate*[66] the award of damages represented the value of the claimants' destroyed barque together with a sum for the loss of profits that would have been secured under a charter she was about to undertake. Jeune P. considered that it would only be if the claim was uncertain and speculative[67] that such losses could be excluded. It was also made clear by Sir Robert Phillimore in *The Northumbria*[68] that where a vessel was sunk with a cargo on board, the freight she would have carried was recoverable, in addition to the value of the ship, though it was necessary to deduct the expenses, such as the crew's wages, that would have been incurred in order to complete the voyage.

In *The Harmonides*[69] Gorell Barnes J. had to consider the problem of a   6–037
vessel which had no market value: an Atlantic liner 35 years old. He concluded that damages had to be assessed on the basis of the value of the vessel to her owners as a going concern at the time she was sunk, mentioning such factors as the amount of capital invested, the amount of depreciation and the amount of profits. This approach also commended itself to the House of Lords in *Liesbosch Dredger v. S.S. Edison*,[70] the leading authority on the measure of damages in cases of destroyed goods. The Liesbosch was a dredger being employed by her owners in pursuance of a contract to carry out construction work at Patras harbour. She was sunk and lost as a consequence of admitted fault by the steamship Edison. Lord Wright held that the measure of damages was: "the value of the ship to her owner as a going concern at the time and place of the loss."[71] The restriction on consequential losses placed by Dr. Lushington in *The Columbus* was not accepted. The damages were to comprise:

"(1) the market price of a comparable dredger in substitution; (2) costs of adaptation, transport, insurance, etc. to Patras; (3) compensation for disturbance and loss in carrying out their contract over the period of delay between the loss of The Liesbosch and the time at which the substituted dredger could reasonably have been available for use in Patras, including in that loss such items as overhead charges, expenses of staff and equipment, and so forth thrown away, but neglecting any special loss due to the appellants' financial position.[72] On the capitalised sum so assessed, interest will run from the date of the loss".[73]

This approach tends to blur the distinction between the basic measure of   6–038
damages and consequential losses, though the risk of potential overlap was noted by Lord Wright, who recognised the need to exercise care.

---

[65] (1849) 3 Wm. Rob. (Adm.) 158 at 164.
[66] [1899] p. 165. See also *The Racine* [1906] p. 273.
[67] On this basis he distinguished *The Columbus*.
[68] (1869) L.R. 3 A. & E. 6.
[69] [1903] P. 1. See also *The Ironmaster* (1859) Swab. 441.
[70] [1933] A.C. 449.
[71] *ibid.* at 464.
[72] On this aspect, see *supra* 4–041 *et seq.*
[73] [1933] A.C. 449 at 468.

"The value of prospective freights cannot simply be added to the market value but ought to be taken into account in order to ascertain the total value for purpose of assessing the damage, since if it is merely added to the market value of a free ship, the owner will be getting *pro tanto* his damages twice over. The vessel cannot be earning in the open market, while fulfilling the pending charter or charters."[74]

He went on to underline the impossibility of laying down any universal formula, given the variety of types of vessel and the uses to which they may be put.

6–039   True value can therefore really only be determined on a case-by-case basis. One or two examples may be helpful in illustrating issues that may arise. In *Moore v. DER Ltd*[75] the claimant's car was written off as a result of the defendant's negligence. It was held that he acted reasonably in buying a new car, delivery of which took significantly longer than would have been the case had he purchased an eighteen-month-old secondhand vehicle of the same make, since he distrusted secondhand cars, and always bought new cars, which he changed every two years. He was therefore able to recover the cost of hiring a car during the lengthy period that elapsed before a new model was available. In *The Fortunity*[76] the defendant sank the claimant's motor cruiser, which was one of a fleet used for hiring out to holiday-makers for cruising on the Norfolk Broads. It was impracticable to hire an adequate substitute, or build a new vessel, in time for the 1959 season, so the earnings for that season were lost. The court awarded damages based on the market value of the vessel to the trade, plus the estimated loss of profit for the 1959 season. It has been argued[77] that this fails to take account of the principles set out in *Liesbosch*, in that the market selling price should have included the loss of profit on future engagements, but it seems that the court's explanation of the market selling price comprised, in the words of Hewson J.:[78]

"the price which a hirer of crafts in the trade would pay in the expectation of a reasonable return on his capital, and not taking into account the fact that she was already fixed with considerable bookings for the next season with a virtual certainty of full employment throughout the season."

6–040   Otherwise, as Lord Wright made clear in *Liesbosch*, the nature of the goods and the purpose for which the claimant held them, will guide the court. The market value approach will be especially significant where the goods are possessed as a commercial investment with a view to ultimate resale, whereas if the main significance of the goods to the claimant lies in the use he would have put them to in his possession, the cost of replacement

---

[74] *ibid.* at 464.
[75] [1971] 1 W.L.R. 1476.
[76] [1961] 1 W.L.R. 351.
[77] Burrows *op. cit.* at 161.
[78] [1971] 1 W.L.R. 351 at 356.

may be more apposite. The true value to the owner is the goal to be kept in mind at all times by the court.

The above cases all concern claims brought by the owner of goods. **6–041** Where the claimant's interest is limited, the position is governed by sections 7 and 8 of the Torts (Interference with Goods) Act 1977. The effect of these provisions is to enable the defendant to restrict the extent of the claimant's claim to his interest in the goods. In *O'Sullivan v. Williams*[79] it was held, without reference to the Act, that where a bailor had recovered damages (by way of settlement) against the defendant who negligently destroyed his car, a bailee could not recover damages representing her losses arising from the same accident, but if the bailee had some interest in the property enforceable against the bailor, then the bailor was required to account appropriately to the bailee.

5. DAMAGE TO GOODS

Where goods are damaged by the defendant's tortious conduct, the gov- **6–042** erning principle is the diminution in the value of the goods, but this, it seems in every case, is represented by the reasonable cost of repair rather than by an attempt to calculate the actual difference between the goods' value before and after the damage. As was pointed out by Greer L.J. in *The London Corporation*[80] "... *prima facie*, the value of a damaged vessel is less by the cost of repairs than the value it would have if undamaged". Though in many ways an attractive solution, this is not without its difficulties, as will be seen below. It is clear that if the goods are so damaged that repair is not reasonable, the court will regard it as a case of constructive total loss, and the principles applicable to cases of destruction of goods, discussed above, will govern the situation. It is also clear that, if there can be shown to be a diminution in the market value of goods on top of the cost of repairs, this may be recoverable if proved by appropriate evidence.[81]

As was stated above, it must be reasonable to repair. If the cost of **6–043** replacement is less than the cost of repair, then replacement will *prima facie* be the reasonable course of action. Thus, in *Darbishire v. Warran*[82] the claimant, whose car had been damaged by the defendant, incurred repair costs of £192 (plus hiring charges) though the market value of the vehicle at the time was £85. It was held that he had acted unreasonably and he was limited to recovery of the market value (*i.e.* £85 plus hiring charges). Exceptionally however the cost of repair may be recovered even where it exceeds the market value. In *O'Grady v. Westminster Scaffolding Ltd*[83] the claimant incurred expenditure of £253 in repairing his car, a 1938 or 1939 M.G. (in addition to £208 spent on hiring substitute cars). The

---

[79] [1992] 3 All E.R. 385.
[80] [1935] P. 70 at 77.
[81] See *Payton v. Brooks* [1974] R.T.R. 169 at 174, 176.
[82] [1963] 1 W.L.R. 1067. See also *Italian State Railways v. Minnehaha* (1921) 6 Lloyd's Rep. 12.
[83] [1962] 2 Lloyd's Rep. 238.

market value of the car prior to the accident was £180–£200. The court, in awarding the cost of repairs, stressed the particular value of the car to the claimant; during the period he owned it the engine was replaced on three occasions, the coachwork had been completely renewed and other work had been done. In the words of Pennycuick J. in *Darbishire*:[84] "It is as though someone had elected to drive around in a mechanised replica of the Lord Mayor's coach." In effect the car was regarded as a unique article, and no comparable article could have been purchased. Again, in *Algeiba v. Australind*[85] repair costs which exceeded market value (cost of replacement less value in damaged state) were awarded, since the ship was of special value to her owners, being particularly well-equipped for the work they used her for, and given the considerable difficulty of finding a replacement at the time.

6–044   Not only must repair be the reasonable option, the cost of repair must itself be reasonable. Thus, in *The Pactolus*[86] the court, in concluding that the repairs must be necessary and the charges not excessive, held that the award must be limited to the ordinary rate for the job. In addition it was held that the claimant in such a case was entitled to a complete repair of all the damage done even if the effect was to render the goods more valuable than they were prior to the damage occurring.[87] Though it is probably right to conclude that the claimant in such a case is overcompensated,[88] it is suggested that this is preferable to making a deduction from the award to deprive the claimant of the overcompensation, since he did not choose to have damage inflicted on his goods and should not be out of pocket as a result.

6–045   For the cost of repairs to be awarded, the court does not require the repairs already to have been carried out. The goods' value has been diminished by the damage whether or not repairs have been effected. It must follow therefore that the award will be made even if the goods are never repaired. So, in *The Glenfinlas*,[89] after the vessel in question was damaged, temporary repairs were carried out. Before permanent repairs could be carried out the ship was requisitioned by the Government and subsequently struck a mine and sank. The defendant admitted liability for the cost of the permanent repairs. However, on the principles discussed above[90] where the claimant's goods have already been damaged by an earlier tortfeasor, the claimant can not recover damages from the second tortfeasor where the repairs his negligence has necessitated are the same as the repairs (as yet not carried out) necessitated by the negligence of the first tortfeasor.[91] On

---

[84] [1963] 1 W.L.R. 1067 at 1079.
[85] (1921) 8 Lloyd's Rep. 210.
[86] (1856) Swab. 173.
[87] See also *The Gazelle* (1844) 2 Wim. Rob. 279.
[88] cf Burrows *op. cit.* pp. 166–7, who argues that the claimant would only really be benefited in such a case if he were to sell the goods. Surely however, even if he retained the goods for his own use he would benefit from their likely extended lifespan.
[89] [1918] P. 363, n. See also *The Endeavour* (1890) 60 L.T. 840; *The London Corporation* [1935] P. 70.
[90] *supra* paras. 4–020 *et seq.*
[91] *Performance Cars Ltd v. Abraham* [1962] 1 Q.B. 33.

the same principles, where, as in *Organic Research Chemicals v. Ricketts*,[92] where a garage whose services were engaged to repair the engine of a car which had broken down, in fact caused further damage to the engine, it was held liable for the difference between the cost of a new engine and the cost of repairing the defect which caused the initial breakdown.

In two interesting cases concerning damage to London buses, the question arose as to the recoverability of overhead charges where the claimant repairs damaged goods himself. In *London Transport Executive v. Court*[93] it was held that the claimant could not recover for overhead expenses which would in any event have been incurred. In *London Transport Executive v. Foy Morgan & Co.*[94] a claim for recovery of overhead expenses was allowed, having been worked out reasonably and properly which, in the light of the earlier case, must mean that some extra expense beyond that which would normally have incurred must have been shown.   6–046

As we saw earlier,[95] the Torts (Interference with Goods) Act 1977 limits the recovery of damages for destruction of goods where the claimant is a person with a limited interest in the goods. Those principles apply equally to cases where the goods are merely damaged.   6–047

6. CONSEQUENTIAL LOSSES

(1) Loss of profit-earning goods

Inevitably the issues that arise under this heading frequently concern remoteness of damage, and in general the cases discussed below are but particular applications of the principles discussed elsewhere.[96] Early cases allowed recovery of lost profits on the basis of "demurrage", (a term more commonly employed in charterparties to denote the amount payable by the charterer to the shipowner per day for improper detention of the vessel) comprising the generalised losses suffered by the owner. Thus in *The Hebe*[97] a claim for demurrage of £56 was not supported by the evidence: the claimant could not substantiate the claim he made that the vessel, if undamaged, would have made two voyages with full cargoes. An award of £30 was upheld under that heading, without specifying the losses it was designed to reflect. In *The Gazelle*[98] it was emphasised by the court that in aiming at the proper sum to be awarded for demurrage there must be deducted from the gross freight the expenses incurred in earning the freight, *i.e.* the net loss of profits. In assessing demurrage in *The Black Prince*[99] Dr.   6–048

---

[92] *The Times*, November 16, 1961.
[93] [1954] C.L.Y. 888.
[94] [1955] C.L.Y. 743.
[95] *supra* para. 6–041.
[96] *supra* paras. 4–025 *et seq.*
[97] (1847) 2 Wm. Rob. 530.
[98] (1844) 2 Wm. Rob. 279 at 284.
[99] (1862) Lush. 568. See also *The Kingsway* [1918] P. 344, where it was held that in addition to demurrage being payable for the four days during which temporary repairs were carried out to the vessel, a further award was made for loss of time during the period when permanent repairs would subsequently be effected.

Lushington related it to the value of the ship, equating it to interest in excess of £36 per cent per annum on the proven value of the ship of £25,000 and arriving at a figure of £25 per day. He also stated that the duration of the relevant period for which demurrage was payable was the number of days the vessel was thrown out of her usual employment.

6–049   Later cases demonstrate the more specific losses that may be recovered under this head. In *The Argentino*[1] the owners of the Argentino were able to show that as a consequence of the damage done to her in a collision she would be unable to fulfil a subsequent charter. It was held that they could recover the lost profits. Lord Herschell said:[2]

> "it . . . is no doubt the usual course, to award damages under the name of demurrage in respect of the loss of earnings which it must reasonably have been anticipated would ensue during the time of detention. But where such a claim is made as in the present case, the owner cannot, I think, be allowed in addition, as a separate item, demurrage in respect of the time the vessel was under repair."

He went on to emphasise that it would be necessary to set off against the award for loss of profits the amount that the claimant could have earned, having lost the particular contract, from the use of the repaired vessel during any of the time covered by the lost voyage when the vessel was available to him.

6–050   It must follow that if the damaged chattel would have been operating unprofitably during the time of repair, damages for loss of profits will not be awarded. Thus in *The Bodlewell*[3] the damaged vessel was working at a loss in order to establish a new trade. No loss of profits could therefore be shown during the period of repair, and in addition it was held that the profits it was hoped to make when the trade was established were too remote[4] to be recoverable.

6–051   Where profits have been lost, the courts have had to grapple with a range of complexities arising from particular fact situations. For example, where freight rates rise substantially over a short period of time, how should this be reflected in the award of damages? In *The Soya*[5] the claimant's vessel was damaged in a collision while proceeding to a port of loading under a charterparty. After 20 days of repairs she was able to complete this charter. During the period of repair the claimant agreed a further charter to be carried out subsequently, at a significantly higher rate of freight, due to a sharp rise in the freight market. But for the collision the vessel would have completed the earlier charter and embarked upon the later charter 20 days earlier. The Court of Appeal awarded damages on the basis of the rate of freight prevailing at the time of the collision, concluding that the loss

---

[1] (1889) 14 App. Cas. 519.
[2] *ibid.* at 523–4.
[3] [1907] P. 286. See also *The Black Prince* (1862) Lush. 568; *Admiralty Commissioners v. SS. Valeria* [1922] 2 A.C. 242.
[4] As Ogus points out (*op. cit.* at 80) the issue would have been better categorised as lack of certainty rather than remoteness.
[5] [1956] 1 W.L.R. 714.

resulting from the delay in embarking on the more profitable charter was too speculative and remote. Subsequently Brandon J. in *The Naxos*[6] interpreted the judgment of Lord Evershed M.R. in *The Soya* as meaning that where the rate of profit under the charterparty whose commencement was delayed by the need for repair was reasonably representative of the vessel's earning capacity during the period of delay, it could and should be taken as the basis of calculation of the lost profits. However, if the rate was unusually low or unusually high, and therefore not reasonably representative, the court could and should seek other evidence of earning capacity, for example, by taking the average over a number of voyages. In the instant case the judge used as a basis for calculation the average of the profit rates from the three voyages before and after the period of detention of the vessel for repair, reducing it slightly (from £518 to £500). It is suggested that this represents a fairer approach than that which would follow from too rigorous an application of the decision in *The Soya*.

As we have seen, the duty to mitigate will require account to be taken of profits which were actually earned or should have been earned during the period when the goods are out of action. There must, however, be a causal connection between the accident and the earning of the alternative profit by the claimant. In *The World Beauty*[7] the claimant's vessel was damaged while engaged on a charterparty (the first charterparty) which was due to be completed in September 1958. She had also been prospectively engaged on another charterparty (the second charterparty) which was to commence between August 1 and October 31, 1958. The damage occurred in April. Her owners acted in mitigation, chartering another vessel to fulfil the first charterparty. The repairs on the damaged vessel were completed in time to enable her to embark (by agreement) on the second charterparty, which was advanced by three months. The defendant argued that the large profits made by the claimant in taking up the second charter three months early had to be set off against the losses sustained by the claimant. The Court of Appeal held however that the only benefit to the claimant was the advancement of the second charterparty by three months, as the profit would have been earned anyway, irrespective of the accident.   6–052

Issues of causation also arise where the claimant makes use of the time during which the repairs necessitated by the defendant's tort are carried out to effect other repairs. A claim may be made in such a case for dock expenses and loss of use and profits, and the House of Lords made it clear in *Carslogie S.S. Co. v. Royal Norwegian Government*[8] that the defendant will either be liable in full or not at all for whichever head of damage is claimed: no question of apportionment arises. Thus, in *Carslogie* the vessel in question received temporary repairs which rendered her seaworthy, but ran into heavy weather on the way to the port where permanent repairs were to be carried out. This caused her to suffer damage making her unseaworthy and requiring immediate repair. When she reached her destination both sets of repairs were carried out concurrently, taking a total of 30   6–053

---

[6] [1972] 1 Lloyd's Rep. 149.
[7] [1970] P. 144.
[8] [1952] A.C. 292.

days. If the collision damage had been carried out separately, it would have required 10 days. It was held that the defendants were not liable for damages in respect of the 10 days detention, since the heavy weather damage was not a consequence of the collision, and there was no loss of profitable time sustained by the claimants by dint of the fact that for 10 of the 30 days during which repairs were being effected the vessel was also undergoing repairs necessitated by the collision. By contrast, in *The Acanthus*[9] the claimants carried out improvements to their vessel while it was in dry dock being repaired, without causing delay or increasing the dock expenses. It was held that they were entitled to take advantage of this opportunity without being required to contribute to the costs of the dry docking and repairs, which remained entirely the responsibility of the defendant.

(2) Loss of non-profit-earning goods

6–054   No difficulty in general arises under this heading where the claimant has acted reasonably in hiring a substitute or has incurred expenses reasonably. Where the claim is one purely for loss of use, the matter is less clear-cut. For example, in *The Mediana*[10] a lightship belonging to the claimant (a harbour board) was damaged due to the defendant's negligence. While the lightship was being repaired it was replaced by another lightship owned by the board, which it kept for just such an emergency. For the defendant it was argued that damages should be limited to the cost of removing and repairing the damaged vessel, since the claimant had mitigated its loss by use of the substitute vessel. The House of Lords held that, in the words of the Earl of Halsbury L.C.[11] "where by the wrongful act of one man something belonging to another is itself so injured as not to be capable of being used or is taken away so that it cannot be used at all, that of itself is a ground for damages." He went on to say that this was: "a ground for real damages, not nominal damages at all."[12] It has been persuasively argued[13] that no damages should be awarded in such a case, since there is no loss suffered by the claimant, but the House of Lords regarded the broad principle as being independent of the particular facts, though admitting that in many cases it might be concluded that there had really been no damage at all. It might in addition be argued that the prudence of the claimant in maintaining a reserve lightship should not operate to the benefit of the defendant, by analogy to the non-deductibility of first party insurance benefits paid to an injured claimant in a personal injury case.[14]

6–055   In any event, the law has been clear since *The Mediana* that a claim for loss of use can be made, though the court in that case was more concerned with establishing the general principle than with the details of quantum. Subsequently in *The Marpessa*[15] a dredger belonging to the claimant dock

---

[9] [1902] P. 17.
[10] [1900] A.C. 113. See also *The Greta Holme* [1897] A.C. 596.
[11] [1900] A.C. 113 at 116.
[12] *ibid.* at 118.
[13] Burrows *op. cit.* p. 165.
[14] See *infra* para. 9–046.
[15] [1907] A.C. 241.

and harbour board was damaged. The dredger was out of action for nine days. The House of Lords held that the loss sustained by the claimant was the value of the work which would have been done by the dredger during those nine days. In quantifying this loss, the court equated the daily value of the dredger's daily services to the claimant to the daily cost to it of maintaining and working the dredger, plus its daily depreciation. More specifically, in *Admiralty Commissioners v. S.S. Chekiang*[16] the House of Lords did not consider that the registrar had misdirected himself in calculating damages for loss of use on the basis of five per cent per annum on the estimated capital value of the ship at the time of the collision. In a penetrating analysis of the problems of assessing damages in such cases, Lord Sumner pointed out the need to differentiate between the different types of vessel and their different uses, and concluded that:

> "except in cases very strictly comparable with the present case, or in cases where admissions are made, the Admiralty should be required, as part of their claim, to give evidence of the character of the ship, to explain what her duties are and the true relation of the original cost to her duties at the time of the damage, and so to enable a clear judgment to be formed of the appropriate rates of depreciation and of interest."[17]

In *Birmingham Corporation v. Sowsbery*[18] Geoffrey Lane J. pointed out   6–056
the difficulties inherent in both the *Marpessa* approach and the *S.S. Chekiang* approach.

> "The former [based on the cost of maintaining and operating the chattel] puts a premium upon inefficiency. The higher the cost of maintaining the omnibus the greater will be the damages. In other words, there can be no guarantee, if the point is contested, that the standing charge cost represents the true value of the vehicle to the claimant, and consequently the damages may be too high. The latter method [based on interest on capital and depreciation] will produce unduly differing results according to the age of the vehicle and the amount by which it has depreciated at the time of the accident. In the case of a long-lived chattel such as a ship this may not be important. In the case of an omnibus, which depreciates rapidly, it may produce results both illogical and unfair to the owners."[19]

The court regarded the cost of maintenance and operation basis as preferable in the circumstances; it provided a reasonably stable basis for calculation and did not suffer from possible fluctuations in capital value and interest rates. The claimants were accordingly held to be entitled to the

---

[16] [1926] A.C. 637. See also *The Hebridean Coast* [1961] A.C. 545, where a rate of 7% was approved.
[17] [1926] A.C. 637 at 649–650.
[18] [1970] R.T.R. 84.
[19] *ibid.* at 86–87.

daily standing charge cost of £4 11s multiplied by 69 (the number of days the damaged bus was off the road being repaired).

6–057   It is difficult therefore to be dogmatic about the test likely to be employed in any particular case. The appropriateness and desirability of the apposite test must depend upon the circumstances of the case, and all one can do is to echo the words of Willmer L.J. in *The Hebridean Coast*[20] that "there is no special sanctity about any particular method of arriving at the appropriate sum."

7. MISAPPROPRIATION OF GOODS

6–058   Unlike other aspects of the law concerning injury to property rights, the measure of damages where goods have been misappropriated depends to an extent upon the relevant cause of action. Though the Law Reform Committee in 1971[21] recommended the replacement of detinue, conversion and trespass by a single tort of wrongful interference with chattels, the ensuing Torts (Interference with Goods) Act 1977, retained trespass and conversion as separate torts, detinue however being subsumed within conversion (an effect of this was to extend to the claimant the possibility of obtaining an order for redelivery of the goods). As damages under the 1977 Act are to be assessed according to the methods appropriate to conversion, the element of damages for detention that formed part of a claim in detinue is no longer available and the time at which the value of the goods is to be taken which was previously different as between the two is now assimilated. Apart from minor differences, discussed briefly below,[22] the measure of damages for conversion and trespass is the same, and in the discussion which follows, references to conversion, which has long been the main action, can be assumed to include trespass, though it should be borne in mind that the 1977 Act brings them both within the phrases "wrongful interference" and "wrongful interference with goods."

Normal measure of damages

6–059   The long-established basis for the measure of damages in cases of misappropriation of goods is the market value of the goods. Thus, in *Caxton Publishing Co. Ltd v. Sutherland Publishing Co Ltd*[23] Lord Roche said: "There is no dispute but that the measure of damages is the value of the thing converted at the time of the conversion." The use of the term "value" is however no more than a starting point in assessing the precise measure of damages in any given case, since it may depend upon such factors as the nature and extent of the claimant's interest in the goods, whether or not the defendant has retained the goods and whether it is the market selling or the market buying price that is to be taken (which in addition gives rise

---

[20] [1961] A.C. 545 at 559.
[21] 18th Report (1971) Cmnd. 4774.
[22] *Infra* para. 6–080.
[23] [1939] A.C. 178 at 192.

to the question of the time at which the value is to be taken). Generally the courts speak in terms of the market value, *i.e.* the selling price of the goods. Thus, in *Chubb Cash Ltd v. John Crilley & Son*[24] the defendant, in executing a distress warrant, converted a cash register which it believed to belong to the debtor but in fact had been hired to him by the claimant under a hire purchase agreement. The register was sold at public auction by the defendant, and it was held that, in the absence of any other evidence as to its value, the measure of damages in conversion was the amount it realised at auction.

In *France v. Gaudet*[25] the claimant bought champagne lying at the 6–060 defendant's wharf at 14s per dozen and agreed to sell it for 24s per dozen. The defendant subsequently refused to deliver the wine. It was held that in ordinary circumstances the measure of damages would be represented by the price paid by the claimant for obtaining other goods of the same quality and description, but the market did not admit of such a possibility; the court thus awarded the price of the sub-sale; 24s per dozen being regarded as the actual value which, in the circumstances, the champagne had acquired. The market value, had there been a market, would therefore have been the buying price rather than the selling price. This approach was reiterated in *Hall v. Barclay*[26] where Greer L.J. said:[27]

> "where you are dealing with goods that can be readily bought in the market, a man whose rights have been interfered with is never entitled to more than what he would have had to pay to buy a similar article in the market."

There was no market for the goods with which the case was concerned (experimental davits), however, and the cost of replacement was therefore awarded.

As has been pointed out,[28] the decision as to whether the buying or sel- 6–061 ling price of the goods is to be taken as the market value should depend upon which more accurately gives effect to the principle of *restitutio in integrum*. If, as in *France v. Gaudet*, the goods are held with a view to future sale, the compensatory principle is surely best reflected, where there is no market in which a replacement can be bought, by awarding the selling price. If however the goods are held with a view to retention for the claimant's own purposes, as in *Hall v. Barclay*, the buying price is appropriate, as it will also be where the claimant intended to sell the goods and there is a market in which he can purchase a replacement. In *The Arpad*[29] however, the Court of Appeal regarded the actual resale price of wheat which the defendant converted as being too remote, and awarded merely the market

---

[24] [1983] 1 W.L.R. 599. See also *Hall v. Barclay* [1937] 3 All E.R. 620.
[25] (1871) L.R. 6 Q.B. 199. See also *The Arpad* [1934] P. 189.
[26] [1937] 3 All E.R. 620.
[27] *ibid.* at 623.
[28] Ogus *op. cit.* p. 145; Burrows *op. cit.* p. 168.
[29] [1934] P. 189. Followed by the Court of Appeal in *Sales Lease Ltd. v. Davis* [1999] 1 W.L.R. 1664. *Cf. Nigerian National Shipping Lines v. Mutual Ltd, The Windfall* [1999] 1 Lloyd's Rep. 664.

selling price (the market price having fallen considerably) at the date arranged for delivery. *France v. Gaudet* was regarded as an authority merely for the proposition that in the absence of other evidence the cost of resale might be treated as the value of the goods. With respect, there seems to be much merit in the dissenting judgment of Scrutton L.J. in *The Arpad*, who regarded the point as turning essentially on the difference between the contractual and tortious rules on remoteness of damage.[30]

6–062   Exceptionally there may be no market value for the goods converted. In *Caxton Publishing Co v. Sutherland Publishing Co*[31] the claimant had the copyright in a literary work, extracts of which were contained in a book published by the defendant, in breach of the claimant's copyright. It was held that the act of binding the infringing sheets in the book was the act that comprised conversion. The court did not accept that the fundamental principle that the measure of damages was the value of the goods converted should be qualified by assessing the value to the owner of the goods. Goods did not have a diminished or no value to the owner because he had no machinery for selling it. The value was not necessarily the price for which the owner could sell the goods. The court concluded that the value might properly be calculated by taking a proportion of the value of the volume into which the claimant's property had been incorporated (with an allowance for expenses which it was proved had been properly and necessarily incurred after the act of conversion) and multiplying that proportion by the number of copies sold.

6–063   Particular problems arise concerning the time at which the value of the misappropriated goods is to be taken. The fluctuating nature of the value of goods is the main factor giving rise to difficulty, but problems may equally arise as a result of improvements made to the goods by the defendant or a third party. The basic rule, as stated in a number of cases, is that the time when the goods are converted is the time at which the market value of the goods is to be assessed.[32] Taking that as a starting point, it is necessary to consider what the effect on this principle is where there are fluctuations in the value, where the goods are improved and where the goods are returned.

6–064   Where market fluctuations have caused the value of the goods to fall after the date of conversion, the measure of damages will depend upon whether the deprivation of the goods was temporary or permanent. In two decisions[33] the Judicial Committee of the Privy Council held, in cases where defendants converted claimants' shares, replacing them subsequently with shares bought at a lower price, the market having fallen, that the defendants were liable for the market value at the time of conversion. From this of course would have to be deducted the value of the shares received, at the time of receipt.

---

[30] *The Arpad* involved alternative claims in contract and tort.
[31] [1939] A.C. 178.
[32] See *e.g. Mercer v. Jones* (1813) 3 Camp. 477: *Henderson v. Williams* [1895] 1 Q.B. 521; *Solloway v. McLaughlin* [1938] A.C. 247. *Cf.* however *Greening v. Wilkinson* (1825) 1 C. & P. 625.
[33] *Solloway v. McLaughlin* [1938] A.C. 247 and *BBMB Finance (Hong Kong) v. Eda Holdings* [1990] 1 W.L.R. 409. The fact that in the latter case the defendant inexplicably did not make a profit, was regarded as irrelevant.

In both of the above cases, the deprivation was permanent. In *Brandeis Goldschmidt & Co Ltd v. Western Transport Ltd*[34] the claimant claimed delivery up of its copper, detained by the defendant, and damages for wrongful detention. The defendant duly complied with an order for delivery up of the copper, but argued that the claimant was entitled to nominal damages only, and not to damages reflecting the fall in the value of copper during the period of detention. The claimant had acquired the copper not for resale but for use in its business, as a raw material, and adduced no evidence of what would have happened to the copper had it not been detained, nor when it would have been processed and sold. The Court of Appeal held that there was no universal rule for assessing damages for wrongful detention of goods, and the claimant was entitled to recover damages only for losses which were proved to have resulted from the detention. Nominal damages only were therefore recoverable for the infringement of their right to possess the goods.

Earlier cases of detinue[35] where the fall in the market value during the period of wrongful detention was awarded were regarded as explicable on the basis that there was a reasonable inference that the claimants intended resale on the market at a profit. In *BBMB Ltd*, however, the Board explained the decision in *Brandeis* as being concerned with damages caused by temporary deprivation of possession and use of property, in contrast to cases where the property is converted permanently by the defendant. It is clear from cases such as *Williams v. Archer*[36] that in an appropriate case damages representing the fall in market value can be awarded, even though the deprivation of possession is merely temporary. It would appear however from the decision in *BBMB Ltd* that where the deprivation is permanent, that measure, *i.e.* the difference between market value at date of default and at date of judgment will always be awarded.   6–065

The question of the effect on quantum of a rise in the value of the goods subsequent to the conversion arose for consideration in *Sachs v. Miklos*,[37] where the defendant agreed to store the claimant's furniture without charge. Subsequently the claimant ceased to keep in touch with the defendant, and, when the defendant needed the room in which the furniture was stored she tried, without success, to contact him via an address provided by his bank manager and by telephone. The defendant sold the furniture for £15. Later the claimant demanded the return of his furniture, the value of which had greatly increased in the meantime. The Court of Appeal held that, though it was decided in *Rosenthal v. Alderton & Sons Ltd*[38] that in a case of detinue a defendant who failed to return goods to a claimant must pay the value of those goods assessed at the date of the judgment in his favour, it would not necessarily be the case that this was the appropriate test for all cases. "The question is what is the plaintiff's loss, what damage he has suffered, by the wrongful act of the defendants."[39] If the claimant   6–066

---

[34] [1981] Q.B. 864.
[35] *Williams v. Archer* (1847) 5 C.B. 318; *Williams v. Peel River Co* (1887) 55 L.T. 689.
[36] *supra* n. 35.
[37] [1948] 2 K.B. 23. See also *Rosenthal v. Alderton & Sons Ltd* [1946] K.B. 374.
[38] [1946] K.B. 374.
[39] [1948] 2 K.B. 23 at 39.

did know, or ought to have known, via the letters sent to him, that the defendant intended to sell the furniture, then the significant rise in value which subsequently occurred was not damage he could recover as flowing from the wrongful act. In such circumstances he would be in breach of his duty to mitigate and would be able to recover no more than the price the goods fetched at that time. The case was remitted to the judge to find whether or not the letters were received by the claimant or came to his knowledge. In such a case, where a rise in value is a consequence of the wrongful act of the defendant, the rise will be assessed as consequential losses, the basic value being the market value at the date of conversion, as was emphasised by Diplock L.J. in *General and Finance Facilities v. Cooks Cars*.[40]

6–067   The next situation for discussion is that concerning cases in which the value of the misappropriated goods has been increased by the defendant or by a third party. In *Munro v. Willmott*[41] the defendant permitted the claimant to leave her car in the defendant's yard. It was contemplated that this would be for a short period only, but in fact the claimant left her car there for several years. After various unsuccessful efforts to communicate with the claimant, the defendant, who needed the space, decided he had to dispose of the car, so he spent £85 on it in order to make it saleable, and sold it for £100. Later the claimant discovered what had happened, and sued the defendant in conversion. The judge found that at the date of judgement the value of the car was £120, whereas, had the defendant not done work on it, it would only have been worth £20. He awarded damages of £35, being the difference between the value at date of judgment and the expenditure of the defendant and representing the true value of the property which the claimant had lost.

6–068   Whether or not the defendant in such a case would still be allowed the benefits of any increase in value resulting from improvements effected by him depends upon the proper interpretation of section 6(i) of the Torts (Interference with Goods) Act 1977. This provides as follows:

> "if in proceedings for wrongful interference against a person (the 'improver') who has improved the goods, it is shown that the improver acted in the mistaken but honest belief that he had a good title to them, an allowance shall be made for the extent to which, at the time as at which the goods fall to be valued in assessing damages, the value of the goods is attributable to the improvement."[42]

6–069   This provision does not protect a person such as the defendant in *Munro* who is well aware that he has no title to the goods. Such a defendant would, under section 12 of the Act, be entitled, as a bailee, to sell the bailor's goods without incurring a liability in conversion, provided reason-

---

[40] [1963] 1 W.L.R. 644 at 649.
[41] [1949] 1 K.B. 295. See also *Reid v. Fairbanks* (1853) 13 C.B. 692.
[42] The section also makes provision for a similar allowance to be made in proceedings against a purchaser in good faith from the improver, and also where the purchaser seeks recovery of the purchase price because of failure of considerable. The section applies to sales, bailments and other dispositions of goods.

able efforts have been made to trace or communicate with the bailor, but the bailee must account to the bailor for the proceeds of sale, less any costs of sale. However the section is silent on the possibility of the bailor, as in *Munro*, being entitled to deduct the increase in value resulting from improvements effected by him.

In *Highland Leasing v. Paul Field*[43] R.M. Stewart Q.C.[44] stated that sec- 6–070 tion 6 did not change the common law rules and, in effect, followed *Munro* in a case where, again, improvements had been made by a defendant who did not believe he had good title to the goods. The commentators are split on the question whether section 6 has the effect of precluding an allowance, in a *Munro*-type case.[45] Tentatively it is suggested that the preferred view is that section 6(1) does not preclude a *Munro*-type claim, on the basis that, as is argued in Halsbury,[46] the sub-section is not expressed as being declaratory of the existing law, nor is it expressed as being in place of it.

Similarly it is unclear what effect, if any, section 6(1) has on the line of 6–071 cases involving unauthorised mining where it has (usually successfully) been claimed that the defendant can deduct the cost of severing and raising the minerals from the value of the minerals at the pit's mouth.[47]

A further situation where problems of assessment may arise occurs where 6–072 the goods are returned to the claimant, whether by order of the court or where, under section 3(2)(b) of the Torts (Interference with Goods) Act 1977 the defendant elects to return the goods and pay consequential damages. Section 3(7) of the Act provides that where, under section 6(1) or (2) an allowance is to be made in respect of an improvement to the goods and an order for delivery is made, the court may assess the allowance to be made in respect of the improvement and, as a condition for delivery of the goods, order that allowance to be made by the claimant. Prior to the Act, there were conflicting dicta in detinue cases,[48] which the Act resolves in favour of the view expressed in the *Peruvian Guano* case, but is silent on the issue of expenses incurred in improving goods. In any event, such an allowance will only be feasible in the circumstances envisaged by section 6(1), so the "mistaken but honest belief" requirement will in such a case act as a limitation on the range of cases where improvements have been effected.

Complexities, especially at common law, arose where the claimant was 6–073 not the owner of the goods, but had a limited interest, such as bailee or pledgee. The Torts (Interference with Goods) Act 1977 resolves a number of these difficulties, but common law rules still have a significant role to play. At common law the defendant might find himself liable to more than

---

[43] [1986] C.L.Y. 3224.
[44] Presumably sitting as a Deputy High Court Judge.
[45] Clerk and Lindsell (17th ed., 1995) para 13-129; McGregor, *op. cit.* para. 1398 believes an allowance can only be made in the cases envisaged in the Act; *Halsbury's Laws* Vol. 45 para 1458, agrees with R.M. Stewart Q.C. in *Highland Leasing.*
[46] *ibid.* n. 45 at fn. 10. See also *Halsbury's Laws* Vol. 44 para. 1438.
[47] See *Jegon v. Vivian* (1871) L.R. 6 Ch. App. 742; *Livingstone v. Rawyards Coal Co.* (1880) 5 App. Cas. 25.
[48] *cf. Peruvian Guano Co. v. Dreyfus* [1892] A.C. 166 at 176 per Lord Macnaghten and *Glenwood Lumber Co. v. Phillips* [1904] A.C. 405 at 412 per Lord Davey.

one claimant. In *The Winkfield*[49] the Court of Appeal accepted that a defendant who had paid full damages to the bailee could not be liable to the bailor, but it was unclear whether this applied in other cases of limited interest. Section 7 of the Act, however, precludes double liability of a wrongdoer where either one of two or more rights of action for wrongful interference is founded on a possessory title, or the measure of damages in an action for wrongful interference founded on a proprietary title is or includes the entire value of the goods, although the interest is one of two or more interests in the goods. The effect of the section is to require a claimant who has recovered more than would have been his proper share of the goods' value on an apportionment to account for the excess to another who has a right to claim;[50] and in addition, where such an account has been made, to require that person, where he himself has made a successful damages claim, to reimburse the claimant to the extent of the overpayment.[51] Section 7(4) provides, as an example of this, the situation where a converter of goods pays damages first to a finder of the goods, and then to the true owner. The finder is unjustly enriched unless he accounts over to the true owner under 7(3) and then the true owner is unjustly enriched and becomes liable to reimburse the converter of the goods.

6–074   At common law a converter was not allowed to argue the *jus tertii* against a claimant in possession of the goods, the effect of which was that he could not argue for a reduction in damages to the extent of the third party's interest in the goods. The *jus tertii* could however be set up where the claimant relied only on an immediate right to possession. It does not follow from this however that such a claimant was precluded from claiming the full value of goods. A broad reading of *The Winkfield*[52] supported by the decision of the Privy Council in *The Jag Shakti*[53] favours the view that a claimant with a right to possession could claim the full value of the goods: whereas *Bloxham v. Hubbard*[54] was interpreted by some[55] as restricting such a claimant to the extent of his interest in the goods. Such debate is now academic in the light of section 8 of the Torts (Interference with Goods) Act 1977, which enables the defendant in an action for wrongful interference to show that a third party has a better right than the claimant as respects all or any part of the interest claimed by the claimant, or in right of which he sues. The section empowers the provision of rules of court[56] relating to proceedings for wrongful interference, enabling the third party to be brought into the proceedings, and enabling the court to divide the damages between the claimant and the third party in accordance with the provisions of section 7 of the Act.

6–075   The Act will however have no application in the situation where the defendant himself is the other person who has an interest in the property,

---

[49] [1902] P. 42.
[50] s. 7(3).
[51] s. 7(4).
[52] [1902] P. 42.
[53] [1986] A.C. 337. See also McGregor *op. cit.* para. 1428; Clerk and Lindsell *op. cit.* 13-141 n. 73.
[54] (1804) 5 East. 407.
[55] See Palmer: Bailment (2nd ed., 1991) pp. 340–351.
[56] See R.S.C. Ord. 15r. 10A, which makes such provision. See now also C.P.R. r. 191(2).

for example when a bailor retakes goods from his bailee, since the Act is concerned, in section 7, with double liability to two or more claimants, and section 8 gives the defendant the ability to show that a third party has a better right than the claimant. In cases where the claimant relies on possession, the usual example being a bailee claiming against a bailor who has retaken the goods, he is limited to recovering only to the extent of his interest in the goods.[57] Where the claimant relies on an immediate right to possession, rather than possession itself (in practice, the owner suing the person in possession or a third party), the cases seem to draw a distinction between the situation where goods held as security are disposed of, and that where the contract is one of sale or hire purchase. As regards the latter category, in *Chinery v. Viall*[58] the defendant agreed to sell sheep to the claimant on credit. He retained possession of the sheep and sold them to a third party. It was held that this amounted to a conversion which was compensated by assessing the loss sustained by the claimant by not having delivered to him the sheep at the agreed price, *i.e.* the value of the sheep minus the price the claimant would have had to pay for them if they had been delivered to him.[59] Similarly, in cases of hire purchase such as *Wickham Holdings v. Brooke House Motors*,[60] the courts have held that a finance company deprived of its goods by an act of conversion is entitled to compensation for the loss of its interest and no more. Thus, in *Wickham Holdings*, "X" hired a car from the claimant under a hire-purchase agreement. He wished to trade it in with the defendant car dealers for another car. The defendant contacted the claimant, who said the settlement figure was £270 (there was £274 10s outstanding). The defendant accepted the car from X in part exchange for another car, and sold it on. The defendant forgot to send on the £270 to the claimant. The judge awarded the claimant £365 being the trade value of the car at date of judgment, and £75 damages for detention. The Court of Appeal held that he was entitled only to the balance outstanding on the hire purchase price which was £274 10s, this being the amount the claimant had lost.

By contrast, where goods are held as security, the effect of an act of conversion, *e.g.* by a bailee with a lien over the goods, may be to entitle the owner not only to immediate possession, but also to recovery of the full value of the goods, without any obligation to deduct the debt owed to the defendant.[61] However, where a pledgee wrongfully sells or re-pledges goods, as in *Donald v. Suckling*[62] such action does not put an end to the

6–076

---

[57] See e.g. Brierly v. Kendall (1852) 17 Q.B. 937.

[58] (1860) 5 H. & N. 288.

[59] Perhaps unsurprisingly this is the same as the measure of damages for non-delivery by a seller in breach of contract.

[60] [1967] 1 W.L.R. 295 overruling *United Dominions Trust (Commercial) Ltd v. Parkway Motors Ltd* [1955] 1 W.L.R. 719. See also *Belvoir Finance Co. v. Stapleton* [1971] 1 Q.B. 210.

[61] See *e.g. Mulliner v. Florence* (1878) 3 Q.B. 484. It should be noted however that, though in *Mulliner* the improper sale determined the lien, there is usually a statutory power of sale nowadays for a lien holder; *e.g.* Sale of Goods Act 1979, s. 48; Torts (Interference with Goods) Act 1977, s. 12, s. 13, Sched. 1.

[62] (1866) L.R. 1 Q.B. 585. See also *Halliday v. Holgate* (1868) L.R. 3 Ex. 299. *Cf. Johnson v. Stear* (1863) 15 C.B. (N.S.) 330, though this is regarded as a questionable authority: see McGregor *op. cit.* para. 1433, n. 92.

contract of pledge, and the pledgor cannot therefore claim in conversion until he has paid or tendered the amount owed. In such cases it is, of course, still open to the owner of the goods to sue for the amount owing, whereas, as was pointed out by Bramwell B. in *Chinery v. Viall*,[63] "it would be singular if the same act which saved the vendee the price of the sheep should vest in him a right of action for their full value without deducting the price."

6–077   Finally, in considering the problems arising from the concept of "value" in cases of misappropriation of goods, one or two further instances of particular situations can be drawn from the case law; thus it was held in *Morison v. London County and Westminster Bank*[64] that where a negotiable instrument has been converted, the measure of damages is normally the amount of the instrument, and a defendant who has diminished its value through his misconduct[65] will not be allowed to avail himself of such diminution. It has been doubted[66] whether old authorities (*e.g. Loosemore v. Radford*)[67] holding that, on a conversion of title deeds the full value of the estate may be awarded (though this would be reduced to a nominal sum on the return of the deeds) would be followed today, given the unlikelihood that loss of title deeds would lead to loss of the land they represent, and that the appropriate measure would be the value of the deeds as curiosities, plus any consequential losses that were not too remote.

6–078   Where goods are returned by the defendant to the claimant before the action has proceeded to judgment, a cause of action is already vested in the claimant, and the return of the goods (assuming redelivery is accepted by the claimant)[68] can only take effect as mitigation of the damages. As we have seen, in *Solloway v. Mclaughlin*[69] delivery of an equivalent article to that converted (in the instant case shares) may have the effect of reducing the damages, and it was established in *Hiort v. London and North Western Railway*[70] that a transaction which is, in the words of Bramwell L.J.[71] "equivalent to a return of the goods" may be treated as a redelivery and reduce the damages accordingly. However, sums received by the claimant from the converter of the goods must be received specifically on account of the converter's liability: hence in *Edmondson v. Nuttall*[72] the defendant converted looms belonging to the claimant, a weaver, and sold them to satisfy a judgment he had against the claimant for debt. It was held that the claimant was entitled to recover the full value of the looms. If the claimant refuses to accept redelivery, he will be able to recover nominal damages (assuming the goods are tendered in their pre-conversion state and

---

[63] (1860) 5 H. & N. 288 at 294.
[64] [1914] 3 K.B. 356. The explanation of the rule by Phillimore L.J. at 279 appears broad enough to encompass cases where the instrument is not negotiable.
[65] *e.g.* by striking out a signature on it: see *M'Leod v. M'Ghie* (1841) 2 Sc. N.R. 605.
[66] Clerk & Lindsell on Torts (17th ed., 1995) para. 13-133.
[67] (1842) 9 M. & W. 657 at 659.
[68] See *infra* for the situation where the claimant refuses to accept redelivery.
[69] [1938] A.C. 247 *infra* para. 6–079.
[70] (1879) 4 Ex. D. 188. See also *Plevin v. Henshall* (1833) 10 Bing. 24; *Underwood v. Bank of Liverpool* [1924] 1 K.B. 755; *Lloyds Bank v. Chartered Bank of India, Australia and China* [1929] 1 K.B. 40.
[71] (1879) 4 Ex. D. 188 at 196.
[72] (1864) 17 C.B. (N.S.) 280.

there are no consequential losses). In *Fisher v. Prince*[73] it was held that in such a case the proceedings will be stayed where the goods are handed over and costs are paid, though it was emphasised in *Tucker v. Wright*[74] that if the value of the goods was disputed, a stay would not be granted.

It is perfectly possible for a claimant whose goods have been misappro- 6–079
priated to claim in trespass, but the measure of damage will be the same as in conversion, subject to a couple of possible differences.[75] Likewise, in general damages for wrongful distress will be measured in the same way as in cases of conversion. However, where the case involves irregular, rather than illegal distress (*i.e.* where the distress is not wrongful from the start but, though initially legal, is subsequently conducted in a wrongful manner), the normal measure of damages will be the value of the goods less the rent due,[76] whereas in cases of illegal distress there need be no deduction of the rent due by the claimant.[77] Also, in cases of irregular distress a failure by the claimant to show actual damage will not entitle him to nominal damages,[78] but he will lose the action.[79] Finally, in cases of replevin, an action under which a party whose goods have been taken out of their possession may obtain their immediate return, subject to an action to decide who has the right to their possession, the measure of the award of damages to a successful claimant will be the same as in other cases of misappropriation where the goods have been redelivered. In *Smith v. Enright*[80] it was held that, in addition to consequential losses the claimant was entitled to compensation for annoyance and loss of reputation, though *Lonrho v. Al Fayed (No.5)*[81]suggests that such losses might not be recoverable today.

---

[73] (1762) 3 Bur. 1363.
[74] (1826) 3 Bing. 601.
[75] *i.e.* (a) In cases involving the seizing of fixtures under an illegal distress, it was held in *Clarke v. Holford* (1848) 2 C. & K. 540, where the claimant claimed in conversion, that only their value as chattels was recoverable, whereas in *Moore v. Drinkwater* (1858) 1 F. & F. 134, where the claim was in trespass, their greater value as fixtures was recoverable; (b) where goods (or their equivalent, or the proceeds of their sale) are redelivered, this does not reduce the damages in trespass, in contrast to the position in conversion (*Rundle v. Little* (1844) 6 Q.B. 174); though it seems right to agree with McGregor (*op. cit.* para. 1453) that the case is either wrong or decided on a point of pleading.
[76] See *Biggins v. Goode* (1832) 2 C. & J. 364.
[77] See *Keen v. Priest* (1859) 4 H. & N. 236.
[78] As would be the case if the distraint was illegal: see *Lamb v. Wall* (1859) 1 F. & F. 503.
[79] See *Rodgers v. Parker* (1856) 18 C.B. 112.
[80] (1894) 63 L.J.K.B. 220.
[81] [1993] 1 W.L.R. 1489.

CHAPTER 7

DAMAGE TO ECONOMIC INTERESTS

In this chapter we examine the law concerning the measure of damages in   7–001
cases where the loss sustained by the claimant is a "pure" economic loss in
the sense that it is not a consequence of physical damage to the person or
to property. For our purposes, physical damage is taken to include damage
to reputation and wrongful interference with goods or land, which receive
separate coverage. Our concern in this chapter is with economic losses
where there is no (intervening) injury to the person, property or reputation
of the claimant. Such a loss may arise, in general, either from the commission of a tort whose essential function is to protect economic interests, such
as passing off or intimidation, or as an aspect of the losses recoverable
following commission of a tort which protects other interests as well, such
as negligence and misrepresentation.

1. INTERFERENCE WITH CONTRACTUAL RELATIONS

Certain torts, either by definition or general usage, concern interference   7–002
with contractual relations, and the appropriate measure of damages in such
cases will reflect the nature of the contractual interest adversely affected.
In particular the action for inducement of breach of contract, inaugurated
in *Lumley v. Gye*,[1] will frequently give rise to a claim for the profits lost
on account of the breach induced by the defendant's action. Thus, in *Goldsoll v. Goldman*[2] "S" induced Goldman to breach covenants he entered
into with Goldsoll not to deal in jewellery. Neville J. stated[3] that if the
breach procured was one which must in the ordinary course of business
cause damage to the claimant, then the claimant might succeed without
proof of any particular damage. Neville J. went on to suggest that the loss
of orders resulting from the carrying on of the rival business was recoverable, and awarded damages of £10, the evidence of damage being "of a
somewhat general character." This implies that if specific losses can be
proved they will be recoverable.

A rather different type of loss was held to be recoverable in *Bent's*   7–003

---

[1] (1853) 2 E. & B. 216.
[2] [1914] 2 Ch. 603.
[3] *ibid.* at 615. See also *Exchange Telegraph Co v. Gregory & Co* [1896] 1 Q.B. 147.

Brewery Co v. Luke Hogan[4] where the defendant, a trade union official, sought to induce managers of public houses to provide confidential details of takings and wages bills. A declaration was granted restraining the union from seeking the information. Lynskey J. considered that the likely damage was that the claimant brewery companies might be compelled to pay more for the services of their managers if the information were disclosed.

7–004 Expenditure reasonably incurred on account of the tort may also be recoverable. In *Bristol Motor Trade Association v. Salvadori*[5] the claimants sought to control price inflation of cars by means of a requirement that purchasers of new cars covenant not to resell within twelve months of purchase. The defendants induced purchasers to resell cars to them in breach of covenant and then sold them on at much higher prices. Roxburgh J. held that expenses incurred in "unravelling and detecting the unlawful machinations of the defendants"[6] on the part of the claimants, who maintained a large investigation department, were recoverable. This was of course limited to the money actually expended in investigating the particular cases complained of, impossible though precise quantification was.

7–005 In an appropriate case loss of profits and expenses may be combined in a claim. In *Falconer v. ASLEF and NUR*[7] the claimant was awarded damages both for inconvenience to himself and unavailability to his business and wasted expenditure when a strike called by the defendants prevented British Rail from carrying out its contract to provide him with rail travel.

7–006 Though none of the cases on inducement of breach of contract concerns awards for anything other than pecuniary losses, it is arguable that since in other respects the rules on assessment of damages are the same for all cases of tortious interference with contract, it may be said, on the authority of *Pratt v. British Medical Association*,[8] a case on conspiracy, that non-pecuniary losses may be recoverable. In that case, McCardie J. said:[9] "The court or jury, once financial loss be proved, may award a sum appropriate to the whole circumstances of the tortious wrong inflicted." The humiliation and menace suffered by the claimant were regarded as a recoverable loss.

7–007 It must be doubted however whether this can stand with the views expressed by the Court of Appeal in *Lonrho plc v. Fayed (no. 5)*,[10] also a case on conspiracy. In making it clear that injury to reputation could not form part of the claimant's claim save in an action for defamation, Stuart Smith L.J. said:[11]

> "nor can they recover damages for injured feeling . . . In the case of the personal plaintiffs, they allege no pecuniary loss, so in my judg-

---

[4] [1945] 2 All E.R. 570. See also *The Kalingrad*, [1997] 2 Lloyd's Rep. 35.
[5] [1949] Ch. 556.
[6] *ibid.* at 569.
[7] [1986] I.R.L.R. 331. A much criticised decision for its potential scope. See however Trade Union and Labour Relations Consolidation Act 1992, s. 235A.
[8] [1919] 1 K.B. 244.
[9] *ibid.* at 291.
[10] [1993] 1 W.L.R. 1489.
[11] *ibid.* at 1505.

ment they have no cause of action and injured feelings would simply be an adjunct of injury to reputation."

Dillon L.J. said:[12]

". . . if the plaintiffs want to claim damages for injury to reputation or injury to feelings, they must do so in an action for defamation, not in this very different form of action."

The better view would therefore appear to be that non-pecuniary losses are not recoverable in a tortious claim for interference with contract.

It is clear that the type of pecuniary losses recoverable in cases on induce-   7–008
ment of breach of contract are also recoverable in cases of conspiracy. Thus it was made clear in *Lonrho plc v. Fayed (No. 5)* that loss of profits and expenses were recoverable.[13] As regards intimidation, the third of the trilogy of torts falling under the heading of interference with contract, in the leading case, *Rookes v. Barnard*[14] the issue of damages was to be resolved on a retrial. In *Morgan v. Fry*[15] the claimant suffered a loss of earnings, as will not be uncommon where intimidation is proved, and was able to recover the earnings from the employment from which he was dismissed as a consequence of the intimidation, the court assuming that he would have remained in that employment for a further five years, and deducting the wages he was subsequently earning in different employment.

2. INFRINGEMENT OF INTELLECTUAL PROPERTY RIGHTS

Under this general heading falls to be considered the measure of damages   7–009
for a number of torts where the claimant's intellectual property rights have been infringed. In such cases the essential recoverable loss is the loss of profits occasioned by the defendant's tort. Non-pecuniary losses will not be recoverable.

In passing off cases Goddard L.J. emphasised in *Draper v. Trist*[16] that a   7–010
"fair and temperate"[17] sum may be awarded for the fact of the passing off, though no doubt the greater the detail provided of losses the greater the award is likely to be. Loss of profits could not be awarded in *Draper*, since the case concerned sale of a large quantity of deceptive goods to a middleman, with no evidence of resale to the public, but the claimant could be compensated for the damage to his business by the presence of those decep-

---

[12] [1993] 1 W.L.R. 1489 at 1496. *cf.* the views of the Court of Appeal in *Joyce v. Sengupta* [1993] 1 W.L.R. 337 at 348 and 351, a case concerning malicious falsehood.
[13] See also *British Motor Trade Association v. Salvadori* (n. 5, para. 7–004), esp. at 569. See also *Standard Chartered Bank v. Pakistan National Shipping Corporation (No. 3)* [1999] 1 Lloyd's Rep. 747.
[14] [1964] A.C. 1129.
[15] [1968] 1 Q.B. 521 (reversed as regards liability: [1968] 2 Q.B. 710).
[16] [1939] 3 All E.R. 513.
[17] *ibid.* at 527.

tive goods on the market. Damage to goodwill could also form part of the award, as had earlier been held in *Spalding Bros v. A. W. Gamage Ltd*[18] where the award of loss of profits seems to have included the cost of counter-advertisements, thus suggesting that expenditure reasonably incurred in efforts to mitigate the damage will be recoverable, though, as McGregor points out,[19] in making such an award the court would have to bear in mind the need to avoid double recovery. In essence the same principles will apply to cases involving infringement of trademarks, patents, copyrights and design rights, though the application of those principles to particular torts may vary depending on the nature of the right protected. Thus, where a patent is infringed, damages for lost manufacturing profits will be awarded where the claimant would have manufactured the invention with a view to making a profit, whereas if he would have permitted others to use the invention in return for royalties, the lost royalty profits will be awarded. In *General Tire and Rubber Co v. Firestone Tire and Rubber Co*[20] the House of Lords disagreed with the Court of Appeal, which had upheld the judge's view that the basis of the award was a fair and reasonable royalty, and held that the basis was what royalty would actually have been paid, there being evidence of actual agreements made by the respondent patentees, which was at a lower figure than the fair and reasonable rate. What the defendant would have had to pay rather than what the court considers he should have had to pay is the relevant criterion therefore.

7-011   Where the claimant would have manufactured the invention itself, the courts have stressed the importance of concentrating on the profits the claimant itself would have obtained.[21] In *United Horse-Shoe and Nail Company Ltd v. John Stewart & Co*[22] the respondents sold horse-shoe nails in infringement of the appellants' patent. As was pointed out by Lord Watson,[23] quantum in such a case is always a matter of estimate, given the impossibility of ascertaining precisely what would have been the patentees' sales and profits in the ordinary course of business. On the facts of the case, the patentees' claim for compensation arising from the reduction in their prices which they alleged was necessary and a direct result of the respondents' unlawful acts, was not allowed, since they were aware of the respondents' identity and their infringement of the appellants' patent rights and must have realised that they could obtain redress in the form of the loss they had suffered. It was also necessary to take account of the efforts of the respondents which enhanced their sales to the extent that it could not be said that the appellants would have sold as many nails as did the respondent had there been no infringement. By contrast the claimants in *American Braided Wire Co v. Thomson*[24] were entitled to recover all the

[18] (1918) 35 R.P.C. 101.
[19] *op. cit.* at p. 1262–3, n. 8.
[20] [1975] 1 W.L.R. 819.
[21] For discussion of the alternative remedy of an account see *infra* para. 7–012 *et seq.*
[22] (1888) 13 App. Cas. 401.
[23] *ibid.* at 413. See also *Watson Laidlaw & Co v. Pott, Cassells & Williamson* (1914) 31 R.P.C. 104 at 112.
[24] (1890) 44 Ch. D. 274. See also *Leeds Forge Co v. Deighton's Patent Flue Co* (1908) 25 R.P.C. 209.

profits they would have made if all the sales they made, and also the sales made by the defendants in infringement of the claimants' patent, had been made by the claimants at their original prices. In contrast to the *United Horse Shoe* case, where the claimants were claiming for a reduction which was clearly not caused by the defendant's acts in the instant case, the claimants had been compelled to reduce their prices as a consequence of price reductions by the defendant, and it was found by the Official Referee that, but for the competition by the defendant, the claimants would have sold at the original prices.

Clearly this is an area of the law where the equitable remedy of an 7–012 account has a role to play. This form of relief, whereby the defendant is required to account to the claimant for the profits he has made out of his unlawful conduct, is considered in more detail elsewhere.[25] It was suggested however in *Watson, Laidlaw & Co v. Pott, Cassels and Williamson*[26] that, quite apart from an account, the claimant, though he had not lost profits as a consequence of the defendant's use of his patent, should nevertheless be entitled to recover the market value of the use by way of damages. The court suggested the analogy of taking a horse and returning it to the owner in the same condition, basing the claim on the fact of the unauthorised use. Such an approach was however disapproved by the House of Lords in the *General Tire* case,[27] where it was viewed as bordering on the punitive, and it would seem in any event to risk conflicting with the principle as expressed by Cotton L.J. in the *American Braided Wire Co* case[28] that a patentee who succeeds cannot get both an account of profits and damages, or, as expressed by Professor Cornish, "in respect to any one infringement the claimant should not be entitled to be both reimbursed and compensated".[29]

In cases of infringement of copyright and design rights, the damages are 7–013 at large. Lord Wright M.R. in *Sutherland Publishing Co Ltd v. Caxton Publishing Co Ltd*[30] stated that this comprised "the depreciation caused by the infringement to the value of the copyright as a chose in action." Typically this will be represented by the loss of profits, as in *Birn v. Keene*[31] but much will depend upon the facts of the case: thus in *Stovin-Bradford v. Volpoint*[32] an architect whose copyright in drawings and plans was infringed was awarded damages assessed on the basis of the sum he might fairly have charged for a licence to use his drawings in constructing the building.

The relevant legislation concerning remedies for infringement of copy- 7–014 right is the Copyright Designs and Patents Act 1988. Section 96 (2) of the Act provides:

"In an action for infringement of copyright all such relief by way of

---

[25] *Supra* para. 5–070 *et seq.*
[26] (1914) 31 R.P.C. 104. See also *Gerber Garment Technology v. Lectra Systems* [1997] R.P.C. 443.
[27] *Supra* n. 20 at 833 per Lord Wilberforce.
[28] *Supra* n. 24 at 287.
[29] "Intellectual Property" (3rd ed., 1996) at 2.42.
[30] [1936] Ch. 323 at 336.
[31] [1918] 2 Ch. 281.
[32] [1971] Ch. 1007.

damages, injunctions and accounts or otherwise is available to the plaintiff as is available in respect of the infringement of any other property rights."

7–015   Section 97(2) provides:

"The court may in an action for infringement of copyright having regard to all the circumstances, and in particular to—
(a) the flagrancy of the infringement, and
(b) any benefit occurring to the defendant by reason of the infringement, award such additional damages as the justice of the case may require."

7–016   In *Redrow Homes Ltd v. Betts Brothers plc*[33] the appellants accepted that they could not recover both damages and an account of profits under section 96(2), but argued that section 97(2) provided an independent remedy of additional damages which was *sui generis* and could therefore be sought in addition to an account of profits. The House of Lords disagreed, holding that the unavailability of an award of damages under section 97(2) in addition to an account was entirely consistent with the basic principle that an award of damages is inconsistent with an account. The election as between an account or an inquiry as to damages does not have to be made until after liability has been established.[34] As regards the object of the award of damages under section 97(2), the House of Lords in *Redrow Homes*[35] did not find it necessary to express a view, though Lord Clyde considered it to be "more probably" aggravated rather than exemplary damages. Given the lack of any express characterisation of the award of damages under section 97(2) as exemplary, Lord Clyde's view appears preferable.

7–017   A final aspect of damages to economic interests in connection with property rights concerns cases where there has been a breach of confidence. In *Seager v. Copydex Ltd (No. 2)*[36] Lord Denning M.R. held, in a case where the claimant imparted confidential information to the defendants which they used in breach of their obligation of confidence, that the damages were to be assessed at the value of the information taken by the defendants. This depended on the nature of the information. If it was of a kind which could be obtained by employing a competent consultant, then its value was the fee which the consultant would charge. If it was more special, such that it could not be obtained from a consultant, then its value would be measured by the price a willing buyer who desired to obtain it would pay. If however the information concerns a process which the claimant would have manufactured itself, the loss of profits will be the appropriate measure of damages.[37] The Court of Appeal in *Dowson* did not consider that the nature of

---

[33] [1999] A.C. 197.
[34] See *Island Records Ltd v. Tring International plc* [1995] F.S.R. 560. See also *Wienerworld Ltd v. Vision Video Ltd* [1998] F.S.R. 832.
[35] [1999] A.C. 197 at 209.
[36] [1969] 1 W.L.R. 809.
[37] See *Dowson & Mason Ltd v. Potter* [1986] 1 W.L.R. 1419.

the confidential information could be the sole determinant in arriving at the appropriate measure of damages, and considered that *Copydex* did not lay down any principle of law, but was concerned with the appropriate approach to the particular facts of the cases, and fell within the principles espoused by the House of Lords in the *General Tire*[38] case. The appropriate principles for dealing with quantum in cases of breach of confidence are therefore appropriately assimilated within the general principles of measure of damages concerning cases of breach of intellectual property rights.

3. NEGLIGENCE

Pure economic losses may also occur as a consequence of an act, omission or statement which comprises negligence. Cases involving negligent misstatements, falling within the principles adumbrated by the House of Lords in *Hedley Byrne & Co Ltd v. Heller & Partners Ltd*[39] and developed in subsequent cases, will be considered in the discussion of misrepresentation.[40] Losses of this kind resulting from a negligent act or a failure to act are infrequently recoverable, given the courts' view that such losses fall more properly within the domain of contract. In *White v. Jones*,[41] as a consequence of delay by the defendant solicitor in preparing a new will for a testator, the claimants, who would have received legacies under the new will had it been executed prior to the death of the testator, were held to be entitled to claim the amount of the lost legacies from the solicitor. A closer degree of proximity existed in *Junior Books Ltd v. Veitchi Co Ltd*[42] where sub-contractors were held liable on a preliminary issue to a factory owner for non-dangerous defects in the floor they laid, the claim being for the cost of replacing the floor, together with consequential losses including the cost of removal of machinery and loss of profits while the floor was being relaid. The measure of damages in these cases compensates the claimant by putting him in the position he would have been in if the task in question had been performed without negligence, thereby in effect measuring damages in the same way as if the breach of duty had been contractual. The justification for this lies in the fact that the nature of the tortious duty is positively to benefit the claimant by acting without negligence, and the same approach, not surprisingly, can be seen in cases of concurrent liability where for example, a professional such as a solicitor or a surveyor incurs liability to a client for failure to provide proper advice. Thus, in *Perry v. Sidney Phillips & Son*[43] it was held in a case involving a negligent survey of a house that, whether the claim was in contract or tort, the measure of damages was the difference between the price paid by the claimant and the actual market value of the property. In addition, consequential losses may be

7–018

---

[38] *Supra* n. 20.
[39] [1964] A.C. 465.
[40] See below *infra* paras. 7–026 *et seq.*
[41] [1995] 2 A.C. 207.
[42] [1983] 1 A.C. 520.
[43] [1982] 3 All E.R. 705.

recoverable. In *Patel v. Hooper & Jackson*[44] the house which had been negligently overvalued by the defendant was uninhabitable except at a cost which the claimants did not have the resources to contemplate. They were therefore able to recover the costs of their alternative accommodation until such time as they were able to sell the house and acquire another in its place. They were not however entitled to be compensated for mortgage interest payments and insurance premiums, as these comprised expenditure which they would have incurred in any event if they had purchased another property. In essence, the claimant in such a case is entitled to recover the reasonable costs of extricating himself from the purchase.

4. MISREPRESENTATION

7–019   Liability for misrepresentation may arise in the tort of deceit, in the case of fraudulent misrepresentations; in the case of negligent misrepresentations liability may exist at common law and also under statute, where damages may also be awarded in lieu of rescission for innocent misrepresentation.

(1) Fraudulent misrepresentation

7–020   It was emphasised by the Court of Appeal in *Doyle v. Olby Ironmongers Ltd*[45] that the measure of damages in deceit is tortious, the need for clarification of this seemingly obvious point having apparently not arisen in previous cases. A claimant seeking to recover for loss of bargain would therefore have to persuade the court that the statement was a warranty. Otherwise he will be compensated on the basis of putting him into the position he would have been in if the statement had not been made.

Thus, in *Archer v. Brown*[46] the defendant induced the claimant to pay him £30,000 for shares in a company in which in fact the defendant owned no shares at all. The claimant was held to be entitled to recover the purchase price of the shares.[47] A number of cases have had to grapple with the problem of assessing damages where shares have been sold as a consequence of a misrepresentation, not as to their ownership, as in *Archer*, but as to their value. The test adopted by the courts has been to compensate the claimant on the basis of the purchase price of the shares less their

---

[44] [1999] 1 All E.R. 992. See also *Hayes v. James & Charles Dodd* [1990] 2 All E.R. 815.
[45] [1969] 2 Q.B. 158. See also *Smith Kline & French Laboratories v. Long* [1989] 1 W.L.R. 1 (criticised by Burrows *op. cit.* at 173–4).
[46] [1985] Q.B. 401.
[47] In addition he was able to recover interest paid to his bank on two loans and an overdraft incurred by him as a consequence of the defendant's deceit, loss of earnings (the defendant had induced him to enter into a service agreement with the company, and, in the light of that contract's worthlessness he was without work for some time. £2,500 was awarded by way of general damages), expenditure incurred in finding employment, and injury to feelings. See also *Richardson v. Silvester* (1873) L.R. 9 Q.B. 34 where the claimant was held to be entitled to claim damages for deceit where he incurred expenditure in reliance on a fraudulent advertisement by the defendant that he had a farm to let.

actual, or real, value at the time of acquisition,[48] though on the particular facts of *Smith New Court Securities Ltd v. Scrimgeour Vickers (Asset Management) Ltd*[49] it was held to be necessary to depart from the time of acquisition rule because the defendant's fraud continued to operate so as to induce the claimant to retain the shares in question. In that case the figure deducted from the purchase price was the amount subsequently realised by the claimant on the sale of the shares, the court holding that the claimant had acted reasonably in retaining and subsequently reselling the shares in the manner it did.

In *Smith New Court* Lord Browne-Wilkinson set out seven principles applicable to the assessment of damages in cases where the claimant had been induced by a fraudulent misrepresentation to buy property:[50]   **7–021**

"(1) the defendant is bound to make reparation for all the damage directly flowing from the transaction;

(2) although such damage need not have been foreseeable, it must have been directly caused by the transaction;

(3) in assessing such damage, the plaintiff is entitled to recover by way of damages the full price paid by him, but he must give credit for any benefits which he has received as a result of the transaction;

(4) as a general rule, the benefits received by him include the market value of the property acquired as at the date of acquisition; but such a general rule is not to be inflexibly applied where to do so would prevent him obtaining full compensation for the wrong suffered;

(5) although the circumstances in which the general rule should not apply cannot be comprehensively stated, it will normally not apply where either (a) the misrepresentation has continued to operate after the date of the acquisition of the asset or (b) the circumstances of the case are such that the plaintiff is, by reason of the fraud, locked into the property;

(6) In addition, the plaintiff is entitled to recover consequential losses caused by the transaction;

(7) The plaintiff must take all reasonable steps to mitigate his loss once he has discovered the fraud."

This valuable analysis confirms, *inter alia*, the view of the Court of Appeal in *Doyle* that, subject to the duty to mitigate, all direct losses resulting from the fraud are recoverable rather than those that are merely reasonably foreseeable. An important further point was made by Lord Steyn in *Smith New Court*.[51] He said   **7–022**

---

[48] See *e.g. Peek v. Derry* (1887) 36 Ch. D. 541; *McConnell v. Wright* [1903] 1 Ch. 546.
[49] [1997] A.C. 254.
[50] *ibid*. at 267.
[51] *ibid*. at 283.

". . . in an action for deceit the plaintiff is entitled to recover all his loss directly flowing from the fraudulently induced *transaction*. In the case of a negligent misrepresentation the rule is narrower: the recoverable loss does not extend beyond the consequences flowing from the negligent *misrepresentation*."

Hence, in a deceit action it is inappropriate to compare the loss resulting from the transaction with what would have been the position had the represented state of affairs actually existed.[52]

7–023   *East v. Maurer*[53] is an interesting illustration of the limited extent to which, apparently contrary to principle, lost profits may be recovered. The defendant induced the claimants to buy his hairdressing salon on the faith of a false representation that he would not compete with them. This statement was held to have been made fraudulently; the claimants were unable to make the salon profitable, and they ultimately sold the lease. The trial judge awarded them, *inter alia*, the loss of profits during the period in which they had owned the premises. The Court of Appeal held that such an award could only be made if damages were being sought for breach of warranty, and reduced the award from £15,000 to £10,000 for profits which had been foregone, on the basis of the profits which the claimants could have expected to make in another hairdressing business bought for a similar sum.[54] In addition the claimants recovered the price paid for the business less the price they were able to sell it on for, the expenses incurred in buying and selling the business and in carrying out improvements in an effort to make it profitable, and the trading losses.

7–024   In addition awards have been made for non-pecuniary losses in cases of deceit. If personal injury results from the deceit, as in *Wilkinson v. Downton*,[55] where the claimant suffered nervous shock when the defendant falsely informed her that her husband had been seriously injured in an accident, damages will be assessed in accordance with the usual principles pertaining to personal injury.[56] Damages for mental distress have also been awarded in a number of cases: £500 was awarded in *Shelley v. Paddock*[57] where the claimant was defrauded by the defendants into buying a house from them to which they had no title. In *Mafo v. Adams*[58] the defendant landlord deceitfully induced the claimant, his tenant, to leave the rooms of which he was the tenant on the faith of an assurance that alternative accommodation was available elsewhere. The claimant was awarded £100 in deceit for the loss of his tenancy and for the inconvenience he suffered in failing to gain access (together with his wife who was eight months

---

[52] As was done in *Downs v. Chappell* [1997] 1 W.L.R. 426 at 444.
[53] [1991] 1 W.L.R. 461. See also *Burrows v. Rhodes* [1899] 1 Q.B. 816 where the claimant was able to recover *inter alia* loss of earnings where personal injury resulted from a fraudulent misrepresentation, and also *Barley v. Walford* (1846) 9 Q.B. 197.
[54] This has been cogently criticised by Marks (1992) 108 L.Q.R. 386 as being unduly speculative.
[55] [1897] 2 Q.B. 57. See also *Burrows v. Rhodes supra* n. 353.
[56] See *infra* Ch. 9.
[57] [1979] Q.B. 120, affirmed at [1980] Q.B. 348. See also *Archer v. Brown supra* n. 46: £500 awarded); *East v. Maurer* (*supra* n. 53: £1,000 awarded).
[58] [1970] 1 Q.B. 548.

pregnant) to the alternative accommodation, and having to stay with friends for several weeks until he found fresh accommodation.

(2) Negligent misrepresentation under the Misrepresentation Act 1967

Section 2(1) of the Misrepresentation Act provides for an award of dam-   7–025
ages in circumstances where the misrepresentation induces a contract between representor and representee . . .

> "if the person making the misrepresentation would be liable in dam-
> ages in respect thereof had the misrepresentation been made fraudu-
> lently, that person shall be so liable notwithstanding that the misrep-
> resentation was not made fraudulently, unless he proves that he had
> reasonable ground to believe and did believe up to the time the con-
> tract was made that the facts represented were true."

Somewhat surprisingly, early cases on section 2(1) demonstrated some support for a contractual measure of damages under the subsection[59] and in *Watts v. Spence*[60] the contractual measure was actually applied. Sub-sequently however, the tortious measure that surely must have been intended, has been consistently asserted, the Court of Appeal in *Sharneyford Supplies Ltd v. Edge*[61] specifically disapproving *Watts v. Spence*.

As a consequence it should follow that the same measure of damages   7–026
will apply to cases under section 2(1) and at common law for negligent misstatement under *Hedley Byrne & Co Ltd v. Heller & Partners*.[62] In *Royscot Trust Ltd v. Rogerson*[63] however, the Court of Appeal construed section 2(1) as requiring damages awarded under the subsection to be measured as if the defendant had been fraudulent. In many cases, including *Royscot* itself, there will be no difference between an assessment of damages based on negligence and one based on fraud, but, as we have seen, all direct losses are recoverable in a deceit claim, whereas only reasonably-foreseeable losses are recoverable in a negligence claim. The decision on this point in *Royscot* flew in the face of the views of commentators[64] and has been subsequently criticized,[65] essentially on the basis that it enables damages for fraud to be obtained where fraud has not been proved (indeed, all a claimant has to do under the subsection is to prove that a misrepresentation has been made; the defendant then has to prove that it was not made carelessly). As has been pointed out,[66] the Court of Appeal's view is

---

[59] *Gosling v. Anderson* [1972] E.G.D. 709, *Davis & Co (Wines) Ltd v. Afa-Minerva (EMI) Ltd* [1974] 2 Lloyd's Rep. 27 and *Jarvis v. Swan's Tours Ltd* [1973] Q.B. 233.

[60] [1976] Ch. 165.

[61] [1987] Ch. 305. See also *Royscot Trust Ltd v. Rogerson* [1991] 2 Q.B. 297; *Cemp Properties (UK) Ltd v. Dentsply Research and Development Corporation* [1991] 2 E.G.L.R. 197.

[62] [1964] A.C. 465.

[63] *Supra* n. 61.

[64] See *e.g.* Treitel, The Law of Contract (7th ed., 1987) at 278; Chitty on Contracts (26th ed., 1989), Vol. 1, para. 439.

[65] See *e.g.* McGregor *op. cit.* para. 2002; Hooley (1991) 107 L.Q.R. 547.

[66] Oakley [1992] C.L.J. 9 at 11.

consistent with the wording of section 2(1), and it does seem that the essential problem lies in the drafting of the subsection. In *Smith New Court Securities*[67] neither Lord Browne-Williamson nor Lord Steyn was prepared to express a view on the correctness of the decision in *Royscot*, but unless the matter comes expressly before the House of Lords or (unlikely) there is legislative change, the decision of the Court of Appeal remains the law.

7–027 Cases under section 2(1) have usually involved damages being measured on the basis of the difference between the value transferred less the value received: purchase price less market value. In *Naughton v. O'Callaghan*[68] the claimant bought for 26,000 guineas a colt whose pedigree had been inaccurately described in the sales catalogue. By the time this fact was discovered the colt had been run unsuccessfully in several races and its value was only £1,500. The defendant argued that the time of the sale was the date at which the value of the item sold was to be taken, in accordance with the usual principles;[69] the value of the colt as correctly described at the date of sale was 23,500 guineas, and the claimant was entitled therefore only to 2,500 guineas. The court held however that the claimant could recover the difference between the price paid and the value at the time when the misrepresentation was discovered. The general rule, mentioned above, was not applied since its application was essentially geared to depreciations in value which were not connected to the circumstances which existed at the time the contract was made. In the words of Waller J.:[70]

> "what . . . makes this case different from the norm is, first, that what the plaintiff in fact purchased in reliance on the representation in the catalogue was a different animal altogether; second, if they had known of the misrepresentation within a day or so they could, and as I have found would, have sold Fondu (the colt) for its then value; third their decision to keep Fondu and race it was precisely what the sellers would have expected; Fondu was not a commodity . . . .which it would be expected that the defendants would go out and sell; fourth, the fall in Fondu's value if it did not win races was not due to a general fall in the market in racehorses, but was special to Fondu and to be expected if Fondu did not win".

7–028 As an example of the application of the *restitutio in integrum* principle to cases involving *Hedley Byrne* liability, in *Box v. Midland Bank Ltd*[71] the defendant's manager negligently misrepresented to the claimant that he would be able to borrow £45,000 from the bank in order to finance his company to enable it to fulfil a contract. The claimant claimed damages amounting to nearly £250,000. Much of that however represented the gains the claimant would have made if the proposed contract had been carried

---

[67] *Supra* n. 49.
[68] [1990] 3 All E.R. 191. See also *Cemp Properties (U.K.) Ltd v. Dentsply Research and Development Corporation* [1991] 2 E.G.L.R. 197; *McNally v. Welltrade International Ltd* [1978] I.R.L.R. 497.
[69] See *supra* n. 48.
[70] [1990] 3 All E.R. 191 at 197–8.
[71] [1979] 2 Lloyd's Rep. 391. See also *Esso Petroleum Co Ltd v. Mardon* [1976] Q.B. 801.

through, and was irrecoverable in negligence. It was held that he was entitled to only £5,000 which represented what he would have saved out of his eventual overdraft if it had not been for the manager's negligent misstatement.

Consequential losses will also be recoverable. Thus, in *Naughton* the claimant was able to recover the training fees and cost of the upkeep of the colt up to the date on which he discovered its true pedigree. The defendant argued that expenditure would have been incurred anyway on a horse purchased at the sales in question, but the judge held that the claimant was entitled to say that the horse he bought was not the horse on which he would have spent any money training or keeping and therefore that was money spent only in reliance on the misrepresentation made. Again, in *Cemp Properties (U.K) Ltd v. Dentsply Research & Development Corporation*[72] the Court of Appeal emphasized that where the difference between price paid and market value did not fully compensate a claimant for his loss, he was entitled in addition to consequential losses. The case concerned misrepresentations regarding the rights of adjoining owners to a property to light and air, which led the claimant to buy the property. By the time these rights were revealed to the claimant it had started to redevelop the site. The difference in value was £150,000, to which was added as consequential losses the expenses thrown away by having to modify plans, and additional costs, such as redesign fees incurred, and compensation for delayed completion.

7–029

Non-pecuniary losses were awarded in *McNally v. Welltrade International*[73] where liability was held to exist under the Misrepresentation Act and at common law on the basis of the defendant's misrepresentation that the claimant was suitable for a position in Libya. He was awarded *inter alia* £400 for worry and inconvenience, and £200 was awarded to the claimant in *Chesneau v. Interhome*[74] for distress and inconvenience occasioned when the facilities at a holiday home fell short of their represented quality. The benefits of such awards must be balanced against their potentially disastrous categorization by the courts as comprising a claim "where the damages . . . consist of or include damages in respect of personal injuries to the plaintiff or any other person" under section11(1) of the Limitation Act 1980, and hence being subject to the three year limitation period created by the section.[75]

7–030

(3) Innocent misrepresentation

The common law has never provided a remedy for damages for an innocent (*i.e.* non-fraudulent and non-negligent) misrepresentation. Section 2(2) of the Misrepresentation Act however provides as follows:

7–031

"where a person has entered into a contract after a misrepresentation

---

[72] [1991] 2 E.G.L.R. 197. See also *Downs v. Chappell* [1996] 3 All E.R. 344.
[73] [1978] I.R.L.R. 497.
[74] (1983) 134 N.L.J. 341.
[75] See *Oates v. Harte Reade and Co* [1999] P.I.Q.R. P. 120.

has been made to him otherwise than fraudulently, and he would be entitled, by reason of the misrepresentation, to rescind the contract, then, if it is claimed, in any proceedings arising out of the contract, that the contract ought to be or has been rescinded, the court or arbitrator may declare the contract subsisting and award damages in lieu of rescission, if of opinion that it would be equitable to do so, having regard to the nature of the misrepresentation and the loss that would be caused by it if the contract were upheld, as well as to the loss that rescission would cause to the other party".

7–032   A clue to the measure of damages under section 2(2) can be found in section 2(3), which provides:

"Damages may be awarded against a person under subsection (2) of this section whether or not he is liable to damages under subsection (1) thereof, but where he is so liable any award under the said subsection (2) shall be taken into account in assessing his liability under the said subsection (1)".

7–033   The impression section 2(3) gives is that damages under section 2(2) are likely to be less that those awarded under section 2(1) which would have the merit of according with the instinctive feeling that innocence is less culpable than negligence. But it is far from clear what measure of damages locates itself somewhere between *restitutio in integrum* and nothing. Some guidance can however be found in the decision of the Court of Appeal in *William Sindall plc v. Cambridgeshire County Council*,[76] where the discussion of section 2(2) was *obiter*, since the court held that the claim for misrepresentation failed. The case concerned the sale by the council to the claimant, a building company of land whose value had declined significantly by the time the claimant had obtained planning permission. The alleged misrepresentation consisted in a failure to disclose, in a reply to inquiries before contract, the existence of a nine-inch foul sewer buried under the land. The court would, had it found for the claimant, have exercised its discretion under section 2(2) to grant damages in lieu of rescission in the circumstances of the case, taking the view that the proper measure was the cost of remedying the defect or the reduced market value attributable to the defect. Hoffman L.J.[77] made the point that section 2(1) is concerned with the damage flowing from having entered into the contract, whereas section 2(2) was concerned with the damage caused by the property not being what it was represented to be. Evans L.J. agreed, expressly stating[78] "[The contract measure] becomes the correct measure in circumstances where the claimant is entitled to an order for rescission, but rescission is refused under s.2(2) of the Act". The rationale for this view is derived from the Tenth Report of the Law Reform Committee[79] which led

---

[76] [1994] 3 All E.R. 932.
[77] *ibid.* at 954.
[78] *ibid.* at 962–3.
[79] "Innocent Misrepresentation" (Cmnd. 1782).

to the enactment of the Misrepresentation Act. The Court of Appeal's analysis has been subjected to powerful criticism by McGregor[80] on the basis that a claimant should not be able to claim the benefit of his bargain when there is no warranty, and that the monetary equivalent of the rescission that has been precluded should form the basis of the award. The debate is finely balanced, but it is thought that the view of the Court of Appeal is the more persuasive.

A final issue concerning damages for innocent misrepresentation concerns the limited monetary compensation, termed an "indemnity", which the courts may award together with rescission. Its ambit is neatly illustrated by *Whittington v. Seale-Hayne*,[81] where the claimant was induced to take a lease of premises on the faith of a misrepresentation by the defendant landlord's agents that the premises were sanitary and in a good state of repair. The defendant was liable to indemnify the claimant for the rent, rates and repairs which he carried out under covenants in the lease, as obligations created by the contract which was rescinded, but the claimant, who used the premises to breed poultry, could not recover for the value of stock lost as a consequence of the insanitary condition of the drainage, nor for loss of profit on sales, loss of breeding season, or services on behalf of their manager, who became ill as the water was insanitary, as these losses were matters of damages—and therefore potentially recoverable today under section 2(1)—and did not arise out of obligations necessarily created by the lease.

7–034

---

[80] *op. cit.* at paras. 2014–2022. See however the judgment of Evans L.J. in *Sindall* [1994] 3 All E.R. 932 at 962–3.
[81] (1900) 82 L.T. 49. See also *Newbigging v. Adam* (1886) 34 Ch. D. 582.

CHAPTER 8

DAMAGE TO REPUTATION, MENTAL DISTRESS AND PHYSICAL INCONVENIENCE

This chapter considers the circumstances in which compensatory dam-   8–001
ages may be awarded for any damage to reputation, mental distress or
physical inconvenience which has been occasioned by the defendant's tort.
These are non-pecuniary losses incapable of being calculated on a precise
mathematical basis. What guidance there is upon quantification suggests
that the amount may be dictated more by policy as much as anything else.
So in the sphere of damages for injury to reputation the recent trend has
been to discourage large awards and instead try and bring awards more in
line with those appropriate in the personal injuries field.[1] And in relation
to awards for physical inconvenience and mental distress it has been said
on more than one occasion that such awards should be "modest",[2] no
doubt reflecting the policy that persons should be of "customary phlegm"[3]
when it comes to matters of the mind.

In the field of personal injuries the claimant may suffer physical incon-   8–002
venience and mental distress as a consequence of the injury. These matters
are given special treatment, however, in the context of damages for personal injuries and are considered under the headings of pain and suffering,
and loss of amenities of life. Because of the specialist nature of damages
for personal injuries, detailed discussion of these particular non-pecuniary
losses is to be found in Chapter 9 *infra*.

1. DAMAGE TO REPUTATION

Damage to reputation consists of injury to society's feelings towards the   8–003
claimant, rather than injury to the claimant's own feelings. A restrictive
approach has been taken by the courts towards recovery for damage to
reputation. Generally the tort of defamation is viewed as the proper avenue
through which to claim for damage to reputation. In *Lonrho Plc. v. Fayed*

---

[1] See *John v. MGN Ltd* [1997] Q.B. 586, in the context of awards for defamation and
Thompson v. Commissioner of Police of the Metropolis [1998] Q.B. 498, in the context of
awards for malicious criminal prosecution.
[2] For example in *Watts v. Morrow* [1991] 1 W.L.R. 1421 and *Saunders v. Edwards* [1987]
2 All E.R. 651. See discussion on these cases below.
[3] *Bourhill v. Young* [1943] A.C. 92 *per* Lord Porter at 117.

(No 5)[4] the Court of Appeal refused to recognise a claim for damage to reputation in conspiracy. Dillon L.J. said:

> "In my judgment, if the plaintiffs want to claim damages for injury to reputation or injury to feelings, they must do so in an action for defamation, not in this very different form of action. Injury to reputation and to feelings is, with very limited exceptions, a field of its own and the established principles in that field are not to be side-stepped by alleging a different cause of action."[5]

8–004   As regards the very limited exceptions, they would appear to be restricted to malicious prosecution and false imprisonment.[6] The decision in *Thurston v. Charles*,[7] which suggested that an award could be made in cases of conversion, was disapproved of by the Court of Appeal in *Lonrho*. Beyond cases of defamation, malicious prosecution and false imprisonment, it is therefore doubtful that a claim for damage to reputation exists as a separate head of non-pecuniary loss. By contrast claims for pecuniary losses consequent upon damage to reputation would appear to be recoverable using other torts, even if the non-pecuniary damage to reputation itself is not.[8]

(1) Awards for damage to reputation in defamation

8–005   The majority of slanders are only actionable upon proof of special damage. Damages can therefore be awarded for the pecuniary losses consequent upon the damage to reputation, but it is unclear whether an award can additionally be made in respect of the non-pecuniary damage to reputation itself.[9] By contrast libels and those slanders not requiring proof of special damage are actionable *per se* and damages are available for both the non-pecuniary and pecuniary consequences of the defamatory statement.[10]

8–006   Historically, claimants in defamation have always had a right to trial by jury, and the level of damages that the jury could award were at large. The

---

[4] [1993] 1 W.L.R. 1489.

[5] *ibid.* at 1496C. See also *Joyce v. Sengupta* [1993] 1 W.L.R. 337, where the Court of Appeal adopted the same approach towards attempts to claim damages for injury to reputation at large using malicious falsehood.

[6] These exceptions were endorsed by the Court of Appeal in *Lonrho*.

[7] (1905) 21 T.L.R. 659.

[8] Economic loss suffered as a result of damage to reputation may in some cases be recovered in negligence (*Spring v. Guardian Assurance* [1995] 2 A.C. 296), malicious falsehood (*Joyce v. Sengupta* [1993] 1 W.L.R. 337), and conspiracy (*Lonrho Plc v. Fayed (No. 5)* [1993] 1 W.L.R. 1489).

[9] No authority seems to cover the point explicitly. See *McGregor*, para. 1888, and *Gatley on Libel and Slander* (9th ed., 1998), Sweet & Maxwell, para. 5.10: "There is some authority both ways but the matter has never perhaps been fully considered." For example, in favour of recovery is the dictum of Martin B. in *Dixon v. Smith* (1860) 5 H. & N. 450 at 453; and the dictum of Lord Wensleydale in *Lynch v. Knight* (1861) 9 H.L. Cas. 577 at 598, cited with apparent approval by Sir Donald Nicholls V.-C. in *Joyce v. Sengupta* [1993] 1 W.L.R. 337 at 348D; that general injury to reputation could be taken into account also appeared to be assumed by the *Report of the Committee on Defamation* (Faulks Committee) (Cmnd. 5909, 1975) para. 86; against is the dictum of Williams J. in *Brown v. Smith* (1855) 13 C.B. 596 at 600.

[10] Although there may be difficulties associated with proof of pecuniary losses.

Defamation Act 1996 introduced a new mechanism to dispose of claims on a summary basis where it appeared to the court that there was no defence to the claim which had a realistic prospect of success, and where there were no other reasons that the claim should not be tried.[11] This part of the Act came into force in February 2000.[12] The new procedure may not be used, however, unless the court is satisfied that summary relief would adequately compensate the claimant,[13] or unless the claimant asks for summary relief.[14] Damages are restricted to £10,000[15] and for that reason alone few claimants are likely to opt for summary relief. Moreover, given the scale of jury awards in recent years, £10,000 is unlikely to be regarded as adequate compensation in many circumstances. Awards made by juries look set to continue as the norm.

In *John v. MGN Ltd*[16] Sir Thomas Bingham M.R. stated the aim of an   8–007
award of compensatory damages in defamation proceedings:

> "The successful plaintiff in a defamation action is entitled to recover, as general compensatory damages, such sum as will compensate him for the wrong he has suffered. That sum must compensate him for the damage to his reputation; vindicate his good name; and take account of the distress, hurt and humiliation which the defamatory publication has caused. In assessing the appropriate damages for injury to reputation the most important factor is the gravity of the libel; the more closely it touches the plaintiff's personal integrity, professional reputation, honour, courage, loyalty and the core attributes of his personality, the more serious it is likely to be."[17]

By leaving the quantification of the award to the jury, the size of some   8–008
awards in recent years has literally been "at large". In *Sutcliffe v. Pressdram Ltd*[18] the jury awarded £600,000 to the wife of the serial killer known as the "Yorkshire Ripper", following publication of a defamatory article in *Private Eye* magazine. The Court of Appeal described the award as "very substantially in excess of any sum which could reasonably have been thought appropriate to compensate the plaintiff."[19] Similarly, in *Rantzen v. Mirror Group Newspapers Ltd*[20] the claimant, a well-known television personality, was awarded £250,000 following publication of a defamatory newspaper article in *The People*. The Court of Appeal said that "Judged by any objective standards of reasonable compensation or necessity or proportionality the award of £250,000 was excessive."[21] The award was substituted by one of £110,000.

---

[11] s. 8(3).
[12] ss. 8 to 10 of the Act, dealing with summary disposal of a claim, came into force on February 28, 2000.
[13] s. 8(4).
[14] s. 8(4).
[15] s. 9(1)(c).
[16] [1997] Q.B. 586.
[17] *ibid.* at 607F.
[18] [1991] 1 Q.B. 153.
[19] *ibid.* per Nourse L.J. at 185E.
[20] [1994] Q.B. 670.
[21] *ibid.* per Neill L.J. at 696C.

8–009   Concerned at the scale of jury awards, the Court of Appeal has attempted to inject an element of realism into the jury's deliberations. A series of decisions between 1989 and 1995 grappled with the issue of how juries could best be directed in the hope that a sensible award might be arrived at. In the first of these decisions, *Sutcliffe v. Pressdram Ltd*,[22] Lord Donaldson of Lymington M.R. advocated what could be described as a "rationalist approach" on the part of the jury. His Lordship said:

> "What is, I think, required, is some guidance to juries in terms which will assist them to appreciate the real value of large sums. It is, and must remain, a jury's duty to award lump sums by way of damages, but there is no reason why they should not be invited notionally to 'weigh' any sum which they have in mind to award."[23]

Guidance on the "real value" of large sums could be provided by pointing out to juries what the weekly, monthly or annual income would be of an invested sum equivalent to a potential award. Alternatively, if the jury had in mind a smaller sum they should be invited to consider what they could purchase with this, and consider whether such an award was appropriate compared to the actual damage to reputation suffered.

8–010   In *Rantzen v. Mirror Group Newspapers Ltd*[24] the Court of Appeal was confronted with another jury award of magnitude. Whilst approving of the approach advocated in *Sutcliffe*, it was acknowledged that there was a need for some sort of comparative guidance to be given to juries concerning awards made in other cases. Rejecting guidance based upon other jury awards, Neill L.J. said that substituted awards of damages made on appeal by the Court of Appeal[25] "would provide a corpus to which reference could be made in subsequent cases . . . The decisions of the Court of Appeal could be relied on as establishing the prescribed norm."[26] Neill L.J. hoped that in the course of time a series of decisions would establish some standards as to what were "proper" awards.

8–011   In *John v. MGN Ltd*[27] it was observed by Sir Thomas Bingham M.R. that a framework of Court of Appeal awards with which comparison could be made would not be established quickly. In the five-year period since the decision in *Rantzen* there had only been two other substituted awards made by the Court of Appeal. Moreover, juries were continuing to award vast sums.[28] It was conceded by the Court of Appeal that it would be proper for counsel and judge to draw the jury's attention to awards made in personal injuries actions which the jury could consider when determining the correct quantum of award. The attention of juries may be drawn to awards for particular personal injuries, and juries may properly be asked to con-

---

[22] [1991] 1 Q.B. 153.
[23] *ibid.* at 179A.
[24] [1994] Q.B. 670.
[25] Pursuant to s. 8(2) of the Courts and Legal Services Act 1990.
[26] [1994] Q.B. 670 at 694C.
[27] [1997] Q.B. 586.
[28] Such as for example the sum of £750,000 awarded to Graham Souness, June 15, 1995, *The Guardian*, June 16, 1995, front page.

sider whether the injury to reputation of which the claimant complained could fairly justify any greater compensation. Sir Thomas Bingham M.R. remarked:

> "It is in our view offensive to public opinion, and rightly so, that a defamation plaintiff should recover damages for injury to reputation greater, perhaps by a significant factor, than if that same plaintiff had been rendered a helpless cripple or an insensate vegetable. The time has in our view come when judges, and counsel, should be free to draw the attention of juries to these comparisons."[29]

This marks not just a change of practice but a change of policy, reflective of a concern that the sums being awarded were out of all proportion to the actual injury to reputation suffered. Moreover there appears to have been some effort in *John* to drive home the message to prospective claimants that they should no longer "regard a successful libel action, risky though the process undoubtedly is, as a road to untaxed riches."[30] At the moment then, as regards what is appropriate guidance, juries should be referred to the value of money, any relevant awards substituted by the Court of Appeal and what the equivalent bracket of award may be for a series of personal injuries ranging from moderate to severe. As regards the range of possible awards that the jury could consider, the Court of Appeal in *John* gave its blessing to a procedure whereby counsel for both sides would be able to indicate to the jury the level of award which they respectively considered appropriate. This would be likely to form the upper and lower bounds of a realistic bracket which the judge could direct the jury to consider. But ultimately the jury must be reminded that they must make up their own mind and may reject the upper or lower bracket suggested, although a great variance from any suggested bracket may give grounds for appeal.   **8–012**

It remains to be seen whether jury awards will tumble pursuant to this new guidance, which may lead to more cases being disposed of summarily.[31] Much will depend upon the facts of each case, as is illustrated in a decision subsequent to *John*, *Kiam v. Neill (No. 2)*.[32] Here the Court of Appeal approved a major award to a successful entrepreneur following erroneous claims in a newspaper article that he was a major debtor of a leading bank and had been forced to file for bankruptcy. Beldam L.J. emphasised that the law has always taken a grave view of an allegation of insolvency in a businessman. Judged by the criteria of reasonableness and proportionality, the award of £45,000 for a widespread, grave and irresponsible assertion of insolvency against a prominent entrepreneur was not felt to be excessive.   **8–013**

Whilst the jury must attempt to award a sum which will fairly compens-   **8–014**

---

[29] [1997] Q.B. 586 at 614.
[30] *per* Sir Thomas Bingham M.R. *ibid.* at 611F.
[31] Defamation Act 1996, s. 8. See above for discussion of this section. In March 2000 two ITN journalists were each awarded £150,000 following allegations by *Living Marxism* magazine that they had fabricated footage of a Serb-run detention camp during the Bosnian civil war. *ITN v. L.M, The Times*, March 15, 2000, p. 5.
[32] *The Times*, July 26, 1996.

ate the claimant for the damage to reputation suffered, the jury should be directed upon particular factors relevant to the tort of defamation which may go to aggravate or mitigate the damage suffered. In *Sutcliffe*[33] Nourse L.J. said that:

> "The conduct of a defendant which may often be regarded as aggravating the injury to the plaintiff's feelings, so as to support a claim for 'aggravated' damages, includes a failure to make any or any sufficient apology and withdrawal; a repetition of the libel; conduct calculated to deter the plaintiff from proceeding; persistence, by way of a prolonged or hostile cross-examination of the plaintiff or in turgid speeches to the jury, in a plea of justification which is bound to fail; the general conduct either of the preliminaries or of the trial itself in a manner calculated to attract further wide publicity; and a persecution of the plaintiff by other means."[34]

8–015   In terms of mitigation, general evidence of the complainant's bad character can go to mitigation of damages on the grounds that damages awarded to persons of bad character should be less than those awarded to persons of good character,[35] and any apology which the defendant has offered can also be considered.[36]

8–016   It was restated by the Court of Appeal in *John* that exemplary damages are also available for damage to reputation in defamation, but such awards should be regarded as exceptional and limited to those situations where the act of defamation was intentional or reckless, and where the defendant acted in the hope or expectation of material gain.[37]

(2) Awards in cases of false imprisonment and malicious prosecution

8–017   False imprisonment will often result in some damage to the claimant's reputation and an element to compensate for this can be built into an award of damages. In *Walter v. Alltools Ltd*[38] Lawrence L.J. said that:

> "The general principle, in my view, is that any evidence which tends to aggravate or mitigate the damage to a man's reputation which flows naturally from his imprisonment must be admissible up to the moment when damages are assessed. A false imprisonment does not merely affect a man's liberty, it also affects his reputation. The damage continues until it is caused to cease by an avowal that the imprisonment was false."[39]

---

[33] [1991] 1 Q.B. 153.
[34] *ibid.* at 184E.
[35] *Speidel v. Plato Films Ltd* [1961] A.C. 1090.
[36] The Libel Act 1843, s. 1.
[37] See discussion on this in Ch. 5 *supra*.
[38] (1944) 171 L.T. 371.
[39] *ibid.* at 372.

Malicious prosecution is actionable only upon proof of one or more of   8–018
three types of damage, one of which is "damage to a man's fame, as if the
matter whereof he is accused be scandalous."[40] This was put in modern
terms in *Clark v. Chief Constable of Cleveland Police*[41] by Roch L.J.:

> "Compensation for malicious prosecution has three aspects. First,
> there is the damage to a person's reputation. The extent of that damage
> will depend upon the claimant's actual reputation and upon the gravity
> of the offence for which he has been maliciously prosecuted."

The institution of criminal proceedings will usually involve damage to
reputation and will attract compensation accordingly.[42] The same is true of
petitions to wind up a company.[43] Whether the improper institution of
other types of proceedings will involve damage to reputation is a matter
for scrutiny in each case. So in *Wiffen v. Bailey and Romford Urban District Council*[44] it was held that a complaint issued under the 1875 Public
Health Act against the claimant for failure to abate a nuisance was not a
proceeding necessarily and naturally involving damage to his fair name
sufficient to support an action for malicious prosecution.[45] The House of
Lords held in *Gregory v. Portsmouth City Council* [2000] 2. W.L.R. 306,
that it was unnecessary and undesirable for the tort of malicious prosecution to be extended to civil proceedings generally, or to disciplinary proceedings, save in a few special cases of abuse of the civil legal process.

As with defamation, the level of award in cases of false imprisonment   8–019
and malicious prosecution will obviously be dependent upon the extent
of the damage to reputation and the particular aggravating or mitigating
features.[46] Another similarity with actions in defamation is the right to trial
by jury. In *Thompson v. Commissioner of Police of the Metropolis*[47] the
Court of Appeal laid down guidance for the assistance of trial judges when
directing juries on the appropriate level of quantum in actions for false
imprisonment and malicious prosecution against the police. It was
emphasised that the guidelines were designed to establish some relationship
between the figures awarded in this area and those awarded for personal

---

[40] *Savile v. Roberts* (1699) 1 Ld. Ray. 374 at 378 per Holt C.J.
[41] *The Times*, May 13, 1999.
[42] See for example *White v. Metropolitan Police Commissioner, The Times*, April 24, 1982,
1982, where awards for damage to reputation were made for false imprisonment and malicious prosecution.
[43] *The Quartz Hill Consolidated Gold Mining Co v. Eyre* (1883) 11 Q.B.D. 674.
[44] [1915] 1 K.B. 600.
[45] cf. *Rayson v. South London Tramways Co* [1893] 2 Q.B. 304 and *Berry v. British Transport Commission* [1962] 1 Q.B. 306.
[46] In *Lunt v. Liverpool City Justices* (unreported, March 5, 1991), Bingham L.J. took as
relevant the fact that "the damage to Mr Lunt's reputation was of a relatively minor kind
since his imprisonment was not the subject of any widespread publicity, nor was he arrested
in the face of anybody of the public and those to whom it was known (mainly his inner
circle of relatives and friends) would appreciate that it was imprisonment that flowed not
from any accusation of crime but from a non-payment of rates. Nonetheless, Mr O'Connor
is in my judgment entitled to submit that any form of imprisonment gives rise to a stigma
and that stigma is not removed until the reputation of the imprisoned party is vindicated
in an appropriate manner".
[47] [1998] Q.B. 498. See *supra* para. 5–037.

injuries, reflecting the concern expressed by the Court of Appeal in *John v. MGN Ltd*[48] in relation to bloated defamation awards. The guide figures provided for basic compensatory damages were global, therefore consisting of an element for damage to reputation.[49]

8–020   The Court of Appeal emphasised that the level of basic compensatory damages would depend upon the circumstances and degree of harm suffered, but in straightforward cases of wrongful arrest and imprisonment the starting point was likely to be about £500 for the first hour during which the claimant had been deprived of his liberty. After the first hour an additional sum should be awarded, but that sum should be on a reducing scale so as to keep the damages proportionate with those payable in personal injury cases. As a guideline, for a claimant who had been wrongly kept in custody for 24 hours, £3,000 should normally be regarded as appropriate for this alone. For subsequent days the daily rate would be on a progressively reducing scale.

8–021   In cases of malicious prosecution the figure should start at about £2,000 and for prosecution continuing for as long as two years, the case being taken to the Crown Court, an award of about £10,000 could be appropriate. If the malicious prosecution resulted in a conviction, a larger award would be justified. Where aggravated damages were claimed the figure was unlikely to be less than £1,000, but in the ordinary way the aggravated damages would not be expected to be as much as twice the basic damages except, perhaps, where on particular facts the basic damages were modest. If the jury considered that the case was one for the award of damages other than basic damages, (for example aggravated or exemplary) then they should usually make a separate award for each category. All of these figures would require adjusting in the future for inflation, and given that the guidelines were laid down in early 1997, a modest increase would seem appropriate.

8–022   The *Thompson* guidelines provided the starting point for the Court of Appeal's deliberations in *Barnett & Wilkinson v. Chief Constable of West Yorkshire*[50] where the claimants had been lawfully arrested but then subjected to false imprisonment for a period of 11 and 12 and a half hours respectively. The jury awarded £200 to each claimant but this was raised to £600 and £400 respectively despite the guidance in *Thompson* that the starting point for the first hour was £500, reaching £3,000 after 24 hours. There were certain mitigating factors to be taken into account, however. First, the fact that the claimants had been initially lawfully arrested removed what was described as the "front-end loading" of the damages, namely the initial shock of being arrested and locked up. Secondly, both claimants had been arrested and detained on other occasions and the experience would therefore not have been as shocking as it might have been to a person experiencing arrest and detention for the first time. Wilkinson's

---

[48] [1998] Q.B. 586.
[49] It was said in *R. v. Governor of Brockhill Prison, ex p. Evans (No. 2)* [1999] 2 W.L.R. 103 at 116B, that there can be two elements to an award of damages for false imprisonment; the first being compensation for loss of liberty and the second being the damage to reputation, humiliation, shock, injury to feelings and so on which can result from the loss of liberty.
[50] [1998] C.L.Y. 1451.

more extensive record and greater familiarity with life in custody justified his lower award.

Another illustration of the court's application of the guidelines is *Clark 8–023 v. Chief Constable of Cleveland Police*[51] where an award of £500 for malicious prosecution of a public order offence was raised to £2,000. Bearing in mind the *Thompson* starting figure of £2,000, rising to £10,000 for prosecutions continuing for as long as two years and culminating in the Crown Court, the Court of Appeal substituted the £2,000 figure after taking into account the claimant's bad character and the fact that the proceedings lasted for only 11 months and proceeded no further than appearances in the Magistrates' Court.

The guidelines provided by the Court of Appeal in *Thompson* may not 8–024 always be applicable, however, as was illustrated in *R. v. Governor of Brockhill Prison, ex parte Evans (No. 2)*[52] where the appellant was lawfully imprisoned but then subjected to false imprisonment following incorrect calculation of her release date. *Thompson* was distinguished: although there had been false imprisonment, there was no damage to reputation, humiliation, shock or injury to feelings. The appellant had been properly sentenced to a term of two years' imprisonment and had no reason to think that she was not perfectly properly incarcerated.

2. MENTAL DISTRESS

"Mental distress" is a term used to describe a wide range of feelings such 8–025 as distress, frustration, anxiety, displeasure, vexation, tension or aggravation.[53] Damages for mental distress caused by the defendant's tort have been awarded in a variety of actions and in principle there would appear to be no reason why damages for mental distress should not be awarded in all actions where mental distress was a reasonably foreseeable consequence of the tort. The authorities have adopted a more restrictive approach, however. So whilst such awards are permissible in claims for defamation or trespass to the person, by contrast in negligence claims arising out of the performance of contractual services the position is more akin to that in contract, and it would seem that such awards may not be made unless one of the objects of the contract or duty was to provide peace of mind. Moreover, there are some situations where damages for mental distress are unavailable on what could be described as policy grounds. For example, mental distress caused through fear for one's own safety, or through grief or anguish is generally not recoverable in tort,[54] although it is important to differentiate mental distress from a recognised psychiatric

---

[51] *The Times*, May 13, 1999.
[52] [1999] 2 W.L.R. 103.
[53] Borrowed from the judgment of Bingham L.J. in *Watts v. Morrow* [1991] 1 W.L.R. 1421 at 1445F.
[54] *Behrens v. Bertram Mills Circus Ltd* [1957] 2 Q.B. 1. Such feelings may in appropriate cases attract awards in cases of trespass to the person or Fatal Accident Act claims.

injury in which case the damage would be treated as a personal injury and different principles would apply.[55]

(1) Examples of awards for mental distress

(a) Actions against solicitors

8–026   Despite the assertion in *Groom v. Crocker*[56] that actions against solicitors lay in contract alone, it is now clear that actions can be brought in both contract and tort.[57] It would appear, however, that damages for mental distress brought about by the solicitor's negligence will only be available in those circumstances where the object of the contract was to provide peace of mind. Whilst the position is not entirely clear, it seems that mere foreseeability of mental distress as a consequence of the solicitor's negligence will alone be insufficient.

8–027   There have been several decisions where a foreseeability-based approach has been adopted by the court. In *Heywood v. Wellers*[58] the claimant instructed the defendants to take steps to protect her from molestation. The defendants' attempts at securing the injunction were wholly ineffective, allowing the molestation to continue and causing the claimant to suffer anxiety and distress, for which the Court of Appeal awarded damages. Whilst Bridge L.J. was of the opinion that the very object of the contract was to provide peace of mind, Lord Denning M.R. and James L.J. seemed to suggest that mere foreseeability of mental distress would be enough to entitle the claimant to damages.[59]

8–028   A similar approach was adopted in *Dickinson v. Jones Alexander & Co*[60] where the claimant instructed the defendant solicitors to commence divorce proceedings. The defendants were aware that the claimant was suffering from an anxiety/depression state brought on by the pressures of her matrimonial situation. The defendants failed to make adequate inquiries of the husband's assets and a settlement was agreed upon which failed to provide the claimant with proper and reasonable financial provision, causing her to suffer financial difficulties and generating further anxiety. In an action against the defendants the claimant included a claim for mental distress. The defendants contended that the claimant's mental distress was unforeseeable. Douglas Brown J. held that the defendants had failed to use professional skill to relieve the claimant from the pressures of her matrimonial situation and having regard to their state of knowledge, it was reasonably foreseeable that the claimant's health problems would be exacerbated if

---

[55] *Alcock v. Chief Constable of South Yorkshire Police* [1992] 1 A.C. 310.
[56] [1939] 1 K.B. 194.
[57] *Henderson v. Merrett Syndicates Ltd* [1995] 2 A.C. 145.
[58] [1976] 1 Q.B. 446.
[59] In *Cook v. Swinfen* [1967] 1 W.L.R. 457, on somewhat similar facts, Lord Denning M.R. held that damages would not be awarded for anxiety on the grounds that this damage was not foreseeable. In *Heywood v. Wellers* [1976] 1 Q.B. 446 at 459C, Lord Denning M.R. said that this decision may have to be reconsidered.
[60] [1993] 2 F.L.R. 521.

they did not achieve a satisfactory resolution of the matter and were negligent.

The foreseeability-based approach was not accepted, however, by Bridge   8–029
L.J. in *Heywood v. Wellers*:[61]

> "There is, I think, a clear distinction to be drawn between mental
> distress which is an incidental consequence to the client of the miscon-
> duct of litigation by his solicitor, on the one hand, and mental distress
> on the other hand which is the direct and inevitable consequence of
> the solicitor's negligent failure to obtain the very relief which it was
> the sole purpose of the litigation to secure. The first does not sound in
> damages: the second does."[62]

The foreseeability approach was also rejected by the Court of Appeal in   8–030
Hayes v. James & Charles Dodd[63] where the defendant solicitors negligently failed to advise the claimants in relation to a property purchase that
there was no right of way over land at the rear of a property. The lack of
access caused the claimants' business venture to fail, subjecting the claimants to vexation and anguish. In an action against the defendants the Court
of Appeal refused to award an amount for mental distress. Staughton L.J.'s
reasons were as follows:

> "I am not convinced that it is enough to ask whether mental distress
> was reasonably foreseeable as a consequence, or even whether it
> should reasonably have been contemplated as not unlikely to result
> from the breach of the contract. It seems to me that damages for
> mental distress in contract are, as a matter of policy, limited to certain
> classes of case. I would broadly follow the classification provided by
> Dillon L.J. in *Bliss v. South East Thames Regional Health Authority*
> [1987] I.C.R. 700 at 718:
>
> > '... where the contract which has been broken was itself a con-
> > tract to provide peace of mind or freedom from distress...'
>
> It may be that the class is somewhat wider than that. But it should
> not, in my judgment, include any case where the object of the contract
> was not comfort or pleasure, or the relief or [sic] discomfort, but
> simply carrying on a commercial activity with a view to profit."[64]

In the later case of *McLeish v. Amoo-Gottfried & Co*[65] Scott Baker J.   8–031
also appeared to endorse the "object of the contract" approach. Here the
claimant was convicted of criminal offences in circumstances where the
defendants admitted that he may well have been acquitted had they conducted his defence properly. The only issue at trial was the assessment of
damages for mental distress. In assessing damages, Scott Baker J. said:

[61] [1976] 1 Q.B. 446.
[62] *ibid.* at 463H.
[63] [1990] 2 All E.R. 815.
[64] *ibid.* at 824A.
[65] *The Times*, October 13, 1993.

"The very essence of the contract to act for the Plaintiff in preparation for and at his trial was to ensure his peace of mind by taking all appropriate steps to secure his acquittal, if possible, and if not, to make the best possible case for him. I have no doubt it was foreseeable that he would suffer mental distress if the Defendants conducted the preparations and trial negligently."

8–032   In *Oates v. Harte Reade and Company*[66] Singer J. raised the issue[67] of whether cases such as *Dickinson v. Jones Alexander & Co* would now stand in the light of the Court of Appeal's decision in *Watts v. Morrow*[68] discussed below in relation to claims against surveyors. This observation carries some force. There seems little reason why the typical solicitor/client relationship should stand on any different footing to the surveyor/client relationship, unless the very object of the solicitor's duty was to obtain peace of mind.

8–033   Arguably then, a foreseeability-based approach is an incorrect basis upon which to decide whether damages should sound for mental distress in actions against solicitors. It is submitted, however, that the courts should be prepared to consider awarding damages for mental distress where the mental distress has been specifically and pertinently brought home to the solicitor beforehand, and is aggravated by the solicitor's negligence. *Dickinson v. Jones Alexander & Co* is an example of the type of situation where such an award may be appropriate. By being made aware of the mental distress and the importance of obtaining a result favourable to the claimant, the object of the contract effectively becomes one to secure peace of mind.

8–034   The cases discussed in this section were actions in contract and it could be argued that they would not bind an action framed in tort, but it seems unlikely that the policy which has been crafted in relation to contractual claims could be undermined in this way. Confirming this view, in *Hayes v. James & Charles Dodd*[69] Purchas L.J. said that "damages of this kind are only recoverable when the subject matter of the contract *or duty in tort* is to provide peace of mind or freedom from distress."[70]

(b) Actions against surveyors

8–035   The leading case on damages for mental distress against surveyors is now *Watts v. Morrow*,[71] a decision based upon contract but which has been held to apply equally to actions framed in tort.[72] The claimants purchased a property in reliance on a surveyor's report negligently prepared by the defendants. Defects in the property were subsequently identified which necessitated expensive repairs and considerable upheaval and distress. The Court of Appeal held that the claimants' mental distress did sound in dam-

---

[66] [1999] P.I.Q.R. P120.
[67] *ibid.* at P126.
[68] [1991] 1 W.L.R. 1421.
[69] [1990] 2 All E.R. 815.
[70] *ibid.* at 826J. Emphasis added.
[71] [1991] 1 W.L.R. 1421.
[72] *Shaw v. Halifax (SW) Ltd* [1994] 2 E.G.L.R. 95, Official Referee's Business.

ages, but only because the distress resulted from physical inconvenience and discomfort caused by the breach of contract. The situation would have been otherwise had there been no inconvenience or discomfort. Bingham L.J. described the correct law as follows:

"A contract-breaker is not in general liable for any distress, frustration, anxiety, displeasure, vexation, tension or aggravation which his breach of contract may cause to the innocent party. This rule is not, I think, founded on the assumption that such reactions are not foreseeable, which they surely are or may be, but on considerations of policy.

But the rule is not absolute. Where the very object of a contract is **8–036** to provide pleasure, relaxation, peace of mind or freedom from molestation, damages will be awarded if the fruit of the contract is not provided or if the contrary result is procured instead. If the law did not cater for this exceptional category of case it would be defective. A contract to survey the condition of a house for a prospective purchaser does not, however, fall within this exceptional category.

In cases not falling within this exceptional category, damages are in **8–037** my view recoverable for physical inconvenience and discomfort caused by the breach and mental suffering directly related to that inconvenience and discomfort. If those effects are foreseeably suffered during a period when defects are repaired I am prepared to accept that they sound in damages even though the cost of the repairs is not recoverable as such."[73]

This maintains the restrictive approach observed in some of the more **8–038** recent decisions concerning negligent solicitors and further casts doubt on a purely foreseeability-based approach in relation to such claims. The earlier decision of *Perry v. Sidney Phillips & Son*,[74] should be regarded as having been decided on the same basis as *Watts v. Morrow*, despite what may appear to be a purely foreseeability-based approach adopted in the judgment of Lord Denning M.R.

(c) Analogous categories

Professional relationships analogous to those between solicitors and sur- **8–039** veyors may be thought to be guided by similar principles as those set out in *Watts v. Morrow*. The issue would be whether the relationship fell into the exceptional category where the object of the contract or duty was to provide peace of mind. Moreover, if foreseeable physical discomfort was occasioned resulting in mental distress, there would appear to no reason why an award should not be made. Negligence on the part of architects and construction engineers, for example, would fall into this category.

---

[73] [1991] 1 W.L.R. 1421 at 1445F.
[74] [1982] 1 W.L.R. 1297.

(d) Trespasses to the person, malicious prosecution and harassment

8–040   Awards in respect of anxiety and mental distress may be made for trespasses to the person. In *Appleton v. Garrett*[75] a dentist was sued in trespass to the person and negligence after carrying out treatment on patients which was both unnecessary and performed without consent. The claimants suffered mental distress and anxiety, and some became distrustful of dentists as a result of the experience. It was held that the claimants were entitled to aggravated damages in respect of this mental distress.

8–041   In *Clark v. Chief Constable of Cleveland Police*[76] Peter Gibson L.J. remarked that "Damages for malicious prosecution are intended to compensate the claimant both for injury to reputation and injury to feelings." In *White v. Metropolitan Police Commissioner*[77] the claimants were awarded aggravated damages for distress and anxiety brought about by malicious prosecution.

8–042   The Protection from Harassment Act 1997 introduced new civil and criminal remedies for victims of harassment. Pursuant to section 3(2) it is specifically provided that in civil claims for harassment "damages may be awarded for (among other things) any anxiety caused by the harassment". Any mental distress suffered at the hands of the harasser therefore sounds in damages. The basis upon which awards should be calculated is unclear, however.

(e) Nuisance and trespass to property

8–043   Awards for mental distress caused by trespass to property are available in appropriate cases, again usually in the form of aggravated damages. In *Ashgar v. Ahmed*[78] the claimants were subjected to enormous suffering, distress and intolerable anxiety when the defendant wrongfully evicted them from their premises, failed to comply with an injunction to re-admit them and threw all their belongings out of the house. The Court of Appeal held that this was about as plain a case for aggravated damages as one could get.

8–044   The position as regards private nuisance is less clear following the ruling of the House of Lords in *Hunter v. Canary Wharf Ltd.*[79] Prior to the ruling there appeared to be no bar to the recovery of damages for mental distress in nuisance claims. Wrongful eviction decisions such as *Ashgar v. Ahmed*[80] and *Drane v. Evangelou*[81] may be viewed as examples. In the latter, Lawton L.J. had said: "To deprive a man of a roof over his head in my judgment is one of the worst torts which can be committed. It causes stress, worry and anxiety."[82]

---

[75] [1996] P.I.Q.R. P1.
[76] *The Times*, May 13, 1999.
[77] *The Times*, April 24, 1982.
[78] (1995) 17 H.L.R. 25.
[79] [1997] A.C. 655.
[80] (1995) 17 H.L.R. 25.
[81] [1978] 1 W.L.R. 455.
[82] *ibid.* at 461F.

In *Hunter v. Canary Wharf Ltd* the House of Lords reaffirmed that nuis- **8–045** ance was a tort directed at the use and enjoyment of land and held that actions in private nuisance could only be brought by persons with an interest in the affected land. Lord Goff said that:

> "It follows that, on the authorities as they stand, an action in private nuisance will only lie at the suit of a person who has a right to the land affected. Ordinarily, such a person can sue if he has the right to exclusive possession of the land, such as a freeholder or tenant in possession, or even a licensee with exclusive possession. Exceptionally however, as *Foster v. Warblington Urban District Council*[83] shows, this category may include a person in actual possession who has no right to be there; and in any event a reversioner can sue in so far his reversionary interest is affected. But a mere licensee on the land has no right to sue."[84]

The ruling therefore excludes the possibility of those without an interest **8–046** in the affected land claiming anything in nuisance, let alone damages for mental distress, although they may be able to bring the act of nuisance within the definition of harassment. Whether even those *with* an interest in land can claim damages for mental distress is, however, now open to question in the wake of *Hunter*. The issues directly in point in *Hunter* were who had standing in an action in private nuisance, and whether interference with television reception was an actionable nuisance.

Their Lordships took the opportunity to make more general comments **8–047** on the law of nuisance beyond those two issues, however. Lord Lloyd and Lord Hoffmann emphasised that private nuisance covered cases of encroachment on land, direct physical injury to the land and interference with the quiet enjoyment of the land. As regards the first and second of these, the correct measure of damages would be the diminution in the value of the land. As regards interference with enjoyment of the land, the correct measure of damage would be loss of amenity value for so long as the nuisance persisted.

> "But inconvenience, annoyance or even illness suffered by persons on land as a result of smells or dust are not damage consequential upon the injury to the land. It is rather the other way about: the injury to the amenity of the land consists in the fact that the persons upon it are liable to suffer inconvenience, annoyance or illness".[85]

On this approach any mental distress suffered by the person with the interest in land would be absorbed into a general award for loss of amenity, the calculation of which "involves placing a value upon intangibles. But estate agents do this all the time."[86]

---

[83] [1906] 1 K.B. 648.
[84] [1997] A.C. 655 at 692C.
[85] *per* Lord Hoffmann *ibid*. 706G.
[86] *per* Lord Hoffmann *ibid*. at 706F.

8–048   Lord Hope appeared to concur with the approach of Lord Lloyd and Lord Hoffmann. Lord Goff did not directly address the point but Lord Cooke dissented on the issue of who had standing to sue and appeared to favour a law of nuisance which would embrace claims for mental distress caused by acts of harassment. Given that their Lordships were not called upon to directly decide the point, it is still open whether damages can be awarded in private nuisance for mental distress. But in the face of a majority opinion on the matter from the House of Lords, it appears unlikely.

8–049   The House of Lords has recently been called upon to consider the tort of nuisance in a slightly different context in *London Borough of Southwark v. Mills, Baxter v. Mayor etc. of the London Borough of Camden*[87] where the claimants were arguing *inter alia* that the local authority landlords were liable in nuisance for noise created by tenants in adjoining properties. The claimants claimed in particular that the noise disturbance had caused them distress. The House of Lords disposed of the claims on the basis of reasonable user. No reference was made in any of the judgments, however, to whether the claims for distress would have sounded in damages.

8–050   The decision in *Hunter* has no application to cases of public nuisance, but the requirement that before damages will be awarded a claimant must show particular or special loss over and above the ordinary inconvenience suffered by the public at large,[88] must necessarily restrict the range of situations in which an award could conceivably be made for mental distress.[89]

(f) Defamation

8–051   Whilst the tort of defamation exists to vindicate the claimant's reputation in the eyes of society, an amount is built in to any award to reflect the claimant's own injured feelings in the matter. In *John v. MGN Ltd*[90] Sir Thomas Bingham M.R. stated:

> "The successful plaintiff in a defamation action is entitled to recover, as general compensatory damages, such sum as will compensate him for the wrong he has suffered. That sum must compensate him for the damage to his reputation; vindicate his good name; and take account of the distress, hurt and humiliation which the defamatory publication has caused."[91]

8–052   Even where any damage to reputation suffered is negligible, *Fielding v. Variety Incorporated*[92] demonstrates that the damages may not be insubstantial if the defamatory statement has caused the claimant anxiety and

---

[87] [1999] 3 W.L.R. 939.
[88] *The Wagon Mound (No. 2)* [1963] 1 Lloyd's Rep. 402, first instance.
[89] In *Halsey v. Esso Petroleum Co Ltd* [1961] 1 W.L.R. 683, the claimant was awarded damages for the disruption to his sleep caused by noisy lorries. Veale J. held that this could be viewed as a case of public nuisance. Disruption to sleep could be viewed as a form of mental distress.
[90] [1997] Q.B. 586.
[91] *ibid.* at 607F.
[92] [1967] 2 Q.B. 841.

annoyance. Here the defendants published an article concerning the claimant's West End play which suggested that the play was a "disastrous flop". This was far from the truth, but the libel had no apparent effect upon audiences who continued to flock to see the show. The claimant received £1,500 in damages. Salmon L.J. said:

> "It seems fairly obvious to me that that article cannot have had any really serious effect upon Mr Fielding's reputation. Nevertheless he is entitled to be compensated, as I say, for the anxiety and annoyance which he very naturally felt at the time".[93]

(g) Malicious falsehood

The Court of Appeal in *Khodaparast v. Shad*[94] has recently confirmed **8–052A** that once a claimant is entitled to sue for malicious falsehood, whether on proof of special damage or by reason of section 3 of the Defamation Act 1952, there is no reason why, in an appropriate case, they should not recover aggravated damages for injury to feelings. Dicta to this effect in *Joyce v. Sengupta*[95] was approved.

(h) Other examples

Damages for mental distress have been awarded in relation to a variety **8–053** of other torts. In *Archer v. Brown*[96] it was held that aggravated damages could be awarded to compensate the claimant for his injured feelings in relation to a claim in deceit. In *Lonrho Plc. v. Fayed (No. 5)*,[97] however, the Court of Appeal held that the claimants could not recover damages for injury to feelings in a conspiracy action; damages for injury to reputation and injury to feelings could only be recovered in an action for defamation.

3. PHYSICAL INCONVENIENCE

There is an obvious overlap between awards for physical inconvenience **8–054** and mental distress as in many cases it will be the physical inconvenience which has created the mental distress. Indeed a global award for physical inconvenience and mental distress will often be made without differentiating between the two.[98] Despite the overlap, awards for physical inconvenience are freely available compared to those for mental distress. In negligence claims against solicitors, for example, provided that such damage is reasonably foreseeable it can be compensated. In *Bailey v. Bullock*[99] the

---

[93] [1967] 2 Q.B. 841 at 855D.
[94] [2000] 1 All E.R. 545.
[95] [1993] 1 W.L.R. 337.
[96] [1984] 2 All E.R. 267.
[97] [1993] 1 W.L.R. 1489.
[98] As it was for example in *Watts v. Morrow* [1991] 1 W.L.R. 1421.
[99] [1950] 2 All E.R. 1167.

claimant instructed the defendants to regain possession of a dwelling house which he had let, the claimant in the meantime being forced to live with his wife and child in a single room of his wife's parents' home. The defendants delayed instituting possession proceedings, the claimant eventually obtaining possession nearly two years later after consulting other solicitors. It was held that the claimant was entitled to recover damages for the inconvenience and discomfort which he had endured during this period as a direct result of the defendant's breach of duty. Similarly in claims against surveyors damages for the foreseeable physical inconvenience suffered through reliance upon the surveyor's report were awarded in *Perry v. Sidney Phillips & Son*[1] and *Watts v. Morrow.*[2] although such claims will be defeated or subject to reduction if it is shown that the physical inconvenience was created through an unreasonable decision on the part of the claimant, for example a decision to live in the property whilst repairs were being carried out when alternative accommodation was available.[3]

8–055   Other examples demonstrate that awards are available where the defendant's actions have foreseeably caused physical inconvenience. So in *Mafo v. Adams*[4] such damages were awarded for the defendant's deceit which caused the claimant to give up his tenancy causing him physical inconvenience. In *Ward v. Cannock Chase District Council*[5] the defendants' negligence caused the claimant and his family to live with a large hole in their roof for six days before being re-housed in temporary accommodation which was grossly inadequate for a family of the size of the claimant's. Scott J. awarded the claimant damages for the discomfort of living first in a house with a hole in its roof, and then subsequently in a house which was grossly overcrowded.

8–056   In relation to claims in private nuisance, it was observed earlier that the decision of the House of Lords in *Hunter v. Canary Wharf*[6] has cast doubt over the ability of a claimant to recover for mental distress. The dictum of Lord Hoffmann, previously referred to, is particularly pertinent in relation to claims for physical inconvenience:

> "But inconvenience, annoyance or even illness suffered by persons on land as a result of smells or dust are not damage consequential upon the injury to the land. It is rather the other way about: the injury to the amenity of the land consists in the fact that the persons upon it are liable to suffer inconvenience, annoyance or illness".[7]

This view, apparently shared by the majority, suggests that claims for physical inconvenience based upon nuisance must now be assessed by reference to the appropriate loss of amenity value of the land, rather than being treated as a separate head of damage.

---

[1] [1982] 1 W.L.R. 1297.
[2] [1991] 1 W.L.R. 1421.
[3] *ibid. per* Ralph Gibson L.J. at 1441G and 1442H.
[4] [1970] 1 Q.B. 548.
[5] [1986] Ch. 546.
[6] [1997] A.C. 655.
[7] *ibid.* at 706G.

By contrast, in cases of public nuisance physical inconvenience will usu-   8–057
ally be the very nub of the claim and provided that the claimant can demonstrate that they have suffered particular or special loss, damages will be
available. In *Halsey v. Esso Petroleum*,[8] for example, the claimant lived
close to an oil storage depot operated by the defendants and was forced to
endure the noise of lorries passing his house as they entered and left the
depot during the night. Veale J. held that as the noise emanated from the
highway, this could be viewed as a case of public nuisance. The claimant
was particularly affected by this noise, and damages would be awarded to
reflect the physical inconvenience caused to the claimant: "a man is entitled
to sleep during the night in his own house."[9]

4. QUANTIFYING DAMAGES FOR MENTAL DISTRESS AND PHYSICAL INCONVENIENCE

There seems to be no clear basis upon which damages for mental distress   8–058
or physical inconvenience should be quantified by the courts. The exception
is distress caused as a result of malicious prosecution or false imprisonment,
where guidance on the appropriate level of global award has now been
provided by the Court of Appeal in *Thompson v. Commissioner of Police
of the Metropolis*.[10] In other cases the matter seems to be one of impression,
although it has been emphasised that awards for mental distress or physical
inconvenience are likely to be moderate. In *Watts v. Morrow*[11] Ralph
Gibson L.J. spoke of the "principle that damages for mental distress
resulting from physical inconvenience . . . should be modest"[12] and Bingham L.J. agreed "that awards should be restrained."[13] Following this
approach, in *Patel v. Hooper & Jackson*,[14] the Court of Appeal upheld an
award of £2,000 to two claimants who had been forced to spend seven
years living in rented accommodation, often substandard, after a property
which they had purchased in reliance on a surveyor's report transpired to
be uninhabitable.

In *Saunders v. Edwards*[15] the claimants claimed against the defendant   8–059
for fraudulent misrepresentation in relation to the sale of a lease on a flat
which the defendant misrepresented to possess a roof terrace. The claimants
included a claim for disappointment and inconvenience. Kerr L.J. said that
awards under this head should be moderate, but added that although moderate, the award should bear some relation to the particular circumstances.
There was no reason why the same sum should be awarded for a spoiled
holiday as where a couple who were getting married and planning a baby
bought a flat which they believed to have a roof terrace. Extreme cases may

---

[8] [1961] 1 W.L.R. 683.
[9] *ibid.* at 701 per Veale J.
[10] [1998] Q.B. 498. Discussed above at para. 8–019.
[11] [1991] 1 W.L.R. 1421.
[12] *ibid.* at 1443E.
[13] *ibid.* at 1445H.
[14] [1999] 1 W.L.R. 1792.
[15] [1987] 2 All E.R. 651.

call for a higher award. So in *McLeish v. Amoo-Gottfried & Co*[16] Scott Baker J. awarded the claimant £6,000 as general damages for the mental distress caused by the defendants' mishandling of his defence which resulted in convictions for assault on police officers and possession of an offensive weapon. And in *Dickinson v. Jones Alexander & Co*[17] Douglas Brown J. awarded the claimant £5,000 for the extreme mental distress caused by the mishandling of the divorce proceedings.

---

[16] *The Times*, October 13, 1933.
[17] [1993] 2 F.L.R. 521.

CHAPTER 9

DAMAGES FOR PERSONAL INJURY

Damages for personal injury* will typically be a consequence of negli- 9–001
gence, but they may also arise out of such torts as nuisance, trespass to the
person and breach of statutory duty (the latter in particular as a consequence of breach of a duty owed by an employer to his employee). The
preponderance of personal injury claims over any other kind of damages
claim has no doubt been an important factor in the creation of significant
divergences from the once-for-all lump sum assessment of damages, discussed above,[1] in the form of provisional damages, interim payments and
structured settlements. These developments reflect also the concern,
expressed judicially and elsewhere on numerous occasions, that, where
damages for future loss are being awarded, in the words of Lord Scarman
in *Lim Poh Choo v. Camden and Islington Area Health Authority*[2] "There
is really only one certainty: the future will prove the award to be either too
high or too low."

The claimant may recover for both pecuniary and non-pecuniary losses. 9–002
In *Jefford v. Gee*[3] it was established that the damages in personal injury
cases should be itemised, as different rates of interest[4] applied to different
heads of loss. Thus non-pecuniary loss, pre-trial pecuniary loss and future
pecuniary losses are to be itemised separately. Further it is necessary to
distinguish between general and special damages,[5] since the amount and
details of the latter (comprising for the purposes of this chapter all pre-trial
pecuniary losses) have to be specifically pleaded, whereas for the former
(non-pecuniary losses and future pecuniary losses and expenses)[6] they do
not.

1. DAMAGES FOR PECUNIARY LOSS

Two basic categories of pecuniary loss may be identified: expenditure 9–003

---

* See generally McGregor *op. cit.*; Burrows *op. cit.*; Kemp & Kemp; Munkman "Damages
  for Personal Injury and Death" (10th ed., 1996). See also the invaluable PNBA "Facts and
  Figures: Tables for the Calculation of Damages" (4th ed., 1999); Butterworths Personal
  Injury Damages Statistics: Nelson-Jones (1999).
[1] *Supra* Ch. 1 paras. 1–024 *et seq.*
[2] [1980] A.C. 174 at 183. See also "Personal Injury Compensation: How much is enough?"
  Law Com. (No. 225, 1994); *Wells v. Wells* [1998] 3 All E.R. 481 at 502 per Lord Steyn.
[3] [1970] 2 A.B. 130.
[4] See *infra* paras. 9–102 *et seq.*
[5] See *supra* Ch. 1 paras. 1–051 *et seq.*
[6] However evidence of amount of lost future earnings and future expenses must be provided.

incurred as a consequence of the personal injury, and lost earnings. These may be further sub-divided into pre-trial and post-trial losses.

(1) Pre-trial losses

9–004   As might be expected, quantification of pre-trial losses presents signific-antly fewer difficulties than assessment of post-trial losses. As regards loss of earnings, the claimant is entitled to recover the net[7] earnings he would have obtained but for the injury. The award will have to take account of increases he would have achieved in his earnings between the time of the accident and the trial as a consequence, for example a likely promotion he would no longer be able to achieve, or a lost bonus. The converse may equally apply: thus in *Rouse v. Port of London Authority*,[8] in assessing pre-trial lost earnings the court took into account the fact that, due to changes in conditions he might well not have been in full employment during the relevant period.

9–005   Pre-trial expenditure which may be recovered is governed by the same principles to be discussed below; again the conjectural element, as with lost earnings, is absent in the case of a claim for pre-trial losses, and the task of quantification is thereby considerably facilitated, the main potential issue for dispute being the reasonableness of the expenditure.

(2) Post-trial losses

(a) Medical and other expenses

9–006   Reasonably-incurred[9] medical and other[10] expenses are recoverable. Medical expenses will include the cost of medical advice and operations, the cost of medicines and appliances (including the cost of maintenance and replacement) and the cost of treatment and care in a hospital or nursing home. The claimant is not required to avail himself of the facilities of the National Health Service;[11] hence, subject to the overriding requirement of reasonableness he may choose private medical treatment; if his needs can and will be met by the National Health Service there will be no claim for medical expenses. The court may take account of the likelihood of use of private or state medical facilities: thus in *Woodrup v. Nicol*[12] the court considered that it was probable that the claimant would obtain half of his physiotherapy on the National Health Service and half privately, and awarded him damages accordingly. Also, as was underlined by Lord Scar-man in *Lim*,[13] there may come a point, in a case of serious injuries, where

---

[7] See *infra* para. 9–023.
[8] [1953] 2 Lloyd's Rep. 179. See also *Carter v. British India Steam Navigation Co.* [1974] 1 Lloyd's Rep. 419.
[9] See Law Reform (Personal Injuries) Act 1948, s. 2(4).
[10] See *infra* paras. 9–007–9–024.
[11] Law Reform (Personal Injuries) Act 1948 s. 2(4). The Pearson Commission Cmnd. 7054 (1978), Vol. 1, para. 342 recommended the repeal of s. 2(4).
[12] [1993] P.I.Q.R. Q104.
[13] *Supra* n. 2 at 188.

it will not be feasible to care for the claimant except in a public institution. The question of recoupment by the NHS of the cost of treating an injured claimant is discussed elsewhere in this chapter.[14]

The courts will seek to avoid over-compensation. Thus in *Shearman v.*   9–007
Folland[15] the claimant, prior to the accident in question, was accustomed to live in hotels, where she paid seven guineas a week for board and lodging. As a consequence of the accident she spent over a year in nursing homes at a cost of twelve guineas a week. The Court of Appeal held that the trial judge had erred in taking into account the whole of the seven guineas in assessing the claimant's damages, but that it would be appropriate to make a deduction in respect of the amount paid to the nursing home for board and lodging (in the absence of evidence concerning this, the court estimated the amount and deducted it). The court pointed out[16] that in the more usual case of a claimant who had a home of his own a deduction would usually be inappropriate since many of his expenses would continue while he was still in hospital. A claim however for "extra nourishment"[17] necessitated by the accident would presuppose credit being given for the usual nourishment for which the claimant would in any event have had to pay.

Further, it is provided in section 5 of the Administration of Justice Act   9–008
1982 that any saving to the injured person which is attributable to his maintenance wholly or partly at public expense in a hospital, nursing home or other institution shall be set off against any income lost by him as a result of his injuries.[18]

In cases of large awards of damages, the need for expert advice as to the   9–009
appropriate investment of a large lump sum and the management of the investment may arise. Thus, in *Anderson v. Davis*[19] the claimant was awarded £400 per annum, with a multiplier of 11 years, for the cost of professional advice on how best to invest his lump sum, and in *Cassel v. Riverside Health Authority*[20] the award included £2,650 per annum, with a multiplier of 18. However, in the light of the decision of the House of Lords in *Wells v. Wells*[21] the question of recovery of the costs of financial management is likely to need review. Prior to the decision in *Wells*, the assumption was that the lump sum would be invested "in a mixed basket of equities and gilts."[22] In *Wells* however it was held that when the court is assessing damages for anticipated future losses and expenses in personal injury cases, it should assume that the claimant will invest his damages in index-linked government stock. Though it was also said that how in fact

---

[14] See *infra* para. 9–071.
[15] [1950] 2 K.B. 43.
[16] *ibid.* at 48–9.
[17] See Munkman: "Damages for Personal Injuries and Death" (10th ed., 1996) at 80.
[18] This reverses *Daish v. Wauton* [1972] 1 Q.B. 262.
[19] [1993] P.I.Q.R. Q87 *cf.* however, *Francis v. Bostock*, November 8, 1995. Kemp & Kemp, Vol. 2 p. 51225, per Russell J.
[20] [1992] P.I.Q.R. Q168. Reported at first instance, *sub nom. Cassel v. Hammersmith and Fulham Health Authority* [1992] P.I.Q.R. Q1.
[21] [1999] 1 A.C. 345. See *infra* para. 9–037 *et seq.* for detailed analysis of the implications of this decision.
[22] *ibid.* at 485, per Lord Lloyd.

the claimant invests his money is irrelevant,[23] it will surely henceforth be inappropriate to argue for the same level of financial management expenses as hitherto. In *Cassel* the services to be provided by the receiver were to include: regular meetings with the parents and child, distribution of income from the fund through a bank account, dealing with tax returns, commenting on investment advice obtained by the Court of Protection, and preparing an annual account and report for the Court of Protection.[24] Much of this expenditure will be unnecessary where the lump sum is simply used to purchase a block of index-linked securities. What if the claimant decides, as he is perfectly entitled to, to ignore index-linked government stock and invest the lump sum in the stock market? Is he then entitled to the pre-*Wells* level of claim for financial management expenditure? It is suggested that he is not so entitled: the assumption upon which the post-*Wells* award is made presupposes a lower level of financial investment and management advice. To some extent this would be mitigated by being able to recover such expenses as may now be recoverable on the basis of the longer multipliers that are the main legacy of *Wells*.

9–010   In addition a claim may be made to recover fees payable to the Court of Protection where the claimant is suffering from a mental instability.[25] Under the Court of Protection Rules 1984 the Court may charge, *inter alia*, a commencement fee[26] and an annual administration fee.[27] Such fees do not appear to be affected by the changes wrought by *Wells v. Wells* and would remain recoverable, but it may be that some transaction fees[28] would no longer be incurred. In its Report "Damages for Personal Injury: Medical Nursing and Other Expenses; Collateral Benefits",[29] the Law Commission favoured the view, adumbrated by the Court of Appeal in *Cassel*, that damages for Court of Protection fees (whether fixed or variable) should be reduced for contributory negligence. The issue awaits detailed consideration by the courts.

9–011   Another aspect of post-accident expenditure concerns the need to make alternative provision for the accommodation of the claimant where his existing accommodation is no longer suitable. In *Roberts v. Johnstone*[30] it was held that the damages to be awarded in respect of the purchase of special accommodation necessitated by the claimant's injuries should not be the net capital cost of the purchase but the additional annual cost over the claimant's lifetime of providing that accommodation. The Court of Appeal decided that the annual cost was to be taken as two per cent of the net capital cost which, if necessarily expended, was not to be reduced by

---

[23] [1999] 1 A.C. 345 at 373.
[24] [1992] P.I.Q.R. Q1 at Q17.
[25] See *e.g. Rialas v. Mitchell* (1984) 128 S.J. 704.
[26] S.I. 1984, No. 2035.
[27] For fees such as these which are related to the clear annual income at the claimant's disposal, only one half of any structured payment or damages or payment intended as part of a series of payments arising from an annuity, insurance bond or similar arrangement made for the benefit of the patient is to be treated as income of the patient (Court of Protection Rules 1984 r. 82A(1), added by S.I. 1992/1899).
[28] Court of Protection Rules 1984 r. 80.
[29] (1999) Law Com. No. 262.
[30] [1989] Q.B. 878.

reason of any element of betterment due to factors not directly related to the claimant's need. However, in *Wells v. Wells*,[31] as a consequence of the House of Lords decision that the return on index-linked government stock represents the best possible indicator of the real return on risk-free investment, it was held that the rate which should now be taken for calculating future accommodation costs is three per cent. If a property is purchased which has to be adapted to the claimant's needs, or existing accommodation requires to be adapted to that end, the full cost of the adaptation should be recoverable, to the extent that it does not increase the value of the property.[32] However, in *Willett v. North Bedfordshire Health Authority*[33] Hobhouse J. considered that the cost of alterations was part of the capital cost of the property, and was included in the two per cent calculation.

Extra expenditure may also arise where living expenses are increased as a consequence of the accident, for example where a specially-adapted vehicle or a wheelchair is necessary, holidays are more expensive, or a lift has to be installed in the claimant's house. In *Cassel*[34] the Court of Appeal disallowed the trial judge's award of £32,500 to provide a swimming pool, in the absence of evidence that it was necessary as part of the claimant's therapeutic treatment: it was more properly regarded as an element in the award for loss of amenity.   9–012

In *Pritchard v. J. H. Cobden Ltd*[35] the claimant argued that, as a consequence of the defendant's negligence he had sustained brain damage, leading to a complete personality change, which led his marriage to break down, causing him financial loss which, he claimed, was recoverable from the defendant. The Court of Appeal held however that, though the breakdown of the claimant's marriage was the result of his injuries, he could not recover losses resulting from any alteration in his financial position resulting from the divorce since the court, in making orders for financial provision and property adjustment was exercising a discretion over the joint assets and resources of the husband and wife, including any damages awarded for personal injuries, by making adjustments to meet their needs following the divorce. This adjustment of the couple's assets was not a loss incurred by the claimant. Further, it would be contrary to public policy and open to abuse to bring into personal injury litigation considerations relevant to matrimonial proceedings. The latter point, justified by O'Connor L.J.[36] on the basis that it would increase evidentiary difficulties and tend to lengthen litigation, seems tenuous in comparison to the loss caused to the claimant: the former appears to ignore the reality of the situation; surely damages to which the claimant might be entitled for losses   9–013

---

[31] [1999] 1 A.C. 345 at 376, see *infra* paras. 9–037 *et seq.* See also (1999) Law Com. No. 262; 4.1–4.17.

[32] *ibid.* n. 30 at 893.

[33] [1993] P.I.Q.R. Q166. See (1999) Law Com. No. 262, para 4.27, agreeing with the approach in *Willett*.

[34] *ibid.* n. 20 at Q181.

[35] [1988] Fam. 22 *Jones v. Jones* [1985] Q.B. 704, also a decision of the Court of Appeal, was not followed.

[36] [1998] Fam. 22 at 39–40. For detailed criticism of the reasoning of the court, see Burrows *op. cit.* at 196–7.

resulting from the divorce could be left out of account in making the divorce orders.[37]

Where property is destroyed or damaged in an accident where personal injury is caused to the claimant, the damages will be assessed on the basis of the principles discussed elsewhere.[38]

9–014   In some cases, expenditure may be incurred or services provided by third parties on the claimant's behalf. In particular this issue may arise in cases where nursing services are provided by the third party, voluntarily and hence without any obligation of reimbursement. In *Donnelly v. Joyce*[39] the mother of an injured child gave up her part-time employment in order to look after him. It was held that the child could recover her loss of wages since the loss to him caused by the defendant's negligence included the existence of the need for the nursing services provided by his mother, and the lost wages represented the proper and reasonable cost of supplying that need. It was said that there was no need for a contractual obligation[40] to be entered into by the claimant to reimburse the third party in such a case, since the loss was the claimant's loss, not that of the third party. In *Cunningham v. Harrison*[41] however, Lord Denning M.R. considered that the claimant should hold the sum awarded on trust for the third party and pay it over to them, focusing therefore on the loss to the third party rather than that of the claimant.

9–015   The issue fell for reconsideration by the House of Lords in *Hunt v. Severs*.[42] In that case the claimant was seriously injured in an accident for which the defendant was responsible. Her claim included a sum for the value of past and future services rendered by the defendant in caring for her at home, and also a sum for travel expenses incurred in visiting her while she was in hospital. The House of Lords held that a claimant could recover as part of her damages in a personal injury claim the reasonable value of services rendered to her gratuitously by a member of her family in the provision of nursing care or domestic assistance made necessary by her injuries. The underlying rationale of that principle is to enable the voluntary carer, who has no cause of action of their own against the tortfeasor, to recover proper compensation for their services. Thus the injured claimant who recovers damages under this head holds them on trust for the voluntary carer; thereby reasserting the rationale of Lord Denning in *Cunningham*. In *Hunt* itself, since it was the defendant who provided the services, the claimant could not receive the cost of those services from the defendant and hold them on trust for the defendant; this would be absurd. Such a conclusion does, however, risk a return to the pre-1973 practice of claimants entering into contracts with defendant carers to remunerate them for the cost of their services; though this has been judicially deprecated[43]

---

[37] See however (1999) Law Com. No. 263, recommending no change.

[38] *Supra* Ch. 6.

[39] [1974] Q.B. 454. See also *Roach v. Yates* [1938] 1 K.B. 256; *Cunningham v. Harrison* [1973] Q.B. 942.

[40] As in *Haggar v. de Placido* [1972] 1 W.L.R. 716.

[41] [1973] Q.B. 942.

[42] [1994] 2 A.C. 350.

[43] See *e.g.* Sir Thomas Bingham M.R. in the Court of Appeal in *Hunt v. Severs* [1993] Q.B. 815 at 831; *Housecroft v. Burnett* [1986] 1 All E.R. 332 at 343 per O'Connor L.J.

there is nothing in the ratio of the decision of the House of Lords in *Hunt* to prevent such an arrangement, followed by a claim for special damages for the cost of the services provided or to be provided, being made. Altern- atively claimants may engage professional carers, supplied at the full com- mercial rate, which may have the doubly disadvantageous effect of increas- ing the cost to the defendant and depriving the claimant of care by a close relative who may well be a more appropriate carer than a professional. In *Hardwick v. Hudson*[44] the wife of an injured claimant who normally worked for two days a week in the garage her husband co-owned, worked an extra twenty hours a week without pay. He claimed damages to include the gratuitous work she had done. It was held, however, that no award under that head should be made. The wife could have charged the business for her increased services, and the commercial reasons behind the decision not to charge for her services made the case very different from one where voluntary services were provided in a domestic environment; in such cases entry into a formal contract would not normally be contemplated, and personal physical care could often be most effectively and economically provided by a family member or friend.

In its 1999 Report: "Damages for Personal Injury: Medical, Nursing and Other Expenses; Collateral Benefits",[45] the Law Commission examined in some detail the principles and policy applicable to cases of gratuitous care. It was the Commission's view, in the light of earlier consultation[46] that the proper rationale was the remuneration of the carer, rather than a loss to the claimant. It was not thought to be appropriate to give the gratuitous carer a direct claim against the tortfeasor given the extra complication and expense that would entail, as well as the potential adverse effect on the claimant's claim. The trust approach of *Hunt v. Severs* was thought to be problematic, given the difficulty of seeing how it could cope with the uncertainties of the future,[47] and the Law Commission preferred the approach whereby the claimant is put under a personal legal obligation to account to a relative or friend for care provided. This obligation would be limited to past care however, on the basis that extending it to future care runs the unacceptable risk of compensating the carer at the expense of undercompensating the claimant where the circumstances turn out differ- ently from those contemplated at trial.[48] Damages would still be recover- able for future gratuitous care, but with no attaching legal obligation on the claimant. The decision in *Hunt v. Severs* should be reversed as regards the denial in that case of a claim for the defendant gratuitous carer, bearing in mind the factors discussed above.[49] Draft legislation is attached to the Report to enable implementation of these proposals, thus enabling a heavily criticised[50] decision to be rectified.

A further issue in cases where care is gratuitously provided is the amount

9–016

9–017

---

[44] [1999] 3 All E.R. 426.
[45] Law Com. No. 262 para. 3.44–3.76.
[46] Consultation Paper No. 144 (1996).
[47] *ibid*. at para 3.50.
[48] (1999) Law Com. No. 262 para 3.59.
[49] *Supra* paras. 9–015–9–016.
[50] See *e.g.* Kemp (1994) 110 L.Q.R. 524; Reed (1995) O.J.L.S. 133.

that the court will award under this head. The matter came in for detailed examination in *Housecroft v. Burnett*[51] where it was held that in assessing "the proper and reasonable cost"[52] of supplying the claimant's needs, the assessment would fall between two extremes:

(a) the full commercial rate[53] for supplying the needs by employing someone to do what the relative does;

(b) assessing the cost as nil, as where the claimant is to be cared for under the NHS.

9–018　It would seem however, from the judgment of O'Connor L.J. in *Housecroft*[54] that the commercial rate could be employed as a ceiling where a relative had given up gainful employment to look after the claimant, though the reported cases have generally involved a lesser figure; thus in *Nash v. Southmead Health Authority*[55] a reduction of one third was applied to the commercial rate; in *Fairhurst v. St Helens and Knowsley Health Authority*[56] a reduction of a quarter was applied. In *Fitzgerald v. Ford*[57] the trial judge had awarded one-and-a-half times the earnings of the husband who had given up his job to look after his wife, but this was reduced to the actual net earnings lost by the Court of Appeal, though such an award was upheld in *Hogg v. Doyle*[58] given the exceptionally extensive nature of the care afforded by the claimant's wife, who was herself a nurse.

9–019　A further aspect of this type of claim is where expenditure is incurred by a third party, such as the travel expenses, totaling £4,429, incurred by the defendant in *Hunt* in visiting the claimant. Such expenditure, provided it is reasonably incurred, is recoverable,[59] though wages foregone by a relative in visiting the claimant are irrecoverable as being too remote.[60] Following *Hunt* such expenditure, like the value of services provided, will be held on trust by the claimant for the third party, unless the person incurring the expenditure is the defendant.

9–020　Another category of expenditure occasioned by negligence which causes personal injury is where the claimant's ability to carry out household services such as housekeeping, home maintenance and gardening is wholly or partially lost. In *Daly v. General Steam Navigation Co Ltd*[61] the claimant claimed for the partial loss of her ability, both pre- and post-trial, to do housework. As regards the pre-trial period, it was held that she could not recover damages by reference to the amount it would have cost to employ the necessary domestic help when she had not in fact employed such help (her husband and his sister in fact did the work). The pre-trial loss had to

[51] [1986] 1 All E.R. 332.
[52] *per* Megaw L.J. in *Donnelly v. Joyce* [1974] Q.B. 454 at 462.
[53] See *e.g. Taylor v. Glass* (23 May, 1979); Kemp & Kemp, Vol. 2, para. 1-715.
[54] [1986] 1 All E.R. 332 at 343.
[55] [1993] P.I.Q.R. Q156.
[56] [1995] P.I.Q.R. Q1.
[57] [1996] P.I.Q.R. Q72.
[58] March 6, 1991; Kemp & Kemp, Vol. 2, para. A2-006/1.
[59] See *e.g. Walker v. Mullen*, *The Times*, January 19, 1984.
[60] *ibid.* See also *Kirkham v. Boughey* [1958] 2 Q.B. 338.
[61] [1980] 3 All E.R. 696.

be assessed as part of her general damages for pain, suffering and loss of amenity by considering the extent to which her difficulties in carrying out housework due to her injuries had increased those damages. As part of the overall award the claimant was awarded £930 which represented an actual pre-trial loss, comprising the sum lost by her husband in giving up his part-time employment. The justification for this was found in *Donnelly v. Joyce*[62] and hence, in the light of *Hunt* it would now have to be held on trust by her for him being regarded as part of his loss.[63] As regards future loss of housekeeping ability, this was the estimated cost of employing domestic help for eight hours a week during her life expectancy, even if she did not use the sum awarded to pay for domestic help. The illogicality of this approach was admitted by the court.[64] The Law Commission[65] has recommended that such cases should entail compensation as a past pecuniary loss where the claimant has reasonably paid someone to do the work, and as a future pecuniary loss where the claimant can show that he/she would reasonably pay someone to do the work. As with the Commission's recommendations on gratuitous care, a claimant should be under a personal liability to account to a friend or relative for past work done, but not as regards future work (the same recommendation is made, *mutatis mutandis*, as concerns hospital visits).[66] Any claim for non-pecuniary losses (pain suffering and loss of amenity)[67] might include a sum in respect of past and/or future reduced inability to do work in the home. Again, these are sensible suggestions which will further tidy up a somewhat confused area of the law.

A further head of claim that may be made in the case of a young unmarried woman who suffers serious personal injuries, as in *Moriarty v. McCarthy*[68] where the claimant sustained injuries resulting in paraplegia, comprises compensation for the loss of opportunity of marriage which deprives her of the support of a husband during the period she would have reared and brought up her family. The claimant was awarded £7,500 by way of general damages for this loss, which was the figure by which her loss of future earnings claim was reduced, in comparison to the sum a man of her age would have been awarded, to take account of the period when she would have been bringing up her children.   **9–021**

Medical and other expenditure may of course be a matter of future as well as past loss. With the increasing emphasis on rehabilitation, identified recently by the Law Commission,[69] it may be expected that claims for past and future expenditure will increase, though the corollary to this should be diminishing claims for lost future earnings, as claimants return to work   **9–022**

---

[62] [1974] Q.B. 454.
[63] See Law Com. No. 144 para. 2.37.
[64] [1980] 3 All E.R. 696 at 70 per Bridge L.J.; who regarded the matter as one of practical reality rather than logic. See Burrows *op. cit.* pp. 195–6 for convincing criticism of the decision.
[65] Damages for Personal Injury: Medical, Nursing and Other Expenses; Collateral Benefits (1999) Law Com. No. 262 para 3.91.
[66] *ibid.* at para 3.98. This should also extend to visits by the defendant: para. 3.100.
[67] See *infra* paras. 9–068 *et seq.*
[68] [1978] 1 W.L.R. 155.
[69] (1999) Law Com. No. 262 para. 1.17.

earlier than might otherwise have been the case. Here, as with loss of future earnings, an inevitable element of conjecture arises, and the courts have evolved techniques designed to quantify such losses. The same approach is applicable to all kinds of pecuniary loss and is considered in detail below.[70]

9–023   As regards future pecuniary losses, some general, preliminary points must be made. As regards lost earnings, the claimant is entitled to recover the net lost earnings, this being the case for both pre-trial and post-trial earnings, the object being *restitutio in integrum* as closely as possible. This has been an established principle since the decision of the House of Lords in *British Transport Commission v. Gourley*[71] where it was held that an award of damages in a personal injuries action for loss of earnings (past and/or future) must take into account the tax which would have been paid by the claimant had he not been injured. This principle was extended to national insurance contributions in *Cooper v. Firth Brown Ltd*[72] and to employees contributing to a compulsory pension scheme in *Dews v. National Coal Board*.[73] In *Gourley* Earl Jowitt emphasised the need to make a broad estimate when determining what the tax would have been if the money had been earned, equating the difficulty of so doing with the impossibility of accurate assessment of damages for non-pecuniary loss.[74] Though the analogy is not an exact one, the computation, especially in cases of long-term future loss is fraught with the difficulties inherent in the lump-sum system. Lord Goddard in *Gourley* did not consider that it would be right to take into account possible future changes in tax rates,[75] though if the claimant's future earnings levels would take him into a higher tax bracket, at current rates, that could not be ignored.

9–024   In *Gourley* Lord Reid reasserted the traditional approach to the assessment of future losses of the lump-sum award, albeit that; "such damages can only be an estimate, often a very rough estimate, of the present value of his prospective loss."[76] As we shall see, some inroads have been made into this principle by provisional damages[77] and structured settlements,[78] but in most cases of personal injury damages the traditional lump-sum award remains. In projecting forward over the life of the claimant as it would have been, quite apart from the inherent impossibility of doing so with any degree of accuracy, the courts have striven within that context, for as great a degree of accuracy as possible. An issue that arises is that of future inflation, and whether it is appropriate for the court to seek to estimate and take account of future inflation. The traditional approach, as exem-

---

[70] See *infra* paras. 9–026 *et seq.*
[71] [1956] A.C. 185.
[72] [1963] 1 W.L.R. 418.
[73] [1988] A.C. 1. In fact it would appear from the speech of Lord Griffith, with whom his brethren all agreed, that contributions under a voluntary scheme would equally fall to be deducted: *ibid.* at 16–17.
[74] [1956] A.C. 185 at 203–4.
[75] *ibid.* at 209.
[76] *ibid.* at 212.
[77] See *infra*, para. 9–096 *et seq.*
[78] See *infra*, para. 9–089 *et seq.*

plified in a number of cases,[79] has been to ignore future inflation as a factor, on the basis that it is very difficult to estimate future inflation rates, and that in any event the traditional method by which the present value of lost future earnings is calculated would automatically take into account future rates of inflation. Discussion of the accuracy or otherwise of this view has happily been rendered academic by the decision of the House of Lords in *Wells v. Wells*,[80] in which it was held that in assessing damages for anticipated future losses and expenses the court should assume that the claimant will invest his damages in index-linked government stock, thereby effectively solving the problem of inflation.

For some years it has been argued that actuarial evidence would assist   9–025
the courts in assessing future pecuniary loss[81] but the courts traditionally resisted this suggestion[82] despite the publication of the Ogden Tables in 1984.[83] These tables form part of a report produced by a working party which consisted of representatives of actuarial associations and English and Scottish lawyers under the chairmanship of Sir Michael Ogden Q.C. The aim of the report was to produce greater accuracy in estimating future financial loss, and it contains a number of valuable actuarial tables, produced by the Government Actuary. As is discussed below,[84] the Ogden Tables have been very influential in persuading the courts to assume investment in index-linked government stock, but, as a precursor to that, they have also increasingly persuaded the courts to take account of actuarial evidence, thereby increasing the likelihood of an accurate assessment of the future life expectancy of the claimant. Thus, judicial notice of the Tables was taken in Scotland in *O'Brien's Curator Bonis v. British Steel Corporation*[85] and in England in *Mills v. British Rail Engineering*,[86] and in *Hunt v. Severs*[87] Lord Bridge accepted that the practice had changed in recent years, and actuarial tables now figured more prominently in the evidence on which courts relied. As a consequence of a recommendation by the Law Commission,[88] section 10 of the Civil Evidence Act 1995[89] provides:

> "(1) The actuarial tables (together with explanatory notes) for use in personal injury and fatal accident cases issued from time to time by the Government Actuary's Department are admissible in evidence for

---

[79] See *e.g. Taylor v. O'Connor [1971] A.C. 115; Cookson v. Knowles [1979] A.C. 556; Lim Poh Choo v. Camden and Islington Area Health Authority [1980] A.C. 174.* See also *Wells v. Wells [1998] 3 All E.R. 481* at 516 per Lord Hutton.

[80] [1999] 1 A.C. 345. For detailed discussion see *infra* paras. 9–037 *et seq.*

[81] See *e.g. Prevett (1972) 35 M.L.R. 140, 257.*

[82] See *Auty v. National Coal Board [1985] 1 All E.R. 930* at 939 per Oliver L.J.

[83] Actuarial Tables with explanatory notes for use in Personal Injury and Fatal Accident cases HMSO May 1985 Third Edition 1998.

[84] *infra* paras. 9–039 *et seq.*

[85] 1991 S.L.T. 477.

[86] [1992] P.I.Q.R. Q130. See also *Read v. Harries [1995] P.I.Q.R. Q25* (a fatal accident case).

[87] [1994] 2 A.C. 350.

[88] "Structural Settlements and Interim and Provisional Damages" Law Com. No. 224 (1994) paras. 2.9–2.15.

[89] Enacting clause 6(2) of the draft Bill attached to the Law Commission's Report.

the purpose of assessing, in an action for personal injury, the sum to be awarded as general damages for future pecuniary loss."

Though this provision is not yet in force, it has had the effect of ensuring that the Tables are regularly used in personal injury cases[90] and hence that appropriate consideration is given to actuarial evidence.

(b) Calculation of future pecuniary losses

9–026   The discussion that follows is applicable to all future financial losses; though the illustrations may be of lost future earnings or of future expenses, the essential principles are the same for both. As regards future earnings, however, it should be pointed out that such a claim may include lost opportunities to make other work-related profits, such as profit-sharing arrangements with the employer, or options to buy shares in the employer company, and also lost benefits such as a company car, free accommodation or free (or reduced price) company or other goods. Such losses must of course be shown to have been precluded by the accident. In addition a claim may be made for loss or diminution of pension rights or retirement gratuities. The capital value at the date of future retirement has to be calculated by finding the value at that date, estimating life expectancy at the date, and taking the appropriate number of years' purchase. The capital value thus calculated then has to be reduced to its present value.

9–027   The method employed by the judiciary to convert lost future earnings into a lump sum is to multiply the net annual loss (the multiplicand) by a multiplier, which is the figure which, based upon the number of years of duration of the lost earning power, is discounted so as to take into account the fact that the lump sum is being paid immediately, rather than being spread over a number of years, as would have been the case had the accident not occurred. The object of the exercise is to provide a lump sum which, when invested will equal the income lost during the working life of the claimant, assuming a combination of interest payments and gradual withdrawal of capital, hence leaving nothing in the fund at the end of the period.

(i) Multiplicand

9–028   As was stated above, this figure comprises the net annual loss. It was held in Cookson v. Knowles[91] that the starting point is the amount the claimant would have been earning at the date of the trial. If the claimant will be able to earn in the future that must be taken into account. Although, as we have seen, the court will not take account of future inflation, it will assess the multiplicand on the basis of the net annual average future earnings; hence account will be taken of promotion prospects. Thus, in Ratnasingam v. Kow Ah Dek[92] the Privy Council held that an allowance of one-

---

[90] See Wells v. Wells [1997] 1 All E.R. 673 at 698 per Hirst L.J.
[91] [1979] A.C. 556.
[92] [1983] 1 W.L.R. 1235.

third should be made for the chance that the claimant, a teacher, would have been successful in a promotion examination. An example of the kind of detailed analysis that may be necessary can be seen in *Biesheuvel v. Birrell*.[93] The claimant had been offered a permanent post with Deloitte Touche after a distinguished academic career, and had a very promising future in financial or management consultancy. Two periods were taken separately for the assessment of lost future earnings. The former, from date of trial to the age of 36 (essentially up to the age of equity partnership) took a figure of £64,400 net per annum; the latter, from age 36 to likely retirement age of 55, took bands of £200,000 gross from 36–38, £250,000 from 38–40; £300,000 from 40–45; £350,000 from 45–50 and £400,000 from 50–55. Beyond that, it was thought likely that the claimant would have continued to work, as a non-executive director or as a consultant, earning £100,000 per annum gross for 10 years. The total for these 29 years came to £7,150,000, resulting in a multiplicand for that period of £153,000 net. In addition a claim for lost pension rights could be made.[94] Conversely, it may be necessary to take account of the risk of diminished future earnings, as was mentioned in *Rouse v. Port of London Authority*[95] where account was taken by the court of the likelihood that the claimant would not have earned his pre-accident earnings during a period when there was less than full employment in the docks where he worked.

As can be seen from the judgment in *Biesheuvel* and many other cases, 9–029 extensive use is made of comparables, as well as seeking projections from employers of the likely career progression of the claimant but for the accident. In addition the previous employment and academic record may assist in indicating the potential earning capacity.

Especial difficulties in assessing quantum may arise in cases where the 9–030 claimant is self-employed, in particular where his business is in its early years and its potential is uncertain. Proper accounts must be produced for the court to be satisfied that the claim has been properly quantified;[96] if this is done, as in *Lee v. Sheard*,[97] where the claimant was one of the two directors of a private company and held nearly half the share capital and due to his absence on account of his injuries the turnover and profits of the company diminished sharply, a claim can succeed for the diminution in the distributions he received from the company. The court did not accept the argument that the loss was in reality a loss to the company; the claimant was not an employee, and the company was not entitled to recover its loss. However it will not always be appropriate to assume that the entirety of the deterioration in a company's profits can be attributed to the absence of the claimant; many other factors such as trade or seasonal conditions may also be relevant and hence need to be taken into account. If the claimant derives a financial advantage from the accident, this must be set off against his losses. Thus, in *Bellingham v. Dhillon*[98] the claimant, who owned a

---

[93] [1999] P.I.Q.R. Q40.
[94] See *supra* para. 9–026.
[95] [1953] 2 Lloyd's Rep. 179.
[96] See *Ashcroft v. Curtin* [1971] 3 All E.R. 1208.
[97] [1956] 1 Q.B. 192. See also *Jason v. Batten (1930)* [1969] 1 Lloyd's Rep. 281.
[98] [1973] Q.B. 304.

driving school, lost the opportunity of buying an expensive indoor driving simulator as a result of the defendant's negligence. He was later able to buy the same simulator as liquidated stock at a greatly reduced price. It was held that from the loss of estimated profits he would have gained from the use of the simulator during the period before he bought it secondhand there had to be deducted the profits he in fact made from it. Problems may arise from the way in which the claimant organises his business affairs. In *Kent v. British Railways Board*[99] the claimant and her husband were working partners in a business. For taxation purposes it had been arranged with the Inland Revenue that they should be assessed on the profits of the business as to 60 per cent on the husband and 40 per cent on the claimant. It was held that she could not recover 100 per cent of the past and future losses, as that would effectively give her husband a right of recovery, but she was awarded 50 per cent, on the basis of the presumption of equality in section 24 of the Partnership Act 1890, which was not rebutted by the arrangement with the Inland Revenue. In *Ward v. Newall Insulation Co Ltd*[1] the claimant and his partner, for tax purposes, made their wives partners in their business, though they played no active part. It was held, allowing an appeal against the judge's decision that the claimant's loss of earning capacity was only 25 per cent of the partnership profits, that it was clear that the Inland Revenue were not concerned whether the agreed structure accurately reflected what was put into the partnership, that in practice the claimant and his partner could have apportioned to themselves whatever percentage of the profits they thought fit, and hence that he was entitled to 50 per cent.

9–031   Where the claimant is not employed at the time of the accident, the initial question to answer must be the reason for the lack of employment. It may be that, though he is seeking work, the claimant has been unemployed for a sufficiently lengthy period that it is not realistic to argue that he would have had reasonable prospects of obtaining work but for the accident.[2] Alternatively he may have a criminal record such that any legitimate earnings he might have had would be outweighed by the savings made as a result of being boarded in prison.[3] Where there are prospects of employment, the court has to assess the degree of likelihood of employment and its likely duration and remuneration.

9–032   Particular difficulties arise where the claimant is a young child. Some cases have adopted an essentially conjectural approach to the multiplicand;[4] others have taken the view that the multiplier/multiplicand approach is inappropriate, and the correct approach is to select a global figure which seems to represent fair compensation.[5] Rather more scientifically, other

---

[99] [1995] P.I.Q.R. Q42.

[1] [1998] P.I.Q.R. Q41.

[2] See *e.g. Hassall v. Secretary of State for Social Security* [1995] 1 W.L.R. 812, where the plaintiffs both accepted that they could not claim for loss of earnings during their period of incapacity as they would not have been able to find work even if they had been fit.

[3] See *Meah v. McCreamer* [1985] 1 All E.R. 367.

[4] See, *e.g. Connolly v. Camden Area Health Authority* [1981] 3 All E.R. 250.

[5] See *Joyce v. Yeomans* [1981] 1 W.L.R. 549. See also *Jones v. Laurence* [1969] 3 All E.R. 267, where the court made an award without any mention of whether or not the multiplier/ multiplicand method was appropriate.

cases have employed the national average wage as a basis for assessing lost future earnings, as in *Croke v. Wiseman*,[6] and also in *Almond v. Leeds Western Health Authority*[7] where the court considered that the claimant was likely to have undergone tertiary education, and used a multiplicand of one-and-a-half times the national average wage. In *Taylor v. British Omnibus Co Ltd*[8] the court made the assumption that the child's earning capacity would be that of his father. Exceptionally, in *Cassel v. Riverside Health Authority*[9] the court found that, having regard to the education which the claimant would have received, to the family history of effort and achievement and the probable nature and extent of his personality and intelligence but for the accident, that a net multiplicand of £35,000 was appropriate, based on the earnings the claimant would have had in a medium-sized City firm of solicitors or accountants. As can be seen from the discussion below,[10] low multipliers are frequently employed in cases of child claimants, to take account of the prospect that they might not have worked.

(ii) Multiplier

Prima facie the multiplier will be calculated on the basis of the likely   9–033
duration of the claimant's disability; thus, if he will not work again, it will be the rest of his working life. The starting point is the date of the trial.[11] Where the claimant's life expectancy has been reduced by the accident, it was previously held, in *Oliver v. Ashman*,[12] that the multiplier was to be calculated by reference to the post-accident life expectancy.[13] However, the House of Lords in *Pickett v. British Rail Engineering Ltd*[14] overruled *Oliver* and held that a claimant was entitled to recover damages for lost future earnings based on the pre-accident life expectancy and hence damages for the "lost years" may be awarded. Thus in *Pickett* itself an award at trial of £1,500 for lost future earnings based on a post-accident life expectancy of one year was remitted for damages to be assessed on the basis of the pre-accident working life expectancy of approximately twelve years. However, as Lord Wilberforce pointed out,[15] it will be necessary to deduct an estimated sum representing the claimant's probable living expenses during the lost years. This follows from the rationale for the decision that the claimant has an interest in providing for his dependents, which he would have done out of his earnings after deducting the amounts he needed for himself. Though it is understandable that the court would wish to see the dependents' interests protected, it is somewhat clumsy and illogical to do

---

[6] [1982] 1 W.L.R. 71.
[7] [1990] 1 Med. L.R. 370. See also *Taylor v. Glass* Kemp & Kemp, Vol. 2, 1-715; *Nash v. Southmead Health Authority* [1993] P.I.Q.R. Q156.
[8] [1975] 2 All E.R. 1107.
[9] [1992] P.I.Q.R. Q168.
[10] *Infra* paras. 9–033 *et seq*. It should be borne in mind that damages recovered by a child are under the control of the court: C.P.R. r.21.11.
[11] Reaffirmed in *Pritchard v. J. H. Cobden* [d1988] Fam. 22.
[12] [1962] 2 Q.B. 210.
[13] In *Oliver* itself it was reduced from about 60 to 30.
[14] [1980] A.C. 136.
[15] *ibid.* at 151.

so via the medium of the claimant's claim, and this illogicality is especially highlighted where there are no dependents. In cases where a young child is the claimant the courts have tended not to make an award for the lost years, and in *Croke v. Wiseman*[16] Griffiths L.J. justified this view on the basis that the child would never have dependents, and adverted also to the particularly difficult nature of the speculation that would be involved in such a case. The effect of the decision in *Pickett* on fatal accident cases led to difficulties that had to be resolved by statute,[17] and it has been suggested[18] that the best solution would be to give a statutory claim to the dependents of a person who has been seriously injured, as well as the existing statutory claim that they have under the Fatal Accidents Act since, as a result of the legislative changes referred to above, damages recoverable for the benefit of the estate of a deceased person in a survival action may not include damages for loss of income after the death.

9–034   As regards calculation of the deduction of the claimant's living expenses in a lost years claim, it may be helpful, as was pointed out by O'Connor L.J. in *Housecroft v. Burnett*,[19] to apply separate multipliers, one for the period during which the claimant is expected to live, and one for the lost years, the multiplicand for the latter being reduced from that for the former by the deducted living expenses. Alternatively the multiplicand may be left in its original form, and the multiplier reduced, though this method is less likely to be accurate. A disparity developed in the immediate post-*Pickett* case law as to whether, in line with the approach taken in fatal accident cases,[20] the relevant deduction should simply comprise the expenses which the claimant would have spent exclusively on himself[21] or whether a proportion[22] or indeed all[23] of his expenditure should be deducted. The matter was resolved by the Court of Appeal in *Harris v. Empress Motors Ltd*[24] where it was held that "the sum to be deducted as living expenses was the proportion of the claimant's net earnings that he spent to maintain himself at the standard of life appropriate to his case."[25] This differs from an expenses deduction in a Fatal Accident Act case in that, under *Harris*, where there is a proportion of the earnings spent on shared living expenses, a *pro rata* part of that proportion is to be allocated for deduction. Given that the rationale for the award for the lost years is essentially the same as

---

[16] [1982] 1 W.L.R. 71 at 82.

[17] See *infra* para. 10–045.

[18] Burrows *op. cit.* at 202. See also McGregor *op. cit.* paras. 1588, 1734, for the view that the wording of the Fatal Accidents Act is broad enough to encompass a claim by the dependants to recover their loss independently of any action by the victim. S. 3 of the Damages Act 1996 makes provision for an award to the dependants of a person who has already received an award of provisional damages: see *infra* para. 10–042.

[19] [1986] 1 All E.R. 332 at 345.

[20] See *infra* para. 10–014.

[21] See *e.g. Benson v. Briggs Wall & Co. Ltd* [1983] 1 W.L.R. 72; *Clay v. Pooler* [1982] 3 All E.R. 570.

[22] See *White v. London Transport Executive* [1982] Q.B. 489.

[23] See *Sullivan v. West Yorkshire Passenger Transport Executive* December 17, 1980, referred to in *Harris v. Empress Motors Ltd* [1983] 3 All E.R. 561.

[24] [1983] 3 All E.R. 561.

[25] *ibid.* at 575 *per* O'Connor L.J.

that in a fatal accident claim; *i.e.* to benefit the dependents, the different treatment of deductible expenses is difficult to justify.

In *Phipps v. Brooks Dry Cleaning Service Ltd*[26] the Court of Appeal had the opportunity to apply the principles set out in *Harris*. It was held that the usual discount in a lost years case would be 50 per cent, though there might be cases where the proportion was less, if, for example, there was a substantial element of savings. There could be no claim for loss of the ability to do DIY and gardening in the lost years; the claimant had not lost anything of value in performing work which would save him expense which he would never incur. It could however be taken account of to a modest extent as a loss of amenity.

9–035

(iii) Discounting the multiplier

In determining the appropriate multiplier, the courts have over many years significantly discounted the *prima facie* figure, to take account of two particular factors. The first of these is, as the award of damages takes the form of a lump-sum, the fact that the claimant would, but for the discount, be receiving immediately the earnings which would otherwise have been spread over a number of years, and benefiting from the interest accruing during that time. He is entitled to the present value of the lost future earnings.

9–036

In *Wells v. Wells*[27] Lord Lloyd explained the approach as follows:

9–037

"The purpose of the discount is to eliminate this element of overcompensation. The objective is to arrive at a lump sum which by drawing down both interest and capital will provide exactly £10,000 a year for 20 years and no more. This is known as the annuity approach. It is a simple enough matter to find the answer by reference to standard tables. The higher the assumed return on capital net of tax the lower the lump sum. If one assumes a net return of 5% the discounted figure would be £124,600 instead of £200,000. If one assumes a net return of 3% the figure would be £148,800. The same point can be put the other way round. £200,000 invested at 5% will produce £10,000 a year for 20 years. But there would still be £200,000 left at the end."

The practical effect of this approach, together with the further discounting designed to take account of the vicissitudes of life[28] led in practice to a maximum multiplier of 18, even on a working life expectancy of 40+ years.

Lord Lloyd went on to describe how the courts have over the years dealt with the problem that money does not retain its value by assuming that future inflation can be taken care of by the claimant investing his lump sum in a mixed basket of gilts and equities. A discount rate of 4.5 per cent was adopted for a number of years on this basis.

9–038

---

[26] [1996] P.I.Q.R. Q100.
[27] [1999] 1 A.C. 345 at 364 in the context of an example of an annual average cost of care of £10,000 on a life expectancy of 20 years.
[28] See *infra* para. 9–042.

9–039   In *Wright v. British Railways Board*[29] Lord Diplock adverted to the recent establishment of index-linked (*i.e.* inflation-proof) bonds, and in *Robertson v. Lestrange*[30] (a fatal accidents case), Webster. J did not accept the argument that the appropriate discount rate was the rate of interest representing the yield currently available from such securities after deduction of the income tax payable on the investment. The practical consequence would have been a very significant increase in the multiplier. Webster J. did not consider that the existence of such securities was sufficient reason to depart from the conventional practice. The case for assuming investment in index-linked government securities (hereafter ILGS) was strongly re-asserted by the Law Commission in 1994,[31] and in three decisions reported in 1996[32] trial judges made that assumption. The Court of Appeal disagreed, reverting to the traditional approach, and thereby reducing significantly the sums awarded.[33] The House of Lords reversed the decision of the Court of Appeal, holding that the award of damages for future losses and expenses should be fixed by assuming that the claimant would invest his damages in ILGS. A claimant investing a lump sum could not be equated with an ordinary investor since, though a substantial proportion of equities was the best long-term investment for the ordinary investor, their volatility over the short term created a serious risk for a claimant who needed the income and a portion of his capital every year to meet his current cost of care. How the claimant in fact chooses to invest his money is irrelevant. Having decided to assume investment in ILGS, the House then had to decide on the appropriate discount rate. The rates of return are published daily in the Financial Times, and from whatever figure is taken there must be a deduction for income tax. In the longer run the rate of return will be determined by the Lord Chancellor, in accordance with the provisions of section 1 of the Damages Act 1996. This states:

> "(1) In determining the return to be expected from the investment of a sum awarded as damages for future pecuniary loss in an action for personal injury the court shall, subject to and in accordance with rules of court made for the purposes of this section, take into account such rate of return (if any) as may from time to time be prescribed by an order made by the Lord Chancellor."

9–040   The section came into force on September 24, 1996, but no rate has yet been prescribed.[33A] In the meantime the House of Lords in *Wells* proposed, on the basis of the then current figures in the context of a falling average gross redemption yield, a guideline rate of return of three per cent net until such time as the Lord Chancellor specifies a new rate under section 1.

---

[29] [1983] 2 A.C. 773 at 782–3.
[30] [1985] 1 All E.R. 950. See also the powerful argument by David Kemp Q.C. at (1985) 101 L.Q.R. 556 and *Anderson v. Davies* [1993] P.I.Q.R. Q87 at 102.
[31] Law Com. No. 224; published after consultation: Consultation Paper 125 (1992).
[32] *Wells v. Wells* [1996] P.I.Q.R. Q62; *Thomas v. Brighton Health Authority* [1996] P.I.Q.R. Q44; *Page v. Sheerness Steel Co. Plc* [1996] P.I.Q.R. Q26.
[33] [1997] 1 All E.R. 673.
[33A] In March 2000 the lord Chancellor's Department issued a Consultation Paper canvassing, *inter alia*, whether the power under s.1 should be exercised, and if so, on what basis.

This decision clearly has very significant implications for multipliers and   9–041
hence for the size of awards generally. For example, in *Page v. Sheerness
Steel*[34] the judge took a whole life multiplier of 24, based on a three per
cent rate of return, which was reduced by the Court of Appeal, employing
the conventional 4.5 per cent rate, to 17.[35] The total award was reduced
by nearly £300,000 on the appeal, but of course the judge's multiplier was
restored by the House of Lords. Lord Lloyd noted the increased burden
that would henceforth be placed on defendants and insurers, and the probability that insurance premiums would have to increase as a consequence.
It seems likely that the Lord Chancellor will prescribe three per cent under
the Damages Act, in accordance with the views of the House of Lords in
Wells. Helpful examples of the extent of the increase in awards can be seen
from a recent recasting of the awards in two maximum-severity cases in
accordance with a three per cent discount rate.[36]

In addition to the discounting designed to take account of the immediate   9–042
award of the lump sum, the courts also take into account the vicissitudes
of life; the risk that the claimant might not have lived to earn his income
over the anticipated working life, or might have lost his employment
through illness or redundancy: though equally, as was pointed out by Lord
Pearce in *Mallett v. McMonagle*[37] the possibilities for good should also be
taken into account. As regards mortality, the now sanctioned use by the
courts of the Ogden Tables[38] should preclude the discounting of the multiplier to take account of the possibility of earlier death, since, based on
population mortality, the tables take account of the chances that the claimant will die young. Also, as was held by the House of Lords in *Wells*, there
is no room for any discount in the case of a whole-life multiplier with an
agreed expectation of life. The explanatory notes to the tables do however
make it clear that they do not take account of other chances of life such as
periods of non-earning due to ill-health or unemployment, though some
guidance is given as to how to adjust for contingencies other than mortality.[39] The supplementary tables in the Ogden Tables indicate a discount of
no more than two per cent for a male in his 20s retiring at 65, and the
same rate is indicated for a man in his 40s working in the south or east
in an occupation of no great risk, contrasting very significantly with the
unscientific approach to be seen from time to time in the caselaw.[40] Interest-
ingly, as early as 1972 a discount of two per cent for contingencies was
being argued for,[41] but, as McGregor points out,[42] courts not taking
account of Ogden have tended to deduct 5–10 per cent from the loss of

---

[34] [1996] P.I.Q.R. Q26.
[35] [1997] P.I.Q.R. Q1 at Q55.
[36] Quantum, September 4, 1998 by Paul Kitson. In one case the total damages would have
    increased by approximately 35%; in the other by approximately 45%.
[37] [1969] 2 All E.R. 178 at 189. See also *Teubner v. Humble* (1963) 108 C.L.R. 491 at 508–
    9 per Windeyer J.
[38] See *supra* para. 9–025. See David Kemp Q.C. and Rowland Hogg [1999] J.P.I.L. 42.
[39] Explanatory Notes to the Ogden Tables. Section C. See also Roderick Denyer Q.C. [1999]
    J.P.I.L. 49 on loss of future earnings and the badly injured child in the light of *Wells v.
    Wells*.
[40] See *e.g. Mitchell v. Mulholland (No. 2)* [1972] 1 Q.B. 65.
[41] *ibid.*
[42] *op. cit.* at para. 1606.

earnings multiplier for contingencies, generally resulting in a reduction of one or two in the multiplier, though, as Munkman points out,[43] deducting the decimals in cases of long future working-life expectancy might be sufficient. In *Worrall v. Powergen Plc*[44] it was held that the whole-life multiplier is to be calculated by reference to Table 11 of the Ogden Tables (3rd ed.), which is based on projected mortality rates, rather than Table 1, based on actual mortality rates deduced from a three-year period, given the emphasis by the House of Lords in *Wells* on the need for a more realistic approach, and the positive recommendation of the Working Party to use Tables 11–20 rather than Tables 1–10.

(iv) Where future earning capacity is restricted

9–043   The claimant may be able to return to work, or to take up similar work, with apparently no continuing loss. However a consequence of his injuries may be to render him more vulnerable on the labour market than he was prior to the accident. He may remain in employment only thanks to the benevolence of his employer, but in a type of employment that is insecure; he may face future operations or time off work due to his injuries; he may be limited in the kinds of alternative work he would be able to do in future due to his injuries. Since the decision of the Court of Appeal in *Smith v. Manchester Corporation*[45] (damages under this head are usually referred to as *Smith v. Manchester* damages) the courts have made separate awards from the award for loss of future earnings under this head, representing their assessment of the extent to which the claimant is hereafter vulnerable on the labour market. In the leading case, *Moeliker v. A Reyrolle & Co Ltd*[46] the Court of Appeal emphasised the need to make an award under this head if there is a substantial or real risk that the claimant will lose his present job at some time before the estimated end of his working life. If there is such a risk, the court must assess and quantify the present value of the risk of the financial damage which the claimant will suffer if the risk materialises, taking into account the degree of risk, the time when it may materialise and the relevant factors, both favourable and unfavourable, which will or may affect the claimant's chances of getting any job, or an equally well-paid job.

9–044   Essentially therefore each case has to be determined on its own facts within this broad framework. It is clear that the claimant need not necessarily be in employment at the time of the injury and/or the trial as in *Dhaliwal v. Hunt*,[47] where the claimant was aged five at the time of the accident, and 11 by the time of the trial, though clearly in such a case the task for the judge is especially speculative. The judge's award of £5,000 was regarded as too low, and a sum of £12,500 was substituted, given the permanent loss of dexterity and clumsiness of the claimant after the accident. In *Dhaliwal* the court endorsed, as one way of approaching an award for handicap

[43] "Damages for Personal Injuries and Death" (10th ed., Butterworths, 1996) at p. 60.
[44] [1999] P.I.Q.R. Q103.
[45] (1974) 17 K.I.R. 1.
[46] [1979] 1 All E.R. 9 esp. at 17 per Browne L.J.
[47] [1995] P.I.Q.R. Q56. See also *Cook v. Consolidated Fisheries* [1977] I.C.R. 635.

on the labour market, the multiplier/multiplicand approach that had been employed by the Court of Appeal in *Gunter v. Nicholas & Sons*.[48] The assessment in that case was effected by multiplying the net annual earnings of £8,000 by a multiplier of two. Either approach is open to a judge, and both appear equally speculative. Clearly it is necessary to avoid any overlap between the award for lost earnings and the *Smith v. Manchester* award,[49] but there is otherwise no preclusion of an award under both heads being made. In *Robson v. Liverpool City Council*[50] it was said that a risk can be "real" within the test set out in *Moeliker v. Reyrolle* even though it is unlikely, and "substantial" does not mean that it is likely to happen on the balance of probabilities. The award in that case to a man of 32 at the date of the appeal, who had in essence lost the sight in one eye in the accident in question, bearing in mind his working history and the fields of work now closed to him, was £2,500. At the other end of the scale, an award of £30,000 was made in *Goldborough v. Thompson and Crowther*[51] to a roofer aged 39 at the date of the accident who would never be able to do heavy work again.

2. DEDUCTION OF COLLATERAL BENEFITS

As a consequence of the general principle that the claimant should be put in the same financial position that he would have been in if the accident had not happened, it is necessary to consider to what extent compensating advantages resulting from the accident should be set off against the damages awarded to him. We have seen already[52] that the award must be net of the tax and national insurance payable by the claimant. A range of sources of collateral benefits exists, and much judicial time has been spent in trying to elucidate principles determinative of the issue of deductibility. Certainly it can be said that there is no general rule that benefits received by the claimant on account of the accident will be deducted; beyond that there is, in the words of the Law Commission, "no single principled test for determining whether collateral benefits are to be deducted or not . . ."[53] Consequently, it appears most appropriate to examine separately the main types of collateral benefit and consider how Parliament and the courts have determined they should be treated.

9–045

(1) Insurance

It was established in *Bradburn v. Great Western Railway Co*[54] that moneys received by the claimant under an accident insurance policy are not

9–046

---

[48] [1993] P.I.Q.R. p. 67.
[49] See *Clarke v. Rotax Aircraft* [1975] 1 W.L.R. 1570; *Frost v. Palmer* [1993] P.I.Q.R. Q14.
[50] [1993] P.I.Q.R. Q78. See also *Watson v. Mitcham Cardboards Ltd* [1982] C.L.Y. 78.
[51] [1996] P.I.Q.R. Q86.
[52] *supra* para. 9–023.
[53] Consultation Paper No. 147 "Damages for Personal Injury: Collateral Benefits" para. 2.5.
[54] (1874) L.R. 10 Ex. 1.

to be taken into account in assessing the damages to be awarded against
the defendant responsible for the accident in respect of which the insurance
payment is made. The essential rationale behind this decision is, as was
said by Lord Reid in *Parry v. Cleaver*,[55] that the claimant has paid for the
insurance, and it would be unjust and unreasonable that it should enure
for the benefit of the tortfeasor. A further justification for the non-
deductibility of insurance payments is, as was said by Pigott B. in
Bradburn[56] that it is the contract, not the accident, which is the cause of
the claimant receiving the payment. In *Hussain v. New Taplow Paper
Mills*[57] Lord Bridge stated the rule as applying where the claimant has paid
the premiums. In *McCamley v. Cammell Laird Shipbuilders Ltd*[58] the
claimant received over £46,000 under an insurance policy taken out on
behalf of the defendant, his employer, by its parent company for the benefit
of employees who were injured at work. It was held that the sum did not
fall to be deducted, but the rationale seems to have been that the payment
was by way of benevolence[59] even though the mechanics required the use
of an insurance policy, and hence the case cannot be said to be conclusive
on the question of whether the claimant must have paid the premiums for
the fruits of an insurance policy to be non-deductible.

9–047   In *Hussain v. New Taplow Paper Mills Ltd*[60] the claimant received full
"sick pay" for thirteen weeks after a work accident from the defendant, his
employer, and thereafter he was contractually entitled to payments equal
to half his pre-accident earnings under the defendant's "permanent health
insurance scheme", to which employees were not required to contribute,
the defendant being reimbursed for payments made under the scheme under
an insurance policy. It was held that the payments received by the claimant
were to be regarded as sick pay, which has long been held to be deductible.[61] In *Page v. Sheerness Steel Plc*[62] the claimant participated in his
employer's contributory pension and life insurance plan. Dyson J., held
that it would be wrong to treat his membership of the scheme as a contract
of insurance within the meaning of *Bradburn*. The claimant did not have a
contract with the insurance company, and he did not pay the premiums.
There was no evidence that he would have received more pay but for the
insurance, or that the existence of the insurance had any effect on his remuneration. It was clear from the claimant's contract of employment that the
whole of his contribution to the scheme was to go to the pension plan, and
it was an essential requirement of the insurance exception that the cost of
the insurance be borne wholly or at least in part by the claimant. The

[55] [1970] A.C. 1 at 14.
[56] (1874) L.R. 10 Ex. 1 at 3.
[57] [1998] A.C. 514 at 527. See also *Hodgson v. Trapp* [1989] A.C. 807 at 819, also per Lord Bridge.
[58] [1990] 1 W.L.R. 963.
[59] And hence non-deductible as a matter of policy; see *infra* paras. 9–048–9–049.
[60] [1988] A.C. 514.
[61] See *Metropolitan Police District Receiver v. Croydon Corporation* [1957] 2 Q.B. 154 and *infra* para. 9–051.
[62] [1996] P.I.Q.R. Q26.

judge's decision was endorsed by the Court of Appeal[63] and by the House of Lords.[64]

(2) Charitable and other payments

As we have noted above, payments to the claimant by way of benevol- 9–048
ence, made on account of the accident, do not fall to be deducted from the award of damages. In *Parry v. Cleaver*[65] Lord Reid justified the non-deductibility of charitable payments on the basis that the tortfeasor should not benefit from the benevolence of others, and because deduction would risk the consequence that, in the words of Sir James Andrews L.C. J. in *Redpath v. Belfast and County Down Ry*[66] "the springs of private charity would be found to be largely, if not entirely, dried up."

A difficult question concerns *ex gratia* payments made to the claimant 9–049
by the tortfeasor. As we have seen, in *McCamley v. Cammell Laird Ship-builders Ltd*[67] the Court of Appeal regarded the payment in that case as a payment by way of benevolence, since it was payable regardless of fault or whether the employer or anyone else was liable. However, O'Connor L.J. cited with approval[68] a passage in the judgment of Lloyd L.J. in *Hussain v. New Taplow Paper Mills Ltd*[69] where the view was expressed that:

> "If an employee is injured in the course of his employment, and his employers make him an immediate *ex gratia* payment, as any good employer might, I see no reason why such a payment should not be taken into account in reduction of any damages for which the employer may ultimately be held liable."

The inference, though it awaits further judicial clarification, is that such a payment will fall to be deducted unless, as in *McCamley*, the court is of the view that the object of the payment was benevolence irrespective of the circumstances in which a qualifying injury occurs.

(3) Sick pay

As we have seen, it was held in *Hussain*, reinforcing earlier authority, 9–050
that where an employee, under the terms of his contract of employment, receives all or some of his wages during a period when he is incapacitated

---

[63] [1997] P.I.Q.R. Q1 at 57.
[64] [1999] 7 A.C. 345 at 381–2.
[65] [1970] A.C. 1.
[66] [1947] N. 1 167 at 170. See also *Liffan v. Watson* [1940] 1 K.B. 556 where it was held that there should be ignored the value of free board and lodging provided by her father to the claimant in connection with the claim for loss of employment which provided free board and lodging.
[67] [1990] 1 W.L.R. 963. *supra* para. 9–046.
[68] *ibid*. at 970–1.
[69] [1987] 1 W.L.R. 336 at 350. The decision was affirmed, on different grounds, by the House of Lords.

for work, the amount of such payments will be deducted from his award of damages for loss of earnings. The fact that the sick pay was provided under an insurance scheme did not deprive it of its essential character. Again, as we have seen in *Page* the claimant had not paid for the permanent health insurance which he received, and hence it fell to be classified as sick pay rather than insurance.

9–051   The cases do not provide clear guidance on the question whether voluntary sick pay should be treated differently from contractual sick pay, though, as has been argued,[70] an inference that may be drawn from *Parry v. Cleaver*[71] is that the two categories are to be treated alike. It is suggested that the issue is best resolved, as in *McCamley*, by a decision by the court as to the object of the payment in the mind of the employer, and that where the employer is the tortfeasor this is likely to be regarded as having the character of sick pay rather than benevolence.

9–052   If the employer makes provision for sick pay in the contract of employment, but provides that sums paid to the employee in this way are to be refunded to the employer if the employee is successful in a claim for damages for lost earnings, the sick pay will not be deductible. In *Dennis v. London Passenger Transport Board*[72] the claimant was, though not under a legal obligation, "expected to repay" the sick pay which he received from his employer. The claimant was prepared to fulfil his moral obligation to reimburse the employer if he was awarded damages, and hence he was held to be entitled to an award of damages for lost earnings, subject to the direction that he reimburse the employer out of the award. An employer does not have a claim against the tortfeasor to recover wages paid to an employee while he is off work due to the tort,[73] and hence the refunding device referred to above is the only way such sums may be recoverable by the employer.

(4) Disability pensions

9–053   In *Parry v. Cleaver*[74] the House of Lords resolved earlier contrasting authorities in holding that a disablement pension, whether contributory or non-contributory, was akin to insurance rather than wages and hence fell to be ignored in the assessment of damages. This decision was affirmed more recently in *Smoker v. London Fire and Civil Defence Authority*,[75] the fact that the defendant was the claimant's employer being regarded as irrelevant. As is the case with sick pay, though there is no claim for the provider of the pension to recover its value from the tortfeasor, it is perfectly entitled in its contract with the claimant to require the claimant to repay the pension to it in the event of a successful damages claim.

---

[70] Atiyah (1969) 32 M.L.R. 397 at 401.
[71] [1970] A.C. 1. *infra* para. 9–053.
[72] [1948] 1 All E.R. 779.
[73] See *Inland Revenue Commissioners v. Hambrook* [1956] 2 Q.B. 641.
[74] [1970] A.C. 1.
[75] [1991] 2 A.C. 502.

(5) Retirement pensions

As regards the state retirement pension, the position has been clear since   9–054
Hewson v. Downs;[76] it is not to be taken into account in assessing damages,
being regarded as within the principle of *Parry v. Cleaver*. However, issues
of some complexity arise where the claimant claims for loss of pension
rights, *i.e.* in cases where the accident has caused pension payments to
begin earlier than had been intended. Thus, in *Parry* it was held that the
claimant's disability pension did not have to be taken into account so as to
reduce the claim for the lost salary. However, as regards the full retirement
pension to which he would otherwise have been entitled, it was held that
the disability pension did have to be taken into account.

The distinction between the treatment of the disability pension before   9–055
and after normal retirement age was that, in the words of Lord Reid:[77]

> ". . . in the earlier period we are not comparing like with like. He lost
> wages, but he gained something different in kind, a pension. But with
> regard to the period after retirement we are comparing like with like.
> Both the ill-health pension and the full retirement pension are the
> products of the same insurance scheme; his loss in the later period is
> caused by his having been deprived of the opportunity to continue in
> insurance so as to swell the ultimate product of that insurance from
> an ill-health to a retirement pension."

In *Longden v. British Coal Corporation*[78] the claimant was forced to   9–056
retire early as a consequence of an accident for which the defendant, his
employer, was liable. The defendant operated a contributory pension
scheme which provided for a retirement pension at the normal retirement
age of 60, but also provided, as an alternative form of benefit, an incapacity
pension where a contributor had to retire early on grounds of ill-health.
The claimant was awarded an incapacity pension under the scheme of
£5,199 per annum at the date of the trial, together with a lump sum of
£10,185.91. If he had continued in employment to the normal retirement
age he would have received an annual pension of £11,080 and a lump sum
of £33,242. In his claim against the defendant he included a claim, comprising the difference between the entitlements, for loss of pension after the
normal retirement age. The House of Lords held that where damages were
claimed for loss of pension after normal retirement age, though no more
could be recovered than the net loss of pension, any disability or incapacity
pension payments received prior to that date did not have to be brought
into account. However, the effect of the lump sum received would be felt
not only in the period up to retirement but also thereafter, and there would
thus be an element of overlap in the period after retirement. It was therefore
necessary to set against the claim for loss of retirement pension an appro-

---

[76] [1970] 1 Q.B. 73.
[77] [1970] A.C. 1 at 20–21.
[78] [1998] 1 All E.R. 289.

priate portion of the lump sum (identified as £1,630) received on retirement on grounds of incapacity.[79]

(6) Redundancy payments

9–057   The authorities are equivocal on the question whether redundancy payments are deductible. In *Wilson v. National Coal Board*[80] the House of Lords held that where it was the injury which was the cause of the tort claim which caused the redundancy, the payment fell to be deducted, but otherwise only exceptionally would such payments be deducted, as they were not designed to compensate for lost earnings, but were for the loss of a settled job. However, the Court of Appeal in *Colledge v. Bass Mitchells & Butler Ltd*,[81] in deducting a redundancy payment from an award for damages for loss of earnings, did not agree with the House of Lords as to the nature of redundancy payments, and it is difficult to disagree with the words of Sir John Donaldson M.R.:

> "... since their Lordships regarded Wilson's position as exceptional, it must be possible to construct a scenario in which the amount of a redundancy payment would not fall to be deducted. Nevertheless, there is only one case in which I can foresee this, namely where the claimant would have been made redundant regardless of the accident."[82]

(7) Social Security benefits

9–058   The rules on deductibility of Social Security benefits were radically overhauled in 1989, and amended further in 1997. The pre-1989 scheme, essentially, though not exclusively, contained in the Law Reform (Personal Injuries) Act 1948[83] was to effect a compromise, based on the level of contribution deemed to have been made by the claimant. Half of the specified benefits for the first five years was to be deducted from the damages award for loss of earnings, representing the rough extent of the employer's contribution, the employee having also contributed approximately a half which,

---

[79] See also *West v. Versil Ltd* [1996] C.L.Y. 4662; *The Times*, August 31, 1996, where it was held that a claimant whose life expectancy had been reduced by asbestosis, and who chose to take his pension at 60 rather than at 65, and for it to be paid on a surviving spouse basis, should not have his damages reduced to take account of his pension rights and the choices he had made in exercising them. The pension contributions that would have been made had he carried on working were not to be deducted from his claim for loss of earnings owing to this early retirement. The widow's pension was not to be deducted as it was bought and paid for by the claimant by the reduction in his own pension.

[80] 1981 S.L.T. 67.

[81] [1988] 1 All E.R. 536.

[82] *ibid.* at 540. See also Law Com. Consultation Paper No. 147 (1997). *Cf.* however *Mills v. Hassalls* [1983] I.C.R. 330. See also the point made by Munkman (*op. cit.* at 108) that a plaintiff who is made redundant but continues to work in other employment has suffered a loss of protection from future redundancy as a result of losing the credits built up during a period of continuous employment, and should be compensated for this loss.

[83] Now substituted by para. 8 of Sched. 2 to the Social Security (Consequential Provisions) Act 1975 and subsequently up to 1989, when it applied only to awards of £2,500 or under.

by analogy with insurance payments, was not deducted. The specified benefits are sickness benefit, invalidity benefit, severe disability benefit (previously non-contributory invalidity pension), severe disablement allowance and disablement benefit. Since 1989, however, this system has only operated if the total damages did not exceed £2,500; where they did, the new system (described below) governed the situation. In 1997 the exemption of awards (or settlements) of £2,500 and below was removed in the Social Security (Recovery of Benefits) Act 1997, the provisions of which are applicable retrospectively to all current cases not decided or settled by the time the Act comes into force.

As regards benefits which were not referred to in the 1948 Act, the House   9–059
of Lords in *Hodgson v. Trapp*[84] held that the matter was one of public policy. Damages awards were paid out of the insurance premiums paid by such groups as motorists, employers, occupiers of property and professionals. Statutory benefits payable to those in need by reason of impecuniosity or disability were funded by the taxpayer. To allow double recovery at the expense of both taxpayers and insurers was incapable of rational justification. The application of this approach can be seen in relation to family income supplement,[85] statutory sick pay[86] and reduced earnings allowance.[87]

In 1989 however the entire system was fundamentally recast, the object   9–060
being to enable the public purse to recoup out of an award of damages the social security benefits which had been paid to the claimant as a consequence of the injury or illness which was the cause of his claim against the defendant. The "compensator" (usually the defendant's insurer) is required, prior to making a compensation payment[88] in consequence of an accident, injury or disease suffered by another person ("the victim") not to do so until (having applied for it) he has been provided by the Secretary of State with a certificate of recoverable benefits.[89] He must then deduct from the

---

[84] [1989] A.C. 807.
[85] *Lincoln v. Hayman* [1982] 1 W.L.R. 488, approving *Gaskill v. Preston* [1981] 3 All E.R. 427.
[86] *Palfrey v. Greater London Council* [1985] I.C.R. 437.
[87] *Flanagan v. Watts Blake Bearne & Co.* [1992] P.I.Q.R. Q144. In *Clarke v. South Yorkshire Transport Ltd* [1998] P.I.Q.R. Q104 it was held that additional heating costs and the cost of having a hairdresser visit the claimant at home had not been shown by the defendant to fall within the attendance and mobility allowances the claimant received and hence no deduction should be made.
[88] *i.e.* where "a person makes a payment (whether on his own behalf or not) to or in respect of any other person in consequence of any accident, injury or disease suffered by the other" (s. 1(1)(a) of the Social Security (Recovery of Benefits) Act 1997, the current legislation. Under s. 1(2)(a) of the Act, the payment is one made "by or on behalf of a person who is, or is alleged to be liable to any extent in respect of the accident, injury or disease".
[89] Set out in column 2 of Sched. 2 to the 1997 Act; disability working allowance, disablement pension payable under s. 103 of the Social Security Contributions and Benefits Act 1992, incapacity benefit, income support, invalidity pension and allowance, jobseeker's allowance, reduced earnings allowance, severe disablement allowance, sickness benefit, statutory sick pay, unemployability supplement, unemployment benefit; attendance allowance, care component of disability living allowance, disablement pension increase payable under s. 104 or s. 105 of the 1992 Act; mobility allowance, mobility component of disability living allowance. It should be noted that reduced earnings allowance was abolished for all accidents or diseases which have occurred since October 1990, but it remains to be paid to persons establishing entitlement prior to that date. Sickness benefit was replaced by incapacity benefit in 1995 but again is payable to those with a prior entitlement. Statutory sick

payment an amount, determined in accordance with the certificate, equal to the gross amount of any recoverable benefits paid or likely to be paid to or for the victim during the relevant period in respect of the accident, injury or disease, and pay to the Secretary of State an amount equal to the total amount of the recoverable benefits.

9–061   The "relevant period" is a period of five years from the date on which the victim first claimed a relevant benefit as a consequence of the disease or, in any other case, five years following the day on which the accident or injury occurred. If a compensation payment is made in final discharge of any claim, the relevant period will end on the date on which that payment is made; five years is therefore the maximum period.

9–062   One reason for the enactment of the 1997 Act was the generally perceived unfairness of the decision in *Hassall v. Secretary of State for Social Security*.[90] The claimants were receiving unemployment benefit at the time they were injured. After the accidents in question they continued to receive approximately the same amount in benefit as before, but on the different basis that they were now incapable of working. It was accepted that they could not claim for loss of earnings during the time of incapacity, as they would not have been able to find work even if they had been fit. However the Court of Appeal held that the Secretary of State was entitled to recoup the amount of the benefit they received due to their incapacity to work.[91] Subsequently it was held in *Neal v. Bingle*[92] that the claimant, who, prior to the accident, was unemployed and in receipt of income support and other social security benefits, was entitled to claim as special damage the loss of the "unrecoupable" benefits (*i.e.* the income support) he was receiving before the accident.

9–063   The decision in *Hassall* was a consequence of the pre-1997 legislation providing that recoupment of benefits fell to be made from the totality of the damages awarded, not linking them to losses of the same nature as the benefit in question. The 1997 Act addresses this problem.[93] Schedule 2 sets out three heads of compensation; compensation for lost earnings, compensation for cost of care and compensation for loss of mobility. The deduction of a particular benefit (the relevant benefits are set out in the Schedule against the relevant head of compensation) is only to be made against the equivalent element of the award of damages. There are no equivalent benefits to be set off against damages for pain, suffering and loss of amenity, and hence an award for such non-pecuniary losses is effectively ringfenced against any recoupment. This benefits the claimant, but not the

---

pay which is paid today is not recoverable from damages, as since 1994 the employer is no longer reimbursed by the DSS. Unemployability supplement is now only paid to those receiving it before April 1997. Unemployment benefit was replaced by the Jobseekers Allowance in October 1996. Mobility allowance ceased in April 1992, but remains payable to persons with an entitlement prior to that date.

[90] [1995] 3 All E.R. 909.

[91] It was said by the Court of Appeal that the way around the problem for the plaintiffs would have been to claim as special damages the loss of entitlement to benefit, *i.e.* the loss of non-recoupable benefits.

[92] [1998] P.I.Q.R. Q1; following a suggestion made by Henry L.J. in *Hassall*, endorsing an idea of Gary Burrell Q.C. in *Quantum* Issue 2/94.

[93] See comments by Gary Burrell Q.C. in *Quantum* Issue 3/97.

defendant, who will still have to reimburse the Secretary of State for all the specified benefits paid to the claimant. It will be necessary, where the case is settled, to demarcate clearly the different heads of damage so the defendant is able to ascertain the amount of recoupment to be made against the relevant amount. The fact that the defendant will always have to pay the non-pecuniary losses in full as well as paying the recoupment sum to the Secretary of State is likely, as has been suggested,[94] to lead the claimant to seek to maximise general damages, where a settlement is being negotiated, and the defendant to minimise them, if there is to be recoupment against loss of earnings.

A helpful guidance was issued by the Compensation Recovery Unit in January 1999 listing damages which might or might not fall within Schedule 2. Damages which might fall within Schedule 2 are; under loss of earnings, loss of past earnings; under cost of care, nursing care and attendance (including holiday/respite care) and inability to cook; under loss of mobility, travel to hospital for treatment, additional costs of travel, including vehicle/powered wheelchair/adaptations to transport/taxi-bus fares (where paid as a result of injury or disease), increased cost of car/additional travel for holiday. Damages listed as not within Schedule 2 are as follows; pain and suffering, loss of future earnings, loss of future care, loss of mobility, loss of expectation of life and bereavement, loss of amenities of life, loss of society, loss of leisure, loss of specific enjoyment, loss or deprivation of privacy, loss of marriage prospects, breakdown of marriage, second home on breakdown of marriage, loss of carrying out DIY, loss of housekeeping capacity, handicap on the labour market (*Smith v. Manchester*), loss of congenial employment, loss of benefits associated with claimant's work, loss of use of motor car, hospital visits other than for treatment, medical expenses (not included in cost of respite or nursing care and attendance), special appliances (except as mentioned in loss of mobility), special diet, special accommodation, paid help (*e.g.* gardener/cleaner), guide dog, Court of Protection fees, actuarial advice and related matters, investment/management advice, loss of financial interest, loss of pension rights. This list should assist parties in negotiations, though the CRU stresses that it is for general guidance only.[95] It should also be noted that there is no offset for contributory negligence; even if the defendant only bears a small percentage of responsibility for the claimant's injuries he will still have to reimburse the Secretary of State for all recoverable benefits.

9–064

Small payments (comprising payments not exceeding £2,500) were, until the 1997 Act, exempt from the recoupment regime, and fell to be dealt with essentially in accordance with the rules set out in the 1948 Act. This exemption was abolished in the 1997 Act, which contains power to make regulations similar to those creating the exemption in the earlier legislation, but it has been suggested[96] that there is at present apparently no intention to implement this.

9–065

As regards social security benefits which do not fall within the list of

---

[94] *ibid.*
[95] See Lewis [1999] J.P.I.L. 11 at 13–14.
[96] Winfield & Jolowicz on Tort (15th ed., by W. V. H. Rogers) at pp. 780–1.

recoverable benefits, the Law Commission[97] thought that such benefits, *e.g.*
community charge relief, would be likely, in the light of the approach
adopted by the House of Lords in *Hodgson v. Trapp*,[98] to be deducted
from damages for the same loss, both as regards past and future payments,
in the absence of express provision in the relevant legislation for double
recovery. This view seems entirely correct.

(8) Rights of third parties

9–066   An important aspect of the Law Commission Report: "Damages for Personal Injury: Medical, Nursing and Other Expenses; Collateral Benefits"[99]
is the discussion of the rights of third parties, who have made a payment
in respect of the accident to the victim, to recover the sum paid if the
victim is successful in a tort claim. Clearly this can be done where there is
contractual or statutory provision for repayment,[1] and also recovery may
be effected where a restitutionary claim can be made, on the basis that the
benefit is provided conditionally, *e.g.* on the basis that the victim does not
succeed in a tort claim; if he succeeds, the condition has failed, and hence
the restitutionary claim can succeed.[2] In its earlier Consultation Paper the
Law Commission canvassed various options for change, but in the 1999
Report concluded that there should be no new statutory right to recover a
(non-deductible) payment from the victim in the event of a successful tort
claim for personal injury, essentially on the basis that it is always open to
the provider to make express provision to enable him to be reimbursed by
the victim from a future damages award.

9–067   A further issue examined by the Law Commission concerns rights of
providers *vis-à-vis* tortfeasors. It was held in *Metropolitan Police District
Receiver v. Croydon Corporation*[3] that a police authority could not recover
from the defendant, whose negligence had caused personal injury to a
police constable, the wages and allowances paid to the constable while he
was incapacitated. The defendant had settled the constable's damages
claim, which did not include a claim for loss of wages. The Court of Appeal
held that, as the constable had been paid his wages, he had not suffered a
loss in that regard for which the defendant could be liable. In its Consultation Paper, the Law Commission, agreeing with Slade J. at first instance,[4]
argued that the tortfeasor in such a case is in fact benefited, but recognised
that the matter is redressable by the ability of the provider to make contrac-

---

[97] Law Com. No. 147 "Damages for Personal Injury: Collateral Benefits" (1997) (1999)
"Damages for Personal Injury: Medical, Nursing and Other Expenses; Collateral Benefits
Law Com. No. 262, para. 10.52.
[98] [1989] A.C. 807; *supra* para. 9–059.
[99] (1999) Law Com. No. 262.
[1] See *supra* para. 9–053.
[2] See *Davies v. Inman* [1999] P.I.Q.R. Q26. The claimant's employer paid his wages while
he was absent from work, on an undertaking that he would reimburse the employer out of
any damages received. It was held that interest was payable on the damages for lost earnings, being held by the claimant, in accordance with *Hunt v. Severs* [1994] 2 A.C. 350,
on trust for his employer.
[3] [1957] 2 Q.B. 154.
[4] [1956] 1 W.L.R. 113. See Law Com. No. 147 at paras. 5.5–5.6.

tual provision for repayment by the victim (or by imposing a condition on the provision of the benefit, as described above). In *Land Hessen v. Gray & Gerrish*[5] the claimant, a German state and the employer of two teachers (one injured, one killed in a road traffic accident), asserted a restitutionary claim in respect of payments it was required by German law to make to the teachers. It was held that the *Metropolitan Police v. Croydon* decision was only binding to the extent of the claimant's claim to emoluments,[6] but not as regards the rest of the claim. It is difficult to justify this decision in the face of the decision in *Metropolitan Police v. Croydon*, but the vast majority of the Law Commission's consultees[7] agreed with the Commission that the reasoning of Slade J. in that case was preferable to that of the Court of Appeal. There was, however, significantly less support for the creation of a new statutory right to recoup the value of deductible collateral benefits from the tortfeasor; again the opportunity to make contractual provision for recoupment was seen as a factor. This analysis however pre-supposes the ability of the provider to make such provision. Where this cannot be done, statutory intervention may be necessary.

Thus, in the case of motor accident cases, the NHS has the right to recoup the cost of the treatment provided to a tort victim from the tortfeasor. Previously sections 157 and 158 of the Road Traffic Act 1988 made provision, in the case of section 157, for a person paying compensation following a motor accident causing injury or death, to pay the reasonable expenses incurred by a hospital in treating the victim's injuries; in the case of section 158 requiring a person using a vehicle at the time of an accident to pay a fee and mileage allowance to a practitioner who administers emergency treatment. Now the Road Traffic (NHS Charges) Act 1999[8] excludes NHS hospitals from sections 157 and 158 of the Road Traffic Act, and makes provision for the payment of NHS treatment received by a victim of a traffic accident,[9] by the person who makes a compensation payment, up to a maximum of £10,000, in respect of the injury or death, to the Secretary of State. A certificate of NHS charges may be applied for before, and if not, must be applied for after a compensation payment has been made, and the amount certified must be paid to the Secretary of State within 14 days from the settlement date, *i.e.* the date the compensation payment is made, if the certificate is issued before that date, and within 14 days of the date of issue of the certificate if it is issued on or after the settlement date. This Act reflects the spirit of the Social Security (Recovery of Benefits) Act 1997 and its precursors in seeking to maximise the efficient use of resources in the accident compensation system.[10]

---

[5] Unreported. July 31, 1998. See Law Com. No. 262 paras. 10.70–10.72.

[6] The meaning of which term is far from clear, as the Law Commission point out, *ibid.* at para. 10.71.

[7] 88% *ibid.* para. 12.28.

[8] See Lewis (1999) 62 M.L.R. 903 for detailed analysis of the Act and criticism of the strategy behind it.

[9] the criterion is that "a person . . . has suffered injury or has suffered injury and died, as a result of the use of a motor vehicle on a road" s. 1(1)(a).

[10] Mention may also be made of s. 17 of the Health and Social Services and Social Security Adjudications Act 1983, which allows local authorities to recover such charge (if any) as they think reasonable from the recipient of the services. In the light of *Avon C.C. v. Hooper* [1997] 1 All E.R. 532 a charge may well be levied where the recipient has a personal

3. NON-PECUNIARY LOSSES

9–068   The effects of an accident on a claimant are extremely unlikely to be only financial. Impairment, disfigurement, loss of functions and pain are just some of the potential non-pecuniary consequences, none of which can be measured in purely financial terms. *Restitutio in integrum*, which as we have seen, poses difficulties enough in compensating for pecuniary losses, cannot be effected by money if the claimant has lost an arm, or is unconscious. Nevertheless, the courts have never doubted the appropriateness of making awards for the non-pecuniary losses suffered by the claimant; they are, after all the essential losses, the most immediate consequences of the accident.

9–069   Two main theoretical approaches to the object of the award of damages for non-pecuniary losses have been identified. The "functional approach"[11] which was adopted by the Canadian Supreme Court in 1978,[12] bases the award on the amount that might be required by the claimant to provide him with reasonable solace for the consequences of the accident. If the claimant is unconscious, no award will be made since his lack of awareness of his misfortune precludes the need to purchase alternative pleasures. The Law Commission[13] convincingly criticised this approach on the basis that it caused problems in developing any kind of tariff system, was limited in its ability to provide compensation for all the non-pecuniary effects of the accident, apparently precluded recovery for past non-pecuniary loss, and placed an undue burden on claimants in having to produce evidence of the cost of the substitute pleasures that would form the basis of the claim. The alternative approach, adopted by English law, is what the Law Commission has termed the "diminution in value" approach[14] whereby a value is placed on the claimant's loss, whatever the use may be to which the damages are put. Under this approach both losses of which the claimant is aware and those of which he is not may be compensated.

9–070   The two main aspects of non-pecuniary loss are pain and suffering and loss of amenity. Before examining in a little more detail what is included within these two terms, it is important to stress that the courts will not itemise the different heads of non-pecuniary loss; and hence it is difficult to identify how much of an award is to be ascribed to pain and suffering and how much to loss of amenity, and, as we shall see, the tariff which has developed for non-pecuniary losses relates to the type of injury in question and has not been sub-divided into pain and suffering and loss of amenity.

---

injury claim. The claimant will need to claim the expenses, both past and future, as where commercial services are engaged. See Stephen Stewart Q.C. [1999] J.P.I.L. 27, and see also *Thrul v, Ray* [2000] P.I.Q.R. Q1 where an indemnity was sought against *Avon. v. Hooper* liability (held to be unnecessary on the facts).

[11] See Ogus (1972) 35 M.L.R. 1; "Law of Damages" (*op cit* p. 195.

[12] *Andrews v. Grand & Toy Alberta Ltd* (1978) 83 D.L.R. (3d) 452; *Arnold v. Teno* (1978) 83 D.L.R. (3d) 609; *Thornton v. Board of School Trustees of School District No. 57* (1978) 83 D.L.R. (3d) 480; contemporaneous decisions known as "the trilogy".

[13] "Damages for Personal Injury: Non-Pecuniary Loss" Law Com. No. 257 (1999) para. 2.5, 2.6.

[14] "Damages for Non-Pecuniary Loss" Law Com. No. 140 (1955).

(1) Pain and suffering

It has been suggested[15] that pain comprises the actual hurt and discom- 9–071
fort caused to the claimant by the injury, and suffering is the consequential
mental or emotional distress, including such emotions as anxiety, fear and
embarrassment. Between 1934 and 1982 it was possible to recover a conventional sum (£1,750 in 1982) where the claimant's life expectancy had
been shortened by the accident. This was abolished as a separate head of
non-pecuniary loss in the Administration of Justice Act 1982 section
1(1)(a), but a claimant's awareness that his life expectancy has been diminished can now form part of the claim for pain and suffering. Other
examples of compensable pain and suffering are embarrassment resulting
from disfigurement,[16] distress[17] and fright.[18]

A claimant who is unconscious[19] is thereby unable to experience pain or 9–072
suffering. Hence an award for non-pecuniary losses in such a case can only
be made for loss of amenities, itself a debatable point, as we shall see. In
such cases, assuming a case of comparable injuries caused to a conscious
claimant can be found, it may be possible to identify the relative assessment
of the two sub-heads of non-pecuniary loss, though such cases are rare,
and in practice it seems preferable to consider the two together. Exceptionally an award may be made for pain and suffering alone; thus in *Phelan v.
East Cumbria Health Authority*[20] the claimant underwent an operation to
his leg without anesthetic. He was awarded £5,000 for the experience on
the operating table, and £10,000 for pain suffering and loss of amenity,
but it is difficult to see what the loss of amenity was since there is no
suggestion in the judgment that the operation had any effect on him beyond
pain and suffering.

(2) Loss of amenity

This head of claim is sometimes referred to as "loss of faculty" or "loss 9–073
of enjoyment of life". This includes matters such as loss or impairment of
any of the five senses, and will extend both to "the physical and social
limitations inherent in the injury itself"[21] and the particular amenities lost
to the claimant, or restricted, such as an inability to pursue particular pas-
times enjoyed prior to the accident. Also compensable under this head of
loss are such matters as loss of ability to carry on an enjoyable occupation,[22] inability to play with his children,[23] loss of marriage prospects[24] and
loss of enjoyment of a holiday.[25]

---

[15] See *supra* n. 14 at 2.10 and McGregor *op cit.* para. 1700.
[16] See *Doughty v. North Staffordshire Health Authority* [1992] 3 Med. L.R. 81.
[17] See *Rourke v. Bardon* [1982] C.L.Y. 793.
[18] See *Thompson v. Royal Mail Lines* [1957] 1 Lloyd's Rep. 99.
[19] "... however caused, whether by the injury itself or produced by drugs or anaesthetics ..." per Lord Devlin in *H. West & Sons Ltd v. Shepherd* [1964] A.C. 326 at 354.
[20] [1991] 2 Med. L.R. 419.
[21] "Damages for Non-Pecuniary Loss" Law Com. Consultation Paper No. 140 (1995) at 2.14.
[22] See *e.g. Hale v. London Underground* [1993] P.I.Q.R. Q30 at Q39.
[23] See *e.g. Hoffman v. Sofaer* [1982] 1 W.L.R. 1350 at 1353C.
[24] See *e.g. Hughes v. McKeown* [1985] 1 W.L.R. 963.
[25] See *e.g. Hoffman v. Sofaer supra* n. 23.

9–074   In *West v. Shepherd*[26] the House of Lords confirmed the decision of the
Court of Appeal in *Wise v. Kay*[27] that an unconscious claimant was able
to be awarded damages for loss of amenity despite his unawareness of the
loss. The essential rationale for this view can be found in the words of Lord
Morris:

> "The fact of unconsciousness does not, however, eliminate the actual-
> ity of the deprivations of the ordinary experiences and amenities of life
> which may be the inevitable result of some physical injury."[28]

The Law Commission in its Consultation Paper on non-pecuniary loss[29]
suggested that non-pecuniary losses should be assessed subjectively, contrary to the view of the House of Lords in *West*. A significant majority of
consultees however preferred the status quo, on the basis that failure to
recognise the loss of amenity would be to undervalue victims and to triv-
ialise their experience, that it would be unjust to award lower compensation for major injuries than for lesser ones, and that there might be problems in determining the degree of awareness of deprivation.[30] In the light
of this, the Law Commission did not recommend any change in the law on
this point.

(3) The tariff system

9–075   As has been noted above, a tariff system has developed for non-pecuniary
losses, on the basis that like-injuries merit like-compensation. It may seem
paradoxical that this can be so, when, as we have seen, pain and suffering
import a significant subjective element, but it is nevertheless possible to
identify bands of levels of compensation appropriate for particular categories of injury; there are limits to the subjective element therefore. The task
has been facilitated by the publication by the Judicial Studies Board in 1992
of "Guidelines for the Assessment of General Damages in Personal Injury
Cases" (now in its 4th edition (1998)), which, based on a detailed survey
of quantum awards collected elsewhere,[31] sets out ranges of compensation
for particular injuries, indicating relevant factors within the particular
bracket that may affect the level of the award. The guidelines, though
extremely helpful, are not, as the Judicial Studies Board has stressed,
designed to do more than provide an indication of appropriate guidelines,
and recourse must still be had to the primary sources.[32] Further, the Court
of Appeal periodically sets out guidelines for quantum in the case of injuries

---

[26] [1964] A.C. 326. The House of Lords reaffirmed this approach in *Lim Poh Choo v.
Camden and Islington Area Health Authority* [1980] A.C. 174.
[27] [1962] 1 Q.B. 638.
[28] [1964] A.C. 326 at 349.
[29] *Supra* n. 21.
[30] See Law Com. No. 247 (1999); paras 2.8–2.19.
[31] See *e.g. Kemp & Kemp, Current Law, Halsbury's Laws Service Monthly Review*, Butterworths Personal Injury Litigation Service.
[32] See *Arafa v. Potter* [1994] P.I.Q.R. Q73 at Q79 per Staughton L.J. *Cf.* however Lord Woolf
M.R. in the introduction to the 1996 edition of the Guidelines.

that occur frequently,[33] thus, for example, in *Housecroft v. Burnett*[34] it was decided that £75,000 was the appropriate award for "a typical middle of the road case of tetraplegia"[35] as at April 1985. The courts are required to take account of inflation in adjusting awards,[36] and will make use of inflation tables, such as that contained in Kemp & Kemp, showing the value of the pound at various dates, and providing a multiplier to enable, for example, the value of a whiplash award of £1,500 in 1993 to be ascertained as of today's date.

Needless to say, no two cases are identical, and, though the guidelines may set out the broad parameters of compensation for injuries of particular types, and individual precedents may provide more precise assistance, it will be necessary to consider a range of factors which will affect the award in the particular case. Some of the more common factors are as follows:[37]

9–076

(a) The age of the claimant

This has at times been suggested as a relevant factor, though the Judicial Studies Board Guidelines make only minimal reference to it. Clearly age may be relevant where the life expectancy of the claimant is such that the duration of pain, suffering and loss of amenity will be less than for a younger claimant. In *Nutbrown v. Sheffield Health Authority*[38] the claimant was aged 72, with a life expectancy at trial to 82, when, as a result of medical negligence, he suffered brain damage. Potts J. considered that it was right to consider what would be an appropriate award to a man in the prime of life, and reduce it to reflect the age of the claimant and his life expectancy, and held that an appropriate award to a man of 30 would be £50,000, and scaled this down to an award of £25,000 to the claimant. In cases of deafness, the Judicial Studies Board Guidelines note that regard must be had to whether the injury or disability is one that the claimant has suffered at an early age, with the result that it has had an effect on his speech, or if it is one that he has suffered in later life. Again, facial scarring is likely to attract a larger award where the claimant is relatively young. As the Law Commission suggest,[39] the better view is that in general age *per se* is not significant except in so far as it relates either to life expectancy, in terms of the duration of the pain, suffering and loss of amenity, or to the fact that the injury is of a kind affecting the old more severely than the young, or vice versa.

9–077

---

[33] See *Wright v. British Railways Board* [1983] 2 A.C. 773 at 784–5.
[34] [1986] 1 All E.R. 332.
[35] *ibid.* at 338.
[36] See *Wright v. British Railways Board* [1983] 2 A.C. 773 at 782.
[37] See Law Com. Consultation Paper No. 140: "Damages for Personal Injury: Non-Pecuniary Loss" (1995); paras 2.25–2.35.
[38] (1993) 4 Med. L.R. 188. See also *Bird v. Cocking & Sons Ltd* [1951] 2 T.L.R. 1260.
[39] *Supra* n. 37 at 2.28.

(b) Pre-existing disability

9–078   Quite apart from the general principles of causation, discussed else-where,[40] the consequences of a pre-existing injury for a claimant may be especially severe. Thus, a claimant who only has one arm and loses the other arm in an accident will be more disadvantaged than a two-armed person losing an arm. The award of damages for non-pecuniary loss will reflect this. Thus, in *Bickerton v. Snare*,[41] the claimant, who was registered blind, sustained a broken leg in an accident. Because of her blindness she was awarded £1,500; had she been in full possession of her faculties she would have been awarded £750. However, a claimant already suffering from a disability, for example, a seriously-injured hand, which has to be amputated as a result of the defendant's negligence, will be awarded merely the difference between a seriously-injured hand and an amputated hand. In *Mustard v. Morris*[42] the Court of Appeal was of the view, in a case where the claimant, who was already unwell with diabetes at the time of the injury which necessitated an above-knee amputation of his left leg, that it would be more appropriate to increase damages in such a case rather than award less than would be awarded to a person who was fit prior to the accident, bearing in mind the reduction in his capacity to bear natural ill health.[43]

(c) Gender

9–079   Although in many cases the gender of the claimant will be irrelevant, it will assume significance in some instances. Disfigurement is the main example of this. In cases of facial disfigurement the Judicial Studies Board Guidelines indicate a top figure of £30,000 for a female, £20,000 for a male, and suggest that for scarring to other parts of the body the principles are the same as those on facial disfigurement. In *Wynn v. Cooper*[44] the Court of Appeal recognised that boys as well as girls suffer embarrassment on scarring, but it is thought that a differential would continue to be maintained.

(d) Circumstances in which injury sustained

9–080   Extra pain and suffering may be caused where the injury is sustained in especially traumatic circumstances. Thus with reference to amputation of all toes the Judicial Studies Board Guidelines state that the position in the bracket would depend, *inter alia* on whether the amputation was traumatic or surgical, and in cases of below-knee amputation of one leg, traumatic amputation in a horrendous accident where the injured person remained fully conscious would come at or towards the top of the range.

---

[40] See *supra* paras. 4–003 *et seq.*
[41] [1963] C.L.Y. 968a.
[42] *Kemp & Kemp*, Vol. 3, para. I2-106 and I2-604. C.A., July 21, 1981.
[43] per Watkins L.J.
[44] [1992] P.I.Q.R. Q140 at Q142.

(e) Duration

This will always be a relevant factor, whether it concerns the duration   9–081
of pain and suffering or loss of amenity. English law has never looked
favourably on the *per diem* approach employed in some states of the U.S.A,
whereby a sum is determined for each day's pain and suffering and multiplied by the number of days it has been experienced and is expected to be
experienced in the future. As Ogus has convincingly argued,[45] there is no
rational foundation for the objective arithmetical process; the figures
chosen are as arbitrary as those reached by any other method. In addition,
such a method ascribes a primacy to the temporal aspect of pain and suffering, rather than treating it, as U.K. law does, as one of a number of
relevant factors. Duration will however be relevant where the injury has
reduced the claimant's life expectancy as well as causing permanent incapacity; thus it was held in *Rose v. Ford*[46] that damages for the loss of the
claimant's leg were limited to the four days she lived after the accident.

Other factors include, in the case of pain and suffering, the intensity of   9–082
the pain experienced by the claimant, and the degree of insight the claimant
has into his or her post-accident circumstances, which may include
awareness of any diminished life expectancy.[47] Loss of ability to pursue
pre-accident hobbies or interests may also be reflected in an augmented
award beyond that which would be made to a person without such
interests.

(f) Multiple injuries

It is generally recognised that multiple injuries pose particular problems   9–083
of assessment. The Introduction to the Judicial Studies Board Guidelines
emphasises the inappropriateness of making separate valuations of the individual elements in a multiple injury case and aggregating the figures to
arrive at a total. The object is to take an overall view of the injuries and
assess the effect they have had upon the claimant, with the main element
being the most serious of the injuries.[48]

(4) Reform Proposals for non-pecuniary losses

For a number of years, concern has been expressed about levels of   9–084
awards for non-pecuniary loss. This has focused not so much on the differentials between different kinds of injury, but rather on the amounts
awarded, especially in cases of particularly serious injury. In 1988
CITCOM (The Citizen Action Compensation Campaign) produced proposals for a Compensation Advisory Board empowered to recommend new

---

[45] *op. cit.* p. 199.
[46] [1937] A.C. 826.
[47] See Administration of Justice Act 1982, s. 1(1)(b).
[48] See *Dureau v. Evans* [1996] P.I.Q.R. Q18; *Brown v. Woodall* [1995] P.I.Q.R. Q36.

levels of compensation.[49] There was a good deal of support, both within and outside Parliament, for these proposals, notably from the National Consumer Council[50] and APIL (the Association of Personal Injury Lawyers). In a Consultation Paper in 1995,[51] the Law Commission, *inter alia*, invited consultees' views on levels of awards and if awards were thought to be too low, the necessary uplift required, whether there should be a legislative tariff and, if not, how the judiciary could be assisted in determining awards. The subsequent report[52] reflects the view of consultees that awards of damages for non-pecuniary loss are too low, as regards cases of serious personal injury (defined by the Law Commission as cases where an award of more than £2,000 would be made for the injury alone, and ignoring contributory negligence).[53] This was regarded as being especially true in cases of very serious injury. The Commission thought it important to take into account public opinion, and a survey was accordingly carried out by the Office for National Statistics, the results of which supported the views of consultees on the excessive lowness of awards. It was also thought important to canvass the interviewees as to whether their views would be different given the knowledge that damages awards were generally paid by insurers, and an increase in awards would have a knock-on effect on the cost of insurance, the cost of compensation therefore being met by a wide cross-section of the public rather than by the defendant. 80 per cent of the interviewees said that knowing this did not alter their views.

9–085   Having also taken into consideration levels of awards in other jurisdictions the Law Commission concluded that, in cases where the current award for non-pecuniary loss would be more than £3,000, damages for non-pecuniary loss should be increased by a factor of at least 1.5 but not more than 2. For awards between £2,000 and £3,000 there should be a series of tapered increases (*e.g.* an award of £2,500 should be uplifted by around 25 per cent). The proposals reflect in particular the views of the public, via the Office for National Statistics Survey, and also reflect the largest measure of consensus among the Commission's consultees.

9–086   The Law Commission favoured the option of implementation of the proposed increase via the Court of Appeal and/or the House of Lords in the context of an appropriate case or series of cases. The Court of Appeal was quick to respond. Arrangements were made to identify as early as possible a group of cases in relation to which the court could express its views on the Law Commission's recommendation, and a five-judge court heard eight appeals jointly, reflecting a range of levels of injury.[54] In addition to the

---

[49] Citizens' Compensation Bill: see *Hansard* H.C. June 22, 1988, Vol. 135, cols 1128–1129; *Hansard* H.C. March 3, 1989, Vol. 148, cols 511–569; Standing Committee C (Citizens' Compensation Bill), May 3, 1989; *Hansard* H.C. July 7, 1989, Vol. 156, cols 583–584 and 637–689.

[50] *Compensation Levels for Pain, Suffering and Loss of Quality of Life* (Ref. PD 30/88); *Compensation Recovery* (Ref. PD 16/L2/95) p. 7.

[51] "Damages for Personal Injury: Non-Pecuniary Loss" Consultation Paper No. 140.

[52] Law Com. No. 257 (1999).

[53] Where the present award would be between £2,000 and £3,000 there should be tapered increases.

[54] *Heil v. Rankin and others*, *The Times*, March 24, 2000.

arguments on behalf of the parties, written submissions were received from, among others, APIL, the ABI and FOIL. The court did not consider it necessary to go as far as the Law Commission had recommended. Bearing in mind the impact of larger awards on the public at large, both in the form of higher insurance premiums and as a result of fewer resources being available for the NHS, it recommended a tapered level of increases, the largest being required for cases of the most catastrophic injuries, with the necessary scale of adjustment required being reduced as the level of existing awards decreased. At the highest level, the court considered there was a neeed for awards for non-pecuniary loss to be increased by about a third; at the other end of the scale there was no need for an increase in awards at present below £10,000. Thus, in two of the cases before it, the court increased awards at trial of £135,000 to £175,000, and in another case an award of £40,000 was increased to £44,000. Use of the RPI would remain appropriate for future updates.

These rulings fall well short of the Law Commission's proposals, no 9–087 doubt to the relief of insurers,[55] and at the time of writing it is not known if there will be further appeals to the House of Lords. Nevertheless, the decision of the Court of Appeal represents a step in the right direction, especially in its recognition of the need to provide significant uplifts in the worse scenario cases.

4. ALTERNATIVE FORMS OF AWARD

As we have seen,[56] the traditional form of award of damages is the once- 9–088 for-all lump sum. The limitations of this form of compensation have been subjected to detailed criticism over the years,[57] focusing especially on its inability to provide more than a rough approximation of the claimant's future losses. To a certain extent this weakness is ameliorated by the fact that the courts now make use of actuarial tables,[58] and the increased multipliers employed as a result of the decision in *Wells v. Wells* to assume investment by the claimant in ILGS. It remains the case however that the lump-sum award carries with it the inevitable likelihood of over-or-under-compensation and the significant risk that the fund will be exhausted during the claimant's lifetime. Consequently various ways have been developed of mitigating the rigidity of the lump-sum approach.

---

[55] ABI figures suggested that a 100% increase in non-pecuniary awards would lead to an increase in motor insurance premiums of 3.8–4.7%, and in employers' liability insurance premiums of 13.8–18% (Law Com. No. 257 (1999) para. 3.65, n. 79).

[56] *Supra* Ch. 1, paras. 1–024 *et seq.*

[57] See, for example, Fleming (1969) 19 U.T.L.J. 295; Report of the Royal Commission for Civil Liability and Compensation for Personal Injury (1978) ("The Pearson Report") Cmnd. 7054, Vol. 1 para. 178; Harris "Remedies in Contract and Tort" (1988) pp. 275–277; Law Com. Consultation Paper No. 125: "Structured Settlements and Interim and Provisional Damages" (1992) para. 2.7–2.8; Lewis: "Structured Settlements: The Law and Practice" (Sweet & Maxwell, 1993), para. 2-07–para. 2-19.

[58] *Supra* paras. 9-025 *et seq.*

(1) Structured settlements[59]

9-089   From time to time the suggestion that the lump sum system be replaced by a scheme of periodic payments has been canvassed. In 1973 the Law Commission concluded that such a system could not fit into the existing tort framework,[60] whereas the Pearson Commission, by a majority, recommended periodic payments for injuries of a serious and lasting nature, and in cases of fatal accidents, the court having a power to award damages as a lump sum or by way of periodic payments.[61] No legislative intervention ensued, but in 1987, as a result of an agreement reached between the Association of British Insurers and the Inland Revenue,[62] a scheme of periodic payments was sanctioned, in the form of structured settlements, a concept which had developed in North America.[63] A typical structured settlement involves the payment of a lump sum, representing part of the agreed lump sum value of the settlement, the balance coming from a series of periodic payments. The great advantage of a structured settlement is that the Revenue has conceded that an appropriately framed agreement is not liable to tax on the periodic payments, as they are treated as instalment payments of the capital sum, rather than being income in the hands of the claimant, and hence taxable. After payment of the initial lump sum, the balance is employed by the defendant's insurer to purchase an annuity or a series of annuities from a life insurance company.

9-090   The Inland Revenue approved four Model Agreements, designed to cover the main types of periodic payment likely to be required: Basic Terms, involving fixed payments and running for a fixed period; Indexed Terms, similar to Basic Terms except that the payments are linked to the Retail Price Index; Terms for Life, where the payments are fixed, running for the rest of the claimant's life (perhaps requiring a minimum number of payments) and Indexed Terms for Life (self-explanatory). These Model Agreements provide for a capital figure to be stated in the agreement, representing the antecedent debt in relation to which the instalment repayments are made.[64] In 1992 in its Consultation Paper on Structured Settlements and Interim and Provisional Damages[65] the Law Commission noted that, though traditionally a structured settlement began with the claim being valued in the conventional multiplier/multiplicand way, there were reports of cases[66] where the reverse occurred, the parties agreeing a structure to cater to the claimant's needs. Thus, rather than as under the conventional approach, agreeing the claim at £1.4 million, paying £400,000 up-

---

[59] There is a growing literature on this subject. See *e.g.* Allen (1988) 104 L.Q.R. 448, Lewis (1988) 15 J. of Law and Society 392; Lewis, "Structured Settlements: the Law and Practice" (1993), Structured Settlements: A Practical Guide (ed. Goldrein and de Haas) 2nd ed., 1997.

[60] Law Com. No. 56 (1973) paras 29–30. Kemp & Kemp Chapter 6A is especially useful.

[61] The Pearson Report (see n. 61 *supra*): Ch. 14. See Cane: Atiyah's Accidents, Compensation and the Law (6th ed., 1999) p. 117.

[62] For the history of this, see Lewis "Structured Settlements: The Law and Practice" (1993) at 4-15–4-20.

[63] *ibid.* at 4-02–4-09.

[64] Lewis *op. cit.* at 13-09.

[65] Consultation Paper No. 125, at 3.17.

[66] See Fiona Bawdon (1992) 6(6) The Lawyer 5.

front and obtaining quotes from the specialists to see what package of monthly payments could be purchased by the resulting £1 million, concentration is focused on the needs of the claimant, the necessary income is determined and a structure is devised accordingly. No doubt the lump sum cost can then be stated in the agreement to satisfy the Inland Revenue's requirements.

Such certainty and flexibility is a welcome aspect of the structured settlement. Having said that, there are, of course, limitations; as has been rightly pointed out, they only have initial flexibility,[67] being able to a significant extent to be tailored to suit the particular needs of the claimant. Thus, it may be possible to include within the structure extra payments designed to meet anticipated future needs such as replacement transport or equipment. However, once determined, the structured settlement cannot be altered, making it vital to anticipate future uncertainties much as is required with a lump sum agreement.[68] A contingency fund is likely to be required, but of course making provision for this will have a knock-on effect on the size or duration of the monthly payments under the agreement. **9–091**

On the positive side, there is the benefit of certainty; the security of knowing that there is an income (index-linked if so desired) for life, or for a fixed period as agreed, which could extend beyond the death of the claimant to benefit his dependents. The fact that tax is not deducted from the periodic payments (unlike the position where a lump sum is invested; the income derived thereby will be taxable) increases the value of the agreement, though it may be discounted to provide a *quid pro quo* for the insurer's agreement to structure. Tax changes in 1995[69] enabled the annuity payments under the agreement to be made directly from the life insurer to the claimant; previously they had to be paid first to the liability insurer who then had to pay them on to the claimant, a process which required the insurer to deduct tax, pay it to the Inland Revenue, gross up the amount paid to the claimant and later reclaim the tax. This cumbersome procedure increased the overall cost of the transaction and no doubt strengthened the insurer's argument for a higher discount percentage. As a consequence of these changes the claimant becomes the policyholder for the purposes of the Policyholders Protection Act 1975, thus giving him greater security in the event that the insurer goes into liquidation. **9–092**

As a consequence of the Law Commission's Report: "Structured Settlements and Interim and Provisional Damages",[70] the Damages Act 1996[71] contains various provisions concerning structured settlements, including, in section 5, a very full definition of "structured settlement". Section 4 of the Act provides enhanced protection for structured settlement annuitants, increasing the guarantee contained in the Policyholders Protection Act 1975 that 90 per cent of the liability of an insurance company in liquidation will be paid to policyholders, to 100 per cent in the case of annuities purchased for persons pursuant to structured settlements. In addition, concerns that **9–093**

---

[67] Law Com. Consultation Paper No. 125 (1992) para 3.19 n. 28.
[68] Law Com. No. 224 "Structured Settlements and Interim and Provisional Damages" (1994).
[69] Finance Act 1995 s. 142 (superseded by s. 150n of the Finance Act 1996).
[70] Law Com. No. 224 (1994).
[71] See Lewis (1997) 60 M.L.R. 230 on the Act and its background.

structured settlements set up by government departments might prove inadequate since such bodies generally use their own resources to fund payments, and they might cease to exist, are allayed by section 7, which empowers the relevant Minister to guarantee the payments. Further protection exists in the National Health Service (Residual Liabilities) Act 1996 which, in section 1, requires the Secretary of State to exercise his statutory powers to transfer, *inter alia*, liabilities of any National Health Service Trust, Health Authority or Special Health Authority which ceases to exist, so as to secure that all of its liabilities are dealt with.

9–094   The Law Commission in its 1994 Report concluded that there should be no judicial power to impose structured settlements, regarding this as premature and fraught with logistical difficulties.[72] Section 2 of the Damages Act does however, again following a recommendation of the Law Commission,[73] empower a court, with the consent of the parties, to make an order under which the damages awarded in an action for personal injury[74] are wholly or partly to take the form of periodical payments. Of course most cases will settle well in advance, but this provision ensures that a case which actually gets to court can still have the award of damages structured.

9–095   Structured settlements are now clearly established as a significant feature of personal injury compensation which may benefit claimants who are attracted by the positive aspects of structuring, and which must be borne in mind by professional advisers as an option, at least in substantial claims,[75] failing which a professional negligence claim is risked. The attractions of structured settlements may vary from time to time, depending on such matters as the level of annuity rates,[76] but they remain, in the words of the Law Commission,[77] "a useful alternative form of arranging an award of damages which should remain available to allow claimants a choice as to how to plan their future."[78]

(2) Provisional damages

9–096   In 1973 the Law Commission recommended legislation to deal with cases where it was possible that the claimant would develop a disease, or his condition would deteriorate. Such "chance" cases would leave the claimant uncompensated, should the contingency occur, unless legislative provision was made to permit the claimant to return to court. This recommendation

---

[72] *Supra* n. 72 at paras 3.37–3.53.
[73] *ibid.* at 3.77–3.78.
[74] See s. 7 of the Damages Act for the definition of "personal injury". It includes fatal accident claims.
[75] In a guidance note issued in October 1992 the Law Society, though clearly recognising that "substantial" could not be defined in this context, indicated that cases conventionally valued at £100,000 plus might be appropriate for consideration of structuring. See Lewis: "Structured Settlements: The Law and Practice (1993) para. 1-30 and Appendix 3.
[76] At their lowest for 30 years, thus rendering structured settlements unattractive, in November 1998: see Taylor *Quantum* Issue 6/98, p. 1.
[77] Law Com. No. 224, para. 3.32.
[78] In March 2000 the Lord Chancellor's Department issued a Consultation Paper canvassing, *inter alia*, views on alternatives to lump sum compensation.

was given legislative effect in 1982, the Administration of Justice Act of that year inserting section 32A into the Supreme Court Act 1981.[79] This provides as follows:

"32A Order for provisional damages for personal injuries   9–097

(1) This section applies to an action for damages for personal injuries in which there is proved or admitted to be a chance that at some definite or indefinite time in the future the injured person will, as a result of the act or omission which gave rise to the cause of action, develop some serious disease or suffer some serious deterioration in his physical or mental condition . . .

(2) Subject to subsection (4) below, as regards any action for damages to which this section applies in which a judgment is given in the High Court, provision may be made by rules of court for enabling the court, in such circumstances as may be prescribed, to award the injured person—

   (a) damages assessed on the assumption that the injured person will not develop the disease or suffer the deterioration in his condition: and
   (b) further damages at a future date if he develops this disease or suffers the deterioration"

The section came into force on July 1, 1985, and applies in all cases,   9–098 including actions begun prior to that date. There is no obligation on the claimant to claim provisional damages rather than a lump sum.[80] A Practice Direction of July 1, 1985[81] requires the judge to specify the disease or type of deterioration which it has been assumed will not occur for the purposes of the immediate award and which will entitle the claimant to further damages if it occurs at a future date. Normally the judge will also specify the period within which the application for further damages must be made, though if a period is specified it may be extended before it expires, on application by the claimant.[82]

In *Willson v. Ministry of Defence*,[83] one of the few reported cases on   9–099 provisional damages, Scott Baker J. held that three questions fell to be considered:

(a) Whether it is proved there is a chance;

(b) Whether it is proved there is a chance of some serious deterioration in the claimant's physical condition; and

(c) Whether the court should exercise its discretion in favour of the claimant in the circumstances of the case.

---

[79] CPR Pt. 41.
[80] Cowan v. Kitson [1992] P.I.Q.R. Q19.
[81] See [1985] 1 W.L.R. 961.
[82] R.S.C. Ord. 37r 8(3).
[83] [1991] 1 All E.R. 638. See also *Molinari v. Ministry of Defence* [1994] P.I.Q.R. Q33.

To comprise a chance, the possibility must be measurable rather than fanciful, and a serious deterioration goes beyond ordinary deterioration. There must be a clear and severable risk rather than a continuing deterioration. The Law Commission[84] considered the potential harshness of this limitation on cases involving gradual deterioration of the claimant's condition, but concluded that there were significant practical problems in defining gradual deterioration. The Commission did however consider that the restriction on a claimant under the current rules of being entitled to make only one application for further damages in respect of each disease or type of deterioration specified in the order for provisional damages[85] might create injustice in certain cases, and recommended that it should be possible to make more than one application where the specified disease or deterioration occurs in more than one position on the body of the claimant, provided that the possible positions are specified at the time when the order is made. Hence, to borrow an example from the Law Commission,[86] if arthritis developed in a leg first, but in an arm later, a claimant who claimed for the former would, under this proposal, be able to claim further damages for the latter, unlike the position under the current rules. This is an eminently sensible proposal, as yet unenacted.

9–100   A further concern of the Law Commission, which has borne legislative fruit, was the issue of whether the dependents of a person who had been awarded provisional damages were precluded from claiming under the Fatal Accidents Act by reason of the provisional award, even though no further award had ever been made. The matter was considered by the Court of Appeal in *Middleton v. Elliott Turbomachinery Ltd*[87] but the matter remained unclear. The Commission's recommendations[88] were enacted in section 3 of the Damages Act 1996, which provides that an award of provisional damages to a person who subsequently dies as a result of the act or omission in respect of which the damages were awarded does not bar a Fatal Accidents Act claim, though if part of the provisional award, or any other damages awarded to the person prior to their death was designed to compensate him for pecuniary loss in a period which in the event falls after his death, that is to be taken into account in assessing the lost dependency of the dependents. The section also provides that no award of further damages made in respect of that person after his death shall include any amount for loss of income in respect of any period after his death.

(3) Interim damages[89]

9–101   Interim damages may be awarded in respect of any claim for damages, but are most frequently awarded in personal injury cases. An award may

[84] "Structured Settlements and Interim and Provisional Damages" Law Com. No. 224 (1994).
[85] R.S.C. Ord. 37r 10(6).
[86] *Supra* n. 87 at 5.21.
[87] *The Times*, October 29, 1990.
[88] *ibid.* n. 87 at 5.37.
[89] CPR, rr.25.6–9. It should be noted that orders for interim payments may only be made in personal injury claims if the defendant is insured in respect of the claim or if the defendant is a public body: CPR r.25.7(2).

be made where the defendant has admitted liability, or where the claimant has obtained judgment against the defendant, or where, if the action proceeded to trial, the claimant would obtain judgment for substantial damages against the defendant. An interim payment shall be in an amount that the court thinks just, not exceeding a reasonable proportion of the likely award, taking into account contributory negligence and set-offs and counterclaims. In *Schott Kem Ltd v. Bentley and others*[90] the Court of Appeal, albeit not in a personal injury case, regarded as sensible the practice that has developed of requiring the claimant to show a need for the interim payment in personal injury cases. The matter was somewhat ameliorated more recently by the Court of Appeal in *Stringman v. McArdle*[91] where it was said that the claimant did not have to demonstrate any particular need over and above the general need that a claimant has to be paid his or her damages as soon as reasonably possible. It would generally be appropriate and just to order a payment when there would be some delay until the final disposal of the case.

(4) Interest

The early power of the courts to award interest on damages,[92] initially **9–102** in cases of debt and certain cases of trespass to goods, developed into a general discretion[93] and subsequently a mandatory provision, in cases of personal injury and wrongful death, in the absence of special reasons. Soon afterwards guidelines were laid down in *Jefford v. Gee*.[94] The following principles have emerged:

(a) Interest is to be awarded or special damages; *i.e.* the claimant's loss of wages and medical expenses up to trial, from date of injury to date of judgment, at half the short-term interest rate on the full amount. This is explained by the fact that much of the claim will be for lost earnings and medical expenses which will occur periodically during the relevant period. Technically, interest arises on the losses as they occur, but this broad brush approach avoids the need for detailed analysis that would otherwise be required, and essentially does justice as between the parties;[95]

(b) No interest is awarded on general damages for loss of future earnings, for the sound reason that those losses have not yet occurred;

[90] [1991] 1 Q.B. 61.
[91] [1994] P.I.Q.R. Q230.
[92] See Civil Procedure Act 1833.
[93] Law Reform (Miscellaneous Provision) Act 1934. See now Supreme Court Act 1981, s. 35A; County Courts Act 1984, s. 69.
[94] [1970] 2 Q.B. 130.
[95] See however *Prokop v. Department of Health and Social Security* [1985] C.L.Y. 1037 where the loss of earnings was complete two or three years before the trial. In the circumstances the Court of Appeal was prepared to approve an award of interest at the full rate. 99 [199] P.I.Q.R. Q128. For comment see Bishop [1999] J.P.I.L. 152 1. See *supra* pp. ?.

(c) Other general damages, *i.e.* for non-pecuniary losses, carry interest from the date when the writ was served to the date of judgment, the rate being 2 per cent.

In *Wadey v. Surrey County Council*[96] it was held that the claimant in a personal injury action does not have to give credit for deductible benefits.[97]

---

[96] [1999] P.I.Q.R. Q128. For comment see Bishop [1999] J.P.I.L. 152.
[97] See *supra* paras. 9–045 *et seq.*

CHAPTER 10

DAMAGES ON DEATH

At common law there could be no claim for damages in cases of death. **10–001**
This was in part a consequence of the maxim: *actio personalis moritur cum persona* (a cause of action dies with the person) and in part a result of the rule expressed in *Baker v. Bolton*[1] that death does not comprise an injury for the purpose of a civil action. Statute subsequently ameliorated the position. As regards the former maxim, the Law Reform (Miscellaneous Provisions) Act 1934 enables the right of action of an injured person to survive his death, it being passed on to his personal representatives. As we shall see, the practical significance of this has diminished significantly in recent years, and the most important piece of legislation is the Fatal Accidents Act 1976, a consolidation of earlier legislation, originating in the Fatal Accidents Act 1846, and amended by the Administration of Justice Act 1982. Under the Fatal Accidents Act claim, a right of action is conferred on the dependants of the deceased, reflecting their loss, not his. Though the way in which damages in fatal accident cases are calculated has some similarities to the method of calculating personal injury damages, discussed above,[2] there are also, as we shall see, significant differences.

Section 1(1) of the 1976 Act as amended provides as follows: **10–002**

> "If death is caused by any wrongful act, neglect or default which is such as would (if death had not ensued) have entitled the person injured to maintain an action and recover damages in respect thereof, the person who would have been liable if death had not ensued shall be liable to an action for damages, notwithstanding the death of the person injured."

It is also important to note that section 2 (1) of the Act provides that the action brought under the Fatal Accidents Act (section 2(3) provides that only one action can be brought) is to be brought in the name of the deceased's executor or administrator; and section 2(4) requires full particulars to be given of the persons for whose benefit the action is brought. Thus, though the claim is that of the dependants, not the deceased, they can only claim if he would have been able to, had he survived. Thus, in *Read v. Great Eastern Railway Co*,[3] prior to his death the deceased had settled his claim against the defendant. As a consequence his dependants had no claim,

---

[1] (1808) 1 Camp. 493.
[2] *Supra* Ch. 9.
[3] (1868) L.R. 3 Q.B. 555.

and the same was true in *Williams v. Mersey Docks and Harbour Board*[4] where the deceased's claim had become time-barred prior to his death. The position will be the same where the deceased had agreed to conditions excluding the defendant's liability to him;[5] but where he had merely agreed to a limitation on the amount of damages recoverable, as in *Nunan v. Southern Railway Co*,[6] this will have no effect on the claim of the dependants, the difference being that in the case of limited liability the deceased would still have had a claim, and that suffices to enable a Fatal Accident Act claim to be made, the limitation being discarded due to the separate nature of the dependants' claim.

10–003 However, there are instances where the extent of the defendant's liability to the deceased may affect the extent of his liability to the dependants. Thus, in *Burns v. Edman*[7] the deceased was a habitual criminal, and the support he provided to his dependants was obtained through criminal enterprise. It was held that the maxim *ex turpi causa non oritur actio* precluded the dependants' claim, though it has been argued[8] that this decision is inconsistent with *Nunan* since the *ex turpi causa* rule would not have prevented the deceased from claiming in respect of his injuries (unless sustained in the course of criminal activity), and the claim of the dependants did not arise *ex turpi causa*. However, public policy also precluded the claim in *Hunter v. Butler*[9] where the support provided by the deceased for his wife included state benefits obtained by fraud and earnings which he had not declared to the Inland Revenue.[10]

10–004 Also, contributory negligence on the part of the deceased will have the effect of reducing the dependants' claim accordingly,[11] although again it can be argued that this is inconsistent with the general rule that the dependants' claim is independent of that of the deceased. In *Dodds v. Dodds*[12] it was held that the negligence of the deceased's wife, which caused his death, did not affect the claims of non-negligent dependants, though she could not claim herself. If she had been only partly responsible for his death, it would seem, on the authority of *Mulholland v. McCrea*,[13] that her claim would have been reduced in proportion to the degree of her responsibility for his death, though there is force to the suggestion[14] that it might be more correct to allow her to claim in full as dependant and adjust the position by claiming against her as joint tortfeasor.

---

[4] [1905] 1 K.B. 804.

[5] See *Haigh v. Royal Mail Steam Packet Co. Ltd* (1883) 52 L.J.Q.B. 640 (a situation much less likely to occur since the enactment of the Unfair Contract Terms Act 1977).

[6] [1924] 1 K.B. 223. See also *Grein v. Imperial Airways Ltd* [1937] 1 U.B. 50.

[7] [1970] 2 Q.B. 541.

[8] "Claims for Wrongful Death", Law Com. Consultation Paper No. 148; para. 2.8. See also McGregor *op. cit.* para. 1739.

[9] [1996] R.T.R. 396. See *Kemp & Kemp*, Vol. 1, para. 25-008.

[10] The widow's awareness of her husband's fraud makes this, as was pointed out by Hobhouse L.J., a stronger case than *Burns*.

[11] Fatal Accidents Act 1976, s. 5. See *Murphy v. Culhane* [1977] K.B. 94.

[12] [1978] Q.B. 543.

[13] [1961] N.1 135.

[14] Munkman, *Damages for Personal Injury and Death* (10th ed., 1996) p. 133.

1. CLAIMANTS UNDER THE FATAL ACCIDENTS ACT

The question who can claim as a dependant is one involving issues of **10–005** law and fact. The Act contains a detailed definition, considered below, of persons whose relationship with the deceased was such as to enable them, as a matter of law, to qualify as dependants, but they must then in addition satisfy the factual test, also examined in detail below, of establishing whether they had, in the words of one of the leading authorities,[15] "a reasonable expectation of pecuniary benefit, as of right or otherwise, from the continuance of the life".

As regards the question of who can be a dependant as a matter of law, **10–006** section 1 (3) of the Fatal Accidents Act[16] provides:

"In this Act 'dependant' means—
  (a) the wife or husband, or former wife or husband[17] of the deceased.
  (b) any person who—

    (i) was living with the deceased in the same household[18] immediately before the date of the death; and
    (ii) had been living with the deceased in the same household for at least two years before that date; and
    (iii) was living during the whole of that period as the husband or wife of the deceased;

  (c) any parent or other ascendant of the deceased;
  (d) any person who was treated by the deceased as his parent;
  (e) any child or other descendant of the deceased;
  (f) any person (not being a child of the deceased) who, in the case of any marriage to which the deceased was at any time a party, was treated by the deceased as a child of the family in relation to that marriage;
  (g) any person who is, or is the issue of, a brother, sister, uncle or aunt of the deceased".

Section 1(5) provides that, in deducing any relationship for the purposes **10–007** of subsection (3):

"(a) any relationship by affinity[19] shall be treated as a relationship by

---

[15] *Franklin v. South Eastern Railway Co.* (1858) 3 H. & N. 211 at 214.

[16] As substituted by s. 3(1) of the Administration of Justice Act 1982.

[17] S. 1(4) provides that being a former wife or husband may result from nullity or divorce. In *Shepherd v. Post Office, The Times,* June 15, 1995, it was held that a divorcee who returned to live with her first husband qualified as a former wife.

[18] See *Pounder v. London Underground* [1995] P.I.Q.R. P. 217. For the purposes of the section a person may live in more than one household at a time. Brief absences will not be fatal to the claim that the deceased was "living" at a particular address during the period immediately preceding his death. The facts must be looked at as a whole.

[19] *i.e.* through marriage.

consanguinity, any relationship of the half blood as a relationship of the whole blood, and the stepchild of any person as his child, and

    (b) an illegitimate person shall be treated as the legitimate child of his mother and reputed father."

10–008   As regards adopted children, section 39(1) of the Adoption Act 1976 provides:

> "an adopted child shall be treated in law—
>
>   (a) where the adopters are a married couple, as if he had been born as a child of the marriage (whether or not he was in fact born after the marriage was solemnised);
>
>   (b) in any other case, as if he had been born to the adopter in wedlock (but not as a child of any actual marriage of the adopter)."

10–009   In its 1999 Report: "Claims for Wrongful Death"[20] the Law Commission recommended retention of the present list of those able to claim, but regarded it as too restrictive, proposing addition to the list of a generally-worded class of claimant, under which any other individual who "was being wholly or partly maintained by the deceased immediately before the death or who would, but for the death, have been so maintained at a time beginning after the death" would be able to claim under the Act. A person would be treated as being wholly or partly maintained by another if that person, "otherwise than for full valuable consideration, was making a substantial contribution in money or money's worth towards his reasonable needs." This definition would enable claims to be brought by persons identified by the Law Commission,[21] as currently being excluded from section 1(3) of the Act, *e.g.* cohabitants living together as husband and wife but who do not satisfy the two years of cohabitation requirement, same-sex couples, non-relatives living together otherwise than in a marriage-like relationship. The range of claimants would therefore be significantly extended by these proposals, in accordance with the view of almost all consultees that the existing list is too restrictive, though, as the Law Commission recognised in its Consultation Paper,[22] it may be difficult for the person bringing the claim to identify all the potential claimants, in the absence of a statutory list.

10–010   It has been clear since *Blake v. Midland Railway Co*[23] that (subject to the statutory award for bereavement, to be considered below), damages under the Fatal Accidents Act are restricted to pecuniary losses; hence the widow in *Blake* could not recover for mental suffering resulting from the loss of her husband, albeit that the wording of the 1846 Act did not preclude an award for non-pecuniary loss. The pecuniary loss recoverable must

---

[20] Law Com. No. 263 para. 3.46.
[21] *ibid.* at para. 3.16.
[22] "Claims for Wrongful Death" Consultation Paper No. 148 (1997) para. 3.35.
[23] (1852) 18 Q.B. 93.

not, however, derive from a business relationship between the deceased and the claimant. In *Burgess v. Florence Nightingale Hospital for Gentlewomen*[24] the deceased and her husband were professional dancing partners. The husband claimed, *inter alia*, for pecuniary losses he sustained as a consequence of having lost his wife as a dancing partner, but it was held that, for a benefit to quality under the Act, it must be one which arises from the relationship between the parties, and there was no benefit arising in the dancing partnership which could properly be attributed to the relationship of the husband and wife. However, if the deceased provides services to the dependant at less than the market rate, the difference between the rate they are paid and the market rate comprises a benefit arising from the relationship, which is therefore recoverable. Thus, in *Malyon v. Plummer*[25] a husband employed his wife at a high wage for part-time casual work. It was held that the work she did merited a salary of £200 per annum; the amount paid to her in excess of that sum was attributable to their relationship as husband and wife and hence formed part of the lost dependency.

It is not necessary to show that the dependant was actually in receipt of **10–011** pecuniary benefits from the deceased at the time of death, although that will very frequently be the case. Nor is it necessary to show that the deceased was under a legal obligation to support the claimant; as we have seen, the criterion is that of a reasonable expectation of pecuniary benefit as of right or otherwise. Hence the possibility that a child of three might in the future contribute to his parents' support was too speculative, and the claim was therefore unsuccessful,[26] whereas where a sixteen year old girl died when nearing completion of her apprenticeship as a dressmaker, it was held that the claim could succeed.[27] *A fortiori* in cases where financial contributions were already being made by the deceased child, as for example, in *Dolbey v. Goodwin*[28] where a son who lived with his mother contributed £4 a week to her support. This decision also emphasises the importance of taking into account the fact that, if the deceased child is single, they are likely to marry and there will thus be a change of emphasis in their responsibilities. The Court of Appeal therefore reduced by approximately half the award of the trial judge, which it regarded as more appropriate if the case had concerned a husband and wife. A promise of financial support may suffice, as in *Piggot v. Fancy Wood Products Ltd.*[29] The nature

---

[24] [1955] 1 Q.B. 349. See also *Sykes v. North Eastern Railway Co.* (1875) 44 L.J. C.P. 191, but *cf. Oldfield v. Mahoney* (1968) Kemp & Kemp para. 21-006, noted at M3-055 and M3-122. See also *Cox v. Hockenhull, The Times*, June 17, 1999.

[25] [1964] 1 Q.B. 330—see also *Franklin v. South Eastern Railway Co.* (1858) 3 H. & N. 211.

[26] *Barnett v. Cohen* [1924] 2 K.B. 461.

[27] *Taff Vale Railway Co. v. Jenkins* [1913] A.C. 1. See also *Buckland v. Guildford Gas Light and Coke Co.* [1949] 1 K.B. 410; *Kandalla v. British European Airways Corporation* [1981] Q.B. 158.

[28] [1955] 2 All E.R. 166. See also *Franklin v. South Eastern Railway Co.* (1858) 3 H. & N. 211; *Dalton v. South Eastern Railway Co.* (1858) 4 C.B., N.S. 296. Occasional financial assistance may suffice, as in *Hetherington v. North Eastern Railway Co.* (1882) 9 Q.B.D. 160; also a one-off benefit may be reasonable: *Betney v. Rowland and Mallard* [1992] C.L.Y. 1786 (daughter; claim for anticipated contribution of deceased parents to her wedding).

[29] Unreported. January 31, 1958 (*Kemp & Kemp* paras. 21-007 and M5-012).

of the parties' relationship may be significant; thus a wife who had deserted her husband and thereby forfeited any right to maintenance was required to show that there were significant prospects of reconciliation had her husband lived.[30]

(1) Calculating the dependency

10–012   In cases where the claim comprises a specific loss, such as the contribution to wedding expenses in *Betney*,[31] the calculation is a simple one. Where the dependency is a continuing one, the matter is more complex. As with personal injury cases, a multiplier/multiplicand method is employed, the multiplicand being the present annual value of the dependency, the multiplier being the likely duration of the dependency, subject to being discounted to take account of the fact that the dependant is receiving an immediate lump sum rather than periodical sums over a period of years, as would have been the case had the deceased lived. In addition, the contingencies of life will be taken into account in determining the multiplier. Occasionally the facts of a case will give rise to too many uncertainties to enable proper calculation to be made by means of the multiplier/multiplicand method. Thus, in *Stanley v. Saddique*[32] the deceased mother had worked and was likely to work in part-time, casual, poorly paid employment which, it was held, could only be assessed as regards her child's lost dependency by the award of a round figure of £5,000. The same approach was adopted to the award for loss of the mother's services, as she was an unreliable mother who had previously abandoned her three young children by her husband and at the time of her death was living with the claimant's father. A "jury award basis" sum of £10,000 was assessed as proper compensation under this head.

(a) Multiplicand

10–013   The fact that many women are now in employment has implications for the traditional approach which assumes that, in cases where the husband has died, he was the breadwinner and, in cases where the wife dies, that the claim will solely be for the loss of her services in the household. However, these assumptions can provide a helpful starting point, and will of course represent the proper approach in appropriate cases. Where the deceased is a husband and father, his pre-death earnings[33] will comprise the starting point for assessing the multiplicand, to which must be added the value of any other benefits he provided, such as work on the family house.[34] In *Cookson v. Knowles*[35] it was held that the award for loss of dependency should be split into two parts, relating respectively to the pre-

---

[30] *Davies v. Taylor* [1974] A.C. 207.
[31] *Supra* n. 28.
[32] [1992] Q.B. 1.
[33] Net of tax and national insurance, as in personal injury cases; see *supra* para. 9–023.
[34] Se *e.g. Crabtree v. Wilson* [1993] P.I.Q.R. Q. 24 (£1,500 per annum under this head).
[35] [1979] A.C. 556.

trial and post-trial periods. This reflects the fact that interest is awarded on the former period,[36] but not on the latter, and also that where events have occurred between the death and the trial the court can "rely on ascertained facts rather than on mere estimates".[37]

Having ascertained the net salary and other benefits provided by the **10–014** deceased breadwinner, it is necessary to identify and then deduct the proportion which the deceased spent on, or used for the benefit of himself.[38] A convention has developed whereby, if the deceased breadwinner had a wife and children, the multiplicand may be assumed to be 75 per cent of his net earnings; if he left a widow and no children (or for the period of the widow's dependency after the children cease to be dependent) $66\frac{2}{3}$ per cent.[39] However each case must be decided on its own facts, and it is always open to argument that the conventional approach should be departed from; thus, in *Owen v. Martin*[40] Stuart-Smith L.J. regarded it as appropriate especially in cases where a stable pattern had been established in a marriage and most of the net earnings were spent on living expenses.[41] It should also be borne in mind that though, as in the case of personal injuries, inflation is to be ignored, likely increases in the deceased's income that it can be shown would have occurred between the date of death and the trial (for the pre-trial multiplicand) and in the future (*e.g.* promotion or moving to more lucrative employment) must be taken into account in assessing the value of the dependency.[42] In addition account will have to be taken of savings that it can be shown he would have made and which his dependants would have inherited, or, as in *Singapore Bus Services (1978) Ltd v. Lim Soon Yong*[43] the fact that his death ended the payment of contributions he and his employer paid into a savings fund, the dependants being the nominated beneficiaries.[44]

As the conventional percentage apportionment suggests, it is assumed **10–015** that the main portion of the money will be allocated to the widow. This however, as has been pointed out,[45] fails to take account of contingencies such as the early death of the widow, leaving the children potentially undercompensated. It would surely be preferable, rather than assuming, as

---

[36] At half the rate on the special account between date of death and trial.
[37] per Lord Fraser in *Cookson v. Knowles* [1979] A.C. 556 at 575.
[38] Alternatively it may be possible to ascertain and add together the value of the actual benefits received from the deceased by the claimants.
[39] See *Harris v. Empress Motors* [1984] 1 W.L.R. 212 at 216–7. The rationale being that broadly the net income is spent as to one-third for the benefit of each and one third for their joint benefit. No deduction is made for the latter since, as O'Connor L.J. pointed out at p. 217, "one cannot buy or drive half a motor car".
[40] [1992] P.I.Q.R. Q151.
[41] *ibid.* at Q160.
[42] See *e.g. Miller v. British Road Services Ltd* [1967] 1 W.L.R. 443; *Mitchell v. Mulholland (No. 2)* [1972] 1 Q.B. 65 at 78–81.
[43] [1985] 1 W.L.R. 1075. See also *Nance v. British Columbia Electric Railway Co. Ltd* [1951] A.C. 601.
[44] As can be seen from *Taylor v. O'Connor* [1971] A.C. 1115 savings may either be included in the annual dependency figure or a separate sum comprising them may be calculated.
[45] McGregor *op. cit.* at para. 1795. The approach adopted in New Zealand in the Death by Accidents Compensation Act 1952 seems preferable: the court has the power to order part or all of the damages to be held on trusts as a class fund for the benefit of the dependants, and may also vary any order it makes.

appears to be the case,[46] that the widow will use part of her award for the benefit of the children, to calculate in respect of each individual the benefit he/she would have derived from the deceased which, even bearing in mind that the dependency of the children is likely to last for a shorter period than that of their mother, should at least increase their proportion of the multiplicand, as in *Robertson v. Lestrange,*[47] where the three children were awarded a total of 60 per cent of the multiplicand, the mother being awarded the remaining 40 per cent.

10–016   It is clear that, where the wife was working before the husband's death, her earnings after his death must be taken into account. In *Coward v. Comex Houlder Diving*[48] the Court of Appeal held that in such a case the dependency of the widow was two-thirds of the deceased's net earnings less one third of her own net earnings, or it was two-thirds of their joint earnings less her own earnings. In the light of this it would seem to follow that where there are also dependent children, in addition to the working wife, the conventional 75 per cent referred to above will be reduced, the children being dependent on the joint incomes.[49]

10–017   Where the deceased is a wife and/or mother, and in other cases where services rather than money were provided by the deceased, a claim can be made for the loss of those services, usually assessed by reference to the cost of employing a substitute, such as a housekeeper[50] or a nanny.[51] Employing a relative to act as housekeeper, as in *Regan v. Williamson,*[52] is a reasonable alternative to hiring a stranger, especially where, as in that case, the relative knows and is attached to the children. In *Mehmet v. Perry*[53] the husband gave up his job to look after the children. In the particular circumstances of the case (two of the children suffered from a rare blood disorder and needed considerable emotional security and support) it was held to be reasonable to assess the damages by reference to his lost wages since this represented the cost of providing his services as a full-time housekeeper. In addition modest awards were made to the children for the loss of their mother, and the fact that they now had only one parent rather than two to look after them, and to the father for the loss of the care and attention of his wife.

10–018   It is important to bear in mind, as in *Regan,* that a wife and mother is "in constant attendance . . . may well give the children instruction on essential matters to do with their upbringing and, possibly with such things as their homework"[54] and thus the value of her services can not be entirely equated with the cost of a housekeeper less the cost of the wife's maintenance. Thus in *Regan* the cost of the housekeeper's services less the cost of keeping the wife was £12.50 per week. This was raised to £20 a week to reflect the

---

[46] See *Thompson v. Price* [1973] Q.B. 838 at 842–3.
[47] [1985] 1 All E.R. 950.
[48] *Kemp & Kemp,* Vol. 1, para. 21-003/2 and Vol. 3, s. M2-232. See also *Crabtree v. Wilson* [1993] P.I.Q.R. Q24.
[49] McGregor *op. cit.* para. 1770.
[50] See *e.g. Jeffery v. Smith* [1970] R.T.R. 279.
[51] See *e.g. Spittle v. Bunney* [1988] 1 W.L.R. 847.
[52] [1976] 1 W.L.R. 305.
[53] [1977] 2 All E.R. 529.
[54] [1976] 1 W.L.R. 305 at 309 per Watkins J.

value of her services as a good wife and mother, and this figure was further increased to take account of the likelihood that she would have returned to work; *a fortiori* if she was already working at the time of her death.[55] In assessing the claim for loss of a mother's services, it should not be forgotten that children of different ages have different needs, and though the cost of a nanny may be a relevant factor where a child is young, valuation by commercial standards becomes increasingly inappropriate as a child grows older and reaches school age, and the nature of the mother's services changes.[56] Compensation cannot be assessed precisely for such a loss; it is "a jury question".[57]

An issue in several cases where, for various reasons, there has been no **10–019** claim by the father, has been whether the full commercial cost of a notional nanny can appropriately be awarded where in fact a relative has stepped in and taken care of the child or children. Where no wages will in fact ever be paid, it has been described as inappropriate and completely artificial to award the cost of a nanny.[58] Awards have been reduced in such cases by devices such as awarding the net pay, and making no award to cover weekends and holidays, when the notional nanny/housekeeper would not be on duty.[59] There is an interrelation between this issue and the thorny problem of collateral benefits: this is discussed below.[60]

(b) Multiplier

The multiplier is assessed as from the date of the death, the number of **10–020** years from the date of death to the trial being applied to assess the pre-trial losses, the amount remaining being the multiplier for post-trial losses. This approach however proved problematic in the case of *Corbett v. Barking Havering and Brentwood Health Authority*.[61] In that case, where a child claimed for loss of his mother at his birth, the judge applied a multiplier of 12, but the child was $11\frac{1}{2}$ at the date of trial, leaving a period of only six months for future losses. Recognising the absurdity of this, the Court of Appeal held that the multiplier could be adjusted to take account of the facts as they were known to be by the date of the trial and increased the multiplier to 15, which, though displaying a commendable flexibility, remains somewhat harsh on the facts.

The duration of the dependency may, of course, vary from claimant to **10–021** claimant. As an example, in *Cresswell v. Eaton*[62] the mother of three children, aged respectively seven, six and four died in a road accident. Simon

---

[55] See *e.g. Cresswell v. Easton* [1991] 1 W.L.R. 1113: referred to by Simon Brown J. as "the disbursement dependency", as distinct from "the services dependency".

[56] See *Spittle v. Bunney* [1988] 1 W.L.R. 847 at 858 per Croom-Johnson L.J.

[57] See *Corbett v. Barking Havering and Brentwood Health Authority* [1991] 2 Q.B. 408 at 419 per Purchas L.J.

[58] See *e.g. Hayden v. Hayden* [1992] 1 W.L.R. 986 at 998; *Corbett v. Barking Havering and Brentwood Health Authority* [1991] 2 Q.B. 408.

[59] See *Corbett supra* n. 57 at 442–3.

[60] *Infra* paras. 10–030 *et seq.*

[61] [1991] 2 Q.B. 408.

[62] [1991] 1 W.L.R. 1113.

Brown J. held it to be likely that the youngest would do A levels and go to university, whereas the elder two would both qualify at 18. Accordingly he adopted a multiplier of 8 for the eldest, 8.5 for the second and 10.5 for the youngest. In *Robertson v. Lestrange*[63] Webster J. adopted a single multiplier, but split it between the period of dependency of the widow and the children and the period when the widow only would be dependant. As regards that latter period the judge used a different multiplicand, which comprised a smaller percentage of a higher income.

10–022   Quite apart from the fact that the children of the deceased will reach an age at which the dependency ceases,[64] other factors may affect the duration of the dependency. Prior to 1971, the re-marriage prospects of the widow could be taken into account, but this was criticised[65] as being unattractive and inappropriate, and section 4 of the Law Reform (Miscellaneous Provisions Act 1971)[66] provides that in a Fatal Accidents Act case, where damages are being assessed in respect of a widow's claim for the death of her husband her actual re-marriage or prospects of re-marriage are not to be taken into account. It can be seen that the wording of the provision does not preclude assessment of the re-marriage prospects of widowers, co-habitants and unmarried women, nor does it preclude taking into account the actual or prospective re-marriage of a widow in assessing her child's claim under the Act. It is also arguably unsatisfactory that the fact of re-marriage, which does not involve the upsetting cross-examination and visual appraisal by the court which were factors leading to the change in the law, in 1971, is ignored. These matters, among others, led the Law Commission in 1997 to canvas possible reforms,[67] ranging from ignoring actual and prospective (re)marriage of the claimant (or another) in all cases to applying a rebuttable presumption as to the prospect of remarriage based on objective statistical probability. In its 1999 Report[68] the Commission recommended that section 3(3) be repealed, and that the prospect that a person will marry, remarry or enter into financially-supportive cohabitation with a new partner should not be taken into account, unless the person is engaged to be married at the time of the trial. The fact of marriage, and the fact of financially supportive cohabitation should be taken into account wherever relevant. The Commission recognised[69] that "creation of any threshold can have the effect that claimants arrange their affairs in an evasive fashion" and hence marriage (or engagement) might be postponed until after the trial, but the reform of section 3(3) of necessity required a compromise between, on the one hand the need to assess damages as accurately

---

[63] [1985] 1 All E.R. 950.

[64] In *Corbett* (*supra* n. 57) the Court of Appeal held that the judge was wrong to limit the child's dependency to the age of 18 on the basis that his chances of proceeding to tertiary education were evenly balanced: the chance had to be evaluated and the multiplier increased as a consequence; which it was, by one.

[65] See *e.g. Buckley v. John Allen and Ford* [1967] 2 Q.B. 637 at 664–5 per Phillimore J.

[66] Re-enacted in s. 3(3) of the Fatal Accidents Act 1976.

[67] "Claims for Wrongful Death" Consultation Paper No. 148, paras. 3.56–3.68. See also the discussion of collateral benefits *infra* paras. 10–030 *et seq.*

[68] "Claims for Wrongful Death" (1999) Law Com. No. 263 para. 4.53.

[69] *ibid.* at 4.47.

as possible, and, on the other hand, the desire to avoid an assessment of the prospects of marriage.

Another relevant factor is that of the prospects of a divorce between the **10–023** dependant and the deceased. In *Owen v. Martin*[70] the court took into account the potential for divorce in a case where the couple had only been married for 11 months, the widow had previously been divorced on the grounds of her adultery, and after the deceased's death, she committed adultery with his senior partner, whom she subsequently married. In the case of a stable marriage the appropriate multiplier would have been 15; on the facts of the case it was held to be 11. The Law Commission[71] recommends that the prospect of divorce or breakdown in the relationship between the deceased and their spouse should not be taken into account unless the couple were no longer living together at the time of the death, or one of the couple had petitioned for divorce, judicial separation or nullity. Under this proposal *Owen v. Martin* would be decided differently, and focus would rightly be placed on the realities of the relationship rather than the potential problems based on inferences from character.

Where a couple have cohabited outside marriage, as in *Drew v. Abassi*[72] **10–024** there may be a reduction in the multiplier; thus in *Drew*, despite the fact that the couple's relationship had been as settled and lasting as any marriage, a multiplier of 13 was adopted rather than one of 15 which would have been applied had the couple been married. The court, in so deciding, bore in mind that, under section 3(4) of the Fatal Accidents Act, in an action concerning dependency where a couple cohabited rather than being married it is to be taken into account that the dependent had no enforceable right to financial support by the deceased as a result of their living together. The Law Commission[73] has recommended the repeal of section 3(4), regarding the policy issues as akin to those in the divorce issue discussed above, and recommends legislative provision to the effect that the prospect of breakdown in the relationship between the deceased and his or her partner should not be taken into account when assessing damages under the Act.

It will be relevant to consider the dependant's expectation of life. An **10–025** extreme example of this is *Williamson v. Thorneycroft*[74] where the widow died before trial. Although damages were to be assessed as at the date of the husband's death, subsequent events which shed light on the reality of the case, such as the widow's death, could not be ignored, and her damages had to be assessed on the basis that her dependency ended on her death. In a case where the dependant is the parent of the deceased, the dependant's life expectancy will also be relevant, also, presumably, where the dependant's health is not good. Clearly the expectation of life of the deceased will be of significance, and use is increasingly made of statistical tables, in particular today the Ogden Tables. As was noted above,[75] section 10 of the

---

[70] [1992] P.I.Q.R. Q.151.
[71] "Claims for Wrongful Death" (1999) Law Com. No. 263 para. 4.66.
[72] [1995] J.P.I.L. 309.
[73] *supra* n. 68 at para. 4.71.
[74] [1940] 2 K.B. 658.
[75] *supra* para. 9–025. S.10 has not yet been brought into force.

Civil Evidence Act makes provision for the admissibility of the Ogden Tables as evidence to assist in the assessment of damages *inter alia* in fatal accident claims. As has been pointed out by the Law Commission,[76] the use of the Ogden Tables does not preclude the taking into account of the individual characteristics of particular cases.[77] In *Rowley v. London and NW Railway*[78] it was said that it was for the defendant to prove the existence of any facts going to diminish the value of the life, and it may be presumed that if it is alleged that there are facts going to increase the value of the life, it is for the claimant to do so.

10–026   Much of what has been said already in the context of damages for personal injury[79] is applicable to fatal accident cases as regards the discounting of the multiplier to take account of the immediate rather than gradual receipt of the benefits of the dependency and also the contingencies of life. As we have seen,[80] the effect of the decision of the House of Lords in *Wells v. Wells*[81] is that the court should assume investment of the lump sum in index-linked government stock, and an immediate consequence of this has been a significant increase in multipliers, representing the difference between the 4.5 per cent discount which had, pre-*Wells*, traditionally been applied and the 3 per cent which was adopted as a guideline rate, pending the prescribing[82] by the Lord Chancellor, of a rate of return in the exercise of his powers under section 1 of the Damages Act 1996.

(2) Funeral expenses

10–027 Since 1934 it has been established, initially by section 2(3) of the Law Reform (Miscellaneous Provisions) Act 1934 and re-enacted in section 3(5) of the Fatal Accidents Act 1976, that the dependants may recover expenses they incur in respect of the funeral expenses of the deceased. The caselaw suggests that the expenses, in order to be recoverable, must be reasonable. The cost of a marble memorial over the deceased's grave was held not be reasonable in *Stanton v. Youlden*,[83] the court allowing only the cost of a stone over the grave for a person in the deceased's position; the cost of embalming was allowed in *Hart v. Griffiths-Jones*,[84] and the expenses of a widow's brother-in-law and his wife, incurred in flying to France (where she and her husband had been on holiday when he was killed) to assist her in returning to England and making arrangement for her husband's body

---

[76] (1994) Law Com. No. 224 para. 2.15.

[77] See *e.g. Hall v. Wilson* [1939] 4 All E.R. 85, where the deceased died shortly before the outbreak of World War 2. It was held that the increased risk of death, had he lived on, must be taken into account. See also however, *Bishop v. Cunard White Star Co. Ltd* [1950] P. 240.

[78] (1873) L.R. 8 Ex. 221.

[79] *supra* Ch. 9.

[80] *supra* paras. 9–037 *et seq.*

[81] [1999] 1 A.C. 345.

[82] As yet still awaited.

[83] [1960] 1 W.L.R. 543.

[84] [1948] 2 All E.R. 729 (a case under the Law Reform (Miscellaneous Provisions) Act 1934 where the claim is brought on behalf of the estate).

to be brought back to England, were held to be recoverable in *Schneider v. Eisovitch*.[85] It should further be noted that even if, as in *Burns v. Edman*,[86] the claim for the dependency fails, or there is no loss of dependency, the reasonable funeral expenses are still recoverable.[87]

(3) Non-pecuniary losses

As we have seen, it was established as long ago as 1852[88] that the claim **10–028** under the Fatal Accidents Act is restricted to recovery of pecuniary losses only, subject only to the introduction in 1982[89] of a statutory claim for damages for bereavement in a limited class of cases. Those entitled to claim are: the wife or husband of the deceased and, where the deceased was a minor who was never married, his parents, if he was legitimate, and his mother, if he was illegitimate. The specified amount recoverable was initially £3,500 but was raised to £7,500 in respect of deaths occurring on or after April 1, 1991.[90] The range of claimants is, as can be seen, very much narrower than that for claimants for loss of dependency under section 1 of the Act. In its 1999 Report "Claims for Wrongful Death"[91] the Law Commission recommended a significant extension of the statutory list. It recommended that the following be entitled to recover bereavement damages: a spouse of the deceased; a parent (including adoptive parents) of the deceased; a child (including adoptive children) of the deceased; a brother or sister (including adoptive siblings) of the deceased; a person engaged to be married to the deceased; a person who, although not married to the deceased, had lived with them as husband and wife, or, if of the same gender, in an equivalent relationship, for not less than two years immediately prior to the accident. The Commission also recommended that, as at present, proof of mental distress should not be required to be proved. The appropriate level of the bereavement award should now be £10,000, linked to the Retail Prices Index; the Lord Chancellor's power to vary the level of damages should thus be repealed. The Commission went on to recommend that the maximum liability of a defendant to pay bereavement damages should be £30,000 (also to be linked to the Retail Prices Index); if there were more than three people with a valid claim, the £30,000 should be apportioned equally amongst them, subject to any reduction for contributory negligence of the bereaved claimant. Under the present law, an award of bereavement damages is not taken into account when assessing damages for psychiatric illness resulting from the death of another, and vice versa. The Law Commission recommends no change to this, nor to the current

---

[85] [1960] 2 Q.B. 430. It was a relevant factor that the widow had agreed to pay their expenses.
[86] [1970] 2 Q.B. 541 *supra* para. 10–003.
[87] Though they may as in *Burns* (and potentially in any case) be subject to a reduction to take account of any contributory negligence.
[88] In *Blake v. Midland Railway Co.* (1852) 18 Q.B. 93.
[89] S. 1A of the Fatal Accidents Act 1976, as inserted by s. 3(1) of the Administration of Justice Act 1982.
[90] Law Reform (Miscellaneous Provisions) Act 1934, s. 1(1A).
[91] Law Com. 263 para. 6.31.

position that a claim for bereavement damages does not survive for the benefit of the bereaved's estate.[92]

10–029   The Law Commission's recommendations go a long way towards meeting the concerns that have periodically been voiced, in particular about the level of bereavement damages and also the range of claimants. The Commission also recommends[93] that the explanatory notes to their replacement clause on bereavement damages should clarify that the function of bereavement damages is to compensate, in so far as a standardised sum of money can, for grief, sorrow and the loss of the non-pecuniary benefits of the deceased's care, guidance and society. Such clarification is helpful, in particular as it would serve to preclude the idea that there is a punitive element to the award, or any reflection of the value of the life of the deceased; in that regard, as the Law Commission note,[94] "no sum of money will be regarded as enough."

(4) Collateral benefits

10–030   As we have seen,[95] the law concerning collateral benefits in personal injury cases is complex and confusing. At first sight, the position as regards fatal accidents is considerably simpler. Thus, section 4 of the Fatal Accidents Act 1976[96] provides as follows:

> "In assessing damages in respect of a person's death in an action under this Act, benefits, which have accrued or will or may accrue to any person from his estate or otherwise as a result of his death shall be disregarded."

This represents a significant shift from the position at common law, whereby, in the absence of statutory provision to the contrary, pecuniary benefits accruing to a dependant in consequence of the death were required to be taken into account.[97] Increasingly exceptions to this developed, initially in the form of private Acts of Parliament arranged by various insurance companies to enable benefits received under their policies not to be taken into account,[98] which led to a demand, subsequently met in the Fatal Accidents (Damages) Act 1908, to extend to all insurance moneys the same protection. Later legislation made non-deductible certain pensions, in the Widows', Orphans' and Old Age Contributory Pensions Act 1929 section 22, and national insurance benefits were rendered non-deductible by the Law Reform (Personal Injuries) Act 1948.

---

[92] At para. 6.62 *ibid.* the Commission recommend that this be made clear in legislation, though it is thought to be sufficiently clear that s. 5 of the Act, requiring "any damages" awarded under the Act to be reduced proportionately to any contributory negligence, entails a reduction for contributory negligence of the deceased.

[93] Law Reform (Miscellaneous Provisions) Act 1934, s. 1(1A).

[94] "Claims for Wrongful Death" Consultation Paper No. 148 (1997).

[95] *supra* paras. 9–045 *et seq.*

[96] As amended by s. 3(1) Administration of Justice Act 1982.

[97] See *Davies v. Powell Duffryn Associated Collieries Ltd* [1942] A.C. 601 at 609.

[98] See *e.g.* General Accident, Fire and Life Assurance Corporation Act 1907, s. 13; Law Commission Consultation Paper No. 148 (1997) para. 2.48.

Though section 4 of the Fatal Accidents Act 1976 gives effect to a recom- **10–031** mendation of the Pearson Commission[99] that benefit derived from the deceased's estate should be disregarded, its wording is so broad as to permit on the face of it, the disregarding of all benefits, which accrue as a result of the death. The breadth of this can be seen from the decision of the Court of Appeal in *Stanley v. Saddique*[1] where a child, whose deceased mother had been unreliable, benefited from the excellent motherly services of his stepmother, which led to him receiving better care than he would have received from his mother. It was held that the word "benefit" in section 4 extended to the benefit now being enjoyed by the claimant, and hence fell to be disregarded in assessing his loss of dependency.

By contrast, in *Hayden v. Hayden*[2] a child whose mother died in a motor **10–032** accident caused by her father, was cared for by her father, who gave up work in order to do so. By a majority the Court of Appeal held that the services provided by the father in replacement of the mother's lost services were not a "benefit" within the ambit of section 4, and hence it was appropriate to take account of the father's services in assessing the loss of dependency. Sir David Croom-Johnson, who sat in both cases, distinguished *Stanley* on the basis that the father in *Hayden* was doing no more than discharging his parental duties, and the question of what is a "benefit" must be a question of fact. Parker L.J. was of the view that no loss had been suffered, since essentially the same services continued to be provided albeit now by the father. McGowan L.J., who dissented, saw the case as falling within the principle elucidated in *Stanley*. He also considered that the possible point of distinction from *Stanley*, that it was the defendant who was providing the services in question, could not affect the position, albeit that the defendant could be said to have lost three times over; he had lost earnings, provided the services and paid damages in respect of the lost services. Such was the effect of *Stanley*.

It is difficult to avoid the conclusion, as expressed by the Law Commis- **10–033** sion,[3] that the majority in *Hayden* were looking for a way to avoid the father's case falling within the ambit of section 4. The two decisions appear to be inconsistent, the problem lying in the very broad wording of the section, which was probably not intended. If it has been so intended, then, as Burrows points out,[4] there would have been no need for section 3 (3) of the Fatal Accidents Act,[5] since it seems clear that an effect of section 4 of the Fatal Accidents Act has been to require the remarriage prospects of a widower to be disregarded in assessing the award of damages to him for the loss of his wife[5] and this must apply equally to the situation of the

---

[99] Cmnd. 7054-1 (1978), paras. 537–539.
[1] [1992] Q.B. 1.
[2] [1992] 1 W.L.R. 986.
[3] Law Com. No. 148 [1997] para. 2.56. In *Hunt v. Severs* [1993] Q.B. 815 at 829 the Court of Appeal found it hard to find a clear ratio in *Hayden*.
[4] *op. cit.* p. 218. See also n. 7 *op. cit.*, referring to the parliamentary background.
[5] *i.e.* the provision requiring the actual remarriage and prospects of remarriage of a widow not to be taken into account. S. 3(3) re-enacts s. 4 of the Law Reform (Miscellaneous Provisions) Act 1971.
[6] In *Topp v. London Country Bus South West Ltd* [1992] P.I.Q.R. P206 the point was not argued. May J. considered he was bound by *Stanley v. Saddique* on this issue.

widow. In *Stanley* Purchas L.J. confronted this argument with the explanation that section 3(3) was left in as being a particularly significant question of policy, but by section 4 Parliament intended to further the departure from ordinary common law assessment of damages for personal injuries. It must be doubted whether this particular approach informed the Court of Appeal in *Hayden* in deciding that appeal as it did, and it is suggested that statutory reform of section 4 is necessary, given the judicial confusion it appears (not surprisingly) to have engendered. The matter was reconsidered by the Divisional Court in *R. v. Criminal Injuries Compensation Board, ex p. K.*[7] where the claimants' mother had been murdered by their father. Subsequently they received at least equivalent care from an uncle and aunt. It was held, following *Stanley v. Saddique*, that the benefit of the uncle and aunt's services fell to be disregarded. Brooke L.J. drew a distinction between the ascertainment of the claimant's loss and the assessment of damages, referring to the analysis by Oliver L.J. in *Auty v. National Coal Board.*[8] Rougier J. emphasised the two points of distinction between *Stanley* and *Hayden*; in *Hayden* the defendant provided the benefits, and, since those benefits were provided by the father, who had a duty to care for the child, they could not be regarded as a benefit arising as a result of the death. This decision provides some clarification, and assists in marginalising *Hayden*, but by no means resolves all the difficulties of how section 4 is to be interpreted. Possible reforms are canvassed below.[9]

10–034   A further potentially problematic issue is that of whether the claimant has suffered a loss at all, which, as we have seen, was the approach of Parker L.J. in *Hayden*. In *Wood v. Bentall Simplex Ltd*[10] Staughton L.J. pointed out[11] that the initial question, prior to any consideration of section 4, was what loss the dependants had suffered; if they had inherited the source of the income upon which they were dependant, they had not lost it. Common sense dictates this conclusion, albeit that, as Staughton L.J. went on to note[12] it will be necessary to establish what parts of the income derived from inherited capital (no loss) and what parts from labour (loss). In this context it is difficult to see how (*pace* Parker L.J. in *Hayden*) a father can entirely replace the services of a deceased mother.[13]

10–035   An aspect of the issue arose for consideration in *Auty v. National Coal Board*[14] where a widow claimed for loss of dependency on the basis that she had lost the chance of obtaining the post-retirement widow's pension to which she would have been entitled if her husband had survived the accident which caused his death and subsequently died in retirement. She was however in receipt of a widow's pension to which she was entitled under his pension scheme. Waller L.J., not surprisingly, concluded that: "she cannot claim for loss of an opportunity to obtain a widow's pension

---

[7] [1999] 2 W.L.R. 948.
[8] [1985] 1 W.L.R. 784. See *infra* para. 10–035.
[9] *infra* paras. 10–039 *et seq.*
[10] [1992] P.I.Q.R. P332. See also *Pym v. Great Northern Railway* (1863) 4 B. & S. 396.
[11] [1992] P.I.Q.R. P332 at P349.
[12] *ibid.*
[13] See *Kemp* (1993) 109 L.Q.R. 173 at 175.
[14] [1985] 1 W.L.R. 784.

at a later date when she has not lost the opportunity of a widow's pension since she is already in receipt of a widows pension."[15] No doubt had she received less under the "death after retirement" pension than she would have received under the "death in service" pension, she would have been able to claim the difference.[16]

The situation was somewhat different in *Pidduck v. Eastern Scottish* 10–036 *Omnibuses Ltd*[17] where a widow became entitled on her husband's death to a lump sum and payment of certain allowances linked to his pension if (as transpired) he died within five years of retiring. The defendant argued that the amounts so received fell to be deducted from her claim for loss of dependency, claiming that she had suffered no loss since she had been dependant, through her husband, on his pension before her death, and was also dependant on his pension after his death. The Court of Appeal disagreed, holding that the benefit the widow received prior to her husband's death was the financial support she received from him, and it was merely incidental that the source of his income was his pension. She had consequently suffered a loss of dependency, and the widow's allowance she received was a benefit within section 4 and this was to be disregarded.

A further potential difficulty of section 4's ambit was neatly side-stepped 10–037 by the House of Lords in *Jameson v. Central Electricity Generating Board*.[18] The deceased contracted malignant mesothelioma in the course of his employment while working at power stations owned and operated by the defendant. He settled a claim (which included a sum in respect of loss of future earnings) against the employer prior to his death in "full and final settlement and satisfaction" of his claim. He died before the money was paid over, and it therefore fell into his estate and was inherited by his widow. A loss of dependency claim was brought on her behalf against the defendant, who joined the employer as third party. The judge and the Court of Appeal held that the claim against the defendant for loss of dependency could proceed, as could proceedings by the defendant against the employer for contribution. The effect of this was that the dependants could recover compensation from the defendant from which, as a consequence of section 4, no deduction would be made in respect of the damages inherited from the deceased, thus entailing a significant element of double compensation. The House of Lords however held that a claimant can recover no more than his loss, and, once the agreed sum had been paid, the claimant's claim against the defendant was satisfied, and, if the claim was for all of the loss for which that defendant, as a concurrent tortfeasor, was liable to him, satisfaction of that claim against him had the effect of extinguishing the claim against the other concurrent tortfeasor. On the facts, as the deceased had accepted the sum in full and final settlement, the claim against the other tortfeasor was extinguished. Hence there could be no claim under the Fatal Accidents Act as the deceased, if death had not ensued, would have had no claim. Lord Hope[19] noted that it seemed unlikely that when section

---

[15] [1985] 1 W.L.R. 784 at 799.
[16] *cf.* however Oliver L.J. *ibid.* at 805.
[17] [1990] 1 W.L.R. 993.
[18] [1999] 1 All E.R. 193.
[19] *ibid.* at 201.

4 was enacted Parliament contemplated that a person could become entitled to double recovery in such circumstance, but, as we have seen, judging from the cases under the section it has proved very difficult to know what Parliament intended and, had the case not proved to be resolvable in the way it ultimately was, it would be perfectly open to a court to interpret section 4 as permitting such double recovery.

10–038   A further example of the potential difficulties engendered by section 4 is the decision in *Malone v. Rowan*,[20] where a widow claimed for the support she would have received from her husband had he lived, given her intention to give up work in order to start a family. Her cause of action accrued before the current section 4 was introduced by the Administration of Justice Act 1982, and it was held that no loss had been suffered, since she would in fact be able to continue to go to work. In its report, "Claims for Wrongful Death"[21] the Law Commission thought it strongly arguable that section 4 would now result in the widow's earning capacity being disregarded. If this view is correct, it would again produce a result which, it is suggested, is unlikely to accord with what was intended by Parliament.

10–039   In the Report the Law Commission recommended the repeal of section 4 and its replacement by a statutory listing of benefits to be ignored, arguing that the law on collateral benefits in fatal accident cases should be as consistent as possible with the common law on collateral benefits in personal injury cases. In its Report, "Damages for Personal Injury: Medical, Nursing and Other Expenses; Collateral Benefits"[22] the Commission concluded that the law in personal injury cases should be left unchanged, and hence the only reforms needed in fatal accident cases were the removal of problems caused by the overinclusiveness of section 4 as currently drafted and the creation of consistency with personal injury cases. The Commission concluded[23] that this could be effected by listing charity, insurance, survivors' pensions and inheritance as non-deductible, except that deduction of the listed benefits should be permitted where not doing so would lead to blatant double recovery, *e.g.* where the deceased supported his dependants from an asset, or income produced by an asset, which is inherited by the dependants.[24] In addition the Law Commission was of the view that there should be recoupment of social security benefits in fatal accident claims, in line with the position in personal injury cases.[25] Clearly in accordance with the Social Security (Recovery of Benefits) Act 1997[26] the benefits[27] should not be set off against the bereavement damages. Social Security benefits would not fall within the ambit of the proposed new section 4; their treatment would, it is suggested[28] fall to be determined in accordance

---

[20] [1984] 3 All E.R. 402.
[21] (1999) Law Com. No. 263 para. 2.51.
[22] (1999) Law Com. No. 262. See *supra* paras. 9–066 *et seq.*
[23] (l1999) Law Com. No. 263, para. 5.39.
[24] *ibid.* para. 5.43. See *Wood v. Bentall Simplex Ltd* [1992] P.I.Q.R. P332, discussed *supra* para. 10–034.
[25] See Law Com. No. 263, para. 5.60 on the confusion that currently exists.
[26] For discussion see *supra* paras. 9–058 *et seq.*
[27] *i.e.* the widow's payment, the widowed mother's allowance, the widow's pension, plus income support and family credit. See Welfare Reform and Pensions Act 1999.
[28] (1999) Law Com. No. 263, para. 5.46 n. 78.

with section 3(1) of the Fatal Accidents Act which, as in *Davies v. Powell Duffryn Associated Collieries Ltd*,[29] has been interpreted as requiring benefits to be deducted against losses on a like for like basis.

A further reform issue arising for consideration concerns the provision **10–040** of gratuitous services, as in *Stanley v. Saddique*[30] and *Hayden v. Hayden*,[31] revisited recently in *R. v. Criminal Injuries Compensation Board, ex p. K*.[32] In *Hunt v. Severs*[33] the House of Lords held that, in a case where gratuitous services are provided, the relevant loss is that of the provider, and the damages which the claimant recovers are held on trust for them. In its Report, "Damages for Personal Injury: Medical, Nursing and Other Expenses; Collateral Benefits"[34] the Law Commission recommends that, instead of a trust being imposed on damages for the gratuitous provision of services, the claimant should be under a personal legal obligation to account for those damages to the provider of the service, but that the legal obligation should exist only as regards past gratuitous services. This restriction is explained on the basis that an equivalent obligation as regards future gratuitous services might run into difficulties where events did not turn out as predicted at trial. As regards fatal accident claims, the Commission on the same basis recommends[35] legislation to provide that damages may be awarded under the Fatal Accidents Act in respect of services gratuitously provided to the dependant, who is to be under a legal obligation to account for damages awarded for past services to a relative or friend who in the past has provided the gratuitous services, but imposing no legal duty on the dependant to pay over the damages awarded in respect of future gratuitous services. In addition, the Law Commission recommends reversing the aspect of *Hunt v. Severs* whereby a claimant cannot recover damages in respect of care provided by the defendant, since a consequence of *Hunt* is that claimants and their carers are encouraged to enter into contracts for the provision of care (which agreements risk being regarded as shams), alternatively claimants hire professionals, thereby needlessly increasing the quantum and discouraging the provision of care by the person or persons often best placed to provide it.[36]

A theme that runs through these proposals is the desirability of promot- **10–041** ing consistency between the rules on collateral benefits in personal injury and in fatal accident cases. There seems to be no logical reason why there should be such radical differences as currently exist between the two, and the views of the Law Commission merit endorsement. In addition the proposals for repealing section 4 and redrafting it with greater precision will facilitate the process of harmonisation.

An unconnected but nevertheless important practical point concerning **10–042** fatal accident claims is contained in section 3 of the Damages Act 1996

---

[29] [1942] A.C. 601. See *supra* para. 10–030.
[30] [1992] Q.B. 1.
[31] [1992] 1 W.L.R. 986.
[32] [1999] 2 W.L.R. 948. See *supra* para. 10–033.
[33] [1994] 2 A.C. 350. See *supra* paras. 9–015 *et seq. Stanley* and *Hayden* both antedate *Hunt*, and *Hunt* was not discussed in *K*.
[34] (1999) Law Com. No. 262. For discussion of this report see *supra* para. 9–016.
[35] (1999) Law Com. No. 263, para. 5.53.
[36] *ibid*. para. 5.54.

which provides that provisional damages awarded to the deceased are to be deducted from an award made under the Fatal Accidents Act.

(5) Claims brought on behalf of the deceased's estate

10–043   At the beginning of this chapter, mention was made of the survival after his death of the right of an injured person to claim, effectively abrogating the old *actio personalis moritur cum persona* rule. Section 1(1) of the Law Reform (Miscellaneous Provisions) Act 1934 provides as follows:

> "subject to the provisions of this section, on the death of any person after the commencement of this Act all causes of action subsisting against or vested in him shall survive against, or, as the case may be, for the benefit of, his estate."

10–044   Thus, on the face of it, the estate may claim for the losses for which the deceased, but for his death, would have been able to claim. Thus pecuniary losses such as lost earnings and medical expenses incurred prior to the death will be recoverable, as will non-pecuniary losses, assuming there was a period between the accident and the death during which there was a loss of amenities and pain and suffering were incurred. It should be recalled that the effect of *Baker v. Bolton*[37] is that life is not an amenity for the loss of which compensation will be awarded. In *Hicks v. Chief Constable of the South Yorkshire Police*[38] where three young spectators were crushed to death at the Hillsborough stadium disaster, the court made no award for pain and suffering incurred prior to their deaths, on the basis that where unconsciousness and death occurred so soon after the injury which caused death, they were in reality part of the death itself and hence no damages were recoverable. In cases where there was a clearly-established period of pain and suffering prior to the death awards have been made: £150 in *Robertson v. Lestrange*[39] for four days pain and suffering; £250 in *Roughead v. Railway Executive*[40] for one day of terrible suffering. Again, awards for loss of amenity have been made; these, of course, on the basis of the principles discussed above,[41] may be awarded even if the claimant is unconscious, but in such a case no award may be made for pain and suffering. Thus, in *Murray v. Shuter*[42] a claimant who was in a coma for over four years was awarded £11,000, and in *Andrews v. Freeborough*[43] a child who was unconscious for a year was awarded £2,000. It is clear that there can be no claim for prospective pain and suffering (which will of course now not be experienced), nor for loss of prospective amenities of life.

---

[37] (1808) 1 Camp. 493.
[38] [1992] 1 All E.R. 690. See also *Bishop v. Cunard White Star* [1950] P. 240.
[39] [1985] 1 All E.R. 950.
[40] (1949) 65 T.L.R. 435.
[41] *supra* paras. 9–073 *et seq.*
[42] [1976] Q.B. 972.
[43] [1967] 1 Q.B. 1. See also *Gray v. Mid Herts Hospital Management Committee* [1974] C.L.Y. 2618 (£5,000 for child unaware of his surroundings during a period of nearly three years).

As regards future pecuniary losses,[44] the rule in *Oliver v. Ashman*[45] effec- **10–045** tively precluded recovery for a number of years, since it based damages for loss of future earnings on the post-accident life expectancy. This decision was, as we have seen, overruled by the House of Lords in *Pickett v. British Rail Engineering*,[46] thereby allowing recovery on the basis of the pre-accident life expectancy. An unforeseen consequence of this, as recognised subsequently by the House of Lords in *Gammell v. Wilson*[47] was that the defendant could be liable both to the dependants in a claim for loss of dependency, and also to the estate for loss of the deceased's future earnings, hence potentially involving a significant element of double recovery. Though that would not have caused problems where the dependants shared in the estate, as what was received by the estate in such a case would be deducted from the dependants' claims,[48] where the dependant and the estate did not overlap there would be at least an element of double liability. The matter was resolved by section 4 of the Administration of Justice Act 1982 (substituting a new section 1(2)(a) in the Law Reform (Miscellaneous Provisions) Act 1934), providing that in a claim under that Act there shall be no recovery of damages for loss of income in respect of any period after the death of the deceased. Hence, as regards the loss of prospective earnings the only claim that can be made in that respect is by the dependants, to the extent of their dependency on the deceased to provide for them out of that income.

As a final point, it should be noted that what was said about structured settlements in Chapter 9[49] applies, *mutatis mutandis*, to fatal accidents.

---

[44] Prospective expenses are not recoverable. However, s. 1(2)9c) of the 1934 Act allows recovery of funeral expenses.
[45] [1962] 2 Q.B. 210. See *supra* para. 9–033.
[46] See [1980] A.C. 136 *supra* para. 9–033.
[47] [1982] A.C. 27.
[48] *Davies v. Powell Duffryn Associated Collieries Ltd* [1942] A.C. 601.
[49] See *supra* paras. 9–089 *et seq.*

CHAPTER 11

THE FUTURE OF DAMAGES IN TORT

The rules and regulations determining damages in tort have remained **11–001** almost static over the last hundred years or so, impervious to developments in other jurisdictions, to the increasing relevance of international and European law, and to overwhelming changes in the structure of society, particularly the changing role of women in the workforce. There have been occasional attempts to bring the law into the twentieth century, such as the amendments brought about by the Administration of Justice Act 1982,[1] but these attempts have done no more than tinker with detail. Opportunities to take a step back and consider the whole picture of remedies for damage tortiously caused have been largely wasted.[2] Much of the work done by the Law Commission and consequent recommendations for change have been ignored.[3]

As the new century begins all this is beginning to change. Damages law **11–002** is being invaded from without and from within. The assault from without has been led by Europe; partly by the enforced recognition of European law and partly by an increased awareness of and sensitivity to the way things are done in other individual European states. Once English law is forced to accommodate European approaches to damages awards, it will be a short step to introducing consideration of developments in other non-European jurisdictions, particularly American and commonwealth law. At this point there will be no option but to accept the challenge of reassessing the objectives and the methodologies of the whole of damages law.

From within the assault has been many-pronged. Lord Woolf's changes **11–003** to the procedural aspects of damages claims[4] will have implications way beyond procedure. Much of the Woolf Report has already been implemented, with both legislation[5] and new procedural rules[6] appearing with remarkable speed after the final report. A wide range of recent legislation will change the face of damages awards and calculation of awards.[7] The

---

[1] *e.g.* by amending the definition of "dependant" for the purposes of the Fatal Accident Act 1976.

[2] The Pearson Commission on Civil Liability and Compensation for Personal Injury Cmnd. 7054, 1978, chose not to examine the appropriateness of no-fault compensation for England and Wales, despite developments which had occurred in New Zealand, Canada and some American states.

[3] *e.g.* the recommendations made by the Commission in *Liability for Psychiatric Illness* (No. 249, 1998).

[4] *Access to Civil Justice* (1996).

[5] Civil Procedure Act 1997, Access to Justice Act 1999.

[6] Civil Procedure Rules 1998.

[7] *e.g.* the Data Protection Act 1998, and the Road Traffic (NHS Charges) Act 1999.

legal profession, frustrated with limitations of conventional damages law, has developed legal practices which have resulted in substantial changes to the way tort damages operate, and has forced formal legal recognition of those practices.[8] The judiciary has also worked from within to change the way in which damages are calculated.[9] Recent changes to funding of litigation, in particular conditional fees and group litigation, will have far reaching implications for tort damages, and professional initiatives such as Bar-Direct, designed to enable clients direct access to counsel without going through a solicitor, and increased rights of audience, will all spill over into the arena of damages. Individual challenges to law and practice are also escalating, eroding traditional practice exclusivity and questioning the profile of the judiciary which makes decisions on issues of damages.[10]

11–004   Although all of these assaults on the law have resulted in change, there has been no consistency in objective or approach to change. Lord Woolf's brief was to reduce the cost of litigation. The effect of the House of Lords in *Wells* was to increase awards to litigants claiming damages for personal injury. The Road Traffic (NHS Charges) Act 1999 will enable an NHS hospital or trust to recover the expenses of treating a road accident victim but will result in substantially increased awards. Structured settlements challenge the "once and for all" rule of damages and may make it possible for awards to be decreased if a "bottom up" approach to awards is developed.

11–005   This chapter will examine some of the more recent developments in the law on damages, and consider the future "whole picture" of tortious damages in England and Wales.

The Human Rights Act 1998

11–006   This Act will do more than introduce the European Convention of Human Rights into domestic law. It will also bring with it the "jurisprudence of the Convention".[11] English law has over time developed its own approach to the interpretation of law and to the authority of previous decisions. Section 2 of the Human Rights Act however, requires that any court or tribunal considering an issue of Convention rights must take into account any "judgment, decision, declaration or advisory opinion of the European Court of Human Rights".[12] Section 3 of the Act requires that domestic legislation be interpreted in a way compatible with the Convention rights.

---

[8] *e.g.* the development of the practice of structured settlements, formally recognised in the Damages Act 1996.

[9] See the judicial recognition of Index Linked Government Securities by the House of Lords in *Wells v. Wells* [1998] 3 All E.R. 481 which resulted in changes to multipliers and to interest awards.

[10] See *e.g.* the claim by Rebecca Edmunds, a pupil barrister at 23 Essex Street chambers, to establish whether the national minimum wage applied to pupillage; see *Edmunds v. Lawson* (2000) I.R.L.R. 18 and the successful appeal by chambers, *The Times*, March 16, 2000.

[11] G. Hoon (Parliamentary Secretary, Lord Chancellor's Department) H.C. Deb. Vol. 313, col. 402 (June 3, 1998), quoted in Leigh and Lustgarten, "Making Rights Real: The Courts, Remedies and the Human Rights Act" (1999) 58(3) C.L.J. 509.

[12] s. 2(1)(a) of the Human Rights Act 1998.

These sections apply to all courts, not just to superior courts. It may be **11–007** that an inferior court considering a case after the Act has come into force will be constrained to decide the issue in accordance with these interpretative provisions, despite domestic precedent which decides otherwise. As has been pointed out, "Freedom for a lower court to depart from the decisions of a higher one in such circumstances has far reaching implications for the doctrine of precedent . . .".[13] Not only will decisions of the European Court of Human Rights need to be taken account of in this way, but also Convention decisions in the other Convention states (over 40 of them) will be relevant to any domestic decision on a rights issue. Thus the domestic law of other European countries will seep into English common law resulting in a process of change which will be unstoppable.

It is not only courts and tribunals which are subject to these provisions. **11–008** Section 6 of the Act makes clear that public authorities must not act in any way incompatible with Convention rights. Section 6(3)(a) includes in the definition of public authority "a court or tribunal". The effect of this is unclear but at the minimum, in the context of an action in tort, any court exercising a discretion will be required to do so in accordance with Convention rights.[14] The Act also contemplates the possibility of an award of damages where a public authority fails to comply with the Act, and provides that in such a case a court "may grant such relief or remedy, or make such order, within its powers as it considers just and appropriate".[15] The award of damages is however subject to qualification: the court must consider the appropriateness of remedies other than damages, and the court must take account of the consequences of an award of damages. The court must be satisfied that the award is necessary to afford satisfaction to the claimant. The court must also take into account the principles of damages awards applied by the European Court of Human Rights, suggesting again that English rules of precedent might not always be applied.

The Human Rights Act will influence both when damages will be **11–009** awarded in tort, and how much those damages will be. Pre-Human Rights Act cases can give us some indication of how this will happen. In *A. v. United Kingdom*[16] a boy who had been caned by his stepfather complained to the European Court of Human Rights when a domestic court failed to convict the stepfather of assault. The boy argued that he was entitled to State protection against abuse. The European Court held that the United Kingdom had failed adequately to protect the claimant, violating article 3 of the Convention, and awarded damages of £10,000 against the United Kingdom.[17] In *McCann v. United Kingdom*[18] the European court found that the shooting of three IRA members by soldiers in Gibraltar violated Article 2 of the Convention in that more force was used than was absolutely

---

[13] See Leigh and Lustgarten, "Making Rights Real: The Courts, Remedies and the Human Rights Act" (1999) 58(3) C.L.J. 509, at 511.
[14] For further discussion of this see Leigh and Lustgarten, *op. cit.*; see also Markesinis (1999) 115 L.Q.R. 47.
[15] s. 8(1).
[16] [1998] F.L.R. 959.
[17] See also *Tyrer v. UK* (1978) 2 E.H.R.R. 1.
[18] (1995) 21 E.H.R.R. 97.

necessary for the achievement of a valid purpose.[19] The court chose only to award costs and expenses and not compensation on the facts but established a right to compensation.

11–010   In *Osman v. United Kingdom*[20] the family of a schoolboy murdered by a stalker complained because the police had known of the risk but taken no steps to protect the boy. The family had tried to sue for damages in domestic law but the Court of Appeal denied a duty of care. On the facts this case failed before the European Court, but the Court made clear that where it is part of the duty of a public authority to protect right to life, if the authority knew or ought have known of a real and immediate risk to the life of an individual from an act of a third party, then the authority would violate the Convention if it failed to do all that could reasonably be expected to provide protection. Such failure might give rise to an award of damages.

11–011   There are many other such cases with respect to the United Kingdom and other Member States. What they illustrate is that is that the Human Rights Act will serve to provide actionable duties and recognition of damage in English law where none previously existed. This will be the case especially in the context of rights to privacy and family life,[21] freedom of expression[22] freedom of assembly and association[23] and discrimination[24] on grounds other than race or sex (which are in theory at least already protected by domestic law).

11–012   More particularly, English courts will be called upon to recognise such duties as a duty on public authorities responsible for public health to take steps to provide protection against life-threatening illness and injury. Article 2[25] may be read as creating a positive duty with respect to the protection of life, requiring the provision of services and facilities for that purpose.[26] Such a duty will have enormous implications for the determination and allocation of health care resources, and claimants in this jurisdiction who have previously had to resort, mostly unsuccessfully, to public law[27] in an attempt to force a health authority's hand in the provision of treatment, may now have a right to damages where such treatment is not provided, even where the resulting damage is distress rather than physical injury. Failure to provide proper medical treatment may also potentially breach Article 3[28] of the Convention, and provide an alternative to the traditional negligence action for inappropriate or substandard medical

---

[19] See para. 2 of each of Arts. 8–11 of the Convention.

[20] (1998) 5 B.H.R.C. 293. Though seee the criticisms of the reasoning in *Osman* by Lord Browne-Wilkinson in *Bassett v. Lafield* L.B.C. [1999] 3 All E.R. 193, at 198e.

[21] Art. 8.

[22] Art. 10.

[23] Art. 11.

[24] Art. 14.

[25] Protecting right to life.

[26] See McBride, "Protecting life: a positive obligation to help" (1999) 24 E.L. Rev. Human Rights Survey 43.

[27] *e.g. R. v. Central Birmingham HA, ex p. Walker* (1992) 3 B.M.L.R. 32.

[28] Prohibition of torture or inhuman or degrading treatment.

treatment.[29] Discrimination in the provision of medical treatment may also give rise to liability under Article 14.[30]

There may now be a duty to warn of risks, or to provide information **11–013** necessary to save life[31] which will impact on the law of negligence, especially in the context of medical information.[32] Persons detained for reasons of mental illness may be accorded new rights to challenge, and claim damages for, detention under Article 5,[33] and given the way in which detention under the Mental Health Act 1983 has been practised in this jurisdiction[34] this may result in a complete rethink of the law on detention of mental health patients. Duties of confidentiality, particularly in the context of medical records, will also be protected by the Act, and may provide a remedy for the subject of a breached confidence beyond that presently recognised by English law.[35]

As well as providing new rights of action, the Human Rights Act may **11–014** also challenge traditional immunities against legal action, such as the immunity of barristers against actions in negligence in relation to court proceedings.[36] The procedural and substantive divisions between public law and private law in the English legal system will also be hard put to survive the changes wrought by the introduction of the Convention into domestic law. There are many areas of damages law and practice which will require reassessment in light of the Human Rights Act. It is too early to be able to fathom the full effect of the Act, but what is clear is that it will have ramifications way beyond the introduction of a language of rights into English jurisprudence.

The laws of European states

It may also be the case that duties and damage recognised in other Euro- **11–015** pean states by virtue of their domestic law will find their way into English law. Examples are the recognition of invasion of personal integrity as a tort giving rise to damages,[37] and rights to business and individual personality, which are protected in German law,[38] and the right to privacy recognised

---

[29] *Tanko v. Finland* 23643/94 (1994) unreported.
[30] *e.g.* discrimination against the aged.
[31] The right to information about risks from radiation was recognised under Art. 2 in *LCB v. UK* (1999) 27 E.H.R.R. 212, although the claim failed on its facts.
[32] At present English law is governed by *Sidaway v. Board of Governors of Bethlem Hospital* [1985] 2 W.L.R. 480.
[33] Right to liberty and security.
[34] See *e.g. R. v. Bournewood Community and Mental Health NHS Trust, ex p. L.* [1998] 3 All E.R. 289; *St George's Health Care Trust v. S. (No. 2); R. v. Collins, ex p. S.* [1998] 3 All E.R. 673. See also Mason & McCall Smith, *Law and Medical Ethics* (5th ed., Butterworths, 1999) Ch. 21.
[35] See *Z. v. Finland* (1998) 25 E.H.R.R. 371.
[36] s. 62, Courts and Legal Services Act 1990.
[37] See Handford, "Moral Damage in Germany" (1978) 27 I.C.L.Q. 849.
[38] See the *Stern* case (B.G.H.Z. 73, 30) where the publishing of the transcript of a telephone conversation was held to breach rights of personality protected under para. 823 of the German Civil Code (BGB), and the *Herrenreiterfall* case (B.G.H.Z. 26, 349) where a picture of a well-known person in an advertisement for a potency medicine, used without consent, gave rise to a successful action for damages.

in French law.[39] Other European states offer far greater protection against personal damage which cannot be categorised as physical or psychiatric, and the concerns of English courts of fraudulent claims and floodgates[40] have played little part in European judgments.

11–016 Similarly, some other European states allow greater recognition of liability for pure economic loss. For example the French Civil Code[41] recognises pure economic loss and loss of chance as types of damage in tort wherever a right has been infringed, and German law, although more cautious than French law on economic loss, will still allow recovery of economic loss in broader circumstances than English law.[42]

11–017 More importantly though, certain historical limitations on claims in English law do not fetter the laws of other European states, and might be difficult to preserve as Britain becomes more subject to the influences of Europe. One example is the barrier between tort and contract which was breached temporarily by the House of Lords in *Junior Books*[43] but firmly restored as a consequence of the decision in *Murphy v. Brentwood*.[44] This tort/contract division has led to anomalies and inconsistencies in recovery particularly of damages for pure economic loss in tort, and has resulted in injustice for victims of builder's negligence causing defects in premises. French law draws no such distinction, and focuses instead on protection of rights and interests, and many actions which would be framed in tort in English law might be framed in contract in French law.[45] Similarly German law is concerned with obligations[46] and the division between contractual and tortious obligations is far more fluid than English law would recognise.

11–018 Another difference is the readiness of European civil law to recognise strict liability for accidents. There is very little common law strict liability in English jurisprudence,[47] and the strict liability introduced by statute[48] has generally been eroded by the introduction of negligence-based tests to determine both liability and defences.[49] Much civil law on the other hand recognises either strict liability or at least a rebuttable assumption of liability by virtue of both statutory interpretation by the courts and of new statutes specifically introducing strict liability. In French law for example, a series of cases beginning with *Jand'heur*[50] led to the interpretation of Article 1384 of the French Civil Code as imposing strict liability for motor vehicles and other "things",[51] which cause injury. In German law the Road

---

[39] Arts. 1382–1383 French Civil Code.
[40] See *e.g. Alcock v. Chief Constable of South Yorkshire Police* [1992] 1 A.C. 310; *White v. Chief Constable of South Yorkshire Police* [1999] 1 All E.R. 1.
[41] Art. 1383.
[42] See Van Gerven, *National, Supranational and International Tort Law: Scope of Protection* (Hart, 1998) Ch. 6.
[43] *Junior Books v. Veitchi* [1983] 1 A.C. 520.
[44] *Murphy v. Brentwood DC* 1990] 2 All E.R. 908.
[45] *e.g.* an action for medical negligence of a public hospital doctor.
[46] See Books I and II of the BGB.
[47] A rare example is liability imposed under the rule in *Rylands v. Fletcher* (1866) L.R. 1 Ex. 265.
[48] *e.g.* the Animals Act 1971 and the Consumer Protection Act 1987.
[49] See *e.g.* s. 2(2) of the Animals Act.
[50] Cass. civ., February 21, 1927.
[51] Such as boat engines—see the *Teffaine* case Cass. civ., June 16, 1897.

Traffic Act 1952 provides strict liability for any user of a car for any damage to person or property arising from operation of the vehicle.

Rules of statutory interpretation differ between common law and civil 11–019 law jurisprudence, and by its very nature civil law is much more statute based than common law, although increasingly statute is being used to remedy flaws in law in this jurisdiction.[52] But perhaps the most important difference between English law and the law of other European states[53] is the level of abstraction of the stated law in civil law jurisdictions and the consequent importance of a sound understanding of legal philosophy to the understanding and practice of law.

Any of these differences may well begin to effect change in English law. Of 11–020 all the states in the European Union, English law constitutes the only common law system, so withstanding the encroachment of the civil law way of doing things will become increasingly difficult. As practitioners and judges become more and more familiar with the legal systems of other jurisdictions, and with the burgeoning literature and commentary on the tort laws of individual European states,[54] then arguments and judgments will increasingly take into account the laws of our neighbours. There is some evidence of this already,[55] and it is inevitable that the influence of Europe will precipitate significant change in the approach of English courts to damages.

Commonwealth and North American law

The availability of legal materials from other jurisdictions at the press of 11–021 a button on the internet, particularly from jurisdictions with common language and legal core, has enabled a vastly increased awareness of developments in law elsewhere. It is not uncommon for law journals and reports now to devote sections to cases and statutes in other jurisdictions.[56] It is increasingly likely that counsel's argument will draw from these readily available sources.

There are many areas of divergence between English law and that of 11–022 other English speaking jurisdictions. Many other jurisdictions have embraced no-fault liability either on a broad scale, as in New Zealand, or for particular circumstances, as is common in some Australian, Canadian and North American states. Courts in other jurisdictions have chosen to reject English authority on such matters as liability for defective premises[57]

---

[52] Examples are the Congenital Disabilities (Civil Liability) Act 1976, the Consumer Protection Act 1987 and the Road Traffic (NHS Charges) Act 1999.

[53] The majority of European states follow broadly the German legal system.

[54] See e.g. Van Buren, *Cases, Materials and Text on National, Supranational and International Tort Law* (Hart, 1998); von Bar, *The Common European Law of Torts* (Verlag C.H. Beck, Munchen, 1998); Vranken, *Fundamentals of European Civil Law* (Blackstones, 1997); Foster, *German Law and Legal System* (Blackstones, 1993); see also Schmid, "The Emergence of a Transnational Legal Science in European Private Law" (1999) 19 O.J.L.S. 671.

[55] See the judgment of Lord Goff in *White v. Jones* [1995] 1 All E.R. 691 where he looks to German law for guidance on a question of duty of care.

[56] e.g. the Medical Law Review, OUP; see also the Journal of Social Welfare and Family Law, Routledge, which now has a European section.

[57] See *Winnipeg Condominium Corporation v. Bird Construction Co. Ltd* (1995) 121 D.L.R. (4th) 193 (Canada); *Bryan v. Maloney* (1995) 128 A.L.R. 163 (Australia); and *Invercargill CC v. Hamlin* [1996] 2 W.L.R. 367 (NZ).

and liability for failure to properly inform in the context of medical treatment.[58] The reasoning of judges in these cases will increasingly resound in
English courts, and it will be difficult for English law to resist the influence
of such decisions.

Woolf

11–023   The Woolf Report[59] was essentially concerned with the process elements
of a claim for damages. However one of the aspects of civil procedure
which most concerned the Committee was the high cost of bringing a claim
to determination, cost which would rebound on the losing party and which
would thus form at least a part of the payment to be made at the end
of the day, and which must be insured against. Additionally, the Report
highlighted delay in getting damages to the victim, with consequent costs,
and the adversarial nature of civil proceedings as major problems in claims
for compensation in tort.

11–024   Among the recommendations in the Report, many of which are incorporated into the Civil Procedure Rules 1998, are measures designed to separate
out both very weak and very strong claims, such that the weak claims can
be disposed of by summary judgment, and the strong ones proceeded with
more quickly and smoothly by disposing of defences early in the process.
These, and other new procedures such as those relating to use of expert
witnesses, will in the long term influence which cases lawyers will be prepared to take on,[60] which cases make it to the courtroom and thus contribute to authority, and what in the way of quantum parties will be prepared
to settle for. The forward to the Civil Procedure Rules 1998 describes them
as "the beginning of . . . the most fundamental change to the civil justice
system since the reforms of Lord Selborne in the 1870s".[61]

11–025   More importantly in this context, it is clear from the Report that litigation for damages should be regarded as the last resort measure for
obtaining compensation for tortious harm. Instead, alternative mechanisms
such as arbitration and mediation are encouraged. Some pilot mediation
projects have already been launched for medical negligence claims[62] and
patent disputes, and private mediators now offer mediation services for
media, libel and financial services disputes.[63] Arbitration is well established
in some construction and insurance disputes.

11–026   The increased use of Alternative Dispute Resolution will affect damages
in tort. Payment of damages as a result of successful ADR need not be
based on legal rules, and quantum need not accord with legal guidelines.
Costs issues are different in the context of ADR, as are evidence requirements and burdens of proof. Were ADR to become the main form of dam-

---

[58] See *Canterbury v. Spence* 464 F. 2d 772 (DC 1972) (US); *Reibel v. Hughes* (1980) 114
D.L.R. (3d) 1 (Canada) and *Rogers v. Whittaker* (1992) 109 A.L.R. 625 (Australia).
[59] *Access to Civil Justice* (1996).
[60] See *infra* on conditional fees.
[61] Lord Irvine, Foreword to the Rules.
[62] *e.g.* the pilot schemes for mediation in Oxford & Anglia, and Northern and Yorkshire
regions. See Easterbrook (1996) S.J. 26 April 410; Polywka (1997) 3 Clinical Risk 80.
[63] See McFarlane (1996) The Litigator 386.

ages negotiation, the basis and amount of damages paid out as accident compensation would develop on very different lines than at present and much of the law discussed in this book would become redundant.

Following the Woolf Report, Sir Peter Middleton published a further **11–027** report on how the government intended to respond to the Woolf proposals.[64] In this report Middleton proposed that the possibility of no-fault compensation, particularly for clinical negligence disputes, be given serious consideration.[65] No-fault compensation schemes designed particularly for medical misadventure are well established in Sweden and Finland[66] and appear to be working successfully. The result of introducing a no-fault scheme would be to change dramatically the criteria and quantum of compensation for personal injury resulting from medical misadventure.[67] The experience of other jurisdictions is that such schemes are expensive, and require enormous political and financial commitment, but that they get damages to a much wider community of injured and deserving accident victims. No-fault schemes for other types of accident such as road accident and congenital injury work well elsewhere[68] and could follow on if the medical scheme were to meet public approval.

Other jurisdictions are also examining ways of improving access to com- **11–028** pensation.[69] Reform initiatives everywhere are aimed at both the substantive law and the procedure which enables the substantive law to operate, and the two issues cannot be looked at in isolation. The implications of procedural changes for civil claimants have been much analysed[70] and these changes will shape a very different law on damages in years to come.

Funding of damages claims

One of the most significant changes in litigation for damages in recent **11–029** years has been in the funding of that litigation. Over the years the legal aid assistance which is essential to enable less well-off members of society even to contemplate embarking on the long road to a damages award has been eroded both in qualification for the scheme and in the amount of funding allocated to it.[71] More recently the Legal Aid scheme has been significantly

---

[64] Sir Peter Middleton, *Review of Civil Justice and Legal Aid* (Lord Chancellor's Department, September 1997).

[65] Ch. 5.

[66] See Ch. 2 above.

[67] See Brazier, "The Case for a No-fault Compensation Scheme for Medical Accidents", in *Compensation for Damage: An International Perspective* (McLean ed., Dartmouth, 1993).

[68] See Ch. 2 above.

[69] See *e.g.* Bendickson, "Canadian Developments in Health Care Liability and Compensation", in *Law Reform and Medical Injury Litigation* (McLean ed., Dartmouth, 1995); the Australian Law Reform Commission, Review of Federal Justice System discussion paper at http:www.alrc.gov/au/news/mb/19992008MB.html; Poythress & Weiner, "Reforming Medical Malpractice Torts: Accuracy, Procedural Justice and the Law as Moral Educator" (1995) The Litigator 385 (on US law).

[70] See *e.g.* *Reform of Civil Procedure—Essays on "Access to Justice"* (Zuckerman & Cranston eds., Clarendon, Oxford, 1995); and Zander, "The Woolf Report: Forwards or Backwards for the New Lord Chancellor?" (1997) 16 C.J.Q. 208.

[71] Cane estimates that in the last 20 years the proportion of population eligible for Legal Aid has fallen from 80% to 40%; Cane, *Atiyah's Accidents, Compensation and the Law* (6th ed., Butterworths, 1999), p. 218.

wound down in the form in which we know it. It is now known as Community Legal Service Funding.[72] From April 2000 Legal Aid assistance has not been available for claimants for damages for property damage, or for personal injury apart from claimants for clinical negligence. Hence the role of Legal Aid assistance in claims for damages in tort is now minimal.

11–030   The main replacement for Legal Aid in this context is the introduction of conditional fee agreements. These are popularly known as "no-win-no fee" agreements but differ from the North American contingency fee arrangements where the lawyer can negotiate a fee based on the damages obtained, and where all parties pay their own costs. Under a conditional fee agreement the client and solicitor negotiate a fee based on an up-lift of the normal solicitor's fee in the case of a successful claim. So the solicitor in such a case would receive the basic fees plus a further amount of up to 100 per cent of those fees. By convention, as recommended by the Law Society, the up-lift should not exceed 25 per cent of the damages awarded. The percentage of uplift is the subject of agreement and will depend on the solicitor's estimation of the likely success of the case.

11–031   The losing party remains responsible for costs, and a court can order that these costs include the uplift.[73] Where a case settles the responsibility for payment of the uplift will be the subject of the settlement agreement. Where the losing party is the claimant, this means that the individual client would despite the no-win-no-fee arrangement find herself responsible for both her own disbursements and the defendant's costs and disbursements, and if such was the case, the risks of litigation would be such that many potential claimants would be limited in their access to the law. To cover this possibility, the development of "costs insurance" has been encouraged to enable clients to insure against the cost of losing the claim.[74]

11–032   Replacing Legal Aid with conditional fee agreements may both increase and decrease the ability of a claimant to seek damages in tort. Some potential claimants, who would not have qualified for Legal Aid but who nevertheless could not have afforded legal fees will now be able to approach a solicitor to take the case on a no-win-no-fee basis.

11–033   However other claimants will be disadvantaged by the removal of legal aid, particularly group claims, where the claims are more complex and the costs of losing more significant.[75] Funding claims through conditional fees may ensure that fewer unwinnable cases are brought to trial thus saving public costs and court time, and of course removing the costs of legal assistance from public responsibility to the open market should free public funds for other purposes.

11–034   The application of conditional fees to counsel is more problematic. Will the barrister be allowed to make a judgment on the likely success of the case, if her payment is contingent on that success? And if so, where does

---

[72] Access to Justice Act 1999.

[73] s. 58, Courts and Legal Services Act 1990 as amended by the Access to Justice Act 1999; Rule 48.9 of the Civil Procedure Rules 1998 provides for the taxing of success fees.

[74] See Prais, "The Future of Legal Costs Insurance" (1996) The Litigator 212; and Grey & Rickman, "The Role of Legal Expenses Insurance in Securing Access to the Market for Legal Service" (Zuckerman & Cranston eds.), op. cit.

[75] See Cane op. cit., p. 217.

this stand with the "cab rank" convention which requires the barrister to take the first case on offer?[76] Will it be a problem that the barrister will now have a financial interest in the outcome of the case? Will this create a conflict of interest with court or client? What will happen to returned briefs—will the fall-back counsel need to reassess success prospects before taking the case on? Will a result of conditional fees be pressure to recognise contractual relationships in the context of the services of counsel?

Conditional fees are not the only new development. Another Woolf initi- **11–035** ative is the introduction of community law centres, supported by charitable and government funds, which provide free legal advice for minor claims. The insurance industry is developing forms of legal claims insurance, particularly in the context of motor and household insurance, which will support claimants for damages. Employment packages now increasingly include perks such as legal claims insurance.

It is clear that the changes in funding of tort claims will have knock-on **11–036** effects for the organisation of the legal profession, and those organisational changes will spill over onto the access claimants have to law, and hence to damages. The ways in which tort claims operate will need to be adjusted to take account of such changes, such that the landscape of damages claims as we have known it will become, in time, very different.

Recoupment

It is increasingly the case that a holistic approach is being taken to dam- **11–037** ages awards. The necessity of an award of damages, and the calculation of how much those damages should be, was for a long time approached as a legalistic calculation without reference to the whole context of the harm. The claimant who stood to benefit from a large insurance payout consequent on the accident may nevertheless be compensated in full, providing in effect double compensation for the same event. The accident victim who had been supported by social services up until trial was paid compensation with very limited obligation to pay back social security payments received.[77] The defendant in a damages claim also benefited from this non-contextual approach: the costs of medical care to an accident victim where it was provided by the NHS were not entered into the damages equation.

This approach, while it may be economically indefensible, was the result **11–038** of a philosophy of community responsibility whereby society was held responsible for a share of the costs of the organisation and risks of living in that society. More recently, in accordance with an emerging philosophy of individual responsibility,[78] there have been increasing moves to pass the

---

[76] See Kunzlik, "Conditional Fees: The Ethical and Organisational Impact on the Bar" (1999) 62 M.L.R. 850.

[77] Under the Law Reform (Personal Injuries) Act 1948 an amount representing half the value of certain specified benefits paid to the claimant over the first five years after the injury was deducted from the award of damages. This money was not repaid to the relevant social services department and while it made some attempt to limit double recovery, it created a benefit only to the defendant in the action.

[78] See Ch. 2 above for further discussion on the relevance of political philosophy to damages awards.

costs of accidents along to those responsible, and to lighten the burden of accidents on the public purse. Of course this is more a matter of form than substance. In the end, whether harm is compensated by insurance or from the public purse, the same person, the ordinary taxpayer, is the ultimate source of funding. But philosophically the difference is important, and politically a government which wants to be seen as limiting public expense will prefer that the costs of accidents at least appear to be attributed to those responsible for them.

11–039   The first major introduction of the new recoupment philosophy into the world of tort damages came with the Social Security Act 1989.[79] For any payment of damages over £2,500,[80] the party responsible for paying the damages, the defendant, became responsible for reimbursing the relevant public authority for social services payments which had been made to the claimant in consequence of the accident. The defendant was required to obtain a certificate detailing the full value of specified social services benefits paid to the claimant for the first five years after the injury and to repay that amount to the Benefits Agency.[81] The 1989 legislation had some flaws.[82] One in particular was that some benefits were so large that they ate up not only the compensation payment for the loss covered by the benefit, but also ate into the award for pain, suffering and loss of amenities, which was intended as a palliative payment. Some accident victims ended up with nothing after the full recoupment exercise had taken place. Many of the wrinkles in the system were ironed out by the Social Security(Recovery of Benefits) Act 1997 which ensures that the non-pecuniary loss award remains intact.

11–040   The second important recoupment measure came in the form of the Road Traffic (NHS Charges) Act 1999.[83] The purpose of this act is to enable an NHS hospital or an NHS Trust which provides treatment services for the victim of a road accident to recover the costs of treatment from the defendant in a claim for damages.[84] Before the introduction of this scheme, there were some limited mechanisms enabling token amounts to be charged by the hospital for providing accident treatment services,[85] but apart from these, the costs of treatment were deducted from the damages award to the benefit of the defendant.

11–041   Under the scheme, the defendant bears the responsibility of obtaining a certificate detailing treatment costs, whether the case goes to court or is settled, and payment of these costs takes place separately from the payment of damages to the claimant. At present, only £10,000 can be charged by the hospital in respect of each patient. The inevitable consequence of this

---

[79] These rules were subsequently incorporated into the Social Security Administration Act 1992.
[80] For lesser amounts the Law Reform (Personal Injuries) Act 1948 continued to apply.
[81] The recoupment procedure is administered by the Compensation Recovery Unit.
[82] See Cane *op. cit.* at p. 328.
[83] See also the Road Traffic (NHS Charges) Regulations S.I. 1999 No. 785; and the Road Traffic (NHS Charges) (Reviews and Appeals) Regulations S.I. 1999 No. 786.
[84] NHS recoupment is, like social services recoupment, administered by the Compensation Recovery Unit.
[85] See Lewis, "Recovery of NHS Accident Costs: Tort as a Vehicle for Raising Public Funds" (1999) 62 M.L.R. 903.

recoupment procedure will be significantly to increase the costs of road accidents to defendant insurers, a cost which will be quickly passed on to premium payers.[86]

More importantly, the two recoupment procedures now in place make **11–042** significant inroads into the rule against third-party claims for damages in tort. If one of the aspects of the new philosophy of compensation is to assess the real costs of accidents and to place the burden of these costs with the accident causer, then why not allow others who have suffered financial loss as the result of an accident to pursue genuine claims for compensation along with the accident victim? What of the relative who gives up highly-paid work to care for the injured person? What of the employer who has suffered the loss of a trained and valuable employee?

The philosophy of recoupment is bound up with the philosophy of fault **11–043** liability. If a defendant at fault cannot be identified then the rationale for imposing these extra cost responsibilities is less strong. Of course liability in the context of road accidents is fault liability in name only, and could more truthfully be described as a form of judicially imposed strict liability.[87] However the insurance culture surrounding compensation for road accidents has been built on an understanding that vehicle drivers are highly likely to bear some legal liability for injuries caused by the vehicle they were driving, and there is a societal acceptance that vulnerability to this type of liability is a general societal risk which we are all prepared to bear.

Conclusion

So, it seems, recent developments in damages law are pulling in different **11–044** directions. On the one hand, fault liability is becoming more firmly entrenched, and the philosophy of attributing full financial responsibility with allocation of causal legal liability is now more so than ever an overt component of tort damages. On the other hand there are calls for reconsideration of no-fault liability in some areas, recognising that in a modern society, where the individual has little real control over the risks she takes or the risks she might expose others to, trying to manipulate a finding of fault is both ethically suspect and practically pointless.

Meanwhile as courts increase the levels of individual damages awards, **11–045** recognising the costs and stresses of accident injury, Parliament has been working to reduce the costs of accidents, particularly as a public expense. As courts continue to frame the law on damages in accordance with English legal precedent, the influence of Europe is such that rules of precedent will become less decisive and judges in domestic courts will be forced to look much more broadly at damages issues.

The supremacy of common law in the context of damages is also under **11–046** threat as a spate of recent legislation impinges on common law rules. Most recently the Health Act 1999 has introduced new statutory duties of health quality, the Healthcare Services Bill 1999 aims to ensure that private med-

---

[86] Lewis *op. cit.* suggests that the added cost to the motor industry will be 2–3%, and that the average insurance premium will rise by £6 to £9.
[87] See the judgment of Lord Denning in *Nettleship v. Weston* [1971] 2 Q.B. 691.

ical treatment provision is at least equivalent to the standard of NHS treatment, and the Contract (Rights of Third Parties) Act 1999 may give rise to actions for damages in contract to persons who were previously forced by rules of privity to sue in tort, further encroaching on the contract/tort divide.

11–047   The face of damages law is changing rapidly. As rights of action for damages expand, the insurance industry will need to reconsider the framework of its coverage. Courts will need to reconsider criteria of damages awards and the appropriateness of quantum rules. Government politicians and economists will need to consider both the effect of recent changes on the public responsibility for tortious harm, especially in respect of the potential liability of public authorities under the Human Rights Act, and the consequences for the private economy of increased liability for accident injury.

11–048   We are, at the beginning of the twenty-first century, in a philosophical cusp where the attractions of both individual responsibility and community responsibility are pulling in different directions, where the historical, comfortable familiarity of the traditional English legal system is confronted with the excitement and inevitability of a move into the European way of doing things. Never has it been more important to take a step back from the details of the law to determine the purpose and objectives of contemporary damages law in a world social, economic and legal context. It is time for another Commission, not limited to damages in tort but looking at the wider question of restitution for harm. The old causes of action and rules of litigation no longer serve us well in an age of technology and globalisation. The changes are inevitable. What is important is that the law keeps abreast of change.

INDEX